How to access the supplemental web study guide

We are pleased to provide access to a web study guide that supplements your textbook, *Contemporary Sport Management, Sixth Edition.* This resource offers multiple interactive learning experiences that will help you more fully understand and apply the concepts covered in each chapter, including activities in which you will thoughtfully consider critical thinking and ethical issues, complete website searches and write essays, and more.

Accessing the web study guide is easy!
Follow these steps if you purchased a new book:

1. Visit **www.HumanKinetics.com/ContemporarySportManagement**.

2. Click the sixth edition link next to the corresponding sixth edition book cover.

3. Click the Sign In link on the left or top of the page. If you do not have an account with Human Kinetics, you will be prompted to create one.

4. If the online product you purchased does not appear in the Ancillary Items box on the left of the page, click the Enter Key Code option in that box. Enter the key code that is printed at the right, including all hyphens. Click the Submit button to unlock your online product.

5. After you have entered your key code the first time, you will never have to enter it again to access this product. Once unlocked, a link to your product will permanently appear in the menu on the left. For future visits, all you need to do is sign in to the textbook's website and follow the link that appears in the left menu!

→   Click the Need Help? button on the textbook's website if you need assistance along the way.

How to access the web study guide if you purchased a used book:

You may purchase access to the web study guide by visiting the text's website, **www.HumanKinetics.com/ContemporarySportManagement**, or by calling the following:

800-747-4457 . . . . U.S. customers
800-465-7301 . . . . Canadian customers
+44 (0) 113 255 5665 . . . . European customers
217-351-5076 . . . . International customers

For technical support, send an email to:
support@hkusa.com . . . . U.S. and international customers
info@hkcanada.com . . . . Canadian customers
academic@hkeurope.com . . . . European customers

D0074438

03-2018

Product: Contemporary Sport Management, Sixth Edition, web study guide

Key code: PEDERSEN-9PNZ2J-OSG

This unique code allows you access to the web study guide.

Access is provided if you have purchased a new book. Once submitted, the code may not be entered for any other user.

Contemporary Sport Management

SIXTH EDITION

Paul M. Pedersen, PhD

Indiana University – Bloomington

Lucie Thibault, PhD

Brock University

EDITORS

HUMAN KINETICS

Library of Congress Cataloging-in-Publication Data

Names: Pedersen, Paul Mark, editor. | Thibault, Lucie, editor.
Title: Contemporary sport management / Paul M. Pedersen, Lucie Thibault, editors.
Description: Sixth edition. | Champaign, IL : Human Kinetics, [2019] | Includes bibliographical references and index.
Identifiers: LCCN 2017031517 (print) | LCCN 2017034238 (ebook) | ISBN 9781492550952 (print) | ISBN 9781492550969 (e-book)
Subjects: | MESH: Sports | Industry--organization & administration
Classification: LCC GV713 (print) | LCC GV713 (ebook) | NLM QT 260 | DDC 796.06/9--dc23
LC record available at https://lccn.loc.gov/2017031517

ISBN: 978-1-4925-5095-2 (print)

The web addresses cited in this text were current as of February 2018, unless otherwise noted.

Acquisitions Editor: Bridget Melton
Developmental Editor: Melissa J. Zavala
Managing Editor: Derek Campbell
Indexer: Karla Walsh
Permissions Manager: Dalene Reeder
Senior Graphic Designer: Nancy Rasmus
Cover Designer: Keri Evans
Cover Design Associate: Susan Rothermel Allen
Photograph (cover): John Giles/PA Images via Getty Images
Photographs (interior): © Human Kinetics, unless otherwise noted
Photo Asset Manager: Laura Fitch
Photo Production Manager: Jason Allen
Senior Art Manager: Kelly Hendren
Illustrations: © Human Kinetics, unless otherwise noted
Printer: Versa Press

Printed in the United States of America   10 9 8 7 6 5 4 3 2 1

The paper in this book is certified under a sustainable forestry program.

Human Kinetics
P.O. Box 5076
Champaign, IL 61825-5076
Website: www.HumanKinetics.com

In the United States, email info@hkusa.com or call 800-747-4457.

In Canada, email info@hkcanada.com.

In the United Kingdom/Europe, email hk@hkeurope.com.

For information about Human Kinetics' coverage in other areas of the world, please visit our website:
www.HumanKinetics.com

E7062

Paul and Lucie wish to dedicate this sixth edition of *Contemporary Sport Management* to Janet B. Parks and to the memory of Jerome Quarterman. Over the course of Dr. Parks' career, she became one of the most influential pioneers, professors, researchers, and leaders in sport management. Besides having a leading role in founding the North American Society for Sport Management (NASSM) and the *Journal of Sport Management*, she had the foresight and dedication nearly three decades ago to develop and publish, along with coeditor Beverly R.K. Zanger, the original version of this textbook. Over the years, she led several revisions of *Contemporary Sport Management* with four coeditors across the various revisions. One of her coeditors through the first four editions was Dr. Quarterman, an accomplished and influential figure in our field until his passing in 2015. This book is dedicated to Dr. Parks and Dr. Quarterman for their impact on the field with the early editions of this textbook and for their leadership and friendship over the years.

Contents

PART I   Introduction to Sport Management

Managing Sport 4

Paul M. Pedersen and Lucie Thibault

Developing a Professional Perspective 30

Sally R. Ross, Brian P. McCullough, and Susan E.C. Simmons

Historical Aspects of the Sport Business Industry 50

Elizabeth A. Gregg, Brenda G. Pitts, and Paul M. Pedersen

Management Concepts and Practice in Sport Organizations 70

Kathy Babiak, Kathryn Heinze, and Lucie Thibault

Managing and Leading in Sport Organizations 94

Shannon Kerwin, Ming Li, and Laura J. Burton

PART II   Selected Sport Management Sites

PART III   Selected Sport Management Functions

Acknowledgments

Paul M. Pedersen and Lucie Thibault would like to express deep gratitude to numerous individuals, groups, and organizations whose collective contributions made this sixth edition of *Contemporary Sport Management* a reality.

This project could not have been accomplished without the input and expertise of the 56 contributing authors, who are national and international leaders and rising stars in various areas of study and segments of the sport industry. The quality of this book is a direct result of the contributors' outstanding efforts. Please refer to the back of the textbook for more information about the activities and accomplishments of the chapter authors.

In addition to welcoming in the new contributors, we would like to thank those who were involved with chapters in the fifth edition (and some in earlier editions as well) but who did not participate in the sixth edition. These previous chapter contributors are Coyte Cooper, Ted Fay, Larry Fielding, Wendy Frisby, Jay Gladden, Sam Olson, David Stotlar, Bill Sutton, and Luisa Velez. Although we hope you are enjoying your retirement, entrepreneurial endeavors, administrative duties, or whatever other activities take the place of your involvement in this edition, we thank you for your foundational work and previous contributions.

We express our sincere gratitude to Ashleigh-Jane Thompson from La Trobe University (Australia) who served as this edition's international profile liaison. She solicited, coordinated, and edited an outstanding group of international vignettes and learning activities for this edition. We sincerely thank those who contributed the vignettes and learning activities that are integrated throughout the chapters: Guillaume Bodet (France), Veerle De Bosscher (Belgium), Sarah Gee (Canada), John Harris (Scotland), Thomas Horky (Germany), Adam Karg (Australia), Elsa Kristiansen (Norway), Sanghak Lee (South Korea), Simon Ličen (Slovenia), Daniel Lock (England), Rosa López de D'Amico (Venezuela), David Maralack (South Africa), E. Esra Erturan Öğüt (Turkey), Dimitra Papadimitriou (Greece), Milena M. Parent (Canada), Richard Parrish (England), Norbert Schütte (Germany), Kamilla Swart (South Africa), Victor Timchenko (Russia), Jasper Truyens (Belgium), János Váczi (Hungary), Geoff Watson (New Zealand), Kong-Ting Yeh (Taiwan), and Masayuki Yoshida (Japan). In addition, we are truly grateful to Corinne Daprano from the University of Dayton for revising and updating the instructor ancillaries and student web study guide. Furthermore, we are appreciative of the time, effort, and input of the sport industry professionals who are featured throughout the textbook: Kristin Bernert, Ross Bjork, Mike Blackburn, Kirsten Britton, Trevor Bukstein, Terri Carmichael Jackson, Scott Crowder, Andy De Angulo, Kyle Dubas, Ashley Feagan, Marshall Fey, Alicia Greco-Walker, Kalen Jackson, Megan Kahn, Nicole Kankam, Donna Lopiano, Ellen Lucey, Mitch Moser, Sheila N. Nguyen, Heidi Pellerano, Keri Potts, Brandon Rhodes, Tracy Schoenadel, Steven J. Silver, Andrew Tinnish, Vernon Walker, and Bill Wise. Students will enjoy—and benefit from—reading the sport management professional profiles included in this sixth edition.

Special notes of appreciation go to our educational institutions and publisher for their outstanding support. We are grateful to Indiana University – Bloomington (IU) and Brock University for providing the resources that facilitated the completion of this book. We are privileged to be university professors and fortunate to work in environments that support our efforts. As always, we extend gratitude to the thousands of students we have had the privilege of teaching across the years. Furthermore, we sincerely appreciate Human Kinetics' remarkable editors and professionals associated with this project, including Skip Maier, Derek Campbell, Denise D'Urso, Kari Testory, Merry Blakey, Nancy Rasmus, Susi Huls, Keri Evans, Kelly Hendren, Matt Harshbarger, Jason Allen, and Dalene Reeder, to name just a few. Although numerous individuals from Human Kinetics have assisted and facilitated this sixth edition, we would like to acknowledge two editors in particular. Bridget Melton, our acquisitions editor, came on board with this sixth edition, and we consider ourselves fortunate that she did. Bridget has been outstanding in terms of leadership, decision making, communication, suggestions, advice, and encouragement. The same is true for Melissa Zavala, the outstanding and supportive development editor for this edition of the textbook. She and Bridget simply made our jobs much easier by always being there with valuable information, assistance, and advice. A special note of appreciation goes out to Myles Schrag, who worked with us on various earlier editions of this textbook and was a part of the initial planning of this sixth edition. Although we definitely miss Myles, he was thrilled to find out that Bridget would be taking his place for this project, and we now understand why he was so happy and comfortable handing this project to her.

Last, in addition to our expression of thanks to Janet Parks for her vision and leadership of this project over the many years until her retirement, we would like to acknowledge our various family members who have provided tremendous support of our work on *Contemporary Sport Management*. In particular, we are grateful for the patience and understanding of Brock, Carlie, Hallie, Jennifer, and Zack.

A Letter to Students and Instructors

Welcome to the sixth edition of *Contemporary Sport Management*. Whether you are a student or an instructor, this letter will provide you with information that explains the goals, updates, and features of this new edition. Many new updates and features make this sixth edition an exciting and valuable resource that we are sure will broaden your understanding of sport management.

Goals of the Book

As with the previous editions, the goal of the sixth edition of *Contemporary Sport Management* is to introduce students to sport management as an academic major and as a professional endeavor. Toward that end, the book provides a broad overview of sport management rather than detailed instructions about how to manage sport enterprises. This distinction is important because the book must meet the needs of two types of students: those who have already decided to major in sport management and those who are still thinking about their choice of a major. If you are currently majoring in sport management, you probably anticipate learning more about the field and particularly about the variety of professional opportunities that await you. Those of you who are currently considering a major in sport management probably want to gain general knowledge about the field before making a final decision. After studying the information in this book, some of you will be even more intrigued with the idea of seeking a career in sport management, and you will pursue the remainder of your coursework with enhanced understanding, insight, and maturity of purpose. Others among you may discover that sport management is not really what you envisioned or is not a field in which you want to work, and you will choose different majors. In either case, the book will have served a valuable purpose.

The sixth edition of *Contemporary Sport Management* contains 21 chapters written by the two of us along with 56 other chapter contributors, 26 of whom are new arrivals for this edition: Nola Agha (University of San Francisco), Natasha T. Brison (Texas A&M University), Laura J. Burton (University of Connecticut), Windy Dees (University of Miami), Brendan Dwyer (Virginia Commonwealth University), Justin Evanovich (University of Connecticut), Elizabeth A. Gregg (University of North Florida), Stacey A. Hall (University of Southern Mississippi), David P. Hedlund (St. John's University), Kathryn L. Heinze (University of Michigan), Millicent Kennelly (Griffith University), Amy Chan Hyung Kim (Florida State University), Nancy Lough (University of Nevada, Las Vegas), Jacqueline McDowell (George Mason University), Kevin Mongeon (Brock University), Ceyda Mumcu (University of New Haven), Brianna L. Newland (University of Delaware), Amanda L. Paule-Koba (Bowling Green State University), Amanda Siegrist (Coastal Carolina University), Susan E.C. Simmons (Indiana University – Bloomington), Danielle Smith (Wasserman), Ryan Spalding (Merrimack College), Sylvia Trendafilova (University of Tennessee), Patrick Walsh (Syracuse University), Nicholas M. Watanabe (University of South Carolina), and James J. Zhang (University of Georgia). All the authors are experts in their fields and are committed to sharing their knowledge with you, the next generation of sport managers. The photographs and biographies of the authors and for Corinne M. Daprano, the subject matter expert for the instructor ancillaries and student web study guide, and Ashleigh-Jane Thompson, the liaison for the international profiles, are included at the back of the book. We hope that seeing their faces and reading about their accomplishments will personalize the material in the chapters and make the book more meaningful for you. We know that you will be impressed with each contributor's experience and depth of knowledge.

Scope and Organization of the Book

The Commission on Sport Management Accreditation (COSMA) is the accrediting body for sport management curricula. This sixth edition of *Contemporary Sport Management* addresses each of the common professional component topical areas that COSMA considers essential to the professional preparation of sport managers. These content areas, according to COSMA's 2016 *Accreditation Principles Manual and Guidelines for Self-Study Preparation*, include sport management foundations (i.e., management concepts, governance and policy, and international sport), functions (i.e., sport operations, sport marketing, sport communications, and sport finance and economics), environment (i.e., legal aspects, ethical aspects, diversity, and technical advances), and experiential learning and career development (e.g., internships, capstone experiences). The book provides basic information in all these content areas (e.g., sport marketing and sport communication are covered in chapter 12, Sport Marketing, and chapter 14, Communication in the Sport Industry). In addition, every chapter includes a sidebar on international aspects of the field and a section on ethics in sport management, which are two requirements of the COSMA standards for accreditation. As you progress through the professional preparation curriculum at your college or university, you will study the content areas covered in this textbook (and those required by programs to meet COSMA standards) in much greater depth.

The 21 chapters in this sixth edition of *Contemporary Sport Management* are organized within the following parts: Introduction to Sport Management, Selected Sport Management Sites, Selected Sport Management Functions, and Current Challenges in Sport Management. Each of these parts begins with a brief description of its purpose, a summary of the information you will find in the chapters, and a For More Information section that identifies additional resources related to the chapter topics. After studying all the chapters, completing the international learning activities and the additional learning activities in the web study guide, and taking advantage of the For More Information sections in the part openers, you should be able to (1) define sport management; (2) discuss the significance of sport as an international social institution; (3) exhibit desirable professional skills and attitudes; (4) describe the nature and scope of professional opportunities in the sport industry; (5) explain a variety of functions that sport managers typically perform; (6) demonstrate an understanding of theories associated with management, leadership, and organizational behavior and of how these theories are applied in sport enterprises; (7) demonstrate critical thinking skills to evaluate major challenges confronting various segments of the industry; (8) explain the relevance of legal, historical, sociological, and psychological concepts to the management of sport; (9) engage in socially responsible activities and make principled decisions through a thorough knowledge of the ethical decision-making process; (10) demonstrate an appreciation of diversity; (11) identify research questions in sport management, demonstrate the ability to analyze and interpret data and published research, and develop an awareness of analytics in sport; and (12) become a member of the profession who will have a positive influence on the way that sport is managed in the future.

Updates to the Sixth Edition

We are gratified that many students over the years have found the first five editions of *Contemporary Sport Management* useful, and we hope that the new, improved version will serve your needs even better. The changes in this edition include the addition of a new chapter (chapter 20, which will introduce you to the various ways sport analytics is used in the management of sport and in the sport industry overall) and other new material (e.g., questions and answers with sport industry professionals) as well as revised and updated sections. We believe that you will appreciate and benefit from the significant modifications and updates. For example, the inclusion of many new social media sidebars is necessary (future sport managers should possess expertise across a variety of social media platforms), relevant (the sport industry has been particularly affected by the social media phenomenon over the past 15 years), and interesting (the topics covered involve some of the unique challenges and opportunities encountered in social media engagement). In addition, each chapter includes practical applications (e.g., sidebars) that provide an example of the direct sport industry application of the content covered.

The textbook has an updated web study guide (WSG). The WSG (which can be accessed under the Student Resources heading at www.HumanKinetics.com/ContemporarySportManagement) provides multiple interactive learning experiences that will help you more fully understand and apply the concepts covered in each chapter. Icons throughout each chapter point you to the following activities:

• *Job announcements*. These fabricated, but realistic, position announcements related to employment opportunities within particular sport settings will help you understand the skills that prospective employers are seeking. You can select the traits and characteristics you think are most applicable to each position. Sport management practitioners then identify the traits and characteristics they think are most applicable to each position.

• *Comprehension activities.* These learning-in-action activities, including matching exercises and multiple-choice questions, will challenge you to complete a specific task that helps drive home the information covered in the chapter.

• *Web activities.* For these activities, you will explore a specific website related to the chapter's content and complete an assignment that connects the website's content to the chapter content.

• *Day in the life.* These activities, which are tied to the professional profiles, ask you to evaluate how professionals spend their time.

• *Portfolio.* The critical thinking and ethics sections in the chapters provide background information that you will use to answer specific questions in the WSG. After completing these questions, you will have built a portfolio that highlights your thoughtful considerations of myriad issues related to sport management.

As noted previously, the sixth edition of *Contemporary Sport Management* has four distinct parts, each of which contains at least five relevant chapters. In the first part, five unique chapters introduce you to sport management. These opening chapters provide an overview of the field and information on becoming an effective and professional sport manager, discuss historical elements of sport management, and address managerial and leadership concepts associated with this dynamic field. In the second part, six chapters detail the major settings that have sport management positions. These chapters examine professional and amateur sport management sites in addition to positions in sport management agencies and sport tourism. The third part has five chapters that convey key functional areas of sport management. These areas involve sport marketing, sport consumer behavior, sport communication, finance and economics in sport, and sport facility and event management. In the fourth part, five chapters examine issues that sport managers currently encounter and that you will face as you enter the sport industry. These challenges (and opportunities) include sport management issues related to law, sociology, globalization, analytics, and research. We believe the organization of the chapters into these four parts will assist you in understanding the field of sport management.

eBook
available at
your campus bookstore
or HumanKinetics.com

Each chapter has been updated, many chapters have been significantly revised, and one chapter is new to this edition. The historical moments at the beginning of each chapter have been updated, and we hope these will capture your attention as they visually communicate historical developments and connections among key events over time. Instructors can incorporate the historical information and the attendant learning activities into their lectures, assignments, and tests.

Although the chapters deal with various competencies that you should acquire as a future sport manager, the ability to make principled ethical decisions and to think critically are essential and are discussed throughout the book. The chapter authors have analyzed ethical and critical thinking issues related to their respective topics. As a future sport manager, you will need to understand ethical principles and moral psychology so you can act in socially responsible ways and effectively deal with the numerous ethical issues you will face. In addition, because of the myriad issues that will confront you throughout your career as a sport manager, you need critical thinking skills to guide you in making sound decisions.

Also, because of the increased attention paid to sport as an international pursuit and the overall activities leading to the globalization of sport, current and future sport managers need an understanding and appreciation of international issues and cultures. Besides offering a specific chapter on international sport (chapter 19) and providing steps to help you prepare for effective involvement in the global community, this edition provides new and revised international profile sidebars in each chapter. Ashleigh-Jane Thompson (La Trobe University, Australia) served as the international liaison; an examination of the variety of individuals, countries, and topics represented will reveal her outstanding contribution to this edition. Each international profile addresses a sport management issue from the perspective of the represented country. We respect the linguistic customs of all countries, so we have retained the voices of the sidebar authors; consequently, they might contain words or expressions that are new to you. We encourage you to take advantage of the opportunities that these features provide to learn more about cultures outside the United States. We hope you will find these essays informative and that they will whet your appetite for learning more about sport and its management in other countries.

Some key features of this sixth edition of *Contemporary Sport Management* are carried over from previous editions. For instance, throughout the chapters, we once again cover diversity in sport management by addressing content, cases, and examples of people of different ages, genders, abilities, social classes, sexual orientations, races, ethnicities, and cultures. The inclusive nature of the text fosters a better understanding and appreciation of the variety of stakeholders that exist in the sport industry.

Although each chapter of the book addresses a particular aspect of sport management, many of the chapters have important similarities. Several chapters address ethical, legal, economic, and communication concerns. By including these topics in several chapters, we hope to reinforce important concepts that you will find useful as you progress in your professional preparation program. Furthermore, some chapters contain real-life scenarios or news stories that illustrate important points. We believe that these features enhance the book.

Each chapter has at least one sport industry professional profile. These features include a photograph of the professional, information on his or her career, and a question-and-answer section. Those featured in this edition include professionals in sport agency management, law, marketing and branding, management, facility and event operations, professional and amateur sport, intercollegiate and interscholastic athletics, sport tourism, for-profit and nonprofit organizations, sport finance, community sport, sport entrepreneurship, and other areas and segments of the sport industry. The following professionals are profiled: Kristin Bernert (NBA New York Knicks), Ross Bjork (University of Mississippi), Mike Blackburn (National Interscholastic Athletic Administrators Association), Kirsten Britton (College of Holy Cross), Trevor Bukstein (NBA Phoenix Suns), Scott Crowder (Pond Hockey Classic), Andy De Angulo (Ransom Everglades School Athletics), Kyle Dubas (NHL Toronto Maple Leafs), Ashley Feagan (Creative Artists Agency), Marshall Fey (Northwest Missouri State University), Alicia Greco-Walker (University of Delaware), Terri Carmichael Jackson (Women's National Basketball Players Association), Kalen Jackson (NFL Indianapolis Colts), Jessica James (University of Florida), Megan Kahn (Alliance of Women Coaches), Nicole Kankam (United States Tennis Association), Donna Lopiano (Sports Management Resources), Ellen Lucey (Bauerfeind), Sheila N. Nguyen (Sports Environment Alliance), Mitch Moser (Duke University Athletics), Heidi Pellerano (Wasserman), Keri Potts (ESPN), Tracy Schoenadel (SMG Insight), Steven J. Silver (Pierce Atwood's Litigation Practice Group), Andrew Tinnish (MLB Toronto Blue Jays), Vernon Walker (National Basketball Association), and Bill Wise (Central Baptist Church, College Station, Texas).

Features of the Book

This text includes the following learning aids to help you understand and retain the information:

- Each chapter begins with learning objectives. These objectives serve as an outline for reading and studying the chapter.
- The Historical Moments section in each chapter lists key moments in the development of the study and practice of sport management such as the establishment of sport organizations, the commencement of sport journals, the arrival of sport leaders, and so on.
- A running glossary provides definitions of key terms at the bottom of the page on which they appear.
- A web study guide (WSG) provides opportunities to practice with the material. We included a wide variety of exercises to accommodate different learning styles and preferences.
- The review questions at the end of each chapter reinforce the key points of the chapter.
- References for each chapter are listed in the back of this textbook, and each part opener includes a For More Information section. We hope you will use the information in these sections for further reading and exploration.

Instructor Resources

Although the preceding sections have outlined how this new edition will be useful to students, note that several items are also useful to instructors. If you have not read the previous sections, please be sure to do so. This sixth edition is supported by the following ancillaries:

- *Instructor guide.* The instructor guide provides a sample syllabus; an explanation of what is included in the WSG, how students should use various WSG activities, and how instructors can use the WSG to prepare for and supplement their classes; an explanation of and a discussion about the importance of critical thinking in sport management; and chapter-by-chapter files that contain lecture outlines, chapter summaries, and additional activities that can be used to supplement the WSG activities.

- *Test package.* The test package includes hundreds of questions in various formats: multiple choice, true–false, fill-in-the-blank, and short answer or essay. These questions are available in multiple formats for a variety of instructor uses and can be used to create tests and quizzes to measure student understanding.

• *Chapter quizzes.* These ready-made quizzes are compatible with learning management systems and can be used to measure student learning of the most important concepts for each chapter. Over 200 questions are included in true–false, multiple choice, and fill-in-the-blank formats.

• *Presentation package plus image bank.* The presentation package includes hundreds of slides that cover the key points of each chapter. You can use these slides as they are presented, but you are encouraged to modify and add to these slides so that they more fully adhere to specific lecture outlines, class structures, and instructor preferences. The image bank includes all the figures and tables from the book separated by chapter. These items can be added to the presentation package, student handouts, and so on.

• *Web study guide.* The WSG provides students with many activities that challenge them to think about careers in sport management, demonstrate an understanding of a chapter's content, complete website searches and write essays, thoughtfully consider critical thinking and ethical issues, and test their comprehension of a chapter's main objectives. All these ancillaries can be found at www.HumanKinetics.com/ContemporarySportMan agement.

Acronyms

AAA: American Automobile Association

AACSB: Association to Advance Collegiate Schools of Business

AAGPBL: All-American Girls Professional Baseball League

AAU: Amateur Athletic Union

ABC: American Bowling Congress

ABL: American Basketball League

ACBSP: Accreditation Council for Business Schools and Programs

ACC: Atlantic Coast Conference

AD: athletic director

ADA: Americans with Disabilities Act

AE: athletic exposures

AEMA: Athletic Equipment Managers Association

AFL: American Football League

AHL: American Hockey League

AIAW: Association for Intercollegiate Athletics for Women

AIHEC: American Indian Higher Education Consortium

AIMS: International Association of Ultramarathons

APR: academic progress rate

AR: augmented reality

ASA: Amateur Softball Association; American Statistical Association

AT: athletic trainer

ATTA: Adventure Travel Trade Association

BAA: Basketball Association of America

BIRGing: basking in reflected glory

BOG: board of governors

CAA: certified athletic administrator; Creative Artists Agency

CAAU: Canadian Amateur Athletic Union

CABMA: College Athletic Business Management Association

CART: Championship Auto Racing Teams

CAS: Court of Arbitration for Sport

CBA: collective bargaining agreement

CCCAA: California Community College Athletic Association

CEO: chief executive officer

CFL: Canadian Football League

CFO: chief financial officer

CFP: College Football Playoff

CFR: Code of Federal Regulations

CIAA: Central Intercollegiate Athletic Association

CIAAA: Canadian Interscholastic Athletic Administrator Association

CLA: Christian liberal arts

CMAA: certified master athletic administrator

CMO: chief marketing officer

CODEME: Mexican Sports Confederation

COM: Mexican Olympic Committee

CONADE: Comisión Nacional de Cultura Física y Deporte, México

CONMEBOL: Confederación Sudamericana de Fútbol

COO: chief operating officer

CoSIDA: College Sports Information Directors of America

COSMA: Commission on Sport Management Accreditation

CSM: contemporary sport management

CSR: corporate social responsibility

CSV: creating shared value

CTE: chronic traumatic encephalopathy

CYO: Catholic Youth Organization

DFS: daily fantasy sports

DOE: U.S. Department of Education

DMO: destination marketing organization

DRL: Drone Racing League

EADA: Equity in Athletics Disclosure Act

ECAC: Eastern College Athletic Conference

ECHL: East Coast Hockey League

ECS: Esports Championship Series

EPA: Environmental Protection Agency

EPL: English Premier League

ESPN: Entertainment and Sports Programming Network

EU: European Union

EUSA: European University Sports Association

F1: Formula One

FBS: Football Bowl Subdivision

FCS: Football Championship Subdivision

FHSAA: Florida High School Athletic Association

FIBA: International Basketball Federation

FIFA: Fédération Internationale de Football Association

FIH: International Hockey Federation

FISU: Federation Internationale du Sport Universitaire

FSG: Fenway Sports Group

FTC: Federal Trade Commission

GATT: General Agreement on Tariffs and Trade

GBR: Great Barrier Reef

GDP: gross domestic product

GLSEN: Gay, Lesbian, and Straight Education Network

GMAT: Graduate Management Admission Test

GOTR: Girls on the Run

GPS: global positioning system

GRE: Graduate Record Examinations

HBCU: historically Black colleges and universities

HRM: human resource management

HWI: historically White institutions

IAAF: International Association of Athletics Federations

IAAUS: Intercollegiate Athletic Association of the United States

IACBE: International Assembly for Collegiate Business Education

IBAF: International Baseball Federation

ICC: International Cricket Council

IF: international sport federation

IHL: International Hockey League

IIT: image identification technology

IMG: International Management Group

INDE: National Institute of Sports

IOC: International Olympic Committee

IPC: International Paralympic Committee

IPL: Indian Premier League

IRS: Internal Revenue Service

ISEP: International Student Exchange Program

IT: information technology

IWFL: Independent Women's Football League

LGBTQ: lesbian, gay, bisexual, transgender, and questioning

LPGA: Ladies Professional Golf Association

MEAC: Mid-Eastern Athletic Conference

MFSHSA: Midwest Federation of State High School Athletic Associations

MLB: Major League Baseball

MLBAM: Major League Baseball Advanced Media

MLBPA: Major League Baseball Players Association

MLS: Major League Soccer

MNF: *Monday Night Football*

MSO: multisport organization

MSOC: Multi-Sport Organizations Council

N4A: National Association of Academic Advisors for Athletics

NAAC: National Association for Athletics Compliance

NABBP: National Association of Base Ball Players

NACE: National Association of Colleges and Employers

NACMA: National Association of College Marketing Administrators

NAFTA: North American Free Trade Agreement

NAIA: National Association of Intercollegiate Athletics

NAPBBP: National Association of Professional Base Ball Players

NASCAR: National Association for Stock Car Auto Racing

NASPE: National Association for Sport and Physical Education

NASSM: North American Society for Sport Management

NAYS: National Alliance for Youth Sports

NBA: National Basketball Association

NBL: National Basketball League

NCA: National Coaches Association

NCAA: National Collegiate Athletic Association

NCCAA: National Christian College Athletic Association

NCPA: National College Players Association

NFHS: National Federation of State High School Associations

NFL: National Football League

NFLPA: National Football League Players Association

NHL: National Hockey League

NHRA: National Hot Rod Association

NIAAA: National Interscholastic Athletic Administrators Association

NIF: Norwegian Olympic and Paralympic Committee and Confederation of Sports

NJCAA: National Junior College Athletic Association

NL: National League

NLL: National Lacrosse League

NLRA: National Labor Relations Act

NLRB: National Labor Relations Board

NPF: National Pro Fastpitch

NSO: national sport organization

NWAC: Northwest Athletic Conference

NWSL: National Women's Soccer League

NZRFU: New Zealand Rugby Football Union

OCOG: Organizing Committee for the Olympic Games

OGGI: Olympic Games Global Impact

OGI: Olympic Games Impact

OHL: Ontario Hockey League

OMTOM: Old Mutual Two Oceans Marathon

OTT: over-the-top (delivery)

PAL: Police Athletic League

PASR: physical activity, sport, and recreation

PAYS: Parents Association for Youth Sports

PFL: Professional Futsal League

PGA: Professional Golfers' Association of America

PR: public relations

PSL: personal seat license

RAA: registered athletic administrator

RMSAA: registered middle school athletic administrator

ROE: return on experience

ROI: return on investment

ROO: return on objective

RWC: Rugby World Cup

SBJ: Street & Smith's SportsBusiness Journal

SBYD: sport-based youth development

SCCA: Sports Car Club of America

SEC: Southeastern Conference

SES: socioeconomic status

SFIA: Sports and Fitness Industry Association

SGD: Sporting Goods Dealer

SHAPE America: Society of Health and Physical Educators

SID: sports information director

SKU: stock keeping unit

SOCOG: Sydney Organising Committee for the Olympic Games

SOS: Spirit of Sydney

SPSS: Statistical Package for the Social Sciences

SRC: sport-related concussions

SSC: School Sport Canada

SSCM: strategic sport communication model

SWA: senior woman administrator

SWAC: Southwest Athletic Conference

TCU: tribal colleges and universities

tDCS: transcranial direct current stimulation

TSN: The Sports Network

TUSF: Turkish University Sports Federation

UEFA: Union of European Football Associations

UFC: Ultimate Fighting Championship

UIGEA: Unlawful Internet Gambling Enforcement Act

UIL: University Interscholastic League

UNEP: United Nations Environment Programme

UNWTO: World Tourism Organization

USAC: United States Auto Club

USBA: United States Boxing Association

USC: United States Code

USGA: United States Golf Association

USLTA: United States Lawn Tennis Association

USOC: United States Olympic Committee

USTA: United States Tennis Association

USVBA: United States Volleyball Association

USWFL: United States Women's Football League

UWLX: United Women's Lacrosse League

VANOC: Vancouver Organizing Committee for the 2010 Olympic and Paralympic Winter Games

VR: virtual reality

WADA: World Anti-Doping Agency

WBA: World Boxing Association

WBC: World Baseball Classic

WBPL: Women's Professional Basketball League

WBS: work breakdown structure

WFA: Women's Football Alliance

WIBC: Women's International Bowling Congress

WLCS: Women Leaders in College Sports

WME: William Morris Endeavor

WME/IMG: William Morris Endeavor/International Management Group

WNBA: Women's National Basketball Association

WNBPA: Women's National Basketball Players Association

WoSIDA: Women Sports Information Directors of America

WPA: win probability added

WPF: Women's Professional Fastpitch

WPFL: Women's Professional Football League

WPS: Women's Professional Soccer

WPSL: Women's Premier Soccer League

WR: World Rugby

WSA: Women Sport Australia

WSF: Women's Sports Foundation

WSG: web study guide

WTA: Women's Tennis Association

WUSA: Women's United Soccer Association

YMCA: Young Men's Christian Association

YOG: Youth Olympic Games

YWCA: Young Women's Christian Association

PART I

Introduction to Sport Management

Professional preparation for

careers in sport management should be built on a strong conceptual foundation. This opening section provides such a foundation because it presents basic, yet important and sometimes overlooked, information and key concepts with which prospective sport managers should be well acquainted. The first three chapters take you through an overview of the field in general, examine professional considerations vital to success in the sport industry, and review key aspects of the history of the field. The last two chapters of this section involve managerial and leadership concepts applied to sport management personnel and sport organizations.

In chapter 1, the editors of this sixth edition, Paul M. Pedersen and Lucie Thibault, provide an overview of the field by introducing sport management as an academic major and a career field. After defining sport and sport management, they delineate the types of sports in the industry and the settings in which sporting activities are found. The authors then segment the sport industry by introducing the Contemporary Sport Management (CSM) Sport Industry Sectors Model. They next discuss several characteristics of sport-related enterprises that distinguish them from other business pursuits and then describe competencies that are essential for success in sport management. Among the competencies examined is a strategy whereby you can develop critical thinking skills and learn to apply them to issues in sport management. The message of this part of the chapter is that sport managers who can think critically about sport-related issues will be competent, reflective professionals who have the potential to become influential agents of change. The chapter concludes with an overview of the opportunities and challenges that sport managers will face in the future. Among the challenges detailed in this part of the chapter are ethics, social responsibility, and principled decision making. The sport management professionals featured in this chapter are Kalen Jackson, the vice chair/owner of the Indianapolis Colts of the National Football League (NFL), and Ashley Feagan, an agent in the sports endorsements and talent sales division of Creative Artists Agency (CAA). In the international profile sidebar, John Harris (Glasgow Caledonian University, Scotland) examines the historical development and continued internationalization of rugby leading up to the 2019 Rugby World Cup in Asia.

Chapter 2 contains information that will help you develop a professional perspective on your studies and your career. Sally R. Ross, Brian P. McCullough, and Susan E.C. Simmons begin by providing a preview of the courses and experiences that you can expect in the preparation program at your college or university. Next, they discuss essential elements of a positive professional perspective: attitude, image, work transition and adjustment, and business etiquette. The authors give special attention to career planning and management and offer sound advice regarding career steps and finding a career that is compatible with your values, interests, and skills. They close the chapter by offering insights on career readiness competencies. Ellen Lucey, the director of consumer and sport marketing at Bauerfeind, is the profiled sport management professional in this chapter. The international profile sidebar contains an essay by Germany's Norbert Schütte (Universität Mainz, Germany). Schütte uses contingency theory to illustrate the sport system in Germany and the development of professional sport management education and opportunities in the country.

The purpose of chapter 3 is to provide a history of sport businesses and market structures so you, as a future sport manager, can understand the significant historical influences on the field and develop strategies for your businesses. Elizabeth A. Gregg, Brenda G. Pitts, and Paul M. Pedersen first present a historical analysis of the commercialization of sport including the rise of management in sport. The authors examine the numerous commercialization models of the developmental periods of the sport business industry. They then discuss the historical aspects of the sport market. Included in this discussion are key watershed events, ranging from endorsement advertising to increased participation and spectatorship, that caused massive changes in the way business in the sport industry was (and is) conducted. The authors then provide an overview of select individuals who were educated and trained in history who had an influence on the development and growth of sport management as a field of study. The professional profiles in this chapter are on Donna Lopiano, the president and founder of Sports Management Resources and the former CEO of the Women's Sports Foundation, and Vernon Walker, the associate manager of event management for the National Basketball Association (NBA). Geoff Watson (Massey University, New Zealand) contributed the international profile sidebar for this chapter; it presents a short overview of rugby and the professionalization of New Zealand's national sports.

In chapter 4, Kathy Babiak, Kathryn Heinze, and Lucie Thibault define the term *organization* and describe three types of sport organizations: public, nonprofit, and commercial. This discussion is followed by explanations of organizational environment, organizational effectiveness, strategic planning, organizational culture, organizational structure and design, and organizational change and innovation. Throughout the chapter, the authors present research on sport organizations and explain how the research findings apply to real-world situations in organizations. Trevor Bukstein, the assistant general manager for the NBA Phoenix Suns, and Brandon Rhodes, associate marketing manager for Gatorade Digital Strategy, are the featured sport management professionals in this chapter. In the international profile sidebar, Milena M. Parent (University of Ottawa, Canada, and the Norwegian School of Sport Sciences, Norway) uses a case study to illustrate the unique aspects of international multisport event organizing committees and the way such organizations are similar to enduring sport organizations.

Organizational behavior, individual aspects of managerial positions and leadership, decision making, authority, power, and diversity in sport organizations are examined in chapter 5. First, Shannon Kerwin, Ming Li, and Laura J. Burton illustrate three approaches to management: scientific, human relations, and administrative. After detailing managerial processes, functions, classifications, and skills, the authors explain theoretical approaches to the study of leadership and end the discussion with the integrative concept of managerial leadership. The authors then present decision making, authority, and power aspects associated with management. They conclude the chapter by covering organizational diversity and the keys to support inclusive diversity practices in sport organizations. The professionals profiled in this chapter are Kirsten Britton, the associate director of athletics for facilities, operations, and events at the College of the Holy Cross, and Jessica James, the assistant director of development and alumni affairs for the College of Liberal Arts and Sciences at the University of Florida. The international profile sidebar is an essay by Kong-Ting Yeh (National Taiwan Sport University) about the recent development and popularity of Taiwanese road running.

Chapters 4 and 5 are important because aspiring sport managers should become familiar with theories of organizational behavior, management, and leadership and should be able to apply these theories in practical settings. Therefore, the last two chapters of this section address the structure and processes of sport organizations and present desirable attributes of managers and leaders in the sport industry. The underlying theme of the two chapters is that managers have a responsibility to themselves, their employees, and their stakeholders to appreciate and apply theoretical concepts that will improve the effectiveness and efficiency of the workplace as well as the quality of the sport product or experience. The knowledge that is gained from these two chapters, combined with what is presented in the first three chapters, will form the foundation of professional preparation for careers in sport management. The opening five chapters also provide the foundation on which the remaining 16 chapters of the book are built.

For More Information

Professional and Scholarly Associations, Institutes, and Organizations

African Sport Management Association (ASMA)

Amateur Athletic Union of the United States (AAU)

Asian Association for Sport Management (AASM)

Birkbeck Sport Business Centre

College Athletic Business Management Association (CABMA)

Commission on Sport Management Accreditation (COSMA)

European Association of Sport Employers (EASE)

European Association for Sport Management (EASM)

European Non-Governmental Sports Organisation (EnGSO)

Global Sport Business Association (GSBA)

The H.J. Lutcher Stark Center for Physical Culture and Sports

Institute for Diversity and Ethics in Sport

Institute for International Sport

International Mind Sports Association (IMSA)

International Olympic Committee (IOC)

International Paralympic Committee (IPC)

International Sport Management Alliance

Japanese Association for Sport Management (JASM)

Josephson Institute Center for Sports Ethics

Korean Society for Sport Management (KSSM)

Laboratory for Diversity in Sport

Latin American Association for Sport Management (ALGeDe)

National Sporting Goods Association (NSGA)

North American Society for Sport History (NASSH)

North American Society for Sport Management (NASSM)

North American Society for the Sociology of Sport (NASSS)

Play the Game

Professional Baseball Employment Opportunities (PBEO)

SHAPE America: Society of Health and Physical Educators

Sport and Fitness Industry Association (SFIA)

Sport Management Association of Australia and New Zealand (SMAANZ)

The Sports Business Institute

World Anti-Doping Agency (WADA)

World Association for Sport Management (WASM)

World Federation of the Sporting Goods Industry (WFSGI)

Select Professional and Scholarly Publications

Academy of Management Journal

Academy of Management Review

Administrative Science Quarterly

Asian Sport Management Review

Athletic Business

European Sport Management Quarterly

Global Sport Business Journal

Global Sport Management News

Harvard Business Review

International Journal of Sport Management

International Journal of Sport Management and Marketing

International Journal of Sport Management, Recreation, and Tourism

International Journal of Sport Policy and Politics

International Journal of the History of Sport

Journal of Applied Sport Management

Journal of Global Sport Management

Journal of the Philosophy of Sport

Journal of Sport History

Journal of Sport Management

Korean Journal of Sport Management

National Sporting Goods Association (NSGA) Now

SGMA Industry Marketplace

Sport, Business and Management: An International Journal

SportBusiness International

Sport History Review

Sport in History

Sport Management Education Journal

Sport Management International Journal: Choregia

Sport Management Review

SportBusiness International

Sporting Goods Intelligence

Sporting Traditions

Sports Business News

Strategic Management Journal

Street & Smith's SportsBusiness Daily

Street & Smith's SportsBusiness Journal

Sport Management Job Market

AthleticLink

Game Face

iHire

Jobs in Sports

Malakye

Monster

North American Society for Sport Management

Online Sports

Quintessential Careers

Sport Business Research Network

Sports Careers

SportsOneSource

TeamWork Online

Women Sports Jobs

Work in Sports

Managing Sport

Paul M. Pedersen
Lucie Thibault

LEARNING OBJECTIVES

- Discuss examples of traditional and nontraditional sport activities.
- Identify settings in which sport activities occur.
- Explain ways of organizing the sport industry.
- Identify three sectors of organizations that operate in the sport industry.
- Discuss unique aspects of sport management and the types of positions available in the field.
- Explain competencies required for success as a sport manager.
- Identify ways sport industry stakeholders can effectively use social media.
- Apply critical thinking skills to a problem in sport management.
- Discuss opportunities and challenges facing sport managers of the future.

KEY TERMS

descriptive
discretionary funds
extreme sports
organizational culture
prescriptive
principled decision making
underrepresented groups
workforce diversity

1949
Baseball business administration offered at Florida Southern University

1964
Stan Isaacs published *Careers and Opportunities in Sports*

1966
First sport administration program established at Ohio University

1970s
Sport Management Arts and Science Society, forerunner of NASSM, conceived

1985
North American Society for Sport Management (NASSM) established

1987
Journal of Sport Management launched

1990
Janet B. Parks and Beverly Zanger published *Sport and Fitness Management,* a forerunner of *Contemporary Sport Management*

1992
NASSM Code of Ethics adopted

1993
NASPE–NASSM curricular standards published

European Association for Sport Management (EASM) established

1994
Pitts, Fielding, and Miller's sport industry segment model introduced

Jackie Robinson, whose legendary life has been well-chronicled in books (e.g., Henry, 2017), movies (e.g., *42*), and productions such as filmmaker Ken Burns' 2016 two-part television series *Jackie Robinson* (for which actor Jamie Foxx did the voiceover), broke the modern color barrier in Major League Baseball (MLB) in 1947 when he stepped onto the field for the Brooklyn (now Los Angeles) Dodgers. Branch Rickey, the hall of fame general manager of the team, had carefully selected and groomed Robinson, who went on to a hall of fame career and was named one of *Time*'s 100 most important individuals of the 20th century. In 1957, the year after Robinson's last at bat, Walter O'Malley (the president and chief stockholder of the Dodgers) anticipated the future growth of organized sport and predicted the need for professionally prepared sport administrators. O'Malley wrote a letter to Dr. James Mason, a faculty member at Ohio University, that stated the following:

> I ask the question, where would one go to find a person who by virtue of education had been trained to administer a marina, race track, ski resort, auditorium, stadium, theater, convention or exhibition hall, a public camp complex, or a person to fill an executive position at a team or league level in junior athletics such as Little League baseball, football, scouting, CYO (Catholic Youth Organization), and youth activities, etc.? A course that would enable a graduate to read architectural and engineering plans; or having to do with specifications and contract letting, the functions of a purchasing agent in plant operations. There would be the problems of ticket selling and accounting, concessions, sale of advertising in programs, and publications, outdoor and indoor displays and related items. (Mason, Higgins, & Wilkinson, 1981, p. 44)

Because of that inquiry, Mason and several of his colleagues created a master's-level sport administration program at Ohio University. Inaugurated in 1966, the Ohio program was the first recorded university-sponsored attempt to provide a graduate-level curriculum that specifically prepared students for jobs in a variety of sport-related industries. The idea caught on, and over the next five decades hundreds of sport management programs were started at universities and colleges around the globe. According to the North American Society for Sport Management (NASSM, n.d.), there are more than 580 universities and colleges offering 484 undergraduate sport management programs, 296 master's programs, and 47 doctoral programs in Africa, Asia, Australia, Canada, Europe, India, New Zealand, and the United States (see table 1.1). Refer to chapter 2 for more information on some of the common characteristics of academic programs in sport management.

This chapter is the first step on your journey toward becoming a sport manager. It includes definitions of basic terms, a discussion of the nature and scope of the sport industry, and explanations of unique aspects of sport management enterprises and careers. You will also learn about desirable sport management competencies and some of the challenges and opportunities that await you as you prepare to take your place among the next generation of sport managers.

Defining Sport and Sport Management

For most of us, *sport* implies having fun, but it can also be work (for a professional athlete), a means of employment (for a sport tourism director), or a business (for a sport marketing agency). If someone questions whether sport is a business, simply refer

1995
Sport Management Association of Australia and New Zealand (SMAANZ) established

2001
European Sport Management Quarterly launched (formerly *European Journal for Sport Management* [1994])

2012
World Association for Sport Management (WASM) formally established

2016
Massachusetts Institute of Technology (MIT) hosted the 10th MIT Sloan Sports Analytics Conference

2018
Over 800 sport management programs (bachelor's, master's, and doctoral degrees) established around the globe

NBA 2K League, a 17-team esports league, launched

1998
Sport Management Review launched

2002
Sport Marketing Association (SMA) established

2013
Global Sport Business Association (GSBA) formed

2017
25th European Association for Sport Management (EASM) conference held in Switzerland

Table 1.1 Sport Management Programs in Selected Continents or Countries

Continent/Country	Bachelor's degree program	Master's degree program	Doctoral program	Total
Africa	1	1	0	2
Asia	12	13	3	28
Australia	13	4	1	18
Canada	16	7	6	29
Europe	15	27	2	44
India	0	1	0	1
New Zealand	4	1	0	5
United States	423	242	35	700
Total	484	296	47	827

Data from North American Society for Sport Management 2018. Available: http://www.nassm.com/Programs/AcademicPrograms

that person to the sport of mixed martial arts. In 2016, the talent agency WME/IMG (William Morris Endeavor/International Management Group, now known as Endeavor) purchased the Ultimate Fighting Championship (UFC) for US$4 billion. Beyond the UFC, the examples of sport as a business are almost endless, ranging from the amateur levels all the way through to the professional ranks (e.g., in 2017 Neymar signed a record-breaking US$265-million deal with Paris Saint-Germain, which also paid a record-breaking US$263-million transfer fee to Barcelona).

Sport takes many forms. Team sports include multiple participants (e.g., soccer, volleyball) working collectively to defeat the opposing team, dual sports include two participants (e.g., wrestling, tennis, badminton) facing each other in competition, and indi-

vidual sports have one participant (e.g., golf, in-line skating, surfing) who may compete with others but focuses on his or her own performance.

What criteria qualify games or activities to be classified as sport? Consider, for example, electronic sports (esports). In 2018 the National Basketball Association (NBA) launched the NBA 2K League, which is an esports league consisting of 17 teams with five players each. Certain universities in the United States have esports degree programs and even offer scholarships to esports athletes, and in certain immigration cases, the U.S. government recognizes professional video gamers as individual athletes. Thus, certain people who play video games at a high level can now call themselves athletes. Around the world, there are professional esports events (e.g., World Cyber Games, Electronic Sports World

Convention) and leagues (e.g., Japan Pro e-Sports Federation, Mexican eSports League). Some of the major players in this sport industry segment are ESL (Electronic Sports League), Activision Blizzard, Riot Games, Twitch, Facebook Live, ELEAGUE, and YouTube Gaming ("Players," 2017). By 2020, esports are projected to reach US$1.49 billion in revenue from sponsorship (US$655 million), media rights (US$340 million), advertising (US$224 million), merchandise and tickets (US$135 million), and game publisher fees (US$133 million) ("Snapshots," 2017). Given that participants are often considered athletes (e.g., training, competition, scholarships) and that there are various professional leagues and events, should we classify video gaming as a sport?

Should the sport classification apply to drone competitions, such as the events of the Drone Racing League (DRL) that are broadcast on ESPN and Sky Sports? Emma Lloyd, group business development director at Sky, said "We're thrilled to be partnering with DRL to help develop this exciting new sport. . . . We're really looking forward to working with the team at DRL to grow the sport and to bring something completely different to audiences across

Nothing New Under the Sun

Lest we be deluded by the notion that contemporary sport management is markedly different from the ancient art of staging athletic spectacles, let us consider for a moment the following description of the games sponsored in 11 BCE by Herod the Great, king of Judea and honorary president of the Olympic Games:

> The games began with a magnificent dedication ceremony. Then there were athletic and musical competitions, in which large prizes were given not only to the winners but also—an unusual feature—to those who took second and third place. Bloody spectacles were also presented, with gladiators and wild beasts fighting in various combinations, and there were also horse races. Large prizes attracted contenders from all areas and this in turn drew great numbers of spectators. Cities favored by Herod sent delegations, and these he entertained and lodged at his own expense. What comes through most clearly . . . is that gigantic sums of money were spent. (Frank, 1984, p. 158)

The success of such an extravaganza relied in all likelihood on the organizational skills of the individuals charged with planning and executing the games. Certainly there was today's equivalent of a general manager, or CEO, to whom all other personnel were responsible. Additionally, assistants who were knowledgeable in economics, accounting, and finance were indispensable if the event was to become profitable. The "business managers" were responsible for obtaining financial support, purchasing equipment (and perhaps even the requisite beasts), furnishing entertainment and lodging for the VIPs, and generally being accountable for the large sums of money that were spent.

Once the financial dimension was secured, there was the challenge of attracting sufficient numbers of contestants and spectators to the games. Enter Herod's "marketing director," armed with unique and unprecedented gimmicks to assure a full complement of participants as well as a full house of onlookers. A new prize structure was devised and, in awarding prizes to musicians as well as athletes, the seeds were sown for the modern spectacle known, among other titles, as the Battle of the Bands. The marketing director must have enlisted the aid of assistants who were responsible for extending invitations, publicizing the games, and keeping records of the day's activities. In the years prior to the printing press, much less the electronic media, informing the public was no small task—to say nothing of offering enticements sufficient to persuade them to journey for days and endure what must have been extremely undesirable traveling conditions. The marketing and promotion people certainly had their hands full!

The parallel[s] could continue—there was a need for crowd control, rules decisions, award ceremonies, and so forth. After all, certain tasks must be performed regardless of the venue in which the event occurs. Now, 2000 years later, we are reminded once again of Solomon's wisdom in proclaiming in Ecclesiastes 1:9 that "there is no new thing under the sun."

Reprinted, by permission, from J.B. Parks and G.A. Olafson, 1987, "Sport management and a new journal," *Journal of Sport Management* 1(1): 1-2.

both TV and digital" (Sky Sports, 2016, para. 9-10). There are numerous drone racing entities such as DR1 Racing (with races broadcast on Fox Sports, beIN Sports, CBS, and Eurosport and a format that includes the DHL Champions Series, featuring teams around the world), MultiGP (with over 20,000 pilots and over 1,100 international chapters), X Class Drone Racing, Freedom Class Giant Drone Racing, International Drone Racing Association, and many more around the globe. Do the formation of teams, the establishment of race objectives, the competitive aspects, and the technological features of drone racing make it a sport?

Is horse racing a sport? What about stand-up paddleboarding, hantis, freediving, pocket billiards, and Texas Hold'em and other table games? We know that softball, tennis, basketball, ice and field hockey, football, and golf are sports. Are they different from sailing, dog racing, marathoning, and scuba diving? If so, how are they different? If not, how are they similar?

A group of researchers (Jenny, Manning, Keiper, & Olrich, 2016), in adapting the work of previous scholars (e.g., Guttmann, Seybert), noted that the defining characteristics of a sport are that it must include play, be organized (e.g., governed by rules), include competition, be comprised of skill and not chance, include physicality (e.g., physical skills), have a broad following, and have achieved institutionalization (e.g., institutional stability as an important social practice rather than a fad). While their characteristics of sport and thus their overall definition might be viewed as somewhat restrictive, other scholars (e.g., Pitts & Stotlar, 2013) have provided broader definitions. For instance, sport management professor Brenda Pitts notes that sport,

> as defined and used in sport management, is a broad concept term used to denote all people, activities, businesses, and organizations involved in producing, facilitating, promoting, or organizing any activity, experience, or business enterprise focused on fitness, recreation, athletics, or leisure; sport products include goods, services, people, places, and ideas. (B.G. Pitts, personal communication, November 18, 2017)

Based on such a definition, sport does not have to be competitive, nor does it always require specialized equipment or rules; in fact, the broad concept of sport can include activities such as working out, swimming, running, boating, and dancing. For this book, we adopt this broader definition (which includes sports covered in the more restrictive definition), and we encourage you to interpret the term *sport* to include an expansive variety of physical activities and associated businesses.

Many people who are employed in business endeavors associated with sport are engaged in a career field known as *sport management.* (Other names for this field include sport administration, sport business management, and athletic administration, but we use sport management.) Several professionals profiled throughout this textbook who are employed in various segments of the sport management field studied sport management as undergraduates (e.g., Ashley Feagan later in this chapter, Alicia Greco-Walker in chapter 16, Kyle Dubas in chapter 20) or graduate students (e.g., Kristin Bernert in chapter 12, Mitch Moser in chapter 15). Sport management—or sport business management, as it is referred to by scholars Brenda Pitts and David Stotlar (2013)—is "the study and practice of all people, activities, businesses, or organizations involved in producing, facilitating, promoting, or organizing any sport-related business or product" (p. 3). Again, this broad definition includes an incredibly wide variety of sport-related careers.

Sport management is also the name given to many college- and university-level academic programs that prepare students to assume positions in the sport industry. These programs provide two additional sources of confusion regarding vocabulary. First, you might have noticed that many professional preparation programs are titled *sport* management, whereas others are called *sports* management. In our view, people prefer one or the other based on the connotations that the words *sports* and *sport* have for them. To many academics, ourselves included, *sports* implies a collection of separate activities such as golf, soccer, hockey, volleyball, softball, and gymnastics—items in a series that we can count. Conversely, *sport* is an all-encompassing concept. It is a collective noun that includes all sport activities. Students often relate well to the parallel with the different connotations of the words *religions* and *religion. Religions* typically connotes several specific faiths or belief systems—different denominations or sects that we can quantify. *Religion*, on the other hand, is a broad term that we can interpret as a general reverence or faith held by any number of people. A second source of confusion is the fact that many professional preparation programs are titled sport (or sports) management whereas others are called by other titles such as sport (or sports) administration. Whether your university's program is labeled as sports management (e.g., Columbia University), athletic administration (e.g., Springfield College), sport

Professional Profile

Courtesy of the Indianapolis Colts.

Title: Vice chair/owner, the Indianapolis Colts

Education: BS (sport management and marketing), Indiana University – Bloomington (IU)

Jackson has been a vice chair and owner of the Indianapolis Colts for five seasons. Before her current role, Jackson served for three years as a vice president of the team. Jackson, who grew up with the Colts, is the president of the Indianapolis Colts Women's Organization. She also represents the team at the league owners' meetings. In August 2016, the National Football League (NFL) and Commissioner Roger Goodell added Kalen to the league's employee benefits committee, where she is responsible for administering club and league benefit plans and is involved in plan design and amendment, benefit and administrative expense payments, and employee eligibility issues. Kalen is on the board of directors for the United Way of Central Indiana and she serves on their community impact committee. Jackson is also heavily involved with the Indianapolis Humane Society and a variety of other local and national nonprofits. Kalen was born and resides in Indianapolis with her husband, Boyd Jackson, and their daughter, Mabel. The following is a snapshot of her development, education, duties, and insights as a leader in the sport industry.

What was your career path?

When describing how I ended up in my current position, the obvious answer would be that I grew up in a family that has had ownership of the Colts since 1972. But on further inspection, I realize that what led me to where I am today is much more complicated than just growing up in the Irsay family. My grandpa, Robert Irsay, bought the Los Angeles Rams in 1972. Only a few months later, he made a trade with Carroll Rosenbloom for the Baltimore Colts. As we all know, this led to the infamous middle-of-the-night move to Indianapolis on March 28th, 1984. When my grandpa passed away in 1997, he left the ownership of the team to my dad, Jim Irsay, who was only 37. I was 9 years old at the time. I guess you could say that the key developments that led me to where I am today started even before I was born.

During my high school and college summers, my responsibilities started with the typical odd jobs of making copies, operating the switchboard, running errands, and just getting to know the basics of how the business of an NFL team works and soaking up everything that I witnessed around me.

I cannot describe the steps that led me to my current position without mentioning my alma mater. I enrolled at IU knowing it had one of the best sport marketing and management programs in the country, which I saw firsthand during my four years there. Shortly after I graduated, I threw myself into the business. While my college education and professors had an immense influence on me and definitely heightened my realization that I was, and always have been, truly passionate about the sport industry, I probably learned more in my first year working full time for the team than I did during my entire time at IU. I say this because in sports it is gaining real-life experiences within the industry that helps you get a pulse on the sport community. It is all about the opportunities in which you choose to partake. What you take away from each experience enables you to grow as a young professional.

When I first started working full time with the Colts, I spent time with employees from every department to learn what their jobs entailed every month out of the year. I eventually landed in sponsorship sales with a role as a sponsorship sales account coordinator, which entails coordination of each sponsorship partner's entire creative inventory in their contract. I did this for about three and a half years while also being involved in general operations of the organization.

As my duties outside of my role as an account coordinator grew, it was time for me to leave my coordination responsibilities behind and focus on the bigger picture. Today, my main role is overseeing our community relations department and helping guide our vision of giving within the community while assisting in public appearances related to said giving. My other responsibilities involve general operations of a variety of departments: marketing, sponsorship, digital media, and tickets.

What characteristics must a person have to be successful in your job?

I think three of the most important characteristics a person must have to be successful in my job are:

1. *Being able think outside the box and take a long view.* We truly are in the entertainment business; therefore, we have to be looking for ways to improve our product even when at the peak of our success. We have to think of innovative ways to keep our consumers engaged and coming back for more. While looking at the present landscape of our organization, we always have to have our eye on the horizon/future of our industry. Our goal is to make sure our product remains unique, competitive, and state-of-the-art while maintaining the highest quality and satisfaction.

2. *Having the ability to multitask [and] be organized and flexible with your time.* For me, my schedule every single day is different, and quite often our industry calls for odd, and long, hours. I think this is part of what makes my job so enjoyable, but sometimes you do have to be prepared to make personal sacrifices for the job at hand.

3. *And lastly, simply being a good communicator and leader.* Healthy communication is something that I feel can be taken for granted. You might think it would be an easy characteristic to have; however, daily we see how miscommunication can cause major problems within departments and between departments throughout an organization, which can lead to lack in efficiency. I have found that good communication leads to healthier office relationships [and] company buy-in to your mission and vision, and [it] creates a more productive work environment.

Which websites, online tools, or resources do you frequently use or refer to?

Our most important tools are our internal resources.

1. Our CRM (customer relationship management) tool: This is a tool that helps us analyze and strengthen our business-to-business relationships (i.e., sponsorships, suites, and ticket outreach).

2. Domo: This is another internal analytics tool that we utilize to help us organize, analyze, and visualize all of our data in order to learn more about our users and how we can better interact and engage with our users/consumers.

3. Lastly, we use the other 31 teams within the NFL as resources frequently when considering a new event, project, potential partnership, etc. to gain insight on specific areas of interest.

Outside of our internal resources, I personally read *Street & Smith's SportsBusiness Journal* as well as a variety of online publications regularly.

What do you consider to be the biggest future challenge in your job or industry?

For me personally, the biggest future challenge in my job would be to overcome the idea of nepotism while being one of the youngest female executives in the NFL. Yes, my sisters and I were handed this unbelievable opportunity to someday take over the Colts, but I have worked very hard, and I plan to continue to work very hard to prove my worth in an extremely competitive industry. Our mom and dad always taught us to live with as much humility as possible, an ideal I try to live by every day.

In regard to our industry, I think our biggest challenge is to continue to remain innovative and unique in an ever-changing entertainment industry where competition only continues to grow. More specifically, the challenge of improving our game-day experience for our consumers, understanding the developing landscape of multiscreen viewing, and learning how to connect with the emergent Generation Z population/consumers.

administration (e.g., University of New Mexico), or sport management (e.g., Brock University), ultimately, the quality of the curriculum is more important than the title of the program.

Nature and Scope of the Sport Industry

Just as there are several definitions of sport, there are many ways to conceptualize the nature and scope of the sport industry. In the following paragraphs, we elaborate on three concepts that, in different ways, provide overviews of sport: (1) types of sports, (2) settings in which sports are found, and (3) models of sport industry segments.

Types of Sports

One way to consider the sport industry is to examine the many types of sports that exist. An awareness of the wide diversity of sport opportunities available to consumers is essential for anyone who anticipates becoming a decision maker in the world of sport. Sport marketers, for instance, must have a good understanding of both traditional and new sports so they can develop effective promotional strategies.

You are already familiar with traditional sports such as rugby, basketball, swimming, volleyball, and tennis. You also know that numerous new sports and physical activities have emerged. In addition to the drone-racing events and the esports leagues noted earlier in the chapter, there are many new, emerging, or rediscovered or reformulated sport activities and sports such as bubble bump football (e.g., International Bubble Football Association), quidditch (e.g., International Quidditch Association), underwater hockey (e.g., World Underwater Federation), pickleball (e.g., International Federation of Pickleball), bossaball (e.g., Bossaball International), and dozens of other often relatively unknown or niche sports activities, events, leagues, and competitions (e.g., beach handball, boomerang, footvolley, paintball). There are also pole sports with a governing body (International Pole Sport Federation) and various international events (e.g., the 2017 Ultra Pole World Championships).

Over the past couple decades, extreme sports such as street luging, base jumping, snowbiking, and sky surfing have become increasingly popular. International sport organizations (e.g., International Olympic Committee), events (e.g., imaginExtreme Barcelona 2018), the mass media (e.g., X Games on ESPN, Dew Tour on NBC), and social media (e.g., videos and photos posted on Stoked's various online platforms) have embraced extreme sports. In addition to sponsored events such as the ones promoted and supported by Red Bull (e.g., Red Bull Cliff Diving World Series in Bosnia, Red Bull Hardline in Wales), fans can watch all types of extreme sports on various websites (e.g., EpicTV) and social media platforms (e.g., Periscope) and on the Extreme Sports Channel. Younger people also enjoy participating in extreme sports.

There is also a heightened interest among adults in participating in ultramarathoning (e.g., thousands of athletes participated in the Marathon des Sables, a six-day foot race through the Sahara), Ironman racing, endurance racing, and survival sport events such as England's Tough Guy and Nettle Warrior. Tough Mudder, an annual obstacle race with over 100 scheduled events around the world, was launched in the United States in 2010 and, according to Rath (2017), is generating US$100 million in revenue. Sport managers of the future should be familiar with these sports and events and should be prepared to make them accessible to even more participants and spectators.

Settings for Sport Activities

Another approach to the sport industry involves examining the many different settings in which sport activities occur. This can provide you with ideas about sites that might need sport managers. The latest edition of the *Sports Market Place Directory* (2017) has more than 14,000 sport-related listings across the following sport industry settings:

- Single sports (e.g., professional leagues, teams, organizations, stakeholders)
- Multisports (e.g., athletic foundations, Olympic sport organizations, sports commissions and conventions and visitors' bureaus, sports halls of fame and museums, state game organizations, high school and youth sports)
- College sports (e.g., college associations, athletic conferences, sport management degree programs)
- Media (e.g., newspapers and magazines; sports business directories; sports radio networks and programs; sports radio stations and satellite radio; sports television, cable, and broadcast networks and programs; sports pay-per-view television; sports television stations and satellite television; sports on the Internet)

---

extreme sports—Action sports that involve adrenaline-inducing exploits and often feature a combination of speed, height, danger, and spectacular stunts.

The sport industry offers sport opportunities ranging from traditional (e.g., basketball) to new (e.g., esports). The multisport court in the photo provides residents with a variety of sport participation options in the Old Town area of Dubrovnik, Croatia, which is surrounded by a wall from medieval times.

Courtesy of Andrea N. Geurin.

- Sport sponsors
- Professional services (e.g., executive search, event planning and security, financial, marketing, consulting, agents and attorneys, medicine, travel, statistical, student-athlete recruiting, ticket services)
- Facilities (e.g., arenas and stadiums, race tracks, facility architects and developers, facility management and concessions)
- Manufacturers and retailers (e.g., equipment, products, software)
- Events, meetings, and trade shows

Sport Industry Segments

A third approach to defining the nature and scope of the sport industry is to create an industry model that shows the relationships among various segments and sectors of the sport industry. Within the various segments of sport management there are segmentation models that are even more specific. For instance, sport communication, which is often considered a segment of sport management, has its own segmentation model (Pedersen, Laucella, Kian, & Geurin, 2017). The strategic sport communication model (SSCM) is detailed in chapter 14. This chapter presents the Contemporary Sport Management (CSM) Sport Industry Sectors Model, which combines the features of three models that represent different approaches to conceptualizing the sport industry: the product type model (Pitts, Fielding, & Miller, 1994), the economic impact model (Meek, 1997), and the sport activity model (Eschenfelder & Li, 2007).

Contemporary Sport Management (CSM) Sport Industry Sectors Model

The sport industry includes three organizational sectors: public, nonprofit, and commercial. These are important categories for the different types of organizations involved in sport and are central to the creation and production of sport products, services, programs, and facilities. In the following paragraphs, we explain the CSM Sport Industry Sectors Model (figure 1.1). In this textbook, sport organizations operating in the public, nonprofit, and commercial sectors are covered.

The model details how three different categories of organizations contribute to the sport industry. The first category, the public sector, includes government-based units, agencies, and departments. These organizations are called public because they are created by the people and for the people. Elected officials and representatives create units to best serve the residents of a town, municipality, region, state, province, territory, or country. Governments provide facilities such as park spaces, recreation centers, and sport areas to their residents, and they develop sport and recreation programs that cater to all residents: children, youth, adults, and older adults. For example, most local governments have a parks and recreation department that provides citizens with sport programs, services, and facilities. In some countries, branches of government provide financial support to nonprofit sport organizations

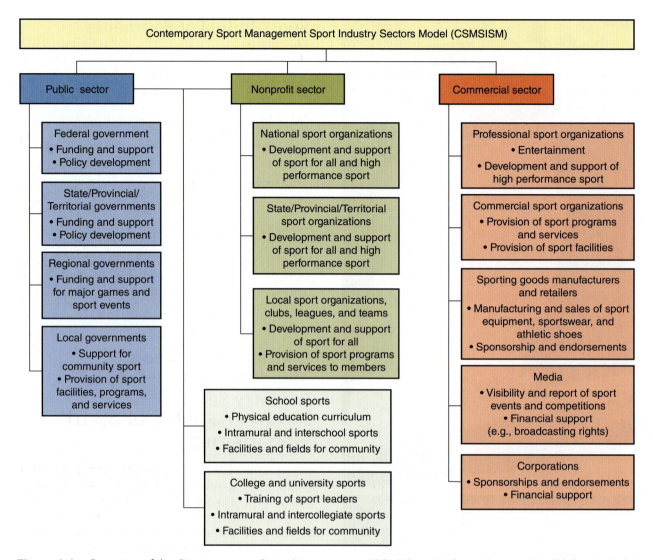

Figure 1.1   Overview of the Contemporary Sport Management (CSM) Sport Industry Sectors Model that includes the primary roles of the organizations.

or provide subsidies to professional sport organizations. In addition, government agencies may develop policies to ensure that everyone has access to sport in a safe environment (e.g., girls and women, people with disabilities, Aboriginal people), policies against doping and cheating, and policies to protect sport participants (e.g., concussion policies).

The second category, the nonprofit sector, includes voluntary organizations whose main purpose is not to make a profit but rather to address a social cause, a special interest, and the needs of members. In many cases, organizations that focus on education, cultural, religious, professional, or public service operate as nonprofit organizations. Numerous sport and recreation organizations are nonprofit organizations. No one reaps financial profit from the work of nonprofits. Members of these organizations elect

people to serve on the executive committee and board of directors, and these people establish the strategic direction of the organizations and fulfill the organization's mandate. Most international, national, state, province, territory, regional, and local sport organizations operate as nonprofit organizations (e.g., the International Olympic Committee, the International Cheer Union, USA Team Handball, Ontario Tennis Federation, the Buffalo City Swim Racers).

Many primary schools, secondary schools, colleges, and universities are government-sanctioned and -funded organizations, and as a result, their mission is to serve and educate all their students. Most schools offer sports (e.g., through the physical education curriculum and through intramural sport and interschool competition), and many primary and secondary schools share their sport and recreation facilities with community groups and local sport organizations. Colleges and universities also contribute to sport through the training of future leaders in sport (e.g., physical education teachers, sport managers, exercise specialists, sport psychologists, coaches, sport researchers) through their various academic programs and offer a range of sport programs and services to their students (e.g., club sports, intramural sports, intercollegiate athletics). In some cases, colleges and universities share their sport and recreation facilities and fields with the community. In figure 1.1, schools, colleges, and universities are located between public sector and nonprofit sector organizations.

The third category, the commercial sector, is composed of organizations whose ultimate objective is generating profit. Many sport organizations and their supporters operate in this sector. Commercial organizations in sport include professional sport franchises, leagues, and other sport entities (e.g., Sky Blue FC, SKA Saint Petersburg, Los Angeles Sparks, Ultimate Fighting Championship); sport providers (e.g., downhill ski resorts, golf, fitness clubs, bungee jumping facilities, zorbing facilities, event management firms, sport marketing agencies, sport facilities contractors and operators); sporting goods manufacturers (e.g., Nike, Russell, New Balance, Head) and retailers (e.g., Dick's Sporting Goods, Foot Locker); sport media (e.g., ESPN, NBC Sports, NFL Network, The Hockey News); and corporations that support sport with sponsorship and endorsements (e.g., Coca-Cola, Visa, McDonald's, Budweiser). Commercial organizations are central to the operations of the entire sport industry and serve an important function to provide sport products and services to the population.

Based on the three previously mentioned models (Eschenfelder & Li, 2007; Meek, 1997; Pitts et al., 1994), we have identified the various products, services, programs, and facilities produced in the different sectors of sport and sport-related organizations that operate within the CSM Sport Industry Sectors Model. Note that some products, services, and programs are produced by organizations in different sectors; for example, high performance sport is produced by national sport organizations in the nonprofit sector and by professional sport franchises in the commercial sector. Colleges and universities also play a role in developing and producing high performance sport. Several organizations from different sectors contribute to community sport, namely nonprofit sport clubs, schools, and local governments.

Collaboration among organizations within and between sectors is central to the success of the sport industry. An example of collaboration is a national sport organization (nonprofit organization) that partners with a professional sport team (commercial organization) to promote its sport among youth. Another example of collaboration is a nonprofit local sport club working with the local government to secure access to sport facilities (e.g., swim club using the local pool to train its members and hold competitions). Through collaboration, multiple organizations with different objectives work together to grow the industry.

In addition to all the different sport organizations, there are countless stakeholders and other peripheral organizations and units that support the sport industry. Stakeholders include members of these sport organizations, sport participants, athletes, coaches, officials, administrators, leaders, volunteers, fans and spectators, corporate sponsors, media, government entities and personnel, and others affiliated with sport and nonsport organizations (e.g., talent agents, contractors, event organizers, government regulators) who can affect or be affected by sport organizations. In the following chapters, you will read about organizations from different sectors of the sport industry as well as various stakeholders.

Unique Aspects of Sport Management

Nearly four decades ago, Mullin (1980) provided insight into three unique aspects of sport management: sport marketing, sport enterprise financial structures, and sport industry career paths. Mullin's three aspects are just as critical today because they still distinguish sport business from other business enterprises and justify sport management as a distinct area of professional preparation. We add a fourth unique aspect of sport to Mullin's list: the enormous power and influence of sport as a social institution.

Sport Marketing

Sport marketing is unique because the sport product is unlike other products that consumers buy. For example, sport is consumed as quickly as it is produced. It is a perishable product that is not accompanied by any guarantees of customer satisfaction. People who provide the sport experience cannot predict the outcome because of the spontaneous nature of the activity, the inconsistency of events, and the uncertainty surrounding the results. Sport marketers, therefore, face unique challenges; for example, they cannot focus their efforts only on the perishable product (e.g., the game). "We're trying to make that connection with the fan throughout the year," noted Joni Smoller, who in 2016 served as president of

Ashley Feagan

Courtesy of Ashley Feagan.

Professional Profile

Title: Basketball marketing agent, Creative Artists Agency (CAA)

Education: BS (sport management and marketing), Indiana University – Bloomington (IU)

After interning with various sport organizations (e.g., Van Wagner Sports Group, Indiana University men's basketball) in college and then working in various entry-level media positions early in her career, Feagan landed a position with CAA in 2013. She worked in assistant and trainee positions with the company before being promoted in 2016 to agent in the CAA Sports Endorsements group. Feagan, who grew up in Rockland County, New York, works out of CAA's New York City office. She focuses on endorsement deals, social media, and public relations for NBA clients. Her work often involves extensive travel to NBA markets and various cities for the NBA All-Star Game, NBA Summer League, NBA Draft Combine, commercial shoots, and games. Feagan embraces travel; as an undergraduate student, she studied sport in Australia and New Zealand during a study-abroad program with the University of Notre Dame Australia. The following is a snapshot of her development, education, duties, and insights as a leader in the sport industry.

What was your career path?

I enjoyed playing high school sports and took a sport marketing class at Tappan Zee High School. While in college, I was inspired by IU alumni and ESPN personality, Sage Steele, to break into the sport industry. I interned for two summers at Van Wagner Sports and one semester with the IU

the National Association of Collegiate Marketing Administrators (NACMA). Smoller, who is in charge of fan experience and sales at Kansas State University, and her colleagues work to keep fans "updated on things like the basketball team's trip to Italy, which has nothing to do with selling tickets, but just staying in touch. It's just constant communication that's not necessarily selling" (Smith, 2016, p. 3).

Sport Enterprise Financial Structures

Most sport businesses are financed differently from other businesses. Typically, the sale of a product or service such as clothing, food, automobiles, or home cleaning finances the business. But, with the exception of sporting goods manufacturers and retailers, sport enterprises earn a significant portion of revenue not from the sale of a service such as a game, workout, or 10K run but from extraneous sources such as

television rights, concessions, road game guarantees, parking, and merchandise. Intercollegiate athletics and municipal recreation sport programs might generate revenue from student or user fees, private donations, taxes, rentals, or licensing fees. Sport managers continually compete for the **discretionary funds** of consumers through the sale of items that might or might not be related to the apparent primary focus of the enterprise. Sport also attracts consumers who spend more money outside the sport arena (e.g., travel, entertainment, souvenirs, equipment) than they spend on the sport itself. This unique financial base requires different practices within the sport setting.

Sport Industry Career Paths

Traditionally, sport management practitioners have been hired based on their affiliations or connections with certain groups such as intercollegiate athletics

---

discretionary funds—Money left over after necessary expenditures (e.g., rent, food, car payment, insurance) have been made.

men's basketball team. Over the years, I have had a passion for health, fitness, and the business of sports in general. I have always had a deep rooted respect for the hard work and dedication athletes put in to perfecting their craft.

What characteristics must a person have to be successful in your job?

Time management and organization are crucial as I have many different responsibilities to balance daily. I set blocks of time in my calendar for cold calls and brand outreach to build clients' endorsement profiles. In addition, I need time to help manage current endorsement deals as well as their social media, public relations, and philanthropic initiatives. Other important characteristics include effective communication, resourcefulness, and adaptability. An agent must communicate openly and honestly with clients, brands, the league, and teams to make sure everyone is on the same page and ready to support the athlete both on and off the court. Resourcefulness and adaptability are also important because the basketball and endorsement landscape are constantly changing. Everything from being traded to a new team or seeing the shift in brand dollars from traditional endorsements to digital content has an impact on an athlete's brand.

Which websites, online tools, or resources do you frequently use or refer to?

I refer to *Street & Smith's SportsBusiness Daily* for industry news and set Google alerts for all of my clients. In addition, I visit websites like NBA.com, Bleacher Report, and ESPN for sports news. LinkedIn is a great resource for sales leads and I use all of the social media platforms for client research.

What do you consider to be the biggest future challenge in your job or industry?

Brands are really now more than ever seeking a tangible return on investment. Companies are spending less on traditional endorsements and moving toward branded lifestyle content and digital initiatives. To be successful, one must consistently recruit new athlete talent to sell to brands. It is also important to be strategic and true to the athlete's personality while building their endorsement portfolio. Consumers and fans are very observant and can see through inauthentic campaigns, which is why as marketers we try to form organic partnerships between brands and athletes.

or professional sport. For example, a basketball star might become a basketball coach and eventually an athletic director. We can find similar career advancement patterns within municipal recreation programs, sport clubs, and professional sport teams. Although it could be argued that some areas of sport are part of a closed society in which obtaining employment might depend less on what the applicant knows and more on whom the applicant knows or what the applicant did on the athletic field, the sport industry is recognizing the value of opening the workforce to a variety of available talent. One of the many positive outcomes of making the switch from a closed society is the advancement of underrepresented groups into management positions. R. Vivian Acosta and Linda Jean Carpenter reported that in 2014 there were 13,963 female professionals working in the intercollegiate athletic job market. The researchers noted that this is the highest number of women ever employed across various positions in college sports

(e.g., athletic directors, sports information directors, coaches) (Acosta & Carpenter, 2014).

Although efforts to break down the previously closed society have diversified the sport management workforce, the sport industry still has work to do before it can be claimed that sport is truly an equal opportunity environment. While there are many notable exceptions where women lead in various sport organizations (e.g., National Basketball Players Association executive director Michele Roberts, Cleveland Browns executive vice president Sashi Brown, MLB senior vice president Kim Ng, ESPN executive vice president and chief financial officer Christine Driessen, NFL chief marketing officer Dawn Hudson, Big East Conference commissioner Val Ackerman, United States Golf Association senior managing director Sarah Hirshland, Baltimore Ravens general manager Ozzie Newsome, Pac-12 Networks president Lydia Murphy-Stephans, Penn State University athletic director Sandy Barbour), there is still a tremendous

---

underrepresented groups—People who traditionally have not been hired in sport management positions (e.g., women, people of color, people with disabilities, Aboriginal people).

need for sport organizations to promote an inclusive workforce by, for example, being more proactive in providing professional opportunities for people of color, women, and people with disabilities. Sport management scholars Sally Ross and Janet B. Parks noted that "the transformation of sport organizations into entities that appreciate and reward the contributions of women will require leaders who value organizational diversity and understand how to manage it" (2008, p. 4). As future professionals in sport management, you may be in positions of authority in which your sensitivity to inequities (e.g., cultural, societal, racial, gender, ability) can lead to expanded workforce diversity and positive changes in the organizational culture of the sport industry. For instance, to increase its workforce diversity NASCAR initiated its Drive for Diversity. A product of the program is Darrell "Bubba" Wallace Jr., who in 2018 became the first full-time African American driver in NASCAR's top division since Wendell Scott in 1971.

Sport as a Social Institution

Sport is a distinctive social activity that is frequently the basis of a person's social identity because it is integrated into everything from education, politics, and family to economy, religion, and media (Coakley, 2017). As such, sport is a social institution of astonishing magnitude and influence. What other social pursuit is allotted several pages in the daily newspaper, has its own slot on every television and radio news program, has its own cable channels, and creates what appears to be an international withdrawal crisis when members of its workforce go on strike? The sheer power of sport mandates that people who wish to manage it acquire a sound understanding of its historical, psychological, sociological, cultural, and philosophical dimensions. Thus, as future sport managers, you need to be aware of the social implications of your actions. Contemporary sport enterprises need well-prepared managers who can make sound management decisions in the context of sport as an exceptionally influential social institution.

Sport Management Competencies

Research suggests that sport management competencies are universal and have remained relatively stable over time (Danylchuk & Boucher, 2003; Horch & Schütte, 2003). Besides emphasizing competencies required for performing traditional

tasks such as personnel management and planning, today's sport management organizations and settings place increased importance on communication skills, technological aptitude, and the ability to interact in a global and multicultural society. A couple of the general competency areas that we cover in this chapter are managerial leadership skills and critical thinking skills.

Managerial Leadership Skills

Although competencies required for specific settings vary depending on organizations and specific assignments, the sport management tasks presented in figure 1.2 provide an overview of industry expectations. Most of the competencies required for these tasks are transferable, which means that you should be able to use them in a variety of vocational settings including sport organizations.

The tasks in the core of figure 1.2 are general sport management responsibilities in which all sport managers must be proficient and, to varying degrees, be able to perform on the job. For example, regardless of whether you work in a sport club, the front office of a professional sport team, a sport association, or an intercollegiate athletic department, you need to demonstrate competence in writing, speaking, and public relations as well as in the other tasks presented in the core.

The tasks listed in the clusters branching out from the core reflect distinctions between two types of responsibilities (i.e., organizational management and communication management). Leadership and management skills are necessary for performing tasks in the organization management cluster. Sport managers need good organizational skills to direct and supervise subordinates in settings such as sport clubs, municipal recreation programs, or sport associations for specific populations (e.g., seniors or people with differing abilities); in intercollegiate athletics and professional sport; and in the business aspect of any sport-related enterprise.

In the communication management cluster, written and oral communication skills are of paramount importance. Although professionals in all segments of the sport industry are expected to have a certain level of communication acumen and expertise to be effective, sophisticated communication management competencies and technological adaptability are especially critical in areas such as sport marketing, media relations, sports writing, and social media (thus, the inclusion of a social media sidebar in each chapter of this textbook).

---

workforce diversity—People of different ages, genders, religions, physical abilities, social classes, sexual orientations, races, ethnicities, and cultures working together in an organization.

organizational culture—Workplace values, norms, and behaviors that produce patterns of behavior unique to an organization.

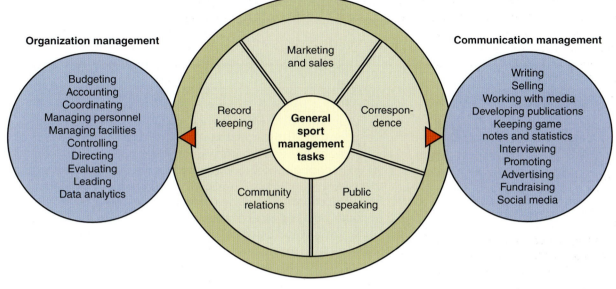

Figure 1.2 Sport management task clusters.

Adapted from J.B. Parks, P.S. Chopra, R.J. Quain, and I.E. Alguindigue, 1988, "ExSport I: An expert system for sport management career counseling," *Journal of Research on Computing in Education* 21: 196-209. By permission of J.B. Parks.

Although tasks requiring similar competencies appear within one cluster or the other, the clusters are not mutually exclusive. The interrelatedness of the tasks within the various clusters is evident in the strategic intersection of management and communication in the sport industry (Pedersen et al., 2017). Take, for example, sport industry practitioners who are employed in the media relations department of a sport organization. Although these professionals belong to the communication management cluster of figure 1.2, they also belong to the organization management cluster because they need to be able to manage and lead personnel (e.g., interns, social media coordinators, photographers, webmasters, statisticians, graphic designers). Conversely, employees in organization management positions need strong communication skills to be successful.

Critical Thinking Skills

An additional competency that sport management students should acquire is the ability to think critically. This skill is developed in sport management programs around the world. Take the University of Miami (UM) as an example: "In our programs, we incorporate critical thinking assignments and activities such as role playing, case studies, and simulations so students can analyze problems or issues from a real-world perspective" stated Windy Dees, a UM sport management scholar and coauthor of chapter 12 (personal communication, September 18, 2016). Winthrop University's president, Dan Mahony,

another sport management scholar and a coauthor of chapter 15, added, "Students who have strong critical thinking skills, high levels of quantitative literacy, decision-making skills, and good written and oral communication skills will be able to succeed in almost any job that they choose" (2008, p. 8). Consider, for example, the following issues sport managers are facing and addressing:

- Should certain protections be implemented to safeguard young athletes from suffering burnout because of high-performance training, intense coaches and parents, and highly competitive situations?

- Should interscholastic athletics be run more as a business (e.g., sponsorship engagement, national television exposure, talent recruitment), and should sport programs be geared for only the talented athletes?

- Should intercollegiate athletes receive salaries? Should alcohol sales be allowed at all sport events, including in college football and basketball facilities?

- Should professional athletes undergo more intensive testing for drugs, and should penalties for failed drug tests be increased?

- Should sport organizations avoid hosting events in areas (i.e., states, countries) that have laws or practices that violate human rights or exclude certain individuals (e.g., anti-LGBTQ laws)?

Social Media and Managing Sport

The sport industry in general and sport managers in particular are increasingly affected—both positively and negatively—by ephemeral social media (e.g., short-lived posts on platforms such as Snapchat) and more permanent social media (e.g., traditional social networking sites such as Facebook). Social media mishaps in sport frequently make the news and hurt sport organizations and affiliated personnel. For example, in 2017, Chelsea F.C. of the English Premier League apologized for one of its player's (Kenedy) Instagram posts, which were considered xenophobic and racist. Kenedy also apologized for his actions. In 2016, an assistant athletic director at a Florida college lost his job after tweeting about how he heckled a professional golfer, and an ESPN analyst was fired over a controversial post on Facebook. In 2015, the social media managers for the Houston Rockets and the Texas Rangers were let go after they posted (separate and unrelated) controversial tweets on the teams' Twitter accounts. The above incidents are only a few of the dozens of social media mistakes that could be used as examples each year. One social media post can certainly embarrass a sport organization and significantly affect or possibly end a sport management career. Although there are regular social media mishaps in sport, sport industry stakeholders have mostly benefited from opportunities presented through social media. For example, fans can interact with like-minded enthusiasts on social networking sites and mobile apps (e.g., Infield Chatter, Reddit Sports, Sports Social, Vole). Future sport managers can establish a marketable personal brand through professional and effective usage of Tumblr, Twitter, Facebook, and other social media platforms. Current sport managers can promote themselves, seek growth opportunities, and network through their use of social networking sites such as LinkedIn, Meetup, and Networking for Professionals as well as sport-specific sites such as Fieldoo. Sport organizations can connect and interact with their stakeholders, engage in source publicity, conduct research, market themselves, engage in cross promotion, and perform damage control through proper use of social media platforms such as Instagram, Google+, Twitter, and Hang w/. What better way for sport organizations at all levels to market themselves and their products, secure free publicity and exposure, and connect with their millions of fans than by posting a training camp story on Snapchat, providing live-streaming video of a press conference via Ustream, uploading behind-the-scenes photos on Instagram, sending a short message on Twitter, pinning a team uniform design to Pinterest, asking a question to fans on Facebook, or posting a highlight video on YouTube? These opportunities did not exist in the past. In each of the following chapters, you can read more about other social media examples and applications in the sport industry.

- Should male and female coaches receive equal salaries if they coach the same sport?
- Should an athlete or an employee of a sport organization be retained and given a second chance if found guilty of domestic violence? Using recreational drugs? Uttering a racist comment? Carrying an unlicensed firearm? Driving while intoxicated?
- Should a professional sport franchise accept public funds to renovate or build a sport facility?
- Should sport organizations place restrictions on the social media activities of their front-office personnel and affiliated athletes?

As managers, you will need exceptional critical thinking skills to make sound decisions about issues such as these and about additional issues that we cannot even conceptualize today. Sound decisions will not be based on expediency, the easy way out, or on what will cause the least turmoil or make the most money. You are most likely to make sound decisions if you make it a point to work toward principled justifications for your beliefs. Becoming a critical thinker is an important step toward learning to provide such justifications for your decisions.

Ideal critical thinkers have certain dispositions or tendencies. We propose that the dispositions offered by Ennis (2015) are especially useful for the critical thinker to pursue. Thus, in synthesizing and combining Ennis' suggested dispositions, we agree that ideal critical thinkers in sport management should

- seek and offer clear statements and clear reasons,
- try to be well informed and use credible sources and observations,

- consider the entire situation and the context,
- be alert for alternatives and be open-minded,
- take a position (or change a position) with sufficient evidence and reasons, and
- seek precision and try to get it right in employing their critical thinking abilities.

The ideal critical thinker cares enough about what others have to say to make an active attempt to uncover and listen to others' reasons and to be sensitive to others' feelings and levels of understanding. An important component of this caring is being truly and seriously open to points of view different from one's own and recognizing that one's own beliefs may not be sufficiently justified. Clearly, achieving this openness is challenging.

What is critical thinking? You probably have encountered the term many times in your daily life and in the classroom. You may also have noticed that when the term is used, its meaning is often unclear. One reason for the confusion is that *it* means different things to different people. Thus, you must understand the meaning of the term as we are using it in this chapter and in the following chapters. Our definition, an adaptation of definitions that are widely used among scholars who systematically study the concept, should be helpful to you in distinguishing between critical thinking and other kinds of thinking. First, to understand what we mean by the term, you need to understand what we do not mean. Critical thinking is not any of the following:

- Simply thinking—Critical thinking is a special form of thinking. For example, developing a good understanding of something is an important dimension of (just) thinking, but it is quite distinct from critical thinking.
- Negative thinking—To many people, critical thinking does not sound agreeable. It sounds negative. But critical thinkers are not naysayers! Critical thinkers are seeking something positive—as solid a basis for their beliefs as they can find in a world full of uncertainty. Criticisms are simply part of their search for better arguments. In this respect, critical thinking, if practiced appropriately, is positive, caring, and productive.
- Creative thinking—Certain aspects of critical thinking require our best creative efforts, which is one of its appealing components. But critical thinking stresses making evaluative judgments rather than the imaginative leaps associated with brainstorming or generating novel ideas or strategies.

Critical Thinking Questions

We have provided examples of what we do not mean, so what *do* we mean by critical thinking? A common feature of all critical thinking activity is the systematic evaluation of arguments (i.e., reasons and conclusions) according to explicit standards of rationality—careful thinking that helps us move forward in a continual, ongoing search to improve our opinions, decisions, or judgments. Critical thinking, as we use the term, refers to the following:

- The awareness of a set of interrelated critical questions
- The ability to ask and answer critical questions at appropriate times
- The desire to use those questions and accept their results as a guide to behavior

Central to your success in becoming a critical thinker is having a good understanding of a

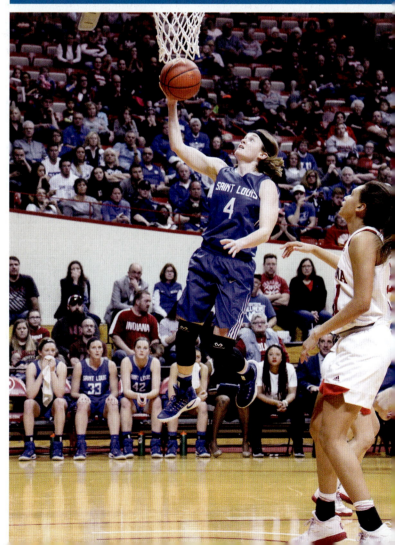

Should these collegiate athletes receive a salary? What are the critical thinking skills needed to argue for and against this question?
Courtesy of Paul M. Pedersen.

set of questions that you need to ask to evaluate someone's reasoning. Although there is no single correct set of critical thinking questions, we have selected eight of them in table 1.2. The discussion of each question is necessarily brief, but you should consult Browne and Keeley (2018) for more in-depth analyses of these and other critical thinking questions.

Table 1.2   Critical Thinking Questions

Question	Discussion
Question 1: What are the issues, and what is the conclusion?	You start the critical thinking process by identifying the issue and the conclusion, which will be either **prescriptive** or **descriptive**. Value preferences will have much greater influence over prescriptive conclusions than they will over descriptive conclusions. For example, values will influence the prescriptive conclusion that there should be more African American athletic directors. Conversely, the descriptive conclusion that only 12.7 percent of NBA team vice presidents and 17.7 percent of the NBA league office professional employees are African American (according to the 2016 report by Lapchick) will depend on empirical evidence.
Question 2: What are the reasons?	Reasons are ideas that communicators use to justify their conclusions. To discover reasons, you need to ask what reasons the communicators give to support their conclusion. You should decide the merits of the conclusion based on the quality of the reasons.
Question 3: What words or phrases are ambiguous?	You cannot determine whether you agree or disagree with someone's reasoning if key terms in the reasoning could have more than one meaning and if those different meanings would influence your reactions. For example, in evaluating a coach's success, if you define success as winning percentage, you may reach a different conclusion than if you define success as motivating athletes to achieve their full potential.
Question 4: What are the value conflicts and assumptions?	Assumptions are ideas that people take for granted. Values are abstract ideas that people see as worthwhile (e.g., honesty, compassion, competition, justice). In many cases, however, values are in conflict such that embracing one value means rejecting another. The following reasoning example illustrates the influence of value conflicts and value assumptions: **Conclusion:** Sport teams should cease using Native American symbols and traditions. **Reason:** These practices are inaccurate, disrespectful to Native Americans, and offensive. **Value assumption:** The value of human dignity is more important than the value of the right of freedom of expression.
Question 5: What are the descriptive assumptions?	Descriptive assumptions are unstated beliefs about how the world is, was, or will be. You discover these assumptions by asking what ideas must be taken for granted for a person to believe the reason is accurate. The following scenario illustrates descriptive assumptions: **Conclusion:** Female athletes perform at higher levels when coached by men rather than by women. **Reason:** Teams with male coaches have won more championships than teams with female coaches because female coaches are not as intense and demanding as male coaches. **Assumptions:** Teams coached by women have had the same recruiting resources as teams coached by men; it is acceptable to attribute standard characteristics to all members of a given group; and intense, demanding coaches are more likely to help female athletes reach their potential (Women's Sports Foundation, 2011).

prescriptive—Concerns about the way the world should or ought to be.
descriptive—Concerns about the way the world is, was, or will be.

Question	Discussion
Question 6: Does the reasoning contain fallacies?	Fallacies are mistakes in reasoning that do not seem to be mistakes. The following claim illustrates a fallacy: Either we raise public moneys to finance a sport stadium, or we will have to move the team to another city. This reasoning assumes that only two choices are available. If, however, it is possible to raise private funds to build the stadium, then the reasoning contains a fallacy.
Question 7: How good is the evidence?	Consider the following claims: The graduation rate of nonathletes is higher than the graduation rate of athletes. Title IX has forced several colleges to drop some men's sports. Participation in sport builds good character. To evaluate such claims, ask how good the evidence is. The greater the quality and quantity of supporting evidence, the more you can depend on it and the more you can legitimately call the claim a fact.
Question 8: What significant information is omitted?	Communicators who are trying to persuade you are likely to select and use information that supports their conclusions. Thus, you need to ask what significant information is missing. Some examples of missing information are evidence that supports different conclusions, alternative value assumptions, and identification of the source of the evidence presented. By seeking missing information, you can decide whether you have enough information to judge the communicator's reasoning.

Based on Browne and Keeley 2018.

Future Challenges and Opportunities

Pedersen and colleagues (2017) noted that "the business of sport continues to expand" (p. 4) and with "the rapid growth of the sport industry" (p. 7) there is "seemingly unending growth in the value of sport as a commodity" (p. 8). The expansion of the sport industry is reflected not only in the introduction of many new sports but also in the increasing opportunities to participate in sports and activities, an upsurge in the number and variety of sport-related publications and social media platforms, enhanced mass media exposure and source publicity of sport activities, growth in the number and types of sport facilities and events, increased interest in sport tourism and adventure travel, and the provision of sport-related goods and services for a greater variety of market segments. New amateur and professional sports have emerged, sport opportunities are being offered to a more diverse population, endorsements and sponsorships are on the rise, sport industry education is becoming more prevalent and sophisticated, marketing and promotion orientation is growing in the sport industry, sport managers are becoming more competent, and the globalization of the sport industry is progressing rapidly.

Although the continued growth and advances in the field will create numerous job opportunities for aspiring sport managers, the future will also present sport managers with many challenges and opportunities, some of which have already emerged and others that we cannot even imagine. In subsequent chapters, you will learn about a variety of such challenges within specific segments of the sport industry. Some challenges will affect all sport managers irrespective of the segment of the industry in which they are employed. These challenges and opportunities are associated with technology, ethics and social responsibility, and the globalization of sport.

Technology

The technology explosion over the past decade has been mind-boggling, and it is only the beginning. For example, artificial intelligence (AI) will increasingly affect the sport industry. As Sennaar (2017) illustrated, the current applications of AI involve chatbots (e.g., the KAI—Kings Artificial Intelligence—system of the NBA Sacramento Kings, which provides virtual assistance to fan inquiries), computer vision (e.g., the Argo AI/NASCAR application to improve safety), automated journalism (e.g., the use of AI to translate data into text that covers games in Minor League Baseball [MiLB]), and wearable tech. Sennaar explored future application of AI in sports by providing examples of AI assistant coaches, smart ticketing, automated video highlights, and computer vision refereeing. Virtual reality (VR) is another example of the growth in sport technology. Who knows what will happen with VR in the coming years; it

A newly formed professional league, the innovative (e.g., half-court play, four-point shot) Big 3 was cofounded by rapper and actor Ice Cube. The league's events include high-level competition between teams and a unique integration of entertainment and sport (e.g., a master of ceremonies, attendance and promotion of celebrity attendees, live music, opportunities for fan engagement). For instance, Ice Cube takes a selfie with a fan who won the opportunity to meet the sport entrepreneur.
Courtesy of Paul M. Pedersen.

is already increasingly being adopted and promoted throughout the sport industry (e.g., VR stadium and fan experiences, VR viewing sport broadcasts, VR in the training and coaching of athletes, VR content through smartphone applications, VR in facility design). AI, VR, and augmented reality (AR) will only become more prevalent with sport organizations and stakeholders. The same applies to social media. There are already myriad ecommerce applications and interactivity opportunities available across social media platforms used in the sport industry. Advances in technology have affected all aspects of the field. For example, technology has provided enhanced experiences for spectators in the stands (e.g., Wi-Fi networks in sport facilities to meet fans' smartphone and tablet demands, massive video boards and state-of-the-art sound systems) and at home (e.g., increased usage of high-definition and 3-D technologies, multiscreen viewing experiences). Technology has also led to better training and care of athletes (e.g., management and editing of training programs, preventive medicine and surgical advancements, fitness activity trackers) and to the safety of all stakeholders

(e.g., protective helmets in football; safer cars, tracks, and methods in auto racing). Sport products (e.g., video games, equipment, transportation, logistics, scheduling, manufacturing), team business, player analytics, and research in sport have all benefited from technology.

In the future, advances in computers and communication technology will play an increasingly significant role in our society and in sport management. This progress will likely be accompanied by acknowledgment of the human need for high-touch activities, many of which the sport experience can provide. The challenge, therefore, is to become proficient in using technology while remaining aware of the need for human interaction in people's lives and understanding how sport can facilitate such interaction.

Ethics and Social Responsibility

Because there are more opportunities to use the platform of sport for good (e.g., charitable work, sport for development, sustainability awareness) while striving to eliminate illegal and immoral incidences in the sport industry (e.g., cheating, criminal activity), many people are calling for greater accountability on the part of sport managers. In recognition of the need for a heightened focus on ethics and social responsibility in sport, DeSensi and Rosenberg (2010) advised that "sport management leaders must view social responsibility as an integral aspect of decisions they make with regard to organizational concerns, the management of funds, the treatment of those in the sport community, and the basic integrity of sport" (p. 10). Along with the call for more socially responsible sport managers, there are now academic courses offered in this area. For instance, George Washington University has a 12-course sports philanthropy academic program "tailored to the unique needs of those who work for professional sports teams, leagues, athlete foundations, sport-related companies with an emphasis on corporate social responsibility, nonprofits using sports for social good and those looking to enter the field" (George Washington University, n.d., para. 1). Overall, sport managers must deal with a multitude of questions that require an understanding

Guidelines for Making Ethical Decisions

Recognize an Ethical Issue

1. Could this decision or situation be damaging to someone or some group? Does this decision involve a choice between good and bad alternatives?
2. Is this issue about more than what is legal or what is most efficient? If so, how?

Get the Facts

1. What are the relevant facts of the case? What facts are not known? Can I learn more about the situation? Do I know enough to make a decision?
2. What individuals and groups have an important stake in the outcome? Are some concerns more important than others? Why?
3. What are the options for acting? Have all the relevant persons and groups been consulted? Have I identified creative options?

Evaluate Alternative Actions

1. Evaluate the options by asking the following questions:
   - Which option will produce the most good and do the least harm (the utilitarian approach)?
   - Which option best respects the rights of all who have a stake (the rights approach)?
   - Which option treats people equally or proportionately (the justice approach)?
   - Which option best serves the community as a whole and not just some members (the common good approach)?
   - Which option leads me to act as the sort of person I want to be (the virtue approach)?

Make a Decision and Test It

1. Considering all these approaches, which option best addresses the situation?
2. If I told someone I respect (or told a television audience) which option I have chosen, what would they say?

Act and Reflect on the Outcome

1. How can my decision be implemented with the greatest care and attention to the concerns of all stakeholders?
2. How did my decision turn out, and what have I learned from this specific situation?

Reprinted, by permission, from *Making an ethical decision*, 2009, Markkula Center for Applied Ethics, Santa Clara University. www.scu.edu/ethics/practicing/decision/making.pdf

of ethical principles and moral psychology. Consider the following questions:

- How can we best achieve gender, race, and class equity in sport?
- Do professional team owners owe primary allegiance to themselves or to the communities that support the team?
- How can we balance academic integrity with the demands of intercollegiate competition?
- Should athletes sacrifice their health for victory?
- Is winning really the bottom line of sport?
- Is intercollegiate sport an entertainment business for public consumption or an extracur-

ricular opportunity for student development, or both, or something else?

The list is seemingly endless, and no doubt you could add your own concerns to it. Regardless of the question or issue at hand, sport management leaders

> must be aware of social issues and problems to establish laudable goals and ensure practices are fair and just. As decision makers, sport managers must treat others with dignity and respect, must ensure that the integrity of sport is maintained, and must pledge to do what is best from organizational and communal standpoints. (DeSensi & Rosenberg, 2010, p. 12)

Code of Ethics, North American Society for Sport Management

The following are some selected canons or principles from NASSM's Code of Ethics. In performing their duties, sport managers should do the following:

- Hold paramount the safety, health, and welfare of the individual in the performance of professional duties.
- Perform services only in their areas of competence.
- Issue public statements in an objective and truthful manner, and make every effort to explain where statements are personal opinions.
- Seek employment only where a need for service exists.
- Maintain high standards of personal conduct in the capacity or identity of the physical and health educator.
- Strive to become and remain proficient in professional practice and the performance of professional functions.
- Act in accordance with the highest standards of professional integrity.
- Respect the privacy of students and clients and hold in confidence all information obtained in the course of professional service.
- Adhere to any and all commitments made to the employing organization. The relationship should be characterized by fairness, non-maleficence, and truthfulness.
- Treat colleagues with respect, courtesy, fairness, and good faith.
- Relate to the students and clients of colleagues with full professional consideration.
- Uphold and advance the values and ethical standards, the knowledge, and the mission of the profession.
- Take responsibility for identifying, developing, and fully utilizing established knowledge for professional practice.
- Promote the general welfare of society.
- Regard as primary their professional service to others.
- Report minor and major infractions by colleagues.

Reprinted, by permission, from NASSM (Butler, PA). Available: https://www.nassm.com/InfoAbout/NASSM/Creed

Rugby World Cup: Japan 2019

John Harris
Glasgow Caledonian University, Scotland

The Rugby World Cup (RWC) was first staged in 1987, when Rugby Union was still an amateur sport. Players had to negotiate time away from their jobs to take part. This competition was an invitation-only event, and there was no qualification process. The tournament was hosted by Australia and New Zealand, and the latter became the inaugural champion by defeating France in the final. The real significance of the World Cup competition was that it created the pathway toward open professionalism. The game became openly professional just eight years after the third RWC in South Africa.

The RWC has developed markedly since this time, and the 2015 event hosted by England (and Cardiff, Wales) was said to have had an economic impact of more than £2 billion. The men who took part were mostly full-time rugby players, and many of them had lucrative endorsement deals with sponsors. This RWC surpassed all previous records in worldwide television viewing numbers, spectator attendance figures, and overall economic impact. As the RWC has developed and become further commercialized and commodified, the international media interest afforded to it has also increased substantially.

The biggest shock of the 2015 tournament, and one of the big upsets in international sport that year, was Japan's victory over two-time World Cup winner South Africa. This was a timely boost for Japan; it will become the first country from outside of the eight foundation nations to host a World Cup competition when the tournament takes place in twelve venues across the country in 2019. The eight foundation nations (Wales, Scotland, South Africa, New Zealand, Ireland, France, England, and Australia) have dominated the sport both on and off the field for more than 100 years. These nations have exerted a tight control in the governance of world rugby, and only four different nations have won the RWC to date. England's victory in 2003 was the only title for a team from the northern hemisphere.

The 2019 event represents a significant development in the continued internationalization of rugby. Japan had hoped to host the 2011 RWC but narrowly missed out to New Zealand under somewhat controversial circumstances. The fact that the tournament will finally take place in Asia is viewed by some as evidence of those leading the governance of the international rugby community finally embracing globalization. Rugby sevens, a shorter and arguably easier to understand version of the game, debuted at the 2016 Olympic Games in Rio. Fiji took the title to win its first Olympic medal in any sport. The Olympic Summer Games take place in Tokyo one year after the RWC, so it will be interesting to see what nations can challenge the status quo in both versions of the sport.

Millennium Stadium in Cardiff (Wales), which staged eight matches during the 2015 Rugby World Cup.
Courtesy of Lestyn James Harris.

In the same vein, Malloy and Zakus (1995) suggested that sport management students should understand the need to "challenge the assumptions, both overt and covert, of sport and society to enable themselves to make ethically sound decisions" (p. 54). The desire and ability to engage in **principled decision making** often distinguishes superior sport managers from their peers.

Now is the time to begin reflecting on ethical concerns because you surely will face them in the years to come. The sidebar Guidelines for Making Ethical Decisions contains an approach developed by scholars in the Markkula Center for Applied Ethics (2009) at Santa Clara University. In subsequent chapters, you will be referred to this sidebar to help you examine ethical concerns in specific sport settings. The guidelines serve as an introduction to the place of ethics in a sport manager's decision-making process.

We are hopeful that in the future, enlightened sport managers will be aware of their social responsibilities and will deliver their services in ways that reflect this understanding (see the sidebar Code of Ethics, North American Society for Sport Management for a listing of NASSM's ethical codebook items covering a sport manager's approach to individual welfare, competency, communication, propriety, integrity, trust, confidentiality, respect, fairness, service, and other canons or principles). For example, sport managers worldwide will be conscious of environmental concerns and will incorporate this understanding into their business practices. Environmental concerns that are important to sport managers include air and water quality, land and water use, waste management, energy management, transportation design and services, accommodation design and services, and the construction of facilities.

Environmental sustainability actions in the sport industry are becoming more prevalent as organizations increasingly recognize the importance and benefits of such initiatives (McCullough, Pfahl, & Nguyen, 2016). The Green Sports Alliance is one of the numerous possible examples. This organization "leverages the cultural and market influence of sports to promote healthy, sustainable communities" (n.d., para. 1). The organization does this "by inspiring sports leagues, teams, venues, their partners and millions of fans to embrace renewable energy, healthy food, recycling, water efficiency, species preservation, safer chemicals and other environmentally preferable practices" (para. 1). In the United States, the Environmental Protection Agency (EPA) provides examples and resources regarding sustainability efforts in the sport industry (Environmental Protection Agency,

n.d.). As can be seen in numerous publicity efforts, many sport entities such as the NFL, intercollegiate athletic departments, and NASCAR actively engage in and promote environmental sustainability efforts.

The social responsibility of future sport managers will include the routine provision of professional child care services in sport facilities and the targeting of previously untapped and undertapped target markets such as women and people of differing ages, abilities, and sexual orientations. The 2016 television drama *Pitch* was a fictionalized account of the first female player in the MLB, and it portrayed various issues and challenges that socially responsible sport management professionals could address in their endeavors to make their sport organizations as inclusive and inviting as possible. Sport managers of the future will also recognize the importance of keeping the sport experience accessible to all socioeconomic groups.

Globalization of Sport

The need to understand and appreciate other countries and cultures cannot be overstated (Danylchuk, 2011; Thibault, 2012). In recognition of this fact, most chapters of this book contain information on the sport industry in other nations. You can take several steps to prepare yourself to interact effectively in the global community. For example, although students in many countries consider mastery of the English language a basic skill, most students in the United States do not master languages of other countries. Consequently, U.S. students can distinguish themselves from their peers by learning a language other than English. Studying in another country for an extended period and completing courses that focus on other cultures are among the additional steps U.S. students can take to broaden their horizons and enhance quality of life. Pursuing this path will also increase your value in the marketplace.

The globalization of sport has many benefits. For example, more countries and athletes are participating in international events. Sport is being used as a vehicle that crosses traditional lines of gender and religion as well as geographical barriers, and it is bringing people around the world together in a common interest. As you contemplate the positive aspects of the globalization of sport, however, you should understand that some advances in international sport have come at the expense of people in developing countries. As with other issues that have been discussed in this chapter, critical thinking from an ethical perspective will be required to address problems such as the exploitation of labor from

---

principled decision making—Basing decisions on the six pillars of character: trustworthiness, respect, responsibility, fairness, caring, and good citizenship (responsible participation in society) (Josephson Institute of Ethics, 2016).

developing nations in the production of sporting goods; the recruitment and migration of athletes that results in a talent drain on their home countries; the effect of the interrelationships among transnational corporations, media, and sport organizations; and the negative effects of sport on the environment (Thibault, 2012).

The future will most assuredly bring change. This can be frightening and is frequently resisted. Progressive sport managers who can anticipate and embrace adaptation will have opportunities to be agents of change who will transform the way that sport is managed. We hope that you will be one of those managers!

For chapter-specific learning activities, visit the web study guide at
www.HumanKinetics.com/ContemporarySportManagement.

Summary

In this chapter, sport is broadly defined and includes new (e.g., esports, drone racing) and traditional (e.g., lacrosse, basketball) competitive activities as well as noncompetitive athletic endeavors. The sport industry can be conceptualized based on the types of sport activities that exist, the settings in which sport occurs, and the industry segments into which various sport businesses and organizations can be categorized. A model of segmentation describes the sport industry and its three sectors: public, nonprofit, and commercial. Four unique aspects of sport management are sport marketing, the sport enterprise financial structure, career paths, and the power of sport as a social institution. Sport managers should possess general, transferable competencies as well as those specific to organization management and information management, and they should be able to think critically.

The next generation of sport managers will face challenges associated with technology, ethics and social responsibility, and globalization. Enlightened sport managers of the future will be competent in the technical aspects of their jobs and will be agents of change in the management of sport and in the larger society.

Review Questions

1. Name three sports that have emerged in the last few years. How has their emergence affected career opportunities in sport management?

2. List and discuss three sport business settings that might represent job opportunities for sport managers.

3. Describe the sport industry model and its three sectors, and provide examples of sport organizations in each sector.

4. Identify three unique aspects of sport management, and explain how each makes the sport business different from other businesses.

5. Explain the task clusters into which sport managers' responsibilities can be classified.

6. Define critical thinking, and explain the benefits of applying critical thinking skills to important issues in sport management.

7. List the dispositions that critical thinkers should possess, and indicate whether you possess each of them. Explain your answers.

8. Define principled decision making, and give examples of when and how sport managers need to make principled decisions.

9. Describe opportunities and challenges in technology, social media, ethics and social responsibility, and globalization that all sport managers will face in the future.

THE BALLPARK OF THE PALM BEACHES

NATIONALS

7	TURNER	SS
2	EATON	CF
34	HARPER	RF
28	WERTH	DH
6	RENDON	3B
11	ZIMMERMAN	1B
32	WIETERS	C
3	TAYLOR	LF
10	DREW	2B

ASTROS

4	SPRINGER	CF
9	GONZALEZ	3B
16	MCCANN	C
11	GATTIS	DH
10	GURRIEL	1B
35	HERNANDEZ	LF
75	KEMMER	RF
28	BRIGNAC	SS
18	KEMP	2B

FAU
MBA IN SPORT MANAGEMENT
Florida Atlantic University Alumni

MPH

STARTING LINEUPS

1:01 PM

	1	2	3	4	5	6	7	8	9	R	H	E		B	S	O
NATIONALS										0	0	0		0	0	0
ASTROS										0	0	0				

Developing a Professional Perspective

Sally R. Ross
Brian P. McCullough
Susan E.C. Simmons

LEARNING OBJECTIVES

- Describe strategies for positioning yourself to be successful in the competitive field of sport management after graduation.

- Identify where entry-level opportunities exist and outline how to gain experience.

- Recognize the importance of professional preparation, professional attitude, and career planning and management.

- Explain the three components of an undergraduate sport management curriculum.

- Describe how students can secure and optimize their involvement in field experiences.

- Discuss ways in which your personal appearance, work transition and adjustment, business etiquette, and social media habits can enhance your employability and advancement.

- Understand the stages involved in career planning.

- Discover several resources that are useful in planning a career in sport management.

KEY TERMS

adaptive skills	explicit norms	job content skills
co-curricular activities	field experience	mock interview
entrepreneur	functional skills	values
etiquette	implicit norms	work ethic

1924
Auditorium Managers Association founded (renamed International Association of Venue Managers)

1966
National Association of Collegiate Directors of Athletics formed

1974
First gathering of the Stadium Managers Association held

Billie Jean King founded Women's Sports Foundation

1978
North American Society for the Sociology of Sport formed

1986
First NASSM conference held at Kent State University

1987
Sport and Recreation Law Association established

Association for Women in Sports Media formed

NASPE published curricular guidelines

1988
Black Coaches Association founded (renamed Black Coaches and Administrators)

Achieving success in most business settings requires specific knowledge, skills, and values that students are expected to begin to acquire as undergraduates. The first step toward developing these essentials to success involves adopting the perspective that you are now more than simply a student. You are a professional. You cannot wait until graduation to begin to accept the responsibilities of being a professional. Your professors expect you to conduct yourself with professionalism while on campus, and you will gain more from your degree program if you behave as a professional rather than just a student. The level of commitment that you dedicate to sport management as an academic pursuit will influence how you approach your coursework, co-curricular activities, and relationships with fellow students and instructors. Students who embody a professional perspective early on in their academic career will benefit through increased knowledge and opportunities. Career readiness should be developed progressively through academic and cocurricular activities that empower you to develop the key competencies that employers seek in job candidates.

The field of sport management is an especially competitive one. Many schools offer a major in sport management, and there are many graduates in this field each year. In addition, students in majors outside sport management may also be interested in working in sport. This means that candidates from a large pool are competing for a finite number of jobs within the sport industry. To achieve success in this competitive environment, students must be willing to plan ahead and put forth a great deal of effort to put themselves in the best position possible.

No matter what type of job you hope to pursue, remember that professionalism begins in the classroom. You must understand and satisfy the requirements and learning objectives of your courses and the expectations of professors. Arrive to class on time, be attentive and prepared, take notes, and show interest. You should also follow the example of professionals and use a day planner, calendar, or organizer in which you can enter assignment due dates, exam dates, work responsibilities, and meetings. Whatever apparatus you use, keep it on hand, update it when necessary, and refer to it often.

Making the decision to focus on your professional perspective will allow you to take advantage of resources available to you and dedicate yourself to developing into a successful professional. This chapter addresses three components of a professional perspective:

1. *Professional preparation.* The courses and experiences that you can expect in your undergraduate curriculum and beyond.
2. *Professional attitude.* How to present a professional image, follow the fundamentals of business etiquette, develop ethical and critical thinking skills, and enter the world of work and be comfortable and productive there.
3. *Career readiness.* Purposeful steps you can take to attain and demonstrate the competencies that broadly prepare college graduates for a successful transition into the workplace.

Professional Preparation

Sport management preparation programs exist at the baccalaureate (undergraduate), master's, and doctoral levels. Baccalaureate programs prepare students for entry-level positions in the sport industry. Master's-level education prepares students for more advanced, specialized responsibilities. The doctorate usually emphasizes research. Students who seek the doctoral degree typically wish to become professors

1995
Korean Society for
Sport Management
founded

1994
Sport Management
Program Review
Council created

2007
College Sport Research
Institute formed

2002
Asian Association for
Sport Management
founded

2010
African Sport
Management
Association
founded

2008
Commission on
Sport Management
Accreditation became
an accrediting body
of sport management
programs

2018
Sixth Global Sport Business Association
conference held on a cruise ship to Cozumel,
Mexico

20th International Conference on Sport
Management and Administration held in Rome

2017
WASM conference held
in Kaunas, Lithuania

or work in some other capacity in a college or university setting.

Currently, you might be enrolled in a sport management undergraduate or graduate program, you might be a high school student, or you might be a college student in another major field who wants to learn more about opportunities in sport management. In any case, you will benefit from an explanation of what to expect in a sport management curriculum at the undergraduate level. Most undergraduate sport management programs include three components: general education courses, major courses, and field experiences.

General Education

The general education component of the undergraduate curriculum is vital because college graduates should be able to demonstrate understanding and capabilities beyond those acquired in their major courses. As a college graduate, you will be expected to express yourself well in writing and verbally. You should understand and be able to discuss—at least on a topical level—areas such as art, literature, history, and social and physical sciences. With a firm foundation provided by general education courses, you should be able to deal with a changing society that reflects the cultural diversity of our world. Awareness of other cultures and an understanding and appreciation of them are essential in addressing the sport management needs of the global community (Chelladurai, 2005). Furthermore, as covered in chapter 1, sport managers are also expected to use critical thinking skills; you can acquire and develop these in general education courses. As you seek to advance your career, the analytical, critical thinking, and leadership skills developed in general education courses will become even more important. These

are some of the career competencies that employers specifically look for when hiring.

Major Courses in Sport Management

Desire for consistency and quality in sport management curricula started in 1986 when NASPE appointed a task force to develop curricular guidelines (Brassie, 1989). NASPE and NASSM jointly served as the program approval agency from 1993 until 2008, when the Commission on Sport Management Accreditation (COSMA) became an accrediting body for sport management curricula.

Sport management programs can be found in schools of education and in departments such as physical education, recreation, hospitality, human movement, and more. In the last two decades, there has been growth in the number of sport management programs housed in business schools (Zaharia, Kaburakis, & Pierce, 2016). These programs commonly seek certifications from the Association to Advance Collegiate Schools of Business (AACSB), the Accreditation Council for Business Schools and Programs (ACBSP), and the International Assembly for Collegiate Business Education (IACBE) to validate their curricula. Regardless of where a sport management program is housed on campus, the curriculum typically contains many business courses, general education courses, and courses specific to the sport context.

One aim of this textbook is to introduce students to areas of study that will prepare them to pursue the sport management curriculum with enhanced insight and understanding. This book addresses topics in the content areas that have been deemed essential by the accrediting bodies of sport management education programs (e.g., COSMA, AACSB). The courses in the sport management curriculum prepare you for a career in one of the many segments of the sport industry. Review the table of contents in this textbook for an overview of the scope of the sport industry and the range of employment opportunities within sport. If you do not enter the sport management field, the course content prescribed in this textbook is sufficiently broad to prepare you to assume positions in a variety of other fields such as advertising, promotions, sales, and communications.

Keeping up with current events in your field is essential to your academic preparation. Although numerous popular media outlets offer sport stories, the popular media should not be the main source of information for the sport management student. One of the most daunting challenges you may have as you develop in your career is to separate your fandom of various sports or specific teams and your role as a future sport manager. Students studying to be sport managers should subsidize any reading from popular media and fan sites with readings from an assortment of trade and academic journals that specifically address sport management issues. One way to discover the most relevant reading material related to your educational and occupational goals is to pay attention to the publications that your instructors use for assignments. Several chapters of this book discuss relevant publications and professional associations specific to various careers in sport management. For examples of such associations, please refer to the sidebar Examples of Sport Management Professional Associations. Membership in one or more of these associations will offer you opportunities to read publications, attend conferences, and access information exclusive to members. Some associations have student branches that provide students with opportunities to gain experience in leadership and governance. Sharing ideas and networking with professionals at all levels will be enjoyable and helpful in your career development. Your instructors can give you advice about which professional associations will be most helpful to you now and in the future.

Additional ways to learn more about your field and gain relevant experience include becoming involved in student activities, gaining on-campus employment, and participating in community service opportunities. Participation in student organizations provides the chance to assume leadership roles and prepare as future professionals. Student-affiliate chapters of professional associations, which are often found on campuses that have sport management programs,

also provide opportunities to network with professionals, visit sport facilities, and learn about ways to gain work experience in sport settings. Students may wish to pursue community service activities such as volunteering with the Special Olympics, working with recreational sport programs, and assisting in community-sponsored events. Furthermore, numerous jobs are available on most college campuses in sport settings such as the student recreation center, the intramural sport office, and intercollegiate athletic department offices.

Cocurricular activities are an important part of professional preparation and have been identified as especially vital to future job success. These experiences can provide valuable skill development in areas such as teamwork, decision making, problem solving, and communication (Peck et al., 2016). Participation in cocurricular activities such as student clubs, intramural sports, and service learning opportunities provides opportunities for leadership and involvement and helps students become well-rounded individuals.

Gaining experience through employment is an important part of professional preparation. Work experience provides students with opportunities to build networks, improve professional skills, establish a greater sense of responsibility, learn more about personal strengths and values, and gain self-confidence. In providing advice on how to launch their careers while in college, one career adviser shared a belief that all students should take as many work and volunteer opportunities as possible before graduating (Scheele, 2005).

The National Association of Colleges and Employers (NACE) projects employment trends. A recent survey by the organization found that more than 80 percent of responding employers said they look for evidence of leadership skills on the candidate's résumé, and nearly as many seek indications that the candidate can work in a team (NACE, n.d.). Employers also cited written communication skills, problem-solving skills, verbal communication skills, and a strong work ethic as important candidate attributes. Students would be wise to involve themselves in work and cocurricular experiences that best prepare them for future careers.

Field Experiences

A **field experience** in sport management is commonly referred to as an internship, and it may include cooperative work experiences (co-ops) or practicum expe-

---

cocurricular activities—Opportunities that are typically outside the academic classroom that complement what students are learning in school.

field experience—A hands-on learning opportunity in which students gain professional experience in an organization, often while receiving class credit.

Examples of Sport Management Professional Associations

Adaptive Sports USA

Africa Sport Management Association

American Sportscasters Association

Asian Association for Sport Management

Association for Women in Sports Media

Athletic Equipment Managers Association

College Athletic Business Management Association

College Sports Information Directors of America

Collegiate Event and Facility Management Association

Council for Responsible Sport

European Association for Sport Management

Global Sport Business Association

Green Sports Alliance

International Association for Communication and Sport

International Association of Venue Managers

International Ticketing Association

Latin American Association for Sport Management

National Association for Coaching Equity and Development

National Association of Academic Advisors for Athletics

National Association of Collegiate Directors of Athletics

National Association of Collegiate Marketing Administrators

National Association of Concessionaires

National Association of Sports Commissions

National Association of Two Year College Athletic Directors

National Recreation and Park Association

NIRSA: Leaders in Collegiate Recreation

North American Society for Sport Management

SHAPE America: Society of Health and Physical Educators

Sport Management Association of Australia and New Zealand

Sport Marketing Association

Stadium Managers Association

Women Leaders in College Sports

Women's Sports Foundation

World Association for Sport Management

riences. A field experience allows students to observe and assist professionals and learn about managerial responsibilities and the scope of the sport organization in which they are employed. Field experience is a common component of the sport management curriculum, and students should expect to be supervised by an on-campus intern coordinator as well as by a professional in the agency providing the experience. Field experiences present excellent opportunities for experiential learning so students can apply what they have learned in the classroom to a real-life situation, thus connecting the theoretical and conceptual with the practical (Cuneen & Sidwell, 1994; Gower & Mulvaney, 2012).

Field experience provides an opportunity to build your professional network. The people in your network can be vitally important to you when you search for jobs in the future. Williams (2003) noted that many sport organizations do not recruit on college campuses or advertise their openings; professional opportunities in the sport industry are "part of the 'hidden' job market" (p. 28). Rather than sift through hundreds or even thousands of applications to find qualified candidates, sport organizations often only let their personal network know about a job opening. Unless you know where to look and are connected to the right people, most of the jobs will go to people who have insider knowledge (Asher, 2011). Given this reality, practical experience in a professional setting is an essential first step into an environment where you might be seeking employment after graduation.

Research has shown that the best field experiences in sport management are those that require interns to expand their knowledge and learn new skills (Dixon, Cunningham, Sagas, Turner, & Kent, 2005). Many students find that their enthusiasm for the field and motivation to excel academically increase because of their internship experience. Students should give

Ellen Lucey

Courtesy of National Basketball Association.

Professional Profile

Title: Director of consumer and sport marketing, Bauerfeind USA

Education: BS (sport marketing and management), Indiana University – Bloomington (IU)

From a young age, Ellen Lucey poured her energy into swimming. She competed through her college years and served as the team's captain. Lucey was known for her competitive spirit and her desire to bring people together through sports. This passion led her to pursue a career in sport marketing. At Lang & Associates, Lucey found her niche as she developed strategies to build a connection between Coca-Cola and POWERADE and the National Hockey League (NHL) based on grassroots marketing efforts.

Lucey then worked for the Coca-Cola Company, where she was involved in brand activation in Super Bowl host cities. As a senior manager, Lucey subsequently took on the challenge of connecting NASCAR fans with the Coca-Cola brand. Next, she leveraged her industry relationships to recruit LeBron James as the spokesperson for Sprite and POWERADE. For the next 10 years, James and Lucey transformed the Sprite brand with their winning combination of skill and swagger.

More recently, Lucey's undergraduate training in kinesiology and her marketing expertise converged when she joined Bauerfeind USA, the top maker of athletic braces and supports. At Bauerfeind, she built a consumer brand from a single idea: helping athletes perform at their best. Based on this model, the trainers' associations from MLB and the National Basketball Association (NBA) now endorse Bauerfeind's products. The following is a snapshot of her development, education, duties, and insights as a leader in the sport industry.

themselves sufficient time to prepare and search for a field experience. Preparing a résumé and cover letters and practicing interviewing skills (i.e., engaging in mock interviews) are essential.

Campus career centers can be valuable sources of assistance in this professional preparation and may have information about available internships. Your campus may also host career fairs or on-campus networking events in which you can interact with alumni and employers offering internships. In addition, many sports teams and organizations hold sport-related job fairs in their venues. Your academic program's internship coordinator may maintain a database of available positions or a list of employers who have provided internships in the past. Your professors can also be a good source of information on planning and preparing for an internship. Although internships have been customary in sport management for quite some time, many academic fields have discovered their value. A NACE student survey found that 65 percent of graduating college seniors from the class of 2016 reported taking part in an internship or co-op (NACE, 2015).

Advanced Education

As you look toward career advancement and additional responsibilities, you may choose, or be asked by your employer, to pursue a graduate degree. Even early in your academic career you may want to begin thinking about an advanced degree. The first graduate degree after the baccalaureate is the master's. Master's degree programs typically require one or two years of additional study. Doctoral-level education builds

---

mock interview—A practice interview in which you can rehearse your responses to questions that interviewers are likely to ask you.

What was your career path?

Joining Coca-Cola was a key move in my career; I started as a contractor but eventually became a full-time employee. Initially, I started with the Super Bowl partnership leading to the NASCAR/Coca-Cola marketing efforts. Ultimately, I turned to managing professional sports for Coke with a primary focus on the NBA and the LeBron James endorsement. Currently, I am responsible for building the Bauerfeind brand directly with the consumer. Although the company has been in the United States for 30 years, they sold their products through medical professionals. With health care changes, we are now selling directly to the consumer. I am now able to take on an entrepreneurial role, sharing my extensive knowledge of brands and partnership building with companies and individuals on a consultative basis.

What characteristics must a person have to be successful in your job?

It is important to stay focused on your goals. I progressed in my career due to continuous dedication to my goals. That singular focus has led to a successful career. In all of my jobs, my favorite part is the relationships I develop that led to win–win partnerships. For example, I used my years of experience and my NBA contacts to forge an endorsement between Bauerfeind and the National Basketball Athletic Trainers Association.

Which websites, online tools, or resources do you frequently use or refer to?

I read the *Street & Smith's SportsBusiness Journal* and also read *Street & Smith's SportsBusiness Daily* every day. This is the best trade magazine for me. I also follow several resources on Twitter such as Turnkey Sports, Sports Business Radio, Bleacher Report, and ESPN Intelligence.

I also follow several sport-related groups on LinkedIn such as Sports Industry Network, *Street & Smith's SportsBusiness Journal/Daily*, NCAA After the Game, Sports Marketers, The Business of Sports, Beyond Sport, and National Sports Marketing Network.

What do you consider to be the biggest future challenge in your job or industry?

A significant challenge for sports is keeping the in-game experience great and affordable. Consumers' in-home watching has improved with better television coverage and access to additional information. However, no one will want to watch a game without the energy of a crowd.

on the background gained at the undergraduate and master's levels. It is much more specialized in its focus and is essential for anyone who aspires to be a college professor. When considering whether to pursue a graduate education, consider the costs associated with graduate study and look for ways to fund graduate education. Be certain that your end goal matches the credentials you seek. In other words, investigate whether your desired workplace setting expects a graduate degree. Note that some degree programs prefer several years of professional experience prior to graduate study.

In choosing a graduate program, consider the location of the program within the university, the industry focus of the program, and the experience and research interests of the faculty. You'll recall that some sport management programs are in departments of physical education or sport management, whereas others are housed in schools of business administration, departments of kinesiology, or other departments. Another important consideration when choosing a graduate program is the industry focus of the program. Some programs are geared toward preparing students for positions in athletic administration within an educational structure (e.g., intercollegiate athletics). Other programs focus on sport management in the private sector (e.g., professional sport) or public sector (e.g., community centers). To be admitted to a graduate program, candidates need to have high grades, be involved in cocurricular activities, have experience in the sport industry, and have high scores on entrance exams such as the Graduate Record Examinations (GRE) or the Graduate Management Admission Test (GMAT). It may be beneficial to look at schools in other geographic regions or athletic conferences. Diversifying your academic setting can afford you new experiences and different perspectives of how sport organizations are run. It is important to consider all options, discuss plans with those working in the field to seek advice, and meet with faculty in programs of interest to determine whether the program is a good fit.

Professional Attitude

Planning your future in sport management includes paying attention to an extremely important element you can control: your professional attitude. Employers commonly share that they cannot teach people to have the mind-set for professional success. Thus, applicants who do not possess this quality are not hired or promoted. To ensure that you are a competitive candidate, one of the things that you must do is demonstrate a positive attitude in your interviews and on the job (Sukiennik, Bendat, & Raufman, 2008). An enthusiastic and professional attitude will not only enhance your opportunities for employment and advancement but also make you a more pleasant person to be around. That alone is a worthy goal. Furthermore, attitudes are demonstrated through behaviors. The following sections examine how behaviors demonstrate what people consider acceptable attitudes and approaches to ethics and critical issues.

Ethical Decision Making

The professional codes of many sport organizations articulate acceptable behaviors. Employees in these organizations are expected to adhere to these codes. The Sport Management Resources website has a well-developed sample policy that addresses ethical and professional conduct of employees (Lopiano & Zotos, 2014). You may want to examine this document as you refer to the guidelines for making ethical decisions presented in chapter 1. In what ways does this organization's code of ethics intersect with the guidelines?

You have no doubt witnessed or read about many breaches of ethical behavior, often by high-profile individuals in spheres such as politics, business, and sport. People who have been caught violating social norms and formal laws can face a variety of sanctions. As discussed in chapter 1, understanding how to examine an issue thoughtfully and maintain an ethical demeanor will serve you well in any environment.

To be successful in a classroom or a place of business, people must understand expectations and recognize norms that regulate group members. **Explicit norms** are formally communicated rules that govern behavior. In college communities, rules are stated in student policy manuals. In classrooms, explicit norms are outlined in the course syllabi and handouts. In a business environment, explicit norms are outlined in documents such as staff handbooks. To gain confidence in any situation, one should review and comprehend an organization's formal policies and procedures.

Seek to understand informal norms, also referred to as **implicit norms**, that serve to "explain the way things happen in an organization" (Harvey & Drolet, 2004, p. 62). These informal norms can be learned, usually by observing other members of the group. As explained by Harvey and Drolet, although these expectations of behavior may be informal, they are extremely important and, in some cases, are more powerful than formal, explicit norms.

An inability to abide by norms combined with a skeptical view of human behavior and pressure to succeed in college may influence students to behave unethically in their own lives. Although some students may be willing to compromise ethics and cheat to receive a better grade than they deserve, they are developing habits and behaviors that may seriously jeopardize their future success. Results based on a survey of college students suggest that "if students do not respect the climate of academic integrity while in college, they will not respect integrity in their future and personal relationships" (Nonis & Swift, 2001, p. 71). Many students, however, have the foresight to understand that ethical behavior in college will serve them well as they develop their professional aptitude. When preparing for a career after college, students have a responsibility to learn academic content and make good decisions on the road to future success.

As a student, you are confronted with ethical dilemmas on a weekly, if not a daily, basis. What are some examples of unethical behavior that you have witnessed as a student in a sport management class? Refer to the guidelines for ethical decision making presented in chapter 1. How might you change your approach to some of the ethical issues that you face (e.g., cheating on a test, plagiarizing an article, forging a signature, explaining an absence to your professor)? How can you apply these guidelines? Why is it important to embrace ethical behavior as a student?

---

explicit norms—Formally communicated rules that govern behavior of group members.
implicit norms—Unstated or informal rules understood and practiced by members of an organization.

Lag of Professional Sport Management in Germany

Norbert Schütte
Universität Mainz, Germany

Many argue that the professionalization of sport management begins when it becomes a distinct field of practice and is recognized as an occupation. Normally this is accompanied by the creation of specialized education programs at universities. In the United States, the first sport management program was established in 1967 at the University of Ohio (Jobling & Deane, 1996). It was not until 18 years later that the first program in Germany was established at the University of Bayreuth (Buchmeier & Zieschang, 1992). Why is there such a big lag?

We can answer this question using contingency theory. The occurrence of new organizational structures and resulting acknowledgment of the need for professional sport managers is considered dependent on the environment in which the sport organizations exist (Donaldson, 2001). What is different in the environment of sport organizations in Germany compared to the United States that contributed to the development of this profession?

First, sport in German schools is organized by sport teachers, and the school teams are not regarded as a high priority. In addition, German universities are mostly run by the government, and thus they are not really competitors. There are championships in sports between the universities, but they are not widely regarded among the German public. In the United States, spectators fill large stadiums, but in Germany, only a few spectators turn out to watch sport championships. Furthermore, in the United States there is enormous media interest, especially by television networks, but in Germany there is no broadcast coverage of these championships. Consequently, university sport in Germany receives little sponsorship, and there is little money in it.

Second, even though professional sport existed in Germany at the beginning of the last century, particularly in sports such as boxing, cycling, and horse racing, most of the sports were considered amateur. It was not until 1963 that Germany's most important sport, soccer, established the first professional league in the country. Given the lag in the development of professional sport in Germany, there was neither the need nor the ability to pay for professional sport managers.

That does not mean that Germany is not a sports country. It has a different sport system that is built on sport clubs. Such clubs were born out of a grassroots movement whereby sport was, and still is, largely supported and provided through voluntary work. The benefit of such an approach is that no money has to be paid. Money is a scarce resource in sport clubs because there is still the idea that sport should be affordable for all (Schütte, 2016). In addition, sport in Germany is largely influenced by the Olympic Movement, and nearly all sport is run by nonprofit organizations that are typically the only ones allowed to take part in the leagues.

The German national football team on their way to get the World Cup in Brazil in 2014. Soccer is the most popular and professionalized sport in Germany.

Courtesy of Gerald Fritz.

Responsible Group Participation

While taking a college class, you are randomly assigned to a three-person group that is required to research a topic and present to the class. All members of the group will work together for one group grade. You have a busy semester with classes and work and family obligations, and finding a time to meet with other group members is difficult. The way that you approach this assignment may indicate how you perform in the workplace. The following are some questions you may want to consider as you embark on this group project. Keep in mind that you will most likely ask yourself similar questions when you are engaged in group work as a professional in the sport industry.

- Will you make the effort to find times to meet with group members so you can play an equal role in the research and presentation?
- Will you avoid group members, ignore their emails and telephone calls, and give excuses for not getting in touch with them?
- Will you allow the other members of your group to do all the work while you take credit for the assignment?
- Will you actively volunteer to take on portions of the assignment, or will you remain silent and hope that other members will do all the work and let you slide?

Critical Thinking Skills

Gaining a thorough understanding about issues is an imperative skill for students and professionals alike. As explained in chapter 1, critical thinking skills can assist a person in a quest to seek the truth. When students cultivate and practice critical thinking skills, they are less likely to act or make decisions out of habit. The development of sound critical thinking skills can allow people to thrive in academic and work environments. Mastering academic content is important, as is learning about social situations, ethics, and values. Those who challenge themselves and take the time to think, reflect, and learn give themselves a much better chance to flourish in their personal and professional lives.

Remember the eight critical thinking questions presented in chapter 1? How can you apply those questions to issues that you are currently confronting as a sport management student? For example, should you confront a friend who uses sexist language while taunting a rival school during a tennis match? Should you join or encourage protesters outside the athletic department when school officials consider an increase in student fees to fund a new basketball arena?

Professional Image

When they first meet you, other people rely on your physical appearance to make judgments about you. Mitchell (1998) explained that studies on the initial impression that people make "show that 7% of that impression is based on what a person says, 38% on how he or she says it, and 55% on what the other person *sees*" (p. 10). Although this way of judging you might seem unfair, and although initial impressions can change after someone gets to know you, you can make a first impression only once—so why not make it a good one?

The impression that you make through your physical presentation during interviews and on the job is related less to physical attractiveness than to other factors, all of which are within your control. The following items are among the many aspects of a professional image.

- *Grooming.* Attention to your grooming can pay off as you present yourself to potential employers. Aspects of grooming to consider include care of hair, nails, and teeth as well as neatness and cleanliness.

- *Attire and accessories.* While in college, you have wide discretion in your choice of clothing and accessories, but as you move into the workplace, you must understand what constitutes appropriate attire. This standard will differ depending on the organization. If you are unsure about what is acceptable attire for your organization, ask your supervisor. Websites on professional dress and business casual dress can be especially helpful. When interviewing for a position, dress in business professional attire unless specifically informed to do otherwise by the interviewing party.

- *Posture.* Your sitting, standing, and walking posture (body language) convey an impression of your attitude. People will draw different conclusions about the attitude of a person who is slouching than one who is sitting upright with feet firmly planted on the floor or leaning slightly forward to indicate good listening skills, interest, and enthusiasm.

- *Social media.* As discussed in this chapter's social media sidebar, your social media presence (e.g., Facebook, Twitter, Instagram, LinkedIn) can influence how you are perceived by current or potential employers.

Work Transition and Adjustment

Now is the time to begin practicing for life in the work environment. How you enter a new sport organization, approach the challenges of your new position, learn the organizational culture, develop working relationships with bosses and colleagues, participate in departmental and team meetings, communicate your ideas to others, and establish your reputation as an employee will have a major influence on your success. Valuable employees display their professional attitudes in the images they project, in the ways they approach work transitions and adjustments, and in their business etiquette. The following sections offer tips on learning your job, understanding organizational culture, demonstrating your work ethic, developing written communication skills, using electronic communication, writing thank-you notes, refining teamwork skills, managing conflict, embracing diversity, being evaluated, and continuing your professional development.

Learn Your Job

When you start a new job, make sure you understand what your duties are and how to proceed. Listen carefully to directions and ask for clarification of any instructions that you do not fully understand before beginning an assignment. Taking notes as you receive oral instructions is perfectly appropriate to ensure understanding and thorough recall of expectations. Set up periodic meetings with your supervisor to confirm and clarify your progress on assignments and to ensure that your work is accurate, thorough, and of high quality. In an entry-level or new job, you are not expected to know everything, but you are expected to show interest and actively learn.

Understand Organizational Culture

As you will learn in chapter 4, each organization has a unique culture; therefore, new employees must learn what behaviors are expected in the workplace. Employee socialization or onboarding programs are often initiated by management to help employees understand policies and procedures and general ground rules to function on the job (Saunderson, 2012). These expectations are sometimes shared during an orientation or stated in an organization's policy manual. Employees also learn unofficial procedures that have evolved over time by observing

etiquette—A system of rules and conventions that regulate social and professional behavior.

Your Social Media Presence

Social media can be an effective tool for establishing a professional network, showcasing your accomplishments, applying for your first job, and advancing your career within the industry. As you progress through your undergraduate education, you should highlight your accomplishments, volunteer opportunities, internships, and employment on various social media outlets (e.g., LinkedIn, Facebook, Twitter, Instagram, Google+, YouTube). Social media sites allow you to showcase a digital résumé that is different from a traditional résumé. Further, as you develop your network, you can keep your colleagues up-to-date on your career through social media. Social media is an essential tool used by sport organizations; therefore, demonstrating you are proficient and savvy in this area can be beneficial in your job search.

Networking on social media makes the sport world much smaller. News about your accomplishments and your weekend festivities can spread quickly. You should keep in mind that whatever you post or are tagged in on your social media profiles can be accessed by current or future employers (e.g., links, photos, videos, comments, posts, tweets). In fact, a CareerBuilder (2016) poll of hiring and human resource managers found that 60 percent of employers use social networking sites to research candidates. That figure is up from 52 percent in 2015, 22 percent in 2008, and 11 percent in the survey's first year in 2006. You should be cautious about the content you post because it can help or hurt your odds of getting a job. Forty-nine percent of hiring managers who screen candidates via social networks said they've found information that caused them not to hire a candidate. When managing your online presence, think about how you can use it to your advantage as a potential employee.

the behaviors of others and listening to stories told about the organization at informal gatherings. A clear understanding of expectations is essential to a fast career start. Astute new employees will recognize the importance of learning the organization's rules and guidelines and will distinguish themselves from others by showing their professional maturity. Professionally mature individuals display good judgment and are more likely to foster healthy workplace relationships and have access to further professional development opportunities (Higuera, n.d.). If you are unclear about expectations within your organization, it is wise to ask for clarification. Kahle-Piasecki (2011) advocated a mentor–mentee relationship between an experienced employee and a new hire to help increase the mentee's knowledge and productivity and enhance performance.

Demonstrate Your Work Ethic

Demonstrate your commitment to the organization, supervisors, and colleagues by enthusiastically completing all job assignments by the agreed-on deadlines, keeping your word, offering assistance, and supporting others in achieving the organization's goals. Your attitude toward work can be referred to as your **work ethic**. A positive attitude toward maintaining high standards usually creates a productive environment in which people take pride in the work and customers, suppliers, and partners want to conduct business (Duggan, n.d.). Identifying qualities and characteristics that you admire in others may help you determine your work values. Strive to do the right thing and gain recognition as a valuable member of the organization.

Develop Your Written Communication Skills

The ability to express thoughts and ideas in writing is one of the most important competencies of a good sport manager. Among the many types of writing that you will have to produce are business correspondence (e.g., memos, email messages, responses to complaints), reports, and technical manuals. Learn to organize your thoughts logically and use grammar and punctuation correctly. Investing time and energy in learning to write well will pay huge dividends when you enter the professional world.

Use Electronic Communication Appropriately   Although email is often used as an informal mode of communication, adherence to the conventions of good business writing is expected in business-related email messages. Good judgment regarding the content of email messages is essential. Use capitalization and punctuation in emails, and make sure you use the spell-checking function. Proofread emails for errors, and ensure that your tone is professional and appropriate. You can practice this when sending emails to your instructors. Always use formal titles (e.g., Dr., Ms., Mr., Professor), use an appropriate greeting, and keep your correspondence professional. Many excellent websites address the proper uses of email and provide tips for composing electronic business correspondence (search using the keywords *netiquette* or *email etiquette*). Your campus career center can also provide advice and guidance on the formatting of professional correspondence.

Thank Others   Take the opportunity to express gratitude to anyone who provides you with information or time. A good practice to follow is to send a note of appreciation within 24 hours of a social or business contact or event. You can send a personal letter of thanks, but in many cases, a well-composed email is appropriate. Making a habit of thanking people who help you will go a long way toward establishing your reputation as a professional.

Refine Your Teamwork Skills

The ability to participate as a valuable member of a team is imperative in any work setting. Tasks and assignments often rely on the talents of a work team, which is a group of people working together to accomplish a task or solve a problem. To be an effective team member, you need to develop skills such as commitment to the task, communication, collaboration, confrontation, consensus building, and caring and demonstrating respect for other team members. Remember to be prompt and provide complete and quality work or feedback in an agreed-on time frame.

Learn to Manage Conflict   Conflict is energy among people; it is not about winning or losing. Conflict is an opportunity to acknowledge and appreciate our differences. Carney and Wells (1995) noted that workplace differences or conflicts are most likely to occur "when workers are under pressure, when their responsibilities are not clear, or when their personal expectations or needs are violated." They added that situations involving conflict "offer ideal opportunities for clarifying personal differences and for team building" (p. 179). If you disagree with a colleague, supervisor, or customer, express yourself without being unpleasant. When handled in a mature, positive way, conflict can be healthy.

---

work ethic—A set of values based on desirable workplace characteristics that include accountability, dependability, initiative, and accomplishment.

Embrace Diversity   Appreciate and celebrate diversity of gender, race, religion, sexual orientation, ability, age, and so on. Do not engage in racist, ageist, or sexist behaviors, and let others know, tactfully, that you do not appreciate such behaviors. Seek to understand and respect the history, values, understandings, and opinions of others. Being inclusive is the right thing to do, and it can benefit an organization's bottom line. A proactive strategy that addresses diversity in an organization is associated with a host of positive outcomes such as improved group processes, better decision making, the attraction of customers, and increased organizational performance (Cunningham, 2016).

Assess Performance   As a new professional, you should welcome the evaluation process, recognizing that the aim of constructive criticism is to improve your performance. Expect to be involved in setting goals that will challenge your learning process. Your progress will be measured on a recurring basis so you and your supervisor can identify appropriate professional development activities to help you perform to the best of your ability. Be prepared to discuss your specific needs for development and strategies to improve your job performance. The most important question to ask your supervisor is what you should be doing to improve your job performance.

Continue Your Professional Development

As the concept of a successful career continually changes in our global sport marketplace, personal flexibility and the ability to adapt to change become even more important. Underlying the assumption that professionals can be flexible and can adapt to change is the concept of lifelong learning. Your professional education is just beginning, and it will continue throughout your life.

You should make an early commitment to lifelong formal and informal learning so you can continue to grow professionally and personally. Participation in business and professional associations (some examples are listed in the earlier sidebar Examples of Sport Management Professional Associations) increases your knowledge and expands your network of associates throughout your career. A well-developed career network is vital to your professional advancement. Your network contacts can provide information, guidance, support, honest feedback, and access to career opportunities. Interaction with sport management colleagues is stimulating and allows you to grow professionally and contribute to your field.

Business Etiquette

The academic environment is a helpful setting in which students can learn and practice professional competencies to bring into the sport industry. Learning technical skills is important, but developing one's interpersonal skills and respectable qualities can maximize employability and career success. Individuals who commit to becoming familiar with the right way to treat other people and can handle any situation with grace and confidence are going to get noticed (Langford, 2016). A commitment to courtesy and respectful behavior will benefit your workplace and will help you achieve your goals. As you prepare for a career in sport management, we encourage you to consider the following reminders of good manners:

- *Telephone.* Answering the telephone in a professional manner includes clearly identifying yourself and your organization or department; giving each caller your full attention; restating important information to check for understanding and accuracy; projecting a tone that is cheerful, natural, and attentive; ending the conversation with agreement on what is to happen next; and following up appropriately. When leaving your phone number on someone's voice-mail system, speak clearly and at a reasonable speed. Remember to leave your name, phone number, and a brief message so the caller will be prepared when she or he returns your call.

- *Voice-mail messages.* Refrain from leaving inappropriate greetings for callers, especially when you are searching for an internship or professional employment. Busy callers do not appreciate long messages, silliness, or loud music in the background.

- *Language.* Practice being inclusive in spoken and written language rather than using gender-biased or racially biased language. In the workplace of the 21st century, employees will interact with managers, clients, and customers who include women, people of color, or people from other cultures. Mastery of inclusive language is a good way to demonstrate your sensitivity and to create a more pleasant workplace (Parks, Harper, & Lopez, 1994).

- *Meeting participation.* Expected behavior in business meetings may vary by organizational culture, but general conventions include being prepared, arriving approximately 10 minutes early, silencing or turning off cell phones, staying on task, participating openly, giving your full attention through active listening, and encouraging others to participate and offer their ideas. Refrain from checking email or other social media sites on your computer, tablet, or phone.

• *Dining etiquette.* Many business meetings and interviews include a meal, and prospective employers, customers, and other business associates will judge your table manners. You will be more comfortable when you know what to expect. First, be prepared to engage in light conversation. Appropriate topics include current events, sports, and the arts. Politics, religion, and sex are taboo topics. Although drinking alcohol is not typically appropriate at a business lunch in the United States, know your organization's policy on drinking alcohol at business functions or follow your host's lead.

• *International experiences.* From an international perspective, good manners can be defined in various ways. Communicating with and relating to people from other cultures requires that you learn the protocols, courtesies, customs, and behaviors of those cultures. To reduce apprehension, investigate the customs prevalent in other countries prior to traveling and before entertaining international visitors. Participating in study-abroad experiences can help students develop cultural competencies. These courses have the potential to transform students' understandings, broaden perspectives, and expand their professional identities (Bai, Larimer, & Riner, 2016).

• *Introductions and greetings.* The host is responsible for introducing those who are meeting for the first time. When making an introduction, use the name of the most senior person first and introduce everyone else to him or her. As a sign of respect, do not use a person's first name until invited to do so. Regardless of your gender, stand when being introduced to others. When shaking hands, both women and men should use a firm grip. Grasp the person's entire hand, not just the fingers, and adjust your grip to the state of health and physical strength of the person you are greeting.

• *Office etiquette.* Many organizations today use dividers rather than walls, so you may find yourself working in a small space with several coworkers. Be conscious of others' needs for privacy and a quiet workplace. Be cautious in your use of music players, speakerphones, and other devices that can be distracting in a small workspace. In addition, refrain from engaging in company gossip. It may be tempting to listen in or indulge in workplace stories, but the best thing to do is remove yourself from the situation or try to defuse gossip when you are unable to get away (Boitnott, 2015).

• *Romantic relationships.* The office is not an appropriate place to engage in flirting or in more overt forms of affectionate behavior. Often, employee handbooks address issues of dating and romantic relationships in the workplace. Furthermore, be aware of your actions, because others can perceive flirtatious behavior as sexual harassment (Pedersen, Osborne, Whisenant, & Lim, 2009).

A positive, professional attitude—as reflected in your professional image, work habits and behavior, and business etiquette—is essential to your future success. Do not underestimate the roles that enthusiasm and positive self-image play in creating a successful professional attitude.

Business etiquette can be enhanced by gaining international experiences. Your interactions with other cultures will broaden your perspectives and help develop your cultural competencies. Consider working or volunteering in a major sport event such as the one shown here, the LPGA Evian Championship in France.
Courtesy of Paul M. Pedersen.

Career Planning and Management

To thrive in today's workforce, employees need to assume responsibility for their career planning and management and be actively involved in developing a career strategy. Gone are the days when college graduates could expect to find jobs immediately after graduation and spend their entire careers working for one organization. If you are a millennial (born between 1980 and 1999), you are likely to move from one company or department to another. As you change positions, you can bring with you best practices and fresh ideas (Pollak, 2017). Pollak cited a leadership survey that found that 80 percent of millennials consider themselves leaders, and a majority want to continue honing those leadership skills. Although frequent job changes may be the norm, you can achieve employment security by continuing to develop new skills through lifelong learning and by assuming personal responsibility for managing your career.

Career Decision Steps

The complex process of making career decisions can be divided into five stages: self-assessment, research, decision making, search, and acceptance (Doyle, 2015). Career planning can be fascinating because you will gain new insights about yourself as well as knowledge about the variety of career options available to you. The following steps will help you in your career planning. You do not have to complete them in the order presented, and you may need to repeat a step or two as you gain new information about yourself and your career options or if you encounter obstacles or barriers.

- *Self-assessment* involves identifying and understanding your personal and work values, interests, abilities, aptitudes, and personality traits and your desired future lifestyle.

- *Research* entails taking a broad look at career fields and researching specific sport management occupations, work environments, and employers that might match your unique career profile as identified through your self-assessment. Online resources are available to explore occupations and help you understand positions of interest to you. It is helpful to speak with people who are involved in or familiar with these occupations. Internships or job shadowing experiences may be helpful.

- *Decision making* is the process of consciously analyzing and weighing all information that you have gathered about yourself and various sport manage-

ment occupations and career paths. At this stage you will make a tentative career decision, formulate educational and vocational goals, and develop plans to achieve them. The more you learn about yourself and the world of sport management, the better and more realistic your educational and career choices will be.

- *The search* involves sharpening the skills that will help you obtain a position to which you aspire. In this stage, you will network with contacts, prepare effective application materials, present yourself professionally in interviews, evaluate and accept a job offer, and adjust to a new position. Acceptance marks the beginning of your career.

An effective way to collect information that can help with occupational decision making is through the completion of a computerized career assessment system. Most college career centers provide an interactive, web-based career guidance and education planning system that helps students with important career planning tasks such as understanding their interests, work values, personalities, skills, and educational preferences; identifying and discovering how their personal qualities relate to occupations; and narrowing their options by interactively exploring and analyzing occupations. Career center professionals can assist you in identifying how your values, interests, personality, and skills align with various occupational choices.

Using a systematic approach, you will be able to conduct a self-assessment and compare occupations to make decisions that are compatible with your values, interests, skills, personality, and desired future lifestyle. For each occupation that you are considering, gather the following information: the nature of the work, work setting and conditions, educational and personal qualifications required, earnings, employment outlook and competition, methods of entering the occupation, opportunities for advancement, opportunities for exploring the occupation, related occupations, and sources of additional information. (Online sources that may be useful in your research are listed in the Sport Management Career Resources sidebar.)

Interviewing professionals on site is another excellent way to gain additional information about jobs and work environments. Most sport managers are willing to help eager college students learn about the field. Through informational interviews, you can gain an insider's view on a sport management position, obtain referrals to other professionals, and create a network of contacts. Identify a sport manager to interview and call to arrange an appointment. Practice asking questions with a friend before you meet with the professional. During the meeting, practice

Volunteering at sporting events can help you decide whether a career in sport management is for you. The NFL Combine Experience event allows fans to participate in interactive experiences ranging from football clinics to virtual reality sessions.
Courtesy of Paul M. Pedersen.

your professionalism. Wear business formal or business casual attire, and be prepared to ask a variety of questions about how you can prepare to enter the occupation and be a successful professional. Remember to take notes. After the interview, send a note of appreciation within 24 hours.

No matter where you are in the career development process, your campus career center has services and programs to help you assess your career goals, find the right academic and experiential programs to achieve those goals, and gain employment after graduation. Career advisors can be extremely helpful in providing guidance and direction in assessing your vocational interests, identifying skills, writing résumés and cover letters, preparing for interviews, and conducting the job search.

Your career center may also be able to help you create a portfolio as evidence of what you have done (and hence what you will be able to do as a professional). Although your portfolio can be a bound collection of work completed during each semester, Gentile (2010) suggests keeping work in an electronic portfolio (eportfolio). There are many online platforms that can help you develop your eportfolio. Regardless of format, the portfolio should include various projects and assignments from sport management courses and any relevant evidence of success in other experiences. Portfolios are valuable in providing examples of skills and knowledge. Fur-

thermore, in the process of creating your portfolio, you will be able to reflect on your competencies and proficiencies. You might want to keep your eportfolio up-to-date as you grow in your profession.

Remember that career planning is not a one-time event. You will continually develop new interests, knowledge, and skills through your coursework, leisure activities, volunteer experiences, jobs, and internships. Throughout your career, you may be motivated to reevaluate your options when changes in duties or work conditions cause you to become less satisfied. You should examine many alternative options and decide what could be a good fit for you. Workplace qualities (e.g., environment, dress code, benefits packages, standard versus flexible work hours, telecommuting arrangements, travel) are constantly changing and are variable from one organization to the next. Understand which employers best suit your style of work and your work–life balance, and consider these factors when making employment transitions. This is part of your career management decision-making process.

Values

Your values are fundamental to career planning, and they indicate what you consider most important in your life. Zunker (2009) stated that a value can be defined as "something that is important or desirable to you" (p. 16). Many factors contribute to your process of learning what you value. These include cultural background, family influences, educational opportunities, religious and spiritual experiences, friends, and peers. One computer-based career guidance system (SIGI-3) that provides clarification of values focuses on the following eight **values** (though there are many more): high income, prestige, independence, contribution to society, security, variety, leadership, and leisure. The choices that you make about your occupational life need to be in harmony with your basic values and belief systems; otherwise, you will not find personal satisfaction in your job.

You should seek an occupation and jobs that will enhance, strengthen, and support the values that you consider important. For example, high school coaches may possess values that are different from those of sport **entrepreneurs**. The coaches may demonstrate the value that they place on facilitating the physical, mental, and moral development of young people, whereas sport entrepreneurs may demonstrate the value that they place on providing a high level of financial security for family members.

Interests

Interests are activities that you enthusiastically engage in and find enjoyable and subjects that arouse your curiosity or hold your attention. Interests are an integral part of your personality and are related to your values. Throughout your life, your personal experiences shape your interests. These interests often lead to competencies in the same areas. When your occupation matches your interests, you experience greater job satisfaction. If you have difficulty identifying or articulating your interests, you might want to seek the assistance of a career advisor at your university career center. Using interest inventories, career advisors can help you assess your measured interests and match those interests with appropriate occupations.

---

values—Indicators of what you consider most important or desirable.

entrepreneur—A person who identifies, organizes, and develops new business ventures.

Sport Management Career Resources

Please refer to the lists in each of this textbook's part openers for additional resources.

Online Resources

Academic Jobs Today

Blue Fish Jobs

Canada's Sport Information Resource Centre

Chronicle of Higher Education: Jobs

HigherEdJobs

Indeed.com

Jobs in Sports

LinkedIn

Major League Baseball Careers

National Alliance of Intercollegiate Athletics: NAIA Careers Center

National Alliance of State Broadcasters Associations

National Association of Collegiate Directors of Athletics: Job Center

National Communication Association

National Hockey League: NHL Hockey Jobs

NBA Career Opportunities

NCAA Market

Occupational Outlook Handbook

Professional Baseball Employment Opportunities

SimplyHired

SportJobMatch.com

Sports Careers

Sports Careers Institute

Sports Job Board

Sports Sales Combine

TeamWork Online

Women Sports Careers

Work in Sports

A Future in Sustainability

Sport has a tremendous effect on the natural environment. For example, consider the pollution that is created through emissions produced in transporting athletes, coaches, officiating crews, broadcasters, game day workers, and fans to an event. Add to that the amount of trash generated, water used, and electricity consumed to provide the best experience for everyone in attendance. What are sport organizations doing to address these issues? Are they doing a good job, or can they do more to reduce their environmental impact?

A focus on the environment positively affects the overall sport experience and can benefit the organization's bottom line. Over the last 10 years, sport management researchers and industry practitioners have looked at new ways to reduce the environmental effects of all types of sport involvement (McCullough & Kellison, 2017). However, some sport managers may not yet recognize the value of environmental sustainability efforts or lack a working knowledge of how to incorporate such initiatives (e.g., waste management, sustainable transportation options, energy efficiency).

Many sport management programs now discuss how environmental sustainability can influence the marketing, management, governance, and financial aspects of an organization. Some programs have gone further to create stand-alone environmental sustainability courses or concentrations. As you continue your sport management education and professional development, you can explore how economic, social, and environmental aspects intersect with sports managers' daily decisions. This knowledge can set you apart from others because you will more thoroughly understand how to contribute to the overall success of your employer.

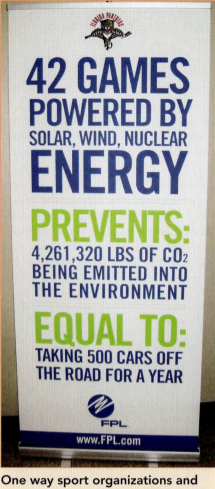

One way sport organizations and sport management practitioners embrace social responsibility and corporate accountability is through their engagement in environmental sustainability efforts.

Courtesy of Paul M. Pedersen.

Skills

A skill is the developed aptitude, ability, or personal quality needed to perform a task competently. The three basic types of skills are job content skills, functional skills, and adaptive skills. **Job content skills** are the specialized knowledge and abilities needed to fulfill a specific job responsibility. Knowing the rules of basketball is an example of a job content skill for a basketball referee. **Functional skills** are general abilities that transfer to many jobs or situations. For example, a referee uses functional skills to make quick, accurate decisions and to resolve player conflicts that occur on the court. **Adaptive skills** are personal attributes or personality traits. For example, a referee must remain calm and poised under stressful conditions.

---

job content skills—The specialized knowledge or abilities needed to fulfill specific job duties.

functional skills—General abilities that transfer to many jobs or situations.

adaptive skills—Personal attributes or traits that enable a person to approach changing workplace situations with flexibility.

Career Readiness for Occupational Success

Findings from a recent survey of employers identified the essential career competencies that employers look for in recent college graduates: critical thinking and problem solving, professionalism and work ethic, teamwork, and communication skills (NACE, 2016). Knowing which skills are required to be successful in today's workplace is a good starting point for assessing your level of skill attainment. After you identify the skills you possess and your level of proficiency, you can develop a plan for enhancing the skills that are most pertinent to your career goals.

For chapter-specific learning activities, visit the web study guide at **www.HumanKinetics.com/ContemporarySportManagement**.

Summary

The three necessary elements for success in sport management are professional preparation, professional attitude, and career planning and management. You can find sport management professional preparation programs at the bachelor's, master's, and doctoral levels. The typical undergraduate curriculum consists of general education and major courses along with field experiences that enable you to apply what you learn in the classroom in sport settings. Master's and doctoral programs will be more specific to your career goals.

Professional attitude is reflected in your personal appearance (e.g., hygiene, posture, self-confidence), adjustment to the workplace (e.g., academic preparation, writing skills, dependability, ethics, work habits), and business etiquette (e.g., telephone calls, emails, thank-you letters). Recruiters evaluate professional attitudes during interviews, and employers evaluate them in performance appraisals.

Career planning consists of self-awareness (e.g., values, interests, skills), occupational exploration (e.g., gathering information from a variety of sources), career decision making, and career implementation. College career centers can provide valuable guidance by directing you to various resources (see also the Sport Management Career Resources sidebar) and helping you create an electronic portfolio. If you are self-aware and eager to research and take advantage of opportunities for professional development, you will best position yourself to be a successful professional.

Review Questions

1. How can professional preparation, a professional attitude, and career planning and management contribute to your success in sport management?

2. List the three components of an undergraduate sport management curriculum. Which elements within each component fulfill the content requirements of the COSMA accreditation standards?

3. Define field experiences. How do they benefit students, employers, colleges and universities, and society?

4. How would you outline an effective plan for finding an optimal field experience in sport management?

5. According to *Job Outlook 2016* (NACE, n.d.), what skills and competencies will you need for a successful career in sport management? Explain how you plan to acquire these skills and competencies while in college.

6. List important elements of personal appearance, work transition and adjustment, and business etiquette. What does your conduct reveal about your personal perspective on each?

7. In your own words, how would you explain the stages of career planning?

8. What are some print and electronic resources that you could use in seeking employment in sport management?

9. How can social media platforms be used in your professional development and in the creation of your personal brand in the sport industry?

Historical Aspects of the Sport Business Industry

Elizabeth A. Gregg
Brenda G. Pitts
Paul M. Pedersen

LEARNING OBJECTIVES

- Identify the major business and market structures that allowed people to develop various historical sport businesses.

- Explain how the sport business industry evolved through the work of several influential people and companies.

- Discuss the influence of technology, marketing, and travel on the sport business industry.

- Understand the importance of communication (e.g., new and social media) to sport stakeholders and organizations.

- Identify the ways in which the sport business industry has been influenced by significant social, cultural, economic, and legal issues.

- Detail how an understanding of the history of sport businesses and market structures can help today's sport managers develop strategies for their businesses.

- Explain how the field of sport management was established in North America, and identify the individuals credited with establishing the discipline.

KEY TERMS

age of organization

brand equity

brand loyalty

brand recognition

decentralized organization

distribution

diversification

market share

vertical integration

watershed events

1862
William H. Cammeyer began charging admission to baseball games

1869
Cincinnati Red Stockings became the first all-professional baseball team

1872
Yale played Columbia in the first intercollegiate football game with an admission charge

1876
Spalding opened the Baseball and Sporting Goods Emporium in Chicago

1910
Philadelphia Athletics' Connie Mack introduced the low-cost producer concept to professional sport

1940
First college basketball doubleheader was broadcasted (NBC): Pittsburgh versus Fordham and NYU versus Georgetown

1951
First live, coast-to-coast broadcast of a sporting event was televised (NBC): college football, Duke versus Pittsburgh

1953
Major League Baseball Players Association formed

1961
Sports Broadcasting Act allowed leagues to negotiate one television contract for all their teams

1966
Roberta Gibb became the first woman to run the Boston Marathon

1967
Kathrine Switzer became the first woman to run the Boston Marathon with a race number

1983
NBA salary cap instituted

In 2017, the Real Madrid Football Club made history when the team won the Union of European Football Associations (UEFA) Champions League title for the second consecutive season. The team is valued at US$3.58 billion, which is slightly below Manchester United (US$3.69 billion) and Barcelona (US$3.64 billion) (Ozanian, 2017). The crown for the most valuable franchise in the sport industry belongs to the Dallas Cowboys. According to *Forbes* (Badenhausen, 2017), the Cowboys are valued at US$4.2 billion. Some of the other most valuable franchises include the New York Yankees (US$3.7 billion), the New England Patriots (US$3.4 billion), the New York Knicks (US$3.3 billion), the New York Giants (US$3.1 billion), the San Francisco 49ers (US$3 billion), and the Los Angeles Lakers (US$3 billion). Examples of other notable franchises are the Washington Redskins in 11th place (US$2.95 billion) and the Chicago Cubs, one of the eight original teams of the National League (founded in 1876), in 18th place (US$2.68 billion). The 50th most valuable team, the Los Angeles Angels of Anaheim, is worth US$1.75 billion.

Albert Goodwill (A.G.) Spalding was a pitcher for the Chicago White Stockings (now the Chicago Cubs) in the inaugural National League (NL) season. That same year, Spalding opened a retail sporting goods store in Chicago a few doors down from the White Stockings. The Baseball and Sporting Goods Emporium (Spalding & Brothers) sold baseball products to professional baseball teams and department stores. As a famous pitcher and a player–coach with the White Stockings, Spalding intended to capitalize on his baseball reputation and coaching position. Ten months later, Spalding & Brothers, Inc., reported a profit of US$1,083 ("Once Upon a Time," 1947). The firm—which pioneered the development of **brand rec-** **ognition** in sporting goods through athlete endorsements and continues such promotional activity today with sports superstar endorsers ranging from softball All-American and Olympian Jennie Finch to professional athlete Damian Lillard—is part of the sporting goods segment of the sport industry that sells more than US$64 billion worth of goods each year (National Sporting Goods Association, 2015).

Franchises such as Real Madrid, manufacturers such as Spalding, and athlete endorsers such as Finch and Lillard are part of a sport business industry that annually produces, advertises, and sells billions of dollars in sport products and services. This chapter provides brief historical sketches in the development of the sport business industry in the United States as well as an overview of the development of the sport management discipline. Because of the size and scope of the industry, this chapter covers only select historical developments. You can read about some historical aspects of the sport business industry not covered in the following pages by referring to some of this textbook's other chapters that include various aspects of history. You can also refer to table 3.1, Rise of Management in Sport, which looks at some of the eras in sport management and the origination dates of a few sport organizations and activities.

Historical Aspects of Commercialization in Sport

This section examines the developmental periods as well as the early commercialization models of the sport business industry. The developmental periods start with the later 19th century and involve issues of urban population growth, consumer demands, modernization, and entrepreneurship. This is followed by

---

brand recognition—A consumer's ability to correctly identify a given product or service by viewing a logo, packaging, tagline, or other product attributes.

an overview of sport business industry commercialization models and especially those associated with the sporting goods segment of the sport industry.

Developments

The 1870s is a good starting point for the discussion of models of commercialization. By this time, several developments were underway that made the emergence of the sport business industry possible. The urban population had grown large enough to support the new sport industry. Changes in response to the urban populace's demand for sport made sustainable commercialization of sport possible; the urban practice of buying sport entertainment had become firmly entrenched. Various sports had become quite popular, which made sport products and services viable for sustained commercial success (Rader, 2009). The process of modernizing sport

Most modern sport organizations were established after the 18th century. The Turf Club, a private entity that acts as the regulatory body for horseracing in Ireland, established in 1790, is one of the exceptions. The INHSC on the building refers to the Irish National Hunt Steeplechase Committee, which is incorporated in the Turf Club.

Courtesy of Paul M. Pedersen.

began in harness racing, horse racing, and baseball before 1870 and experienced exponential growth after 1870 (Adelman, 1986). The modernization process included the specialization of athletic skill, the development of effective organizational structures to present and control sport, the standardization and routinization of the sport product, and an educated citizenry ready to learn about and follow sport in newspapers and popular magazines. The development of the sport business industry was also aided during the last quarter of the 19th century by the growth of per capita income that left consumers with discretionary funds to spend on sport and entertainment.

Technology also influenced the beginnings of a viable sport business industry after 1870. It is difficult, for example, to imagine the development of the sport business industry without railroads to transport teams and distribute products or the telegraph to report scores and solidify business deals. By 1870, all major eastern and midwestern cities were interconnected by rail and telegraph. Technological developments in the newspaper press and printing industry also helped spread information about sport to an increasingly interested middle class. Table 3.1 provides an overview of the rise of management in sport over the years.

Table 3.1   Rise of Management in Sport: Eras and Select Organizations

Era	Year	Example organization*
Rise of organized sport (before 1840)	776 BCE	Olympic Games
	1735	Royal Burgess Golfing Society of Edinburgh
	1754	Royal and Ancient Golf Club of St Andrews
	1790	The Turf Club (Ireland)
Owner/manager (1840-1870)	1845	Knickerbocker Base Ball Club of New York
	1860	The Open Championship (British Open)
Field manager/team president (1870-1900)	1876	National League of Professional Baseball Clubs (NL)
	1894	International Olympic Committee (IOC)
	1894	American Jockey Club
	1894	United States Golf Association (USGA)
	1895	American Bowling Congress (ABC)
Team president/field manager/ business manager (1900-1920)	1900	International Cycling Union
	1903	Tour de France
	1904	International Federation of Football Association (FIFA)
	1904	American Automobile Association (AAA)
	1906	National Collegiate Athletic Association (NCAA)
	1916	Women's International Bowling Congress (WIBC)
	1916	Professional Golfers' Association (PGA) of America
	1917	National Hockey League (NHL)
	1919	Triple Crown Horse Racing

Era	Year	Example organization*
General manager (1920-1950)	1920	National Football League (NFL)
	1921	World Boxing Association (WBA)
	1944	Sports Car Club of America (SCCA)
	1948	National Association for Stock Car Auto Racing (NASCAR)
	1950	Ladies Professional Golf Association (LPGA)
	1950	Formula One (F1)
Management team (1950-1980)	1951	National Hot Rod Association (NHRA)
	1955	United States Auto Club (USAC)
	1954	Rugby League World Cup
	1958	Canadian Football League (CFL)
	1973	Women's Tennis Association (WTA)
	1977	United States Boxing Association (USBA)
	1978	Championship Auto Racing Teams (CART)
	1979	Entertainment and Sports Programming Network (ESPN)
Conglomerate/subsidiary team management (1980-present)	1986	International Floorball Federation
	1987	Arena Football League (AFL)
	1987	National Lacrosse League (NLL)
	1992	English Premier League (EPL)
	1993	Ultimate Fighting Championship (UFC)
	1993	Major League Soccer (MLS)
	1995	X Games
	1996	Women's National Basketball Association (WNBA)
	1997	American National Rugby League
	1998	Women's Premier Soccer League (WPSL)
	2008	Indian Premier League (IPL)
	2013	Fox Sports 1
	2013	National Women's Soccer League
	2016	Drone Racing League (DRL)
	2016	Esports Championship Series (ECS)
	2017	Professional Futsal League (PFL)

*Current name; various organizations had previous names or evolved or merged from other organizations.

Models

Numerous commercialization models in the sport business industry developed over the last few decades of the 19th century. Between 1880 and 1890, 79 companies began to produce sporting goods products. Some companies began with the objective of producing sport equipment. For example, the Nelson Johnson Manufacturing Company was established in Chicago in 1883 to produce tubular skates. Some firms relocated to U.S. soil to produce sporting goods. Two companies, Slazenger and Bancroft, arrived from England in the early 1880s to produce tennis rackets. Several other firms were established to distribute and sell sporting goods. These new corporations competed directly with hardware stores, which began distributing sporting goods during the 1870s. Department stores and mail-order houses started selling sporting goods during the 1880s. Each new entrant into the sport business industry helped to popularize sport, thus developing and expanding the market.

A.G. Spalding & Brothers emerged in the 1880s as one of the first and certainly the most successful of the early sporting goods firms. The diversification of Spalding during the last quarter of the 19th century provides insight into the development of the industry. Spalding & Brothers was the first modern sport business enterprise, and many other companies copied its techniques, methods, and attitudes.

The success of Spalding & Brothers resulted from four interrelated developments within the firm: (1) vertical integration, (2) diversification, (3) the development of a modern management system, and (4) the promotional skills of A.G. Spalding himself. Spalding & Brothers began in 1876 as a retail store, and by the next year, the firm had initiated its practice of **vertical integration** by wholesaling sporting goods from the same store. By 1884, Spalding had established wholesale centers in Chicago and New York to coordinate service for eastern and western markets. By the beginning of the 20th century, Spalding was producing sporting goods equipment in 15 plants in the United States and five plants overseas. Vertical integration meant that Spalding could benefit from economies of scale and scope, thus more effectively coordinating the manufacture and distribution of sporting goods. Vertical integration allowed the company to control resale prices in local stores.

Diversification was another key to the company's success. Spalding began by selling baseball equipment. Its largest contract was with one of the baseball clubs in Chicago, the White Stockings. Within two years, Spalding & Brothers was selling fishing equipment, ice skates, and croquet equipment. During the 1880s, Spalding expanded into football, soccer, boxing, track and field, tennis, boats, canoes, and a variety of sport clothing, uniforms, and shoes. In the early 1890s, Spalding produced the first basketball

---

vertical integration—A company's expansion by moving forward or backward within an industry; expansion along a product or service value chain. The opposite of vertical integration is horizontal integration. Horizontal integration occurs when a company adds new products and services to its organizational structure.

diversification—The act of adding new products to the company's product mix, thus diversifying the company's product offerings.

Under Armour

In 1996, Kevin Plank was a 23-year-old special team's captain on the football team at the University of Maryland. Recognizing that the cotton T-shirt he wore under his uniform frequently became sweat soaked and uncomfortable, Plank began developing an alternative using microfibers. Based out of his grandmother's house, Plank built the prototype of his technologically advanced moisture wicking fabric that changed the sportswear industry. Plank's company was soon named Under Armour and quickly caught the attention of the sport industry and the media. After his first year in business, Plank acquired a manufacturing plant and had about US$100,000 in orders. Two years later, his products were featured in the popular football movie *Any Given Sunday*, which provided Plank with enough capital to purchase advertising time on ESPN. The creative use of product placements allowed Plank to create widespread brand recognition of Under Armour, which in turn generated tremendous market share. Under Armour profited using brand diversification and expanded their product lines from clothing to a wide range of sporting goods. The company now also holds a significant market share of the fitness app industry. In just over 20 years, Under Armour has grown into a US$16 billion corporation.

Professionalism in New Zealand Rugby

Geoff Watson
Massey University, New Zealand

Rugby Union has been New Zealand's national sport almost from the time it was first played there in 1870. The national men's team, known as the All Blacks, is one of the most consistently successful teams in world sport, winning over 70 percent of their games since they first played in 1884. For most of its history, rugby was an amateur game. It famously split in Britain in 1895 when clubs that wanted to compensate players who had to take time off work to play formed their own competition (which subsequently became the game of Rugby League). The professionalization of rugby was not entirely unprecedented; the game had become increasingly shamateur during the 1970s and 1980s as the commercial sector became increasingly involved. It was not until 1995 that it became openly professional when SANZAR, a newly created entity representing the rugby unions from South Africa, New Zealand, and Australia, signed an agreement with Rupert Murdoch's News Corporation for US$555 million for broadcasting rights to future competitions.

The effects of professionalism were far reaching. For the first time, players were contracted to the New Zealand Rugby Football Union (NZRFU). NZRFU had to work hard to secure the loyalty of its top players, many of whom had been approached to join a rival organization, the World Rugby Corporation. Beginning in 1996, SANZAR established a new competition with teams from New Zealand, Australia, and South Africa (Super Rugby, as the competition is now called, presently comprises 18 teams). Whereas New Zealand teams had previously been selected along provincial lines, the new competition operated on a franchise model, meaning players who lived outside a region could be drafted into a team. The flipside to players being better paid and more prominent in the media was that they came under much greater public scrutiny, which is a trend exacerbated by the influence of social media.

The way people watched the game also changed. Fans who had previously watched games on free-to-air television now had to pay subscription fees to watch their teams. Match venues also changed with a movement toward all-seater stadiums and the provision of corporate boxes where sponsors could host clients. Moreover, most international and Super Rugby games in New Zealand now took place at night, which allowed the broadcasters to maximize their audience. A new vocabulary also entered the public consciousness, and the game was referred to as a product. Some people found these changes unsettling, and they vented their frustrations in print and on talk radio.

Despite the rumblings of discontent, professionalism has endured. Arguably, by continuing to pay their subscriptions, most New Zealand sports fans have given it at least tacit approval. Moreover, by contracting leading players directly to the national body and insisting that only players based in New Zealand are eligible for All Black selection, the NZRFU has arguably gained a competitive advantage by ensuring that national coaches have access to players and that New Zealanders continue to see their best players in their own country.

The marketability of the All Blacks has, to a large degree, been based on their heritage. Perhaps the most famous team is 1905-1906 Originals, pictured here, who won 34 of their 35 matches on their tour of the United Kingdom, France, and North America scoring 976 points and conceding only 59.

Negatives and prints from the Making New Zealand Centennial Collection. Ref: MNZ-1035-1/4F. Alexander Turnbull Library, Wellington, New Zealand.

for James Naismith (the inventor of the game of basketball), helped introduce golf equipment into the U.S. market, and became a leading contender in the market. Before the end of the 19th century, Spalding manufactured nearly everything that the sport enthusiast might want or require to improve sport performance or pleasure.

Spalding used popular sport figures to discuss sports rules and to provide instruction in how to develop sport skills. Spalding advertisements promoted the benefits of sport for participants, helping to popularize the motives for active involvement. The company donated trophies for tournaments, track meets, regattas, bicycle races, baseball contests, and league championships. Spalding staff members offered lessons and training for beginners as well as more advanced players and provided advice on the construction of facilities. Spalding employees taught local consumers about club organization and management of tournaments and contests. These services helped expand local markets, brought goodwill to the company, and promoted Spalding products.

The purpose of Spalding & Brothers' promotions was not just to expand the market for sport equipment but also to sell its products. When Spalding received the contract to publish the *National League Official Rules*, the name of the rule book was changed to *Spalding's Official National League Rule Book*, and it advertised Spalding sporting goods equipment. When Spalding obtained the rights to produce the official baseball for the National League, the firm quickly announced to the baseball consumer that only Spalding could produce the real thing. Realizing the significance of being the official producer, Spalding tried to outdistance rivals by declaring its status as the official producer of footballs and soccer balls as well as golf, tennis, and track and field equipment. Spalding's pioneering use of celebrity athletes as endorsers of the company's products resulted in the development of the unique aspect of brand recognition in sporting goods. Spalding's promotional slogans, such as "First make sure it's Spalding and then go buy," further established brand identity.

Other sporting goods entrepreneurs learned from Spalding & Brothers about **decentralized organization** and successful management techniques. When A.G. Spalding purchased the Wilkins Manufacturing Company in 1878, he knew little about the manufacture of baseball bats, croquet mallets, ice skates, or baseball uniforms. To overcome this problem, Spalding retained Wilkins' staff and employees to train

A.G. Spalding was a pioneer in the sport business industry whose name can still be seen on sporting goods used today.

Courtesy of Paul M. Pedersen.

his Spalding & Brothers staff. When Wilkins sold his interest in the company, Spalding had a trained administrative staff ready to take over and run the business. The company adopted the same approach in the development of its retail and wholesale distribution networks. Instead of searching for new employees to manage newly acquired or developed retail and wholesale outlets, Spalding hired managers away from the competition.

By 1894, Spalding had established two divisions, one on the East coast with headquarters in New York City and the other in the Midwest with headquarters in Chicago. Each division was subdivided into major activities: manufacturing, retail, and wholesale. These activities were further subdivided into departments organized around sport categories (e.g., golf department, tennis department). Departments organized and administered their own functional activities such as accounting, purchasing, and advertising. To coordinate activities across divisions and departments, Spalding developed overarching functional departments. The marketing department, for example,

---

decentralized organization—The act of developing separate divisions, subcompanies, or departments that focus on certain tasks or products of the company and can be run autonomously.

coordinated advertising, product promotions, and markdown sales promotions nationwide. A top-level management department observed, standardized, and coordinated management techniques in each of Spalding's retail stores. This matrix organizational design proved highly effective and efficient. It gave Spalding a distinct advantage in management and proved to be an asset in the preparation of future top managers for the company.

Just as sporting goods entrepreneurs in the 1800s learned their trade from model companies such as Spalding & Brothers, entrepreneurs in the intercollegiate athletic system benefited from observing student-athletes and student organizers. Some of the best examples of these entrepreneurs can be found in the early years of intercollegiate football.

Historical Aspects of the Sport Market

Over the years in the sport business industry, **watershed events** have caused massive changes in the way business is conducted. These events have led to new ways of doing activities (e.g., manufacturing) and new strategies and techniques for achieving business success. Although several watershed events illustrate such changes in the sport business industry, the bicycle craze of the 1890s probably provides the most instructive historical example. In 1890, 27 firms manufactured bicycles, and sales competition was relatively low. Beginning developments in ancillary industries were under way during the same period. Dunlop, B.F. Goodrich, Goodyear, Penn Rubber Company, and a few others were beginning to manufacture bicycle tires. Miscellaneous bicycle parts such as bells, seats, and lamps were just beginning to make inroads into consumer markets. Top-grade bicycles sold for US$150. Medium-grade bicycles sold for around US$100. Bicycles were sold primarily through hardware stores, although a few specialty shops and sporting goods stores sold bicycles. Distribution was targeted toward the larger cities in the East and the Midwest. Reason-why advertisements attempting to convince potential customers about the importance of the bicycle for fun, health, fitness, and self-development were placed predominantly in trade magazines. Promotions included trade shows, instructional books, and essay and poster contests.

By 1898, 312 companies were manufacturing bicycles and bicycle parts. Rapid technological improvements in the safety of the bicycle between 1890 and 1895 led firms to emphasize the need for consumers to purchase a new model each year. Bicycle sales skyrocketed after 1893, but so did competition among an ever-expanding number of firms that produced bicycles. Competition spread quickly to ancillary industries as new entrants vied for **market share**. Bicycle accessories also experienced a boom period between 1893 and 1898, prompting the emergence of new firms in the industry. Competition forced bicycle prices down. In 1898, top-grade bicycles could be bought for US$75, middle-grade bicycles for US$40, and low-grade bicycles for US$20. Secondhand bicycles sold for as little as US$3.

Increased competition forced bicycle firms to change the way that they did business. Beginning in 1893, firms stressed marketing and tried to meet customer needs in a variety of new ways. Firms emphasized **brand equity** and tried to establish entry barriers, protect against price cutting, and move bicycles through distribution channels more quickly. Bicycle firms also advertised extensively and became one of the top 10 industries in advertising volume during the 1890s. Systematic advertising became the rule as bicycle companies planned advertising campaigns across a 6- to 12-month period. Firms developed slogans and trademarks to help establish brand-name recognition. They also created new advertising themes to place the bicycle in the mainstream of American social movements and perceived individual needs and wants.

During the last years of the 19th century, the bicycle became an engine of democracy, an escape from the bonds of technology and industrialization, a tool promoting freedom for women, a moral elevator and developer for youth, and an agent for training young men. Advertisers used popular middle-class magazines and newspapers to sell bicycles. Bicycle firms employed traveling salesmen, former athletes, and former bicycle racing stars to visit local shops, sell company products, and establish training facilities. These same traveling salesmen taught locals how to organize bicycle clubs, hold and administer bicycle races, and arrange and coordinate bicycle parades, touring rides, and bicycle cross-country runs. These activities were part of the firm's attempt to increase or protect market share.

The bicycle craze motivated many firms to enter the industry (Fielding & Miller, 1998). Demand for bicycles and bicycle accessories amounted to a product value of US$2,568,326 in 1890. Falling

---

watershed events—Events or developments in an industry that cause significant changes throughout the industry.
market share—The ranked position of a company in a market that is determined by the percentage of a company's product sales.
brand equity—The value of a given brand in the commercial marketplace derived from consumer perceptions of a sport organization's product or service.

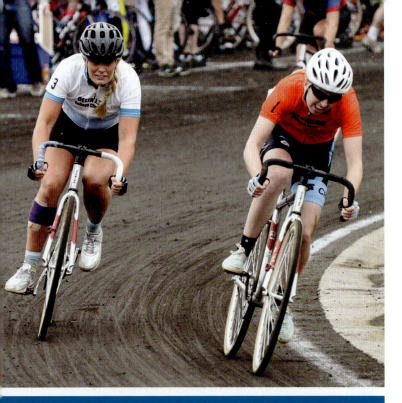

traveling salesmen, and trade show promotions. The bicycle craze taught manufacturers the importance of using national and local marketing and promotional campaigns.

Although the first decade of the 20th century was tough on the bicycle industry, numerous sports were becoming more popular and witnessing tremendous growth (read the critical thinking section at the end of this chapter for more about the growth and popularity of sport at this time). The popularity and growth were particularly evident in baseball, tennis, golf, football, basketball, fishing, target shooting, and roller skating, according to the *Sporting Goods Dealer* (*SGD*), a trade journal that provided monthly marketing reports. The *SGD* periodically reported on what it called the "golf and tennis boom." Companies manufacturing or selling baseball and football equipment reported brisk business throughout the decade.

The growth of sport participation, as evidenced by increased sporting goods sales during the decade, was influenced by the drive to organize sport participation during the age of organization (the decades of the 1880s and 1890s). For example, YMCAs began to organize and market sport during this period, helping to create a youth sport market by the turn of the century. The United States Lawn Tennis Association (USLTA), organized in 1881, promoted tennis for both men and women by sponsoring national tournaments during the 1890s. The USGA offered similar opportunities for male and female golfers. As Betts (1974) explained, the National Canoe Association (1880), the National Croquet Association (1882), the United States Skating Association (1884), and the American Bowling Congress (1895) all promoted participation and organized sport opportunities for men and women before 1900. Men's intercollegiate athletic organizations multiplied during the 1870s, 1880s, and 1890s, codifying rules of play and organizing and administering intercollegiate contests in such diverse sports as football, soccer, track and field, cross country, baseball, and rowing (Smith, 1988). Women's colleges offered sport opportunities during the 1880s and 1890s. Women learned the joys of participation in gymnastics, basketball, golf, tennis, field hockey, and track and field. After graduation, women took with them a desire to continue to participate in sport. Just over a half century later, institutions of higher education began offering women and men opportunities to study sport management.

profits after 1895 were the immediate result of the intensity of competition that increased exponentially each year from 1892 through 1898. After 1898, price wars occurred frequently, disrupting profit margins. Alarmed at shrinking profits, companies sold bicycles and related goods below cost to unload surplus. Despite such efforts, profits declined each year after 1895. By 1897, net earnings were less than half what they had been in 1896. Bicycle prices dropped steadily after 1895. In the eyes of 1899 observers, the bicycle industry was ready for a crash. The collapse happened gradually but was in full force by 1901. By 1909, only 94 companies remained in the bicycle industry.

The bicycle craze and the crash that followed it serve as examples for members of the sport business industry in three key areas. First, the bicycle craze raised questions about how firms coped with the uncertainty created by intense competition. Overproduction and price cutting became watchwords in the sport industry. Second, the influence of the bicycle advertising message, promoting sport in general, convinced sport firms of the necessity of promoting all kinds of sport. Third, the bicycle craze influenced marketing strategy. Successful companies employed a variety of marketing techniques in an integrated marketing strategy. Marketing techniques integrated advertising, sponsorship, and endorsements and included organizing participation through the development of local clubs and local activities, the use of

Segmentation

By the turn of the 20th century, perceptive observers within the sport business industry saw opportunities to make money by selling participation opportunities,

age of organization—A period during the 1880s and 1890s during which companies began to organize and market sport to specific markets such as youth.

charging spectators admission to watch athletes perform, and selling equipment for players to improve performance. The segmentation of sport marketing commenced as sport business leaders recognized that the market for sport participants, sport audiences, and sport equipment purchasers was segmented.

The largest of these segments was the growing number of white, male, middle-class sport enthusiasts in U.S. cities. Middle-class consumers far outnumbered spenders in other segments in the market, and they had the money to buy participation opportunities, tickets to games and matches, and high-priced equipment to perform. Astute observers of the sport scene were also aware of the second important segment: the developing youth market. Periodically, readers of the *SGD* were informed about the necessity of catering to the American boy for two important reasons. First was the fact that the participation rate for boys was up and that an increasing number of boys purchased sport equipment. Second, entrepreneurs realized that today's youth participant would become tomorrow's adult participant. Brand recognition and **brand loyalty** began in adolescence. White upper- and middle-class women constituted a third major segment in the sport market. Marketers were interested in enticing women to participate and purchase golf and tennis equipment, fishing equipment, bicycles, and athletic wear.

Endorsement Advertising

Athlete endorsements today are commonplace, as evidenced by deals between Sloane Stephens and HEAD, Tom Brady and Tag Heuer, Phil Mickelson and Rolex, Serena Williams and Nike, Usain Bolt and Gatorade, Lewis Hamilton and Mercedes, Rafael Nadal and Richard Mille, Danica Patrick and Tissot, LeBron James and McDonald's, Aaron Rodgers and State Farm, Yani Tseng and Adams Golf, and Cristiano Ronaldo and a host of companies. Such endorsements commenced decades ago. For example, in 1917, J.H. Hillerich signed George Herman Ruth, otherwise known as Babe Ruth, to a contract that allowed the sporting goods company Hillerich & Bradsby (H&B) to use Ruth's autograph on its Louisville Slugger bats. Two years later, the Babe Ruth–autographed Louisville Slugger was the leading seller for H&B, outdistancing the sale of any other bat sold in America. The contract with Ruth cost H&B US$100 and a set of golf clubs— probably the most lucrative deal (for a company) in endorsement contract history.

Using an athlete's name to sell a product, particularly a sporting goods product, was not a novel

idea in 1917. Hillerich had signed Honus Wagner, hall of fame shortstop for the Pittsburgh Pirates, to a similar deal back in 1905. Before 1910, Hillerich signed Ty Cobb and Napoleon Lajoie, both future hall of famers, to endorsement contracts. Wagner, Cobb, and Lajoie were chosen to endorse Louisville Slugger bats because they were expert hitters. They were excellent choices for a baseball bat company whose slogan was "the bat that gets more hits." This message, endorsed by the best hitters in professional baseball, sold bats. Advertisers used endorsements by experts to symbolize product quality and to establish brand-name recognition. Product endorsements by experts attracted consumers who wanted to improve performance in some way. Endorsements linked participant performance to product quality.

Hillerich & Bradsby—through Ruth, Cobb, Wagner, Lajoie, and others—took the matter a step further. Ruth was more than simply an expert who informed consumers about bats. He was an icon, a personality, a hero, and a human-interest story. His was a style to be copied, and it symbolized a certain type of individuality. Indeed, vocabulary was created to describe him (e.g., people spoke of "Ruthian feats" to communicate heroic accomplishments). Consumers'

The use of athletes to endorse products has been a common practice for over a century. Tag Heuer is one of many products endorsed by NFL quarterback Tom Brady, who played in his eighth Super Bowl in 2018.
Courtesy of Paul M. Pedersen.

brand loyalty—Faithfulness to a particular brand as evidenced by repeat purchases of one brand over others.

Roone Arledge, Televised Sport, and Entertainment

Finding sports on television at any time of the day is not difficult to do with the rise of televised sport programming overall and the proliferation of sport-focused television networks (SEC Network, Big Ten Network, Pac-12 Network, NBC Sports Network, Longhorn Network, Fox Sports 1, Golf Channel, and so on). The seemingly ubiquitous sport broadcast content available today is a result of a relationship between television and sport that commenced decades ago. In the first half of the 20th century came the arrival of televised sport, starting with a college baseball game in the late 1930s, a variety of sport broadcasts (e.g., Gillette Cavalcade of Sports) in the 1940s, and popular niche broadcasts such as roller derby and wrestling in the 1950s.

In 1960, Roone Arledge proposed to ABC executives a new plan for covering football games. The application of his plan revolutionized how sports were televised during the remainder of the 20th century. Arledge wanted to bring the TV viewer to the game and to get the audiences emotionally involved. He wanted viewers at home to experience the game as though they were at the stadium. Arledge reasoned that even if they were not football fans, they could still enjoy the game. Bringing the consumer to the game required developing a new method for covering the game. Arledge increased the number of cameras from 3 to 12 or more and introduced instant replay. To bring the action up close and personal, he used handheld and isolated cameras. To help duplicate the live atmosphere, Arledge used directional and remote microphones to capture the sounds of the game and crowd.

Arledge believed that televised sport was in the commercial entertainment business. Television programs survived only if they could draw high ratings, support advertising dollars, and generate corporate profits. The same was true for televised sport. This requirement meant that televised games had to attract a variety of viewers. Arledge realized that casual viewers and fans were far more important than avid football consumers because there were more of them. These people required more than just sport to be entertained. Arledge believed that the participants in a sport contest were the essence of entertainment. Sport viewing was experiential. Therefore, Arledge sought to extend the entertainment value of sport beyond the game itself.

Arledge's lessons on improving sport entertainment were copied by others. For instance, the 1970s ushered in the age of the mascot. Later in that decade, the success of the Dallas Cowboys cheerleaders prompted other teams to add cheerleaders to extend the entertainment value of the game. Additional ways that sport was tailored to appeal to more followers included exploding scoreboards, artificial grass, extended schedules and playoff systems, and rule changes to make games more action packed and exciting (Rader, 1984; Roberts & Olsen, 1989).

lower prices for consumers and greater competition among industry members.

Because of the new entrants into the marketplace, leaders in the sporting goods segment of the sport industry soon realized that the industry had become highly competitive and consequently unprofitable by the mid-1920s. The cost of doing business increased, and profits plummeted. To survive, manufacturers resorted to ruinous competitive practices such as price cutting. As the industry moved into the 1930s, sporting goods leaders realized that cooperative efforts were needed to curb competition. Cutthroat competition decreased as industry leaders shared customer credit information, discussed solutions to common problems, and generally cooperated among themselves. These practices increased the individual and collective knowledge about the sporting goods segment of the sport industry. Competitors gained better understanding about the effects of competitive

strategy on industry members and overall profitability.

Increased Participation and Spectatorship

World War II severely curbed the production of sporting equipment, especially goods made from rubber, leather, wood, cotton, and petroleum. Many sporting goods companies attempted to stockpile raw materials; this was a fruitless action because government policy curbed production of sport equipment regardless of material supplies. Rationing was the rule of civilian life during this time. Many sporting and leisure activities were postponed indefinitely, terminated, or affected in other ways. The prestigious Wimbledon championships were suspended from 1940 through 1945. Many male professional athletes were called into military duty, leaving many men's sport teams with less-skilled players. College and high school sport programs were cut back or eliminated altogether.

In both military and civilian life, sport participation became a matter of policy. Inductees into the army and the navy had to be trained. Sport, including highly competitive athletic events, became part of this training as a matter of military policy. The military tried to coerce every soldier and every sailor into the sporting life. Military leaders advised civilian authorities to adopt similar policies as part of the war effort. Postwar Americans sought out entertainment and leisure as sport participants and as spectators. Because of the growing popularity of men's football, a new professional football league began in 1946 and survived for three seasons before merging with the NFL for the 1950 season. In 1949, the men's Basketball Association of America merged with the National Basketball League to become the NBA. The end of the decade was a boom period for professional sports.

During the late 1940s, the color barrier was broken in professional sport, as highlighted in the widely acclaimed 2013 movie *42*. Jackie Robinson signed with the Brooklyn Dodgers in 1945 and in 1947 became the first African American to play any professional sport. In 1946, professional football saw Marion Motley and Bill Willis join the Cleveland Browns and Kenny Washington and Woody Strode play for the Los Angeles Rams. In 1949, Indiana University All-American George Taliaferro became the first African American drafted by the NFL. The following year, professional basketball integrated when Chuck Cooper joined the Celtics and Sweetwater Clifton left the Harlem Globetrotters for the New York Knicks. Several factors influenced the integration process. It was, at least in part, a response to the pressure for integration in the military during World War II. Part of it was also a question of ethics and values and of changing attitudes. Part of it was economics. African Americans constituted a vast, untapped, and inexpensive talent pool. During the decades that followed, team owners became aware that African American talent often meant the difference between financial success and failure, particularly in the 1950s and 1960s as a new breed of owners took control of professional sports. Bill Veeck, an innovator who introduced new techniques to sport managers, was one of the best examples of this new breed of owners and promoters.

World War II brought substantial numbers of women into the army, navy, and coast guard. Athletic competition became part of the training program for women, which copied the men's program. Women were encouraged to participate in competitive athletic programs in volleyball, archery, basketball, bowling, tennis, table tennis, swimming, badminton, and softball. Women's military teams also took on civilian teams.

Women had been competing in industrial leagues since World War I. The 1930s witnessed tremendous expansion in women's industrial leagues and particularly softball leagues. World War II brought more women into more sports. Society's attitude toward the participation of women in sports began to change. An example is the women's professional baseball league. The All-American Girls Professional Baseball League (AAGPBL) was established by Philip K. Wrigley, owner of the Wrigley chewing gum company and the Chicago Cubs, to provide entertainment for sport fans during the war. Made famous by the movie *A League of Their Own*, the AAGPBL enjoyed success from 1943 to 1954. At its peak in 1948, 10 teams played in the AAGPBL, and more than 1 million fans watched them play. The AAGPBL, along with other societal changes in the United States, helped bring about the beginning of a positive change in thinking toward women in sport. Although the AAGPBL is the most well-known women's baseball league, the historical record shows that women played baseball in colleges in 1866 and on professional women's teams in 1867.

Over the succeeding decades, sport participation rates for women grew dramatically. Between 1968 and 1980, high school girls' sport participation increased by more than 500 percent. Participation by women collegians increased nearly as much. The feminist movement of the late 1960s and 1970s prompted tremendous growth in the women's market for sport and sport products. The fitness boom of the 1970s and 1980s also influenced women's interest. Increased participation by women was also a matter of public policy (i.e., Title IX), and the increased opportunities translated into increased sales. Sporting goods manufacturers, distributors, and retailers strove to do their bit for public policy by selling sport shoes, sport equipment, and sport apparel and by promoting participation opportunities for female athletes.

The 1960s and 1970s provided an all-out assault on sexism and the traditional notions and limitations of gendered and sexualized roles. Now, with legislation and the women's rights movement making progress, women in sport charged ahead. But the rights of women in sport were resisted by societal strongholds that clung to old traditions. Not until the 1990s did women in sport in the United States become comfortable with their muscularity and approach equality in pay to men. Along the way, it took Title IX, several lawsuits, and a series of events to reach this point (please read this chapter's professional profile on Dr. Donna Lopiano for some insight into the history and influence one woman has had on intercollegiate athletics and girls and women's sport). In 1978, the Women's Professional Basketball League (WBPL) made history by becoming the first such professional team-sport league. The league lasted three years, folded, started again, went another three years, folded, and then repeated this sequence a few more times. Today, the WNBA, WTA, and other women's professional sports leagues and intercollegiate athletic programs are so popular that they have commercial value and major corporate support. Overall, the 1990s (known as the decade of the female athlete) through well into the second decade of the 21st century have witnessed increased interest in women's sports and increased participation by women in athletic competitions ranging from mixed martial arts, extreme sports, and boxing to football, soccer, and basketball. The sport industry—including media outlets such as ESPN with its *Nine for IX* documentary series (table 3.2)—celebrated the 40th anniversary of Title IX in 2013.

History of the Discipline of Sport Management

As the sport industry matured, the need for professionals trained in the business of sport became apparent. Earle Zeigler, Guy Lewis, Stephen Hardy, and Lawrence W. Fielding, who were educated and trained in sport history, were influential in the development and growth of sport management as a field of study (de Wilde, Seifried, & Adelman, 2010).

These historians adopted ideas, theories, and models originally established at the Harvard Business School and applied them to sport. Throughout the course of his career, Zeigler used history to evaluate present societal conditions and plan for the future. He was instrumental in the introduction of the case study as a learning tool for sport professionals and students to improve critical thinking, create and monitor strategic plans, and identify effective solutions for organizational problems. Zeigler was a founding member of the NASSM and is credited with creating the first Canadian academic programs in sport philosophy, sport history, and sport management at the University of Western Ontario in the early 1950s. In the United States, James Mason founded the sport management program at Ohio University in 1966, and Lewis used business theories, models, and academic curriculum for sport management master's and doctoral programs at the University of Massachusetts in 1971. Hardy, who was also instrumental in the establishment of NASSM, used his research to shed light on the importance of urban areas in the legitimization of sport, the importance of focusing on business history and entrepreneurship in sport management scholarship, and the way large companies in the past influenced large sport firms (Seifried, 2014). Fielding's work, which combined sport business history and sport management, resulted in several models that shaped sport marketing theoretically and pedagogically. Fielding, who for several editions of this textbook led the authorship of this sport history chapter, is, according to de Wilde and

Table 3.2   Documentaries in ESPN's *Nine for IX*

Documentary	Director(s)	Topic
Venus VS.	Ava DuVernay	Venus Williams and equal prize money
Pat XO	Lisa Lax and Nancy Stern Winters	NCAA Division I winningest coach Pat Summitt
Let Them Wear Towels	Annie Sundberg and Ricki Stern	Equal access for female sports journalists
No Limits	Alison Ellwood	Competitive freediver Audry Mestre
Swoopes	Hannah Storm	Collegiate, Olympic, and professional champion Sheryl Swoopes
The Diplomat	Jennifer Arnold and Senain Kheshgi	Figure skater Katarina Witt and the Cold War
Runner	Shola Lynch	Mary Decker's running exploits, pursuits, and challenges
The 99ers	Erin Leyden	Legacy of 1999 World Cup win by the U.S. women's soccer team
Branded	Heidi Ewing and Rachel Grady	Play and image double standards faced by women in sports

Adapted from *Nine for IX*, 2013, espnW. Available: http://espn.go.com/espnw/w-in-action/nine-for-ix/

Social Media and Historical Aspects of the Sport Business Industry

Students may not remember a time when social media did not have a significant influence on the sport industry. However, a search of the leading trade magazines for sport industry practitioners will reveal the entrance of various social media platforms into the field's dialogue. Although an online keyword search of social media mentions in *Street & Smith's SportsBusiness Journal* (*SBJ*) is not going to reveal every article published, the results of the searches on the publication's website do provide a glimpse into the recent rise of social media and its influence on the sport industry.

For instance, *SBJ* first mentioned Myspace, one of the first social media sites, in 2005, and the following year the journal included its first mentions of Facebook and YouTube. Facebook and YouTube are still often used in the sport industry, and Pinterest, Snapchat, Instagram, and Twitter are frequently used by leagues, teams, personnel, fans, and other sport industry stakeholders. For instance, MLB president of business and media, Bob Bowman, reported Twitter is the primary medium for instant news for the league, and Facebook is ideal when the league hopes to reach the largest audience (Spanberg, 2016).

In 2016, Facebook was the most dominant social media site among sport fans, with about 67 percent of the overall digital audience, followed by YouTube (44 percent), Twitter (34 percent), Instagram (26 percent), and Snapchat (10 percent). The growth in social media consumption is expected to increase in the future primarily because of the prevalence of mobile devices (e.g., smartphones, tablets). According to Katz (2016), "mobile is the fastest-growing platform from a sports content perspective, especially for younger fans" (p. 1). Sport teams and leagues spend heavily to capitalize on the social media market. According to *SBJ*, sport analytics firms charge customers between US$50,000 and US$100,000 per year for sophisticated social media data (Spanberg, 2016). Spending on analytics is logical due to the vast revenue potential social media represents. The Chicago Blackhawks, for example, valued their social media presence at US$5.7 million in 2016.

colleagues (2010), "perhaps the best example of an academician who brought sport business history into the realm of sport management" (p. 415). Overall, de Wilde and colleagues argued that "sport business history training can serve to help frame much of the field and is vitally relevant to the study of the sports industry" (p. 406). In particular, they advocated the use of historical case studies within the overall study of sport management.

Critical Thinking in the History of the Sport Business Industry

This critical thinking section relates to the earlier Historical Aspects of the Sport Market section. Reflecting on the business of sport during the first decade of the 20th century, P.R. Robinson (1909), president of the New York Sporting Goods Company, concluded that it had been a good decade. Robinson noted tremendous growth in the popularity of sport, particularly in baseball, tennis, golf, football, basketball, fishing, target shooting, and roller skating. Looking to the future, Robinson saw only good times for the sport

business industry. As times became better, he concluded, the demand for high-priced sporting equipment would increase because people would want to perform more effectively. Was Robinson correct in his predictions? If so, what are some variables a sport industry analyst could use to evaluate success? Outline your response using modern examples through which industry experts currently evaluate the success of a sport business.

Ethics in the History of the Sport Business Industry

Beginning in 1927, Frank Bradsby, president of the Chamber of Commerce of Sporting Goods Manufacturers (later called the SGMA and then the SFIA), led a concerted effort to develop a code of ethics for sporting goods manufacturers. Bradsby was prompted to lead the fight for a code of ethics by several industry-wide trade practices that hurt the image of the industry and curbed profits. Key among these unethical practices were price cutting; selling below cost; tying contracts; giving hidden rebates or discounts to secure sales; commercial bribery; piracy

Vernon Walker

Courtesy of Vernon Walker.

Professional Profile

Title: Associate manager of event management, NBA

Education: BS (sport management), University of North Florida

Vernon Walker had an unconventional path to the league offices of the NBA that included experiences in several sports and job functions ranging from communications to event management to guest services. After internships with the PGA Tour, the Daytona International Speedway, and NASCAR and brief stints with the Jacksonville Jaguars and the Jacksonville Sharks, Walker was selected in the highly esteemed NBA associate program offered to college graduates in their first summer after graduation. The one-year program provided a well-rounded collection of experiences that allowed Walker to collaborate in three-month intervals with the NBA's D-League business development and basketball operations, digital marketing, events, and global licensing finance departments. In June 2013, Walker accepted a position with the NBA as an associate coordinator with the events group, now known as the content group. He coordinates event operations and venue logistics for all major events and games produced by the NBA such as the NBA All-Star Weekend, the NBA Finals, and the NBA Global Games series. Walker also assists with operations of the U.S. men's Olympic basketball team. These duties involve a robust domestic and international travel schedule, and he assists with the development of venue operations, checklists, game operations, preparation of arena directories, trip surveys, and standardizing. A 2012 graduate of the University of North Florida in Jacksonville, Walker obtained his bachelor's degree in sport management with a minor in business administration. The following is a snapshot of his development, education, duties, and insights as a leader in the sport industry.

of trademarks, brand names, and athletic endorsements; piracy of the term *official*; misbranding of products relative to grade, quality, and guarantees; and interference with existing contracts. Through the auspices of the SGMA, Bradsby enlisted several sporting goods leaders (including Julian Curtis of Spalding Brothers; H.B. Canby of Crawford, McGregor & Canby; E. Goldsmith of Goldsmith Sons; and L.B. Icely of Wilson Sporting Goods) to help create a code of ethics for the sporting goods segment of the sport industry. Between 1927 and 1930, leaders in the SGMA established a set of ethical trade practices for sporting goods manufacturers. These practices were endorsed by the entire membership of the SGMA at the industry-wide meeting in 1930. Today, SFIA represents more than 1,000 sporting goods and fitness-related entities (e.g., brands, manufacturers, retailers, marketers), more than 3,000 areas (e.g., locations, plants, distribution centers), more than 375,000 individuals employed in the field, and an industry that generates US$150 billion in wholesale sales (SFIA, n.d.).

For chapter-specific learning activities, visit the web study guide at
www.HumanKinetics.com/ContemporarySportManagement.

Summary

This chapter provided sketches of some of the significant developments that took place starting in the 19th century and described the foundation for the development of the sport business industry in the United States. The key events, innovations, and entrepreneurs

What was your career path?

I started college as an engineering major, not fully knowing what I wanted to do. I paused long and hard to realize that sports were the one thing I was truly passionate about. I was fascinated with the business aspect and how a sports organization could deeply connect with a fan in such a way that would cause them to even spend their last dime on a sporting event due to an emotional connection. As a result, I switched my major to sport management at the start of my junior year. From there, I networked, built relationships, and set up informational interviews. Internships presented themselves and one opportunity led to another.

What characteristics must a person have to be successful in your job?

In my opinion, three key characteristics for success are having an impeccable work ethic, versatility, and humility. Impeccable work ethic is critical because it's the foundation of what you accomplish as a successful employee. Without a strong work ethic, there is no success. Versatility is imperative because the operational nature of the sports industry is so fast paced and constantly evolving. Having a versatile skill set and the ability to thrive in multiple facets of the business will prove to be invaluable to the success of your career. Lastly, exercising humility is what keeps you consistently growing and developing as a professional. Confidence is great, but humility is even greater. It causes you to realize that as much as you may have accomplished, there's still room to accomplish even more. Having a willingness to learn and always being in a mind-set to grow and develop will no doubt enable you to achieve more success.

Which websites, online tools, or resources do you frequently use or refer to?

For general knowledge, current trends, and the overall landscape of the industry, the *Street & Smith's SportsBusiness Journal* is my go-to. LinkedIn is another great tool that I utilize, given the numerous articles that are shared and circulated across that platform. For the sports fan in me, Bleacher Report and ESPN are my most frequently used publications.

What do you consider to be the biggest future challenge in your job or industry?

The biggest future challenge is keeping fans engaged and connected to the brand from an event perspective. Keeping fans coming to events in a world that has become so technology and social media focused is certainly a challenge that involves out-of-the-box thinking and a creative approach. The ability to present new and innovative content at events to engage and entertain fans is a task that must be addressed consistently. The sports industry is constantly changing; being able to keep pace with that is a challenge that must be examined with detail and creativity.

presented here are only a few of the myriad activities and people who have played some crucial roles in the development and history of sport management. The sketches provided in this chapter are useful because history offers many lessons relevant to your studies and your career in the sport business industry.

Review Questions

1. What are some of the ways that the history of the sport business industry can be helpful to a sport management executive today?

2. How has commercialization affected the sport industry over the years, and how is it currently influencing the industry?

3. Who were the sport historians who helped develop the discipline of sport management?

4. How have advances in manufacturing processes influenced the growth of the sport industry?

5. What are some advances in technology and communication that have influenced the development of the sport industry?

6. What factors have affected the growth and development of participatory, spectator, and professional sports for girls and women?

7. How have historical developments related to endorsement and sponsorship marketing affected the sport industry?

4

Management Concepts and Practice in Sport Organizations

Kathy Babiak
Kathryn Heinze
Lucie Thibault

LEARNING OBJECTIVES

- Identify concepts of management theory and understand how these concepts can help leaders and executives better manage their sport organizations.

- Describe the influence of the environment on sport organizations.

- Demonstrate an understanding of organizational effectiveness and how it is measured in sport organizations.

- Demonstrate knowledge of the relationship between the structure and design of sport organizations.

- Describe the importance of strategic planning, organizational culture, and organizational change in managing organizations.

- Identify the key challenges and opportunities of innovation in sport.

- Explain the importance of critical thinking in management concepts and practice in the sport industry.

- Detail the roles ethics and social responsibility play in the management of sport.

- Explain how new media platforms such as social networking applications affect sport industry organizational issues.

KEY TERMS

economies of scale	efficiency	organizational culture
economies of scope	environment	organizational design
effectiveness	organization	organizational structure

or are affected by the actions and practices of the business or organization). Here are some important questions about elements of the specific environment and stakeholders:

- Who are the consumers? What are their preferences?

- Who are the suppliers? How easy is it for the organization to acquire its resources from suppliers? Does the organization deal with labor groups or unions for its workforce?

- Who is the competition? For example, Nike, adidas, New Balance, and Asics are all competitors of Puma. But does Puma have other competitors? What about nonsport shoe manufacturers? Are clothing manufacturers

that also produce leisure wear considered to be Puma's competitors?

- What role does the government play in the environment? The government might be an element of the specific environment through its imposition of legislation and guidelines for the treatment of employees and consumers. Organizations must also provide details to government agencies for taxation purposes.

Clearly, the environment significantly influences and represents a major source of uncertainty for an organization. As a result, leaders and managers must understand the environment and carefully monitor its effects on the organization.

Trevor Bukstein

Courtesy of Phoenix Suns.

Professional Profile

Title: Assistant general manager, Phoenix Suns, NBA

Education: BA (sport management), University of Michigan; Law degree, Georgetown University Law Center

Trevor Bukstein has been assistant general manager of the NBA's Phoenix Suns since 2013. In this role, Bukstein interprets and applies the league's collective bargaining agreement, monitors salary cap management, and oversees trade and contract negotiations. He also helps manage the front office and the training, coaching, and scouting staff. The following is a snapshot of his development, education, duties, and insights as a leader in the sport industry.

What was your career path?

After I graduated from the University of Michigan, I worked at a law firm in Washington, DC, where I began as a paralegal doing litigation work and filing documents. Then, I started supporting the firm's sport agents; eventually, I began working as an agent myself, representing clients from the NBA, MLB, and WNBA. At night, I attended Georgetown University where I took as many sport and entertainment classes as possible including contract drafting, arbitration law, and statutory interpretation.

When I finished my law degree, I accepted a position with the Phoenix Suns as director of basketball operations administration. After three years in this role, I was promoted to the position of assistant general manager. I use my legal background on a daily basis; my job requires expertise in drafting contracts and negotiating agreements with players and other employees (i.e., coaches, and other player personnel). I currently oversee the analytics department where computer and statistics experts run algorithms to provide advanced statistical analyses of individual players and

Organizational Effectiveness

The **effectiveness** of an organization is the extent to which it achieves its goals. A related term, **efficiency**, refers to the achievement of goals using minimal resources. Efficiency implies the minimal use of resources to produce outputs. As a result, concepts of cost–benefit, return on investment (ROI), and budget compared with number of customers served are assessed to evaluate efficiency. Achieving effectiveness is easier than achieving efficiency. In fact, most managers and leaders of organizations rarely achieve efficiency.

For example, the 2016 Rio Olympic and Paralympic Games were effective because members of the organizing committee achieved the objective of hosting the Games. But did the organizers achieve efficiency? Members of the organizing committee barely met deadlines for construction of facilities, encountered the Zika outbreak, and had to address security issues in advance of the Olympic and Paralympic Games. The committee had to spend more resources (i.e., sport-related costs had a US$1.6 billion overrun) to ensure the completion of the facilities before the opening ceremonies (Price, 2016). In sum, effectiveness focuses on results, whereas efficiency focuses on activities.

---

effectiveness—The extent to which goals are achieved.

efficiency—The extent to which goals are achieved using the fewest possible resources.

---

team performance. The daily reports generated by this department are used in decision making around player transactions, coaching, in-game strategy, and player development and acquisition.

My ultimate goal is to become the general manager of an NBA franchise. In order to reach this goal, I need to continue to develop my leadership skills including public speaking and managing organizational culture.

What characteristics must a person have to be successful in your job?

I believe that in my job, the following are important characteristics: industriousness, preparation, strong communication skills (writing, presenting, and supporting ideas), humility, and active listening. The business of sport is win-oriented and focused on the bottom line—and sometimes overlooks the emotional and human elements of the work. I feel it is important to understand and express appreciation for the grueling schedules, challenging tasks, and intensity of people who work in the professional sport industry. Bringing a positive perspective and celebrating others' efforts are important qualities and actions in my line of work. Finally, I believe that a critical quality for anyone working in professional sport is curiosity and lifelong learning, so I read extensively to help me think creatively and understand issues from different perspectives.

Which websites, online tools, or resources do you frequently use or refer to?

I love to read the work of Jon Gordon, which is focused on developing positive leaders in organizations (e.g., *The Energy Bus*, *Training Camp*). I also recommend *Basketball on Paper* by Dean Oliver. Other resources I rely on daily include websites such as http://nyloncalculus.com (for reference information on advanced analytics for basketball), http://nbpa.com/cba (for information on the salary cap, trade rules, and other aspects of collective bargaining), and http://sports-law.blogspot.com (to stay up-to-date on the sports law world).

What do you consider to be the biggest future challenge in your job or industry?

Professional sport teams are always seeking an edge on and off the court through developing psychological advantages for players (e.g., mental skills, mindfulness training), [using] technological innovations (e.g., using wearables to understand and measure training load, heart rate, speed), and using data to structure training programs and developing techniques to prevent injuries (e.g., preventative exercises). Leaders in sport business today have to be effective at scanning the environment and understand the areas that can make a positive impact on performance, ensure the health and well-being of all employees, and ultimately improve the bottom line for the organization.

Evaluating Organizational Effectiveness

Ultimately, managers and leaders want to ensure that the goals set out for the organization are met. Assessing organizational effectiveness, however, is not always this simple. Consequently, several approaches should be considered to evaluate organizational effectiveness. Traditional approaches include the goal approach, the resource-based approach, and the internal process approach. Contemporary approaches include the competing-values approach and the stakeholder approach (Daft, 2016).

Traditional Approaches

The goal approach focuses on the outputs side of the organization. The organization is considered effective if it achieves its organizational goal (e.g., maximizing profits, winning the game, successfully teaching sport skills to students, healing patients) (Daft, 2016). The resource-based approach focuses on the inputs side of the organization. With this approach, the effectiveness of an organization is assessed by its ability to acquire resources from the external environment and transform them into outputs. The logic behind this approach is that without inputs or the ability to acquire them, an organization would be unable to produce outputs (Daft, 2016). The internal process approach focuses on the transformation side of the organization—the ability to process the inputs while considering the internal well-being of the organization. Focusing on the transformation of inputs into outputs helps ensure the organization's stability and long-term survival (Daft, 2016). While traditional approaches contribute to our understanding of effectiveness, they lack nuance and acknowledgment of the complexity of the environment in which the organization operates (e.g., acquisition of various types of resources, multiple measures of success or effectiveness). Thus, a more multidimensional set of criteria must be considered. More contemporary approaches provide this perspective (Daft, 2016).

Contemporary Approaches

Instead of focusing on single parts of the organization (i.e., inputs, transformation, or outputs), the competing-values approach combines elements of all traditional effectiveness approaches by focusing on the value dimensions of focus and structure. The dimension of focus is represented on a continuum from internal to external, whereas the dimension of structure is represented on a continuum from stability to flexibility. An internal focus means that the organization values the well-being of its employees, whereas an external focus values the well-being of the organi-

zation. A stable structure would favor a task-oriented approach, and a flexible structure would favor change and innovation in the organization (Quinn & Rohrbaugh, 1981). With the competing-values approach, the assessment of an organization's effectiveness will be based on its values with respect to the dimensions of focus and structure. In this approach, a leader or manager acknowledges that the assessment or interpretation of organizational effectiveness depends on their position and experience, whose interests they represent, and what values are favored for the organization. The stakeholder approach is based on the premise that several groups, entities, and other organizations have an interest in the focal organization. Various stakeholders will assess organizational effectiveness differently. For example, employees in an organization might not judge effectiveness in the same manner that executives in the organization do or that customers do. For instance, suppliers may judge the organization's effectiveness by the volume of raw materials that they acquire and sell annually, whereas shareholders may consider the value of the shares as their measure of organizational effectiveness. Furthermore, customers may judge effectiveness by the quality and price of the product they purchased, whereas employees may consider wages and benefits when they evaluate organizational effectiveness.

Those who subscribe to the stakeholder approach and the competing-values approach believe that the organization must consider the values and interest of the various groups, or stakeholders, in the organization and consolidate these interests and views to achieve effectiveness (Daft, 2016). As explained by Daft, the stakeholder and the competing-values approaches address the complexities involved in determining whether an organization is effective.

Effectiveness in Sport Organizations

Several sport management researchers have investigated the concept of organizational effectiveness. Wolfe and Putler (2002) examined the perceptions of stakeholders (e.g., faculty members, student-athletes, potential students, college students, members of the athletic department, and alumni) regarding the priorities of intercollegiate athletic programs. These priorities included win–loss record, graduation rates, violations, attendance, gender equity, number of teams, and finances. In a subsequent study, Wolfe, Hoeber, and Babiak (2002) investigated how perceptions of effectiveness differed according to the values of various intercollegiate athletic stakeholders. In a different context, Papadimitriou (2001) evaluated the effectiveness of Greek sport organizations from the athletes' perspectives. Her results showed that athletes perceived their sport organizations' effectiveness to be low because the following factors were poorly addressed: interest in the athlete, long-term planning, caliber of the board, sport science support, and internal and external liaisons. The athletes had different opinions about the sport organizations' levels of effectiveness than did the leaders of those organizations, another group of stakeholders. Shilbury and Moore (2006) examined the competing-values approach in Australian nonprofit sport organizations whose government funding is dependent on measures of organizational effectiveness, but the organizations operate in a more commercialized environment. Their aim was to operationalize the competing-values approach to measure the effectiveness of national sport organizations (NSOs). Their findings indicated that important measures of effectiveness in these organizations included productivity, planning, flexibility, and stability.

Organizational Strategy

The managers and leaders of organizations use strategies or plans to cope with the environment. A plan is a course of action or a direction in which to move the organization from one point to another. The development of a plan involves the following four steps:

1. *Identifying the goals, objectives, and mission of the organization.* The strategy must be congruent with the goals, objectives, and mission.

2. *Determining the strategic objectives.* This step involves assessing what the organization wants to achieve with the strategy and includes the SWOT analysis. As you will learn in chapter 12, a SWOT analysis consists of an assessment of the strengths and weaknesses of the organization and the opportunities and threats in the organization's environment.

3. *Identifying the resources required to implement the strategy.* Without adequate resources, the organization will find it difficult to implement the strategy.

4. *Establishing a timeline and identifying milestones.* A timeline is used for implementing the strategy, and milestones aid in assessing whether the organization is on target to achieve its objectives (Daft, 2016).

Organizations undertake the process of developing a strategy to gain a competitive advantage over competitors. Organizations may achieve this advantage by acquiring scarce resources. For sport organizations, scarce resources may be financial resources, sponsorship opportunities, media visibility, participants or athletes, clients, members and fans, market share, equipment, or facilities. Access to these resources can lead to success in sport competitions or greater profits because of increased fan attendance at games or increased sales of sporting goods. Strategies are extremely important for leaders and managers because they outline the major direction and future activities of the organization. As such, strategies serve as road maps for organizations.

Olberding (2003) investigated the strategies of 33 Olympic sport organizations in the United States. He examined the following elements: each organization's competitive position relative to other U.S. sport organizations, the domestic sport programs, the level of participation in the sport in the country, the costs involved in taking part in the sport, the level of visibility of the sport, the extent to which the sport was entrenched in the grassroots, the opportunities for competitions in the sport, and the new programs being developed within the organization. Using the framework developed by Thibault, Slack, and Hinings (1993) for Canadian sport organizations, Olberding found that U.S. sport organizations used similar strategies (i.e., enhancers, refiners, innovators, and explorers).

Ferkins and Shilbury (2012) explored strategic capability in NSOs. In particular, they were interested in factors that constrained or enabled strategic function. They identified four dimensions that were considered integral to a strategically able board: capable people (human resources), frame of reference (objectives and plan), facilitative board process (practices and structures), and facilitative regional relationships (partnerships).

Some research on strategy has focused on the development of partnerships (also known as interorganizational relationships or strategic alliances) with other organizations as a strategy to retain or gain a competitive advantage. All types of sport organizations (i.e., public, nonprofit, and commercial) are increasingly involved in alliances with other organizations to capitalize on opportunities and access more resources; to increase programs, services, and products offered to members or clients; and to reduce uncertainty.

In the context of sport, several researchers have applied the work of Oliver (1990) on the organizational motives behind the creation of partnerships. Oliver uncovered the following six motives leading organizations to collaborate:

1. *Asymmetry.* An organization's choice to enter into partnerships to exercise power over another organization or its resources.

2. *Reciprocity.* The creation of partnerships to achieve common or mutual goals or activities.

3. *Necessity.* Partnerships created to respond to legal obligations or regulations set by another organization (e.g., government).

4. *Legitimacy.* The creation of partnerships to provide credibility or enhance reputation, image, or authority.

5. *Efficiency.* The need for an organization to improve its input–output ratio; partnerships may be created to decrease the cost of raw materials needed for producing goods and services.

6. *Stability.* The development of partnerships to reduce uncertainty and increase predictability for the organization.

These six motives for partnership creation were featured in research by Babiak (2007) and Turner and Shilbury (2010). Babiak studied a training center for high-performance elite athletes and its network of partnerships to achieve its goal of providing the best possible training environment for these world-class athletes. The training center's motives for developing partnerships with other nonprofit organizations, with public organizations, and with commercial organizations were varied, but these alliances contributed to the center's strategy to enhance the training environment of the athletes. Turner and Shilbury examined the development of partnerships between clubs of the Australian Football League and the National Rugby League with broadcasters. They found different motives for clubs to undertake strategic alliances with broadcasters. Furthermore, the authors discussed the effect of broadcasting technologies on the establishment of partnerships. Given the increasing importance of broadcasters for sport organizations

Brandon Rhodes

Courtesy of Brandon Rhodes, Pepsi Co.

Professional Profile

Title: Associate marketing manager, Gatorade Digital Strategy

Education: BA (sport management) and BBA (marketing), University of Michigan

Brandon Rhodes has a passion for understanding youth culture, and he values the importance of digital technology as a means of communication in youth's interactions. He works arduously to combine innovative practices in enhancing consumer engagement with sport brands. The following is a snapshot of his development, education, duties, and insights as a leader in the sport industry.

What was your career path?

When I started my studies at the University of Michigan (UM), I wanted to be a sport agent. After learning about the breadth of the sport industry, my career goals shifted to a desire to work with athletes from a marketing perspective. While working as an intern for the UM athletic department on the marketing and promotion team, I further realized that I was interested in the strategic aspects of marketing. Around the same time, some of my colleagues and I formed the Michigan Sports Business Conference (MSBC), now one of the top national sport management conferences. Through this experience, I learned how to develop a business plan, pitch an idea, and develop and lead a team. The relationships I developed during the creation of MSBC led to

(e.g., for access to much-needed resources), studies addressing the relationships between sport leagues and clubs with media are imperative.

Organizational Culture

Schein (1985), one of the pioneers of research on culture in organizations, defined organizational culture as "a pattern of basic assumptions—invented, discovered, or developed by a given group as it learns to cope with its problems of external adaptation and internal integration" (p. 9). Schein explained that organizations consider this set of assumptions valid and, as a result, promote them to new members as the appropriate and correct ways to act in the workplace. Daft (2016) explained that organizational culture is "unwritten but can be observed in its stories, slogans, ceremonies, dress, and office layout" (p. 21).

Culture manifests in different ways throughout organizations such as through stories and myths, symbols, language, ceremonies and rites, physical settings, and symbolic artifacts. Stories and myths are narratives that can be based on truth, fiction, or a combination of the two. Symbols consist of events, objects, or acts that convey meanings for the organization. Organizational logos, slogans, and mission statements are symbols. Language refers to the terminology and jargon that organizational members use to communicate with each other. Ceremonies and rites include social events and awards and recognition events that leaders organize. These events often reinforce organizational values. Physical settings include the office space and objects found in the organization. Artifacts are items found in the organization's physical setting. Photographs of past successes, banners, copies of past marketing campaigns, and displays of awards, achievements, and

---

organizational culture—A pattern of basic assumptions that are invented, discovered, or developed by a given group as it learns to cope with its problems of external adaptation and internal integration (Schein, 1985).

---

an internship with Gatorade, where I focused on a sporting goods strategy. This internship turned into full-time employment in the marketing team at Gatorade. I then started on the innovation team, where I interacted frequently with elite athletes to better understand what they were looking for in new products. Then, I moved to the global team, focused on growing the Gatorade brand internationally, particularly through soccer. Now, I am on the digital strategy team, where I work on reaching consumers effectively through different digital channels and tactics.

What characteristics must a person have to be successful in your job?

To be successful in marketing, you need to be able to think critically and make strategic decisions in a fast-paced environment. This process involves understanding both hard and soft data and synthesizing data from different sources. For example, in developing new products, I need to think through the data originating from the science team, product development team, design team, and the marketing campaign and then develop a cohesive strategy. The other set of skills associated with success are emotional intelligence and people skills. I have to consistently and effectively lead and manage teams, including knowing when to make a decision, when to listen, and when to get everyone involved.

Which websites, online tools, or resources do you frequently use or refer to?

I believe the biggest resource in the organization is people—particularly their expertise and knowledge. The value derived from agency partners across public relations, media, and marketing is also very important. In terms of publications, I read the *Street & Smith's SportsBusiness Journal* and *Ad Age* for inspiration and to get up-to-date information. I also attend conferences including MSBC and South by Southwest.

What do you consider to be the biggest future challenge in your job or industry?

With respect to digital marketing, I believe the fragmentation of the media is a big challenge. Different generations watch and consume media in different ways. The challenge is how to capture my target market's (i.e., teen athletes) attention effectively across different platforms, particularly when their media consumption evolves constantly.

Canadian International Multisport Event Organizing Committees

Milena M. Parent
University of Ottawa, Canada, and the
Norwegian School of Sport Sciences, Norway

Imagine an organization that is created knowing it will not last more than 10 years, starts with only a handful of people, grows to tens of thousands within days, and is expected to leave a legacy after it is gone. This is the case of the international multisport event organizing committees in Canada. The 2010 Vancouver Olympic and Paralympic Winter Games Organizing Committees (known as VANOC) was incorporated as a nonprofit organization. Its owners (i.e., the event's rights owners: the Canadian Olympic and Paralympic Committees on behalf of the International Olympic and Paralympic Committees), host governments (the city of Vancouver, the resort municipality of Whistler, the province of British Columbia, and the federal government), and other key partners could not keep any profits that resulted from the Games for their own benefit. These profits, as well as all in-kind resources that remained, were to be distributed as a legacy.

These owners appointed representatives to sit on VANOC's 19-member board of directors, which was the decision-making body of the organization. Reporting to the board were the chief executive officer, executive vice presidents, vice presidents, directors, managers, and coordinators. In all, there were more than 55,000 individuals involved as paid staff, volunteers, contractors, or ceremony participants in 53 functions (e.g., accreditation, sponsorship, sport, and transportation).

VANOC's owners were key event stakeholders. However, VANOC had to work with, and needed the help of, many stakeholder groups with differing interests. Moreover, these stakeholders ultimately determined whether VANOC was successful. The stakeholders included VANOC's paid staff and volunteers, host governments, the community (residents, activists, community groups, schools, tourism organizations), the media (print, radio, TV, electronic, and photographic), national and international sponsors, sport organizations (national and international Olympic and Paralympic committees as well as local, provincial, national, and international sport organizations and federations), the delegations (athletes, delegation support staff), and other stakeholders (e.g., four host first nations, nongovernmental organizations, and consultants).

There is a clear distinction between working for an organization such as VANOC and working for other enduring sport organizations. First, VANOC's structure changed frequently: First it was headquarter-based to create plans, policies, and procedures; then it was venue-based with venue teams enacting the plans, policies, and procedures during Games; and then it went back to being headquarter-based to close the books, decommission the venues, and transfer the legacies. These structural transitions were among the most difficult organizational tasks undertaken by VANOC members. Members quickly learned to operate in a changing environment. Second, VANOC managers' decision-making time decreased until decision making had to be nearly instantaneous during the Games. Managers moved

products are examples of artifacts. The setting and these artifacts are representative of the organization's values and assumptions.

Colyer (2000) investigated organizational culture in nonprofit Australian sport organizations. Her findings revealed the existence of "tensions between two of the main groups of people (employees and volunteers) in sport organizations" (p. 338). She explained that if leaders were to draw cultural profiles of their organizations, they would become aware of tensions and could develop strategies to change the culture and thus enhance organizational effectiveness. She

also discussed the presence of subcultures, which are an important element in any examination of an organization's culture.

Other studies have focused on the values held in sport organizations. Because values are central to an organization's culture, they are often the focus of research. Milton-Smith (2002) discussed the scandals, corruptions, and controversies involving the IOC in the late 1990s and early 2000s. He explained how concerns about the Olympic Games mirror concerns about the movement toward globalization. Concerns regarding "winning at any price;

The National Olympic Committee flags presented by an athlete from each delegation during the closing ceremonies of the 2010 Olympic Winter Games in Vancouver, Canada.

Courtesy of Milena M. Parent.

from an administrative model of decision making during the planning mode to a garbage-can model during the Games and finally to a rational model post-Games. More precisely, VANOC managers moved from a bounded rationality situation to one where uncertainty, organized anarchy, timing, and luck reigned; organizing committee members used a 'fly-by-the-seats-of-your-pants' strategy, looking at the confluence of problems, solutions, and readily available resources (i.e., individuals, information, material, financial, etc.) to address what came at them (cf. Parent, 2010). Then, managers moved into a rational decision-making model, as they had the relevant information needed to make decisions. Thus, working for an organizing committee requires the ability to change decision-making approaches and strategies and being comfortable with uncertainty and risk. Third, it was critical for VANOC employees to consider the Olympic Movement's culture, VANOC's culture, their assigned sports' culture, and their function's culture and then create a specific Games team culture almost instantaneously. Successfully integrating these cultures was critical to effective human resource management.

Although this sidebar focuses on VANOC, the information applies to other international multisport events hosted in Canada and elsewhere (for more information, see Parent, 2008, 2010, 2015, 2016, 2017; Parent & MacIntosh, 2013; Parent, Rouillard, & Leopkey, 2011).

commercial exploitation by MNCs [multinational corporations]; corruption; intense national rivalry; [and] the competitive advantage of advanced nations" were identified (p. 132). In analyzing the case of the 2000 Sydney Olympic Games, Milton-Smith drew on the values espoused by the Olympic Movement and demonstrated how members of the IOC and members of the Sydney Organising Committee for the Olympic Games (SOCOG) violated those values. According to the analysis, the IOC and SOCOG compromised values such as honesty, transparency, objectivity, fairness, dignity, and loyalty. Although it was not the purpose of his work to discuss the organizational culture of the IOC or the SOCOG per se, Milton-Smith explained that the leadership of the IOC cultivated a culture of excess while overlooking questionable and unethical practices of its members. In other words, the Olympic ideals and the core values of the Olympic movement were used as marketing tools to showcase the IOC, but they were never translated into the culture of the organization.

A more recent study on culture in professional sport examined the culture transformation process undertaken by owners and general managers

(Frontiera, 2010). Frontiera considered the link between culture and performance and the influence a leader can have on supporting or changing the culture of a professional sport team. His findings revealed that leaders could recognize a dysfunctional culture manifested in cultural artifacts such as substandard facilities and win–loss records. Competing values were also espoused by members of the organization (i.e., "selfishness, placing too much emphasis on monetary profit and minimizing the value of players" [p. 76]). Leaders in these professional sport teams made efforts to change the existing dysfunctional culture in their own ways by articulating a clear vision for the team or organization, expressing their values clearly, changing personnel, hiring and developing employees, and engaging in explicit communication. Frontiera concluded that cultural understanding is essential for sport leaders to guide and direct the organization in a way that achieves its goals.

Organizational Structure and Design

Organizational structure "designates formal reporting relationships, . . . identifies the grouping together of individuals into departments, . . . [and] includes the design of systems to ensure effective communication, coordination, and integration of efforts across departments" (Daft, 2016, p. 88). When addressing the topic of organizational structure, we usually refer to formal organizations, which are what we typically see when we examine an organizational chart. Figure 4.1 earlier in the chapter is an example of a formal organizational chart for a fictitious professional baseball organization. Note, however, that every organization also has an informal dimension. Formal and informal relationships operate simultaneously within a sport organization. Informal relationships among employees can take many forms, such as employees who have lunch together on a regular basis and discuss everything from sports to company politics. Informal relationships are not officially acknowledged in the structure of the organization but are likely to compete with or support the formal organization. Although the formal organization cannot control informal relationships, encouraging a positive organizational culture, a topic discussed in the chapter, will increase the likelihood of mutual support.

Dimensions of Organizational Structure

Organizational theorists generally agree on three major dimensions of structure: 1) specialization, 2) formalization and standardization, and 3) centralization (Daft, 2016). In the following paragraphs, we define and explain each of these dimensions.

The first structural dimension, specialization, concerns the division of labor, which is the extent to which tasks and duties are divided into separate roles (Daft, 2016). According to Daft, when specialization is high, employees carry out a limited range of tasks and duties, and when specialization is low, individual employees carry out a wide range of tasks. The dimension of specialization is tied to the concept of complexity. There are three levels of complexity: vertical, horizontal, and spatial. Vertical complexity is evidenced by the number of levels that exist between the top executive in the organization (i.e., president, chief executive officer) and the lowest positions and units in the hierarchy (i.e., support positions and departments). The more levels there are, the more vertically complex the organization is. For instance, The Ohio State University Athletic Department has several levels (e.g., executive associate athletic director, senior associate athletic director, associate athletic director) between the athletic director and lower athletic department positions. This indicates a high degree of vertical complexity—and each role within the hierarchical level requires specialized tasks and duties be completed. Horizontal complexity is shown in the number of units that exist across the organization. The NBA's organizational structure has more horizontal complexity with an array of business units including NBA Entertainment, the WNBA, the NBA Development League, and the Global Merchandising Group, all of which have different business functions and specialized foci. Spatial complexity refers to the number of geographical locations in which an organization operates. An organization situated in many locations would be considered spatially complex relative to an organization that operates in a single location. For example, the UEFA, which includes 55 national football (soccer) associations, is more spatially complex than the Confederación Sudamericana de Fútbol (CONMEBOL), which comprises 10 national football associations.

---

organizational structure—Identifies the formal reporting relationships amongst individuals and organizational units, determines the grouping of functions, roles, and departments, and provides designs that enhance communication, coordination, and integration of the work to be achieved within the organization.

Organizational Structure Makes a Difference

According to Daft (2016), structural dimensions refer to the labels that describe the "internal characteristics of an organization" (p. 17). Cunningham (2006) examined the relationship between structural dimensions (i.e., specialization, formalization and standardization, and centralization) and job satisfaction in the context of intercollegiate athletics. Associate and assistant athletic directors of NCAA Division I member institutions were surveyed to examine the extent to which structural dimensions were mediated by job satisfaction. The statistical analyses revealed that the relationship of formalization was partially mediated by job satisfaction and that the relationship between centralization and organizational commitment was fully mediated by job satisfaction. The results demonstrate that specialization, formalization and standardization, and centralization have a significant effect on employee work outcomes in the sport industry.

The second structural dimension includes both *formalization* and *standardization*. These terms are often used interchangeably because high levels of formalization result in standardization. Formalization refers to "the amount of written documentation in the organization" (Daft, 2016, p. 18), including items such as job descriptions, policies, procedures, and regulations as well as employee records of performance. This documentation is often used to control employees' behaviors and activities. As a result, a high degree of formalization leads to a high degree of standardization, because employees who face similar situations will be expected to act in a similar fashion (Daft, 2016). The NCAA, for example, has a high degree of formalization in its guidelines, policies, procedures, and regulations regarding intercollegiate athletic activities in American universities.

Centralization is the third dimension of organizational structure. This concept refers to the hierarchical levels of individuals in the organization who have authority to make decisions (Daft, 2016). When leaders and managers at the top of the hierarchy handle the decision-making activities, the organization is centralized. When decision making is delegated to levels throughout the organization, the organization is decentralized. Typically, organizations are not completely centralized or decentralized; some decisions may be centralized (e.g., hiring and firing of employees, establishing the strategic direction of the organization), whereas others may be decentralized (e.g., purchasing of organizational supplies, marketing strategies for products and services). The following factors affect whether decisions are centralized or decentralized:

- *The cost (in organizational resources) of the decision to the sport organization.* The greater the cost, the more centralized the decision will be.
- *The timing (how much time a sport manager has to make the decision).* The more urgent the decision, the more decentralized it will be.
- *The qualifications of employees.* The greater the number of expert employees involved throughout the sport organization, the more decentralized the decision will be.

Relationships Among the Dimensions of Organizational Structure

Specialization and formalization and standardization are interrelated. For example, high levels of specialization are typically associated with high levels of formalization and standardization. In other words, the greater the number of roles in the organization, the more formalized and standardized the organization will be (e.g., more job descriptions, more policies and procedures). Likewise, when an organization has a small number of roles, formalization and standardization will be low.

The relationship between formalization and standardization and centralization is not as easy to predict. Research in organizational theory has not demonstrated a consistent relationship between the two dimensions. Further, the relationship between specialization and centralization is not always consistent. In situations where specialization is high and thus where roles, tasks, and duties within the organization are narrowly defined, one would expect decentralization of decision making. With low levels of specialization, one would expect centralization of decision making within the organization.

Organizational Design

Daft (2016) defined **organizational design** as the features and traits of an organization that allow it to undertake various activities and achieve objectives. Consider organizational design as the structural configurations that leaders use to arrange an organization's activities and operations so it can reach its goals.

Henry Mintzberg conducted extensive work on organizational design. In a 1979 study, Mintzberg outlined different design configurations for various types of organizations based on the nature of their operations. A sporting goods organization in the business of manufacturing running shoes will be designed differently from a sport marketing agency or an event management business. Mintzberg based his designs on the interplay among five major parts of the organization, which have been simplified as follows:

1. *Top management.* The leadership within the organization
2. *Middle management.* The managers who are between the leadership of the organization and the employees who are directly involved with the production of goods and services
3. *Technical core.* The group of employees responsible for producing goods and services
4. *Administrative support staff.* The employees who provide a support function in the organization
5. *Technical support staff.* The employees who provide technical and technological support to assist in the production of goods and services and introduce innovative practices to enhance existing goods and services or create new ones

Based on the relevance and importance of these five parts of the organization, various designs are proposed. Mintzberg (1979) identified several designs, among them the simple structure, the machine bureaucracy, and the professional bureaucracy. Subsequently, new designs have been added to reflect emerging realities for organizations. Among these new designs are entrepreneurial, innovative, missionary, and political designs.

The simple structure is typically a suitable design for small organizations that have only two major parts: top management and the technical core. Simple structures are characterized by low levels of specialization and standardization and high levels of centralization. A small sport club that operates at the local level might have a simple structure.

The machine bureaucracy is appropriate for sporting goods manufacturers that have high levels

organizational design—The features and traits of an organization that allow it to achieve its objectives.

Organizational Size Matters

The concept of size for sport organizations (or any other type of organization) varies extensively. For most scholars, organizational size is defined as the number of employees, but others may consider the number of sites where the organization is located, the value of its assets, its sales volume, the number of clients it serves, and the number of people affected by its operations. No matter how someone defines organizational size, it is important to note that size affects how an organization is structured. A large organization, for example, will have a more complex structure, whereas a small organization will be less complex. What are the challenges associated with using the number of employees for the interpretation of organization size? Specifically, for sport organizations, should we calculate size as the number of full-time employees? With so many seasonal and part-time workers in sport and numerous volunteers, how does a sport organization adjust its structure to cope with the influx of employees at different times of the year? As future leaders in sport organizations, you are already likely involved as volunteers and part-time employees within sport organizations. You understand the role you play in the organization and the fact that all labor involved in the organization's products, services, programs, and events is critical to the success of the organization. The number of full-time and part-time employees and volunteers in sport organizations should always be considered because these people affect how the organization is structured, what mechanisms (e.g., organizational charts, job descriptions, policies and procedures) are implemented to operate effectively, and how tasks and duties are coordinated to achieve the organization's mission, goals, and objectives.

of specialization, standardization, and centralization. In the machine bureaucracy design, all parts of the organization identified by Mintzberg are important: top management, middle management, technical core, administrative support staff, and technical support staff.

The professional bureaucracy is characterized by an important technical core and administrative support staff along with a limited technical support staff, middle management, and top management. This design would be appropriate for national sport organizations in which professionals (e.g., coaches, sport psychologists, professional administrators) are responsible for the products or services. Decentralization and high levels of specialization and standardization are also characteristics of this design.

Entrepreneurial organizations have a simple design. With a minimal staff, the organization initially has little need for specialization and standardization because the top of the organization coordinates much of the work. As outlined in Sack and Nadim (2002), Starter Corporation, a licensed sport apparel business now owned by Nike, was initially structured as an entrepreneurial organization.

Innovative designs allow greater flexibility than the bureaucratic designs while providing decentralization not found in entrepreneurial organizations. Organizations featuring an innovative design emphasize a climate of creativity for the experts responsible for developing the product or the service. As a result, the power in the organization resides in the experts, who might be allowed to work in creative teams or on special projects. A marketing agency or ad agency with several accounts may exhibit an innovative design.

A missionary organization is designed around its ideology. After employees become indoctrinated into the organization and identify strongly with the organization's ideology, they have the freedom to make decisions. In her research of organizational designs of organizing committees for the Olympic Games (OCOGs), Theodoraki (2001) found evidence of this missionary design.

Organizations with political designs are extremely flexible. They have no definite mechanisms of coordination. Typically, temporary organizations use this design so they can address challenging transitions. An organization bidding to host a major sport event such as a World Cup or international championship, for example, might be designed as a political organization because it addresses needs to secure resources (e.g., funding, facilities, volunteers) and support in the hopes of hosting an event. Table 4.1 outlines the structural profiles of Mintzberg's organizational designs.

Structure and Design of Sport Organizations

Several sport management scholars (e.g., Byers, Slack, & Parent, 2012) have investigated or provided an overview of the structure and design of various sport organizations. For example, Theodoraki (2001) applied Mintzberg's organizational design theories to OCOGs. She explained how the organizational design of OCOGs changed over time. The committees are created seven years before the Olympic Games take place and immediately following the IOC's decision about which bid city will host the Olympic Games. These organizations have a life span of eight years and are typically dismantled one year after the Olympic Games. According to Theodoraki, OCOGs initially display a simple structure (Mintzberg's most basic design). She noted that OCOGs eventually display

Table 4.1   Characteristics of Organizational Designs and Their Structures

Mintzberg's design types	Specialization	Formalization and standardization	Centralization
Simple structure	Low	Low	High
Machine bureaucracy	High	High	High
Professional bureaucracy	High	High	Low
Entrepreneurial	Low	Low	High
Innovative	High	Low	Low
Missionary	Low	High	Low
Political	High	Low	Undetermined

Data from Mintzberg (1979); Slack and Parent (2006).

characteristics of the missionary design during the hosting of the Olympic Games and in the year following. In other words, as the members and employees of the OCOG become indoctrinated and socialized into the organization, they start to work collectively toward the organizational goals without the need for high levels of formalization and standardization or centralization.

Organizational Change and Innovation

Organizational change is the process by which leaders of organizations adopt new ideas and behaviors to enhance their operations, products, services, and programs (Daft, 2016). To remain competitive, relevant, and viable, organizations constantly undergo change. Sometimes, organizational change involves innovation or "a new way of doing things" (Porter, 2008, p. 780). Innovation leads to new or improved products or services or processes that enable organizations to operate more efficiently and effectively. In the following pages, we discuss key frameworks of organizational change and innovation.

Change

One framework of organizational change is the organizational life cycle or the model of organizational growth. This framework is an adaptation of Greiner's (1972) work on the various stages of evolution and revolution that an organization undertakes as it grows and of the work of Quinn and Cameron (1983) on the life cycle of an organization. Figure 4.2 provides a graphic illustration of the evolution and revolution stages as an organization grows. There are four stages of growth for organizations (entrepreneurial, collectivity, formalization, and elaboration), and each of these stages is punctuated by a crisis (i.e., need for leadership, need for delegation with control, need to deal with too much red tape, and need for revitalization). These stages and crises are briefly described next.

- *Entrepreneurial stage.* This stage is based on the vision of the founder of the organization. The founder is investing her or his energies in all aspects of the organization (e.g., management, technical production, marketing, delivery of products or services) to ensure that the organization survives and grows. As a catalyst for progression toward the next growth

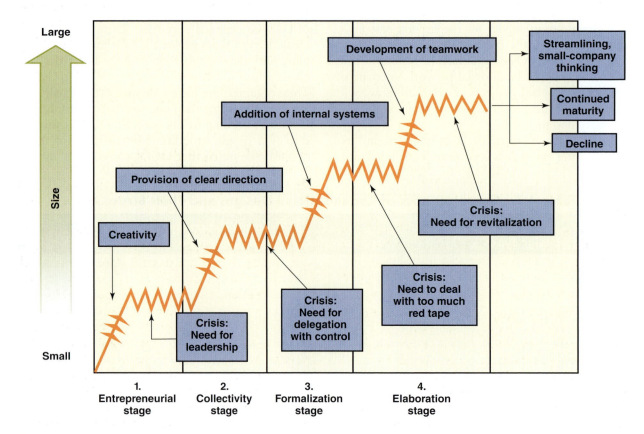

Figure 4.2   Stages of organizational development.
Adapted from Greiner (1972); Quinn and Cameron (1983).

stage, the organization typically undergoes a crisis identified as *need for leadership*. During this crisis, the founder becomes overwhelmed with the quantity of work involved and with the increasing responsibilities that she or he holds within the organization. As a result, the founder who created the organization needs help.

• *Collectivity stage.* In this stage, the leadership crisis has been addressed. The organization is now developing clear goals and establishing its direction. Functional areas, departments, and a hierarchy of authority are created to help divide and assign the work to newly hired employees. Also, formal communication mechanisms are being developed to help in the coordination of the work to be achieved and to address the rapid growth. For progression into the next stage, the organization in the collectivity stage will go through a crisis termed *need for delegation with control*. During this crisis, lower-level employees are limited in their ability to make decisions autonomously. As they gain experience and expertise in their functional areas, they become increasingly frustrated with the strong top-down leadership. During this crisis, leaders develop coordination and control mechanisms within the organization and provide employees with some level of autonomy and decision-making power.

• *Formalization stage.* During this stage, rules and procedures are developed. Job descriptions are created, and communication becomes more formal. Top management executives invest their time in strategic planning and allow middle management the responsibility of managing the operations. Decentralized units may be created and incentive systems for managers may be introduced to enhance the effectiveness of the organization. As the organization increases its levels of formalization and standardization, the crisis of *too much red tape* will surface. With systems and high levels of formalization in place, middle management may begin to experience some constraints in their ability to do their work within the organization. Specifically, too much bureaucracy may paralyze employees and stifle innovation. The organization is large and complex and will require adjustments to reach the next stage.

• *Elaboration stage.* To address the increasing red tape, leaders and managers within the organization undertake collaboration and teamwork. This collaboration occurs across different hierarchical levels, departments or divisions, and functions. Leaders, managers, and employees work together to solve problems. During this stage, formal systems may be simplified in favor of more collaboration among leaders, managers, and employees. As the organization matures, it may experience the *need for revitalization*,

as the organization's alignment with its environment becomes askew. A streamlining of operations may be necessary for the organization to respond better to a changing environment. Also, innovations provide the organization with new energy and spirit.

The various stages involved in an organization's life cycle help us understand the changes that organizations go through as they develop and mature. As reviewed in the previous paragraphs, this life cycle is punctuated with challenges and crises along the way. If leaders respond to these crises, they can lead the organization to success.

Another framework for studying organizational change is the contextualist approach developed by Pettigrew (1987, 1990). This approach acknowledges that change does not take place in isolation or in a brief time. Understanding change is important, but it must be accomplished over the long term by considering three elements: content, context, and process. To acquire a full understanding of change, one must first examine the content of change, which is best done by determining what has changed. The next element of Pettigrew's framework is the context of change. The focus is on determining why the change occurred. Context includes two sections: the inner context and the outer context. Inner context consists of internal elements at play within organizations, such as strategy, culture, and the structure of organizations. Outer context refers to general political, economic, and social forces at work within the organizational environment. After content and context of change have been uncovered, the process of change needs to be examined. The process of change can be assessed by asking how change has occurred. In uncovering the process of change, leadership is a key component because change agents often contribute to the adoption of change within the organization. By answering the what, why, and how, leaders are in a better position to understand change in their organizations.

A few studies have applied Pettigrew's contextual approach to organizational change to the sport context. Specifically, Cousens, Babiak, and Slack (2001) investigated changes in the NBA over a 17-year period, focusing on the relationship marketing approach adopted by the league. The scholars discussed the relevance of Pettigrew's approach to understand the need to foster relationships within and outside the NBA. In another example of Pettigrew's work applied to the context of sport, Caza (2000) examined the adoption of innovative practices in a Canadian provincial sport organization. His investigation focused on the extent to which organizational members were receptive to the implementation of two initiatives. Caza found that Pettigrew's framework was useful in understanding challenges related to the implementation of innovations in the sport sector.

Thibault and Babiak (2005) also used Pettigrew's framework to investigate changes in Canada's sport system. They were specifically interested in examining how and why the Canadian sport system changed to accommodate greater involvement from athletes. They found that increased representation by athletes on decision-making boards of sport organizations, greater funding of athletes, the creation of national sport training centers, and the creation of a forum for athletes to resolve conflicts between themselves and sport organizations or coaches all contributed to an athlete-centered sport system. The authors were able to understand the nature of the change that had occurred in light of the context in which Canada's sport system operated and the leadership role assumed by change agents to bring about the adoption of more athlete-centered change in the sport system.

Innovation

Organizational change often involves innovation. Discovering new ways of doing things can lead to growth and differentiation, and thus strategic renewal (Damanpour & Schneider, 2006). Different types of innovations include product and process innovations. Product innovations relate to the creation of new product designs or the development of new products. Examples of product innovations in sport include the *Street & Smith's SportsBusiness Journal* and motion-responsive sportswear. Process innovations improve the efficiency or effectiveness of organizational processes. Patagonia's Common Threads apparel-recycling program is an example of a process innovation. In sport, process innovations may relate to the game (recruiting, conditioning, and strategy of play) or the entertainment and viewership experience in person (e.g., stadium, arena, ballpark) and at home (e.g., television, streaming). Yoshida and colleagues found that sport event innovativeness, in terms of both product and process, affects consumer behavior (Yoshida, James, & Cronin, 2013). The greater consumers' perceptions of the innovativeness of the sport event, the more likely they are to plan to attend in the future.

Innovations can also be radical or incremental. Radical innovations break unwritten industry rules and are often due to technological change. These innovations are highly disruptive and can transform an organization or industry. Smart technology, for example, has significantly altered the sport business landscape. Incremental innovations, by comparison, are small and evolutionary but can add value and have competitive advantages. Mikasa Sports developed an indoor volleyball with eight, rather than

the usual 18, panels to improve players' control. Mikasa volleyballs became the official balls for many leagues and competitions, including all Fédération Internationale de Volleyball worldwide competitions and the 2012 London Olympic and Paralympic Games. In their study of innovation in community sport organizations, Hoeber and colleagues found that incremental innovations, such as the adoption of social responsibility initiatives and new organizational models, were much more common than radical innovations (Hoeber, Doherty, Hoeber, & Wolfe, 2015).

There are a variety of different sources of innovation. Drucker (2002) outlined some ways that innovation emerges. For example, new ways of doing things can arise accidentally or unexpectedly. The current curved design of hockey sticks was discovered during a Chicago Blackhawks practice in the early 1960s when forward Stan Mikita accidentally broke his stick. Mikita realized the slightly bent stick made the puck move through the air more effectively. Another source of innovation is incongruity, which is the difference between reality as it actually is and reality as it is assumed to be (Drucker, 2002). For example, clap skates were around for a long time but were not considered serious until an Olympic skater noticed junior skaters wearing them. Innovations can also come from process needs. Moneyball player analytics were developed to facilitate the formation of a winning baseball team, particularly under financial resource restrictions. Other sources of innovation include industry, market, and demographic changes and new knowledge. For examples of these innovations in sport, see table 4.2.

Organizational innovation involves significant challenges and thus must be managed carefully. Innovation is risky, and as with organizational change more generally, it may face resistance within and outside the organization (Wolfe, Wright, & Smart, 2006). In addition, funding for innovation can be inadequate, new skills may be necessary, and decisions regarding who will lead projects and their scope and pace are complicated and sometimes contentious. Given these challenges, Kanter (2008) argues for the need to create a culture of innovation. In particular, organizations should use incentives and recognition to promote innovative behavior. Further, a climate of innovation can be fostered through celebrating failure, promoting transparency, and adopting slack time (Kanter, 2008). Regarding specific innovations, a champion can facilitate adoption and implementation. These individuals or groups emerge, often informally, to promote particular innovations within the organization (Howell & Boies, 2004). Comeaux (2013) argues for the role of head coaches as champions of educational innovation for student-athletes to improve student learning.

Table 4.2   Sources of Innovation and Examples in Sport

Sources of innovation	Examples in sport
Unintended or accidental	Toe release bindings for skis were created after ski champ Hjalmar Hvam broke his leg in 1937 and had a brainstorm: bindings that pop you free. His invention led to a significant drop in tibia fractures.
Incongruity	Ski jumpers were using the classic parallel style to maximize style points in competition even when the V technique was proven to result in longer jumps.
Process needs	For the Vancouver Olympic Winter Games, the U.S. team worked closely with the Exa Corporation, evaluating potential bobsled designs with computational fluid dynamics. This involved creating 3D models of the designs through simulators running on supercomputers to evaluate how aerodynamic they were.
Industry and market structure changes	Sport technological applications (videos, information, statistics, chat) were used for an increasingly wired and connected industry.
Demographics	Changes were made to golf to engage younger players (e.g., Wi-Fi on the course, speakers and GPS [global positioning system] on carts, larger holes, foot golf, disc golf). Shaped (parabolic) skis facilitated turns for skiers and were easier on the knees for an aging population.
New knowledge	The introduction of smart technology performance apparel has led to the ability to measure and interpret muscle activity, heart rate, sport performance, and distance travelled (GPS).

Critical Thinking in Sport Organizations

Critical thinking is important in sport organizations. As introduced in chapter 1, sport leaders, managers, and employees with critical thinking skills are better able to solve problems, make informed decisions, and develop comprehensive plans and strategies for the organization. Given the constant flux in the environment, sport managers must adopt a critical thinking approach whereby they can analyze and evaluate information, facts, evidence, assumptions, ideas, and implications.

Numerous sport management scholars have expounded on the importance of developing critical thinking skills. For instance, Boucher (1998) explained that "a true measure of whether [sport management] graduates are truly prepared is *not* the courses listed on their transcripts but whether they have been educated to *think* intelligently and *make decisions* about issues they will face in the dynamic world of managing a sport enterprise" (p. 81). Similarly, Harris (1993) urged sport management educators to give greater emphasis to students' development of critical and reflective competencies. She surmised that such an emphasis would prepare professionals who would be able to "free themselves from traditional ways of identifying and solving problems, [and] to look at problems from new perspectives" (p. 322). In the same vein, Edwards (1999) suggested that critical reflection should receive more attention than it currently receives in sport management so that we can find "new, less oppressive, and more just ways of creating and managing sport" (p. 79). Furthermore, Frisby (2005) proposed that sport management educators become "versed in critical social science theories" so that they can help students become "strong critical thinkers who will make positive contributions to society" (p. 5). The clear implication of all these suggestions is that, as the managers of the future, you will need exceptional thinking skills to make the necessary decisions to deal effectively and responsibly with the myriad challenges that you will encounter. For instance, sport managers will have to make difficult decisions as they address issues regarding where limited funds are invested (e.g., in high-performance sport or sport for all). Thibault (2009) applied critical thinking to her analysis of globalization and sport and encouraged academics and practitioners to consider the "inconvenient truths" of globalization for those without power. This type of critical perspective may allow for different and more effective and appropriate organizational decisions to be made.

Social Media and Management Concepts and Practice in Sport Organizations

Social media and technology networking platforms such as social network applications (e.g., Twitter, Facebook, Instagram, LinkedIn, Snapchat), blogs, social tagging, wikis, microblogs, artificial intelligence, virtual reality, and augmented reality (Kane, 2017) are being adopted by sport organizations at a rapid rate. These new technologies have the potential to advance organizational performance (effectiveness) and improve organizational processes (efficiency) in areas such as cost reduction, enhanced customer relations, and increased access to information accessibility (Parveen, Jaafar, & Ainin, 2016; Treem & Leonardi, 2012).

Communication through social media facilitates the exchange of a broader scope and type of information and sometimes bypasses formal structures and channels. It may also influence communication of thoughts and ideas (i.e., knowledge management [Kane, 2017]), affect values, and possibly shape organizational culture. Treem and Leonardi (2012) explore how new media differ from other forms of traditional computer-mediated communication (e.g., email, teleconferencing). They argue that social media communication benefits organizations because it affords visibility, persistence, editability, and association.

The use of social media in organizations may influence and alter knowledge sharing, socialization (formal and informal connections), and power processes in organizations. Treem and Leonardi identified "three types of information or actions that are made visible through the use of social media in organizations: (a) work behavior, (b) metaknowledge, and (c) organizational activity streams" (p. 150). For example, information about work behavior becomes more readily accessible and easier to find and is shared more easily across organizational boundaries. The visibility of social media provides metaknowledge and data about people who work for the organization (i.e., they share information about their skills and interests). It also allows employees to orient themselves appropriately in the company because they are informed about what is happening around them. The information shared on social media platforms is also persistent—that is, it does not disappear after a user has logged off (like instant messaging or video conferencing). This may foster the development of a common ground in communication settings and in the transmission of complex ideas.

Finally, social media allows for more extensive associations across various levels of the organizational structure, thereby creating social capital and building community and bridges between employees. Ultimately, social media as a technological infrastructure in organizations supports and changes the way people communicate and collaborate (Kane, 2017). The implications of social media for organizational practices, however, have not yet been broadly explored. For example, the effects of social media on organizational structure or culture are areas that are ripe for investigation.

In sport organizations, social media is being used to communicate with external constituents. The focus of much of the research on social media in sport examines this area of marketing, branding, and fandom (see Abeza, O'Reilly, & Reid, 2013; Miranda, Chamorro, Rubio, & Rodriguez, 2014; Stavros, Meng, Westberg, & Farrelly, 2014). Little work, however, has investigated how social media affects internal organizational operations in different types of sport organizations.

Ethics in Sport Organizations

Besides applying critical thinking skills, sport organization employees, managers, and leaders will also need to act ethically. In recent years, several ethical issues have surfaced in the context of sport. For example, incidents involving drugs and cheating in sport, violence in sport, overtraining of children involved in high-performance sport, eating disorders among athletes, recruitment violations within intercollegiate athletic programs, corruption in decision making, athlete hazing, and questionable behaviors from athletes, coaches, and referees on and off the court or field have all affected sport and sport organizations. As mentioned in the section on organizational culture, the Milton-Smith (2002) study of unethical practices by the members of the IOC and OCOG led to serious negative repercussions for both organizations. Although rules, procedures, and codes of ethics were developed within these organizations, those responsible for upholding the standards of the organizations did not respect them. Managers and leaders of sport organizations are constantly facing situations, events, and issues that challenge their ability to make ethical decisions.

An extension of ethical considerations in sport organizations is the broader framing of corporate social responsibility (CSR). Carroll (1999) identified four dimensions of CSR: economic, legal, ethical, and discretionary. His view was that in being socially responsible, organizations should engage in behaviors that serve the organization financially but that are within the boundaries of the law and morally ethical (an obligation to do what is right and fair), and they should be good corporate citizens by contributing to the community and improving the quality of life of those affected by the organization's activities. Porter and Kramer (2006) extended these concepts to consider the role of social responsibility as a source of competitive advantage for organizations and to consider that the capacity exists for companies to maximize their social agendas and, at the same time, advance their business agendas. In this way, ethics and social responsibility are now being woven into the fabric and strategy of many organizational activities. In sport, these efforts are being examined by several authors from many different perspectives including environmental responsibility (Pfahl, 2011; Polite, Waller, Spearman, & Trendafilova, 2012), community involvement and relations (Sheth & Babiak, 2010), fan and customer perspectives (Giroux, Pons, & Mourali, 2015), and philanthropy (Tainsky & Babiak, 2011). The next chapter provides more details on managers' and leaders' involvement in ethical decision making.

For chapter-specific learning activities, visit the web study guide at
www.HumanKinetics.com/ContemporarySportManagement.

Summary

The organizational theory topics covered in this chapter—management concepts, organizational environment, effectiveness, structure and design, strategy, culture, and change—are all important to consider and monitor. Left unchecked, problems in these areas can reduce the effectiveness of a sport organization and, ultimately, lead to its demise. Note that these topics are interrelated. For example, the structure and design of the sport organization may affect, or be affected by, the culture of that organization. Similarly, the ability to develop and implement a strategy or to cope with change may affect, or be affected by, the structure and design of the sport organization.

These interrelationships take on even more complexity considering the roles people play in the development and management of organizations in the sport industry. The following chapter addresses the topic of people and their roles in organizations.

Review Questions

1. How would you define the term *organization*? What are three types of sport organizations?

2. What is the difference between effectiveness and efficiency? What is the best approach to the study of organizational effectiveness?

3. Select one sport organization. How would you describe its structure using the structural dimensions featured in this chapter?

4. What organizational design would be most appropriate for a sporting goods manufacturer? For a sport marketing agency? For an organization bidding for the right to host a major international event?

5. What is the difference between the general environment and the specific environment?

6. Why would sport organizations choose to develop strategies?

7. What are some possible ways that stakeholders can influence sport organizations?

8. In what ways can some organizational cultures be positive for a sport organization? In what ways can other cultures be negative for a sport organization?

9. How could you use Pettigrew's contextual approach to study change in a sport organization of your choice?

10. Describe how some sport businesses view corporate social responsibility as a strategic practice.

11. Describe how new media platforms (e.g., social networking applications) affect organizational issues in the sport industry (e.g., effectiveness, structure, and strategy).

PUNCH BOWL SOCIAL

SINCERITY ALERTNESS INITIATIVE INDUSTRIOUSNESS FRIENDSHIP LOYALTY HONESTY RESPECT

"Success is peace of mind attained only through self satisfaction in knowing you made the effort to do the best of which you're capable." - John R. Wooden

Managing and Leading in Sport Organizations

Shannon Kerwin
Ming Li
Laura J. Burton

LEARNING OBJECTIVES

- Define organizational behavior and its application to the sport industry.
- Differentiate between the terms *management* and *leadership*.
- Understand the components of the contingency theory of leadership.
- Understand the full range of leadership model.
- Understand and discuss the multilevel approach to leadership.
- Understand the role of transformational and servant leadership in sport organizations.
- Understand the concepts of decision making, authority, and power.
- Understand the importance of diversity and creating a culture of diversity in the workplace.
- Understand the importance of ethics and ethical leadership in the workplace.
- Describe the factors that are important in managing an inclusive organization.
- Explain the critical role that theory plays in the management of people within sport organizations.

KEY TERMS

behaviors centered on employees	leadership	participative leadership style
behaviors centered on tasks	leadership context	task uncertainty
contingency theory of leadership	management	transformational leader
ethical leaders	organizational complexity	

1917
Frank Calder named the first president of the NHL

1946
Maurice Podoloff appointed as president of the Basketball Association of America (now the NBA)

1984
David Stern named NBA commissioner (retired in 2014)

1992
Donna Lopiano became the executive director of the WSF (served until 2007)

2005
Valerie Ackerman became the first female president of USA Basketball (served until 2008)

2007
Tonya Antonucci named the Women's Professional Soccer commissioner (served until 2010)

1920
Kenesaw Mountain Landis appointed the first commissioner of the MLB; Jim Thorpe appointed the first president of the American Professional Football Association (now the NFL)

1962
Marvin Miller became the first executive director of the Major League Baseball Players Association

1986
Anita DeFrantz became the first American woman and first African American on the IOC

2001
Jacques Rogge elected as president of the IOC

2006
Roger Goodell named the NFL commissioner

This chapter introduces and examines the roles that individuals play within sport organizations. Thus, this chapter is about organizational behavior, which is the study of individuals and groups in organizations (Robbins & Judge, 2008). According to Schermerhorn, Hunt, and Osborn (2008), organizational behavior "is a multidisciplinary field devoted to understanding individual and group behavior, interpersonal processes, and organization dynamics" (p. 5).

This chapter addresses many topics related to people in the sport management workplace. First, management functions and skills are introduced. These are followed by an examination of leadership and leaders relative to the skills of the sport manager, his or her followers, and the sport context. Then, the concepts of decision making, authority, and power are explained. A conceptual model of leadership development, including the individual, group, and organizational level factors that influence leaders, is explained next. The chapter concludes with discussions of diversity and the value that needs to be placed on diversity in sport organizations, commentary regarding ethics in the sport workplace, and the relevance of critical thinking in managing and leading people in sport organizations.

Theoretical Approaches to Management

The success of sport organizations ultimately depends on how effectively managers apply their management and leadership skills. Hersey, Blanchard, and Johnson (2008) provided one of the most comprehensive definitions of **management** as "the process of working with and through individuals and groups and other resources (such as equipment, capital, and technology) to accomplish organizational goals" (p. 7). Numerous theoretical approaches to management and managing people in organizations have been developed. We classify these approaches into three basic types: scientific management, human relations management, and the process approach (also known as administrative management). In the following paragraphs, we summarize these approaches.

Scientific Management Approach

Early theorists believed that the primary responsibility of managers was to increase workers' output. Frederick Taylor (1911) developed this approach in which the major concern was to scrutinize the performance of individual workers. The key was that workers who produced more than others would receive greater rewards. This approach advocated paying people by the number of units produced or sold rather than by the length of time (e.g., hours) that they worked. In the sport industry, this approach is best illustrated when employees work on a commission basis. For example, a game-day salesperson might earn a commission based on the number of programs sold, and the sport manager would focus on how effective the salespeople are. The scientific management approach considers pay and working conditions to be the most important factors in increasing a worker's performance.

Human Relations Approach to Management

The human relations approach grew out of studies conducted at Western Electric's Hawthorne, Illinois,

---

management—The process of working with and through individuals and groups to accomplish organizational goals.

2008
Jerry Reese became the first African American NFL general manager to win the Super Bowl

2009
Riccardo Fraccari voted into office as president of the International Baseball Federation (IBAF)

2010
Scott Blackmun became the CEO of the USOC

2013
Thomas Bach elected the ninth president of the IOC

2014
Adam Silver became the fifth commissioner of the NBA

Michele A. Roberts became the first female executive director of the NBA Players Association

Becky Hammon became the first female assistant coach in the NBA (San Antonio Spurs)

2016
Alison Overholt named the first female editor-in-chief for *ESPN The Magazine*

Lisa Borders appointed as president of the WNBA

Cathy Lanier became the NFL's senior vice president of security

2017
Carla Williams became the first African American female to hold the athletic director position (University of Virginia) at an NCAA Division I FBS (Power Five) University

plant during the late 1920s and early 1930s (Mayo, 1933). Mayo's research on more than 20,000 employees found that when employees believed they were important, they became more cohesive and productive. The researcher's conclusion was that managers' concern for workers would lead to higher rates of job satisfaction, which would result in better performance and higher productivity (Staw, 1986).

Process Approach to Management

The process approach has been the predominant theoretical framework used in the study and practice of management in recent times. Unlike the scientific and human relations management approaches, the process approach focuses on managing the organization as an entity. Using the process management approach, we review various management functions assumed by managers.

Management Functions

The process approach to management uses a set of ongoing, interactive activities—known as the underlying processes of management—to accomplish the goals and objectives of organizations, departments, or work units. Such processes were first introduced more than six decades ago as POSDCORB (Gulick & Urwick, 1937). POSDCORB is the acronym for planning, organizing, staffing, directing, coordinating, reporting, and budgeting. The original seven processes have since been reduced to five functions: planning, staffing, organizing, directing, and controlling and evaluating (Jones & George, 2009). Figure 5.1 illustrates that these underlying processes

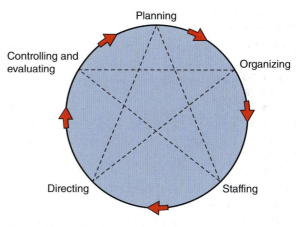

Figure 5.1 The functions of management.

flow in all directions and that decisions made in each component affect all other components. Ultimately, all the processes revolve around the manager's actions and decisions.

In sport organizations, the management process typically starts with planning and ends with controlling and evaluating. Managers might engage in the activities in various sequences, and sometimes they perform several activities simultaneously as they carry out the responsibilities of their jobs. The element common to all the processes, whenever they are performed, is decision making. Table 5.1 provides definitions of each function as well as examples of how the general manager of a private sport club might practice them. The concepts of decision making, authority, and power are covered later in this chapter. We now proceed to a discussion of the classifications of managers.

Table 5.1   Management Process of a General Manager in a Private Sport Club

Underlying process	Definition	Example
Planning	Developing and implementing goals, objectives, strategies, procedures, policies, and rules to produce goods and services in the most effective and efficient manner	The general manager of a private sport club predicts the increase in enrollment at the start of the new year and arranges for the facility to be open 18 hours per day instead of 15 hours per day.
Staffing	Recruiting, selecting, orienting, training, developing, and replacing employees to produce goods and services in the most effective and efficient manner	The general manager advertises the positions: three teaching pros, one maintenance person, and one administrative assistant. The general manager then holds interviews, checks references, makes job offers, and selects the staff needed for the golf program.
Organizing	Arranging resources (e.g., human, financial, equipment, supplies, time, space, information) to produce goods and services in the most effective and efficient manner	After conducting an assessment, the general manager establishes a work unit for teaching golf at the club. The general manager appoints a full-time coordinator who will coordinate three teaching pros and a new golf course with an adequate budget.
Directing	Influencing members (e.g., subordinates, peers, supervisors) as individuals and as groups to produce goods and services in the most effective and efficient manner	The general manager encourages the golf teaching pros to prepare weekend course packages for local executives who have expressed an interest in learning golf skills.
Controlling and evaluating	Evaluating whether the employees are on task and making progress toward achieving the goals and adhering to the guidelines and standards for producing goods and services in the most effective and efficient manner	After three months, the general manager monitors the progress of the new golf program with the pros and discusses ways to make the program more attractive to potential new members.

Classifications of Managers

Although all managers have formal authority for organizing, directing, and controlling the work activities of others, they possess different degrees of authority. In the hierarchy of an organization, managers are usually classified as top level, middle level, or supervisory level.

- *Top-level managers.* The number of managers in this group is small. Also known as executive or senior-level managers, they have the most power and authority. They are usually responsible for the entire organization or a major part of it.

- *Middle-level managers.* Also known as administrative-level managers, these people are usually selected by top-level managers. They are, therefore, accountable to top-level managers and responsible for the employees who are below them in the hier-

archy. The managers at the middle level are generally responsible for managing a department or unit that performs an organizational function and ensuring that the assigned tasks are done efficiently. To their subordinates, middle-level managers are the sources of information and are problem solvers because they know the technical side of the products and services. Middle-level managers are unique because they must be both leaders and followers. They are connected to supervisors and to subordinates.

- *Supervisory-level managers.* These managers, also known as first-line managers or supervisors, report to middle-level managers and are responsible for the employees who work in their units. The employees for whom these managers are responsible can be classified as operatives or technical specialists. Supervisory managers have the least amount of authority. They are primarily responsible for a single area in a work unit, division, or department in which they supervise the work of the operatives or technical specialists. Their duties are to communicate with, inspire, and influence their subordinates to get the job done in the most effective and efficient way. Supervisory managers represent the contact point between the technical specialists (operatives) and middle-level managers.

Examples of titles of managers at these different levels in three types of sport organizations are shown in table 5.2.

Managerial Skills

Managers at all levels possess certain skills that aid in the performance of their day-to-day tasks. As noted by Katz (1974), the skill sets of effective administrators can be broken down into three cate-

gories: conceptual skills, human relations skills, and technical skills. Interestingly, the amount of each skill required by a manager may change from organization to organization and may fluctuate with the level of management (Katz, 1974). Further, managerial skills do not function in isolation; most managers display multiple managerial skills at any given time. A summary of the link between each managerial skill category and the levels of management for the USOC is provided in table 5.3.

A manager's conceptual skills help to identify the root cause of problems rather than simply stating the symptoms of an issue. For instance, to redirect an unmotivated corporate culture, the CEO of the USOC may use his or her human relations skills to communicate with each of the chief officers to develop an understanding of the factors that influence the USOC's corporate culture. Rather than diagnose and label the symptoms (e.g., poor productivity, low

Table 5.2   Selected Titles for Managers at Different Levels in Three Typical Sport Organizations

Levels of management	Professional baseball organization	Investor-owned health and fitness club	Intercollegiate athletic program
Top-level managers (executive or senior level)	President Chief executive officer (CEO) Vice president of business operations Vice president of baseball operations	Owners General managers Regional director of corporate wellness Regional director of health promotion	Board of trustees University president Vice president for athletics Athletic director (AD) Senior associate AD
Middle-level managers (administrative level)	Director of public relations Director of corporate sales Director of marketing operations Team manager Director of scouting	Site manager of corporate wellness Site manager of health promotion	Associate AD Director of development
Supervisory-level managers (first line)	Manager of stadium operations Manager of broadcasting Manager of community relations Manager of baseball administration	Coordinators (supervisors) of aerobics, fitness, golf, pro shop, weight training	Assistant ADs Sports information director Coordinator of athletic training Marketing director Academic coordinator Director of event operations Manager of ticket sales Director of compliance Equipment manager

Table 5.3   Linking Managerial Skills to Levels of Management in the USOC

Managerial skills	Definition	Link to levels of management
Conceptual skills	Possesses the ability to see the organization as a whole Effectively uses analytical, creative, and initiative skills Aids in planning and organizing processes of managers Most often linked to top-level managers	Top-level managers (e.g., the CEO) analyze the state of high-performance sport in the United States to determine a long-term athlete development plan.
Human relations skills	Possesses the ability to work with people (i.e., interpersonal skills) Effectively uses communication and listening skills Aids in planning, staffing, organizing, directing, and controlling/evaluating processes of managers; each process requires interaction with people Most often linked to all three levels of manager	Top-level managers must communicate with each chief officer when planning the budget for each Olympic year. Middle-level managers (e.g., the chief communications and public affairs officer) must communicate with the managing director of information technology (IT) to ensure a plan is in place for the effective use of Twitter for the upcoming Olympic Games. Supervisory-level managers (e.g., the managing director of IT) must work closely with members of his or her research team to evaluate the most effective use of Twitter for the upcoming Olympic Games.
Technical skills	Can perform a job based on the job requirements Effectively uses skills (e.g., computer, IT) required for a given position Aids in completing everyday operational tasks Most often linked to supervisory-level managers	Supervisory-level managers (e.g., the research team within the IT department) must have the computing skills to work with research software and statistics associated with collecting data from potential Olympic Games consumers.

morale) of the issue, the CEO would use his or her conceptual skills to see the big picture and create solutions for the betterment of the USOC as a whole.

A manager's human relations skills help in leading, motivating, and developing cohesion among employees. Within sport organizations, managers at all levels must work with a variety of employees including paid staff, volunteers, and interns. Thus, effective human relations skills are an essential component to the daily operations of sport managers.

A manager's technical skills are directly associated with everyday tasks on the job. For instance, the chief financial officer (CFO) of the USOC must possess technical skills associated with budget management, management of internal and external audits, and

financial planning. More specifically, he or she must also possess human relations skills when communicating with and directing supervisory-level managers responsible for preparing budgets using their technical skills in computer programs such as Microsoft Excel and PeopleSoft.

Leadership

Kane (2014) defined **leadership** as "an influence relationship aimed at moving organizations or groups of people toward an imagined future that depends upon alignment of values and establishment of mutual purposes" (p. 4). Hersey and colleagues (2008) have

---

leadership—A relationship where an individual, or group of individuals, influence others in an effort to inspire stakeholders to move toward an end goal that depends on alignment with values and a mutually beneficial purpose.

defined management as working with individuals and groups while using other resources (e.g., time, money, equipment, facilities) to achieve the goals of an organization. The roles of leaders and managers have both similarities and differences. For example, both roles involve people working with other people. The roles are different with respect to the ways in which leaders and managers accomplish the objectives. Managers are often leaders, but not all leaders are necessarily managers. The term *leader* is broader than the term *manager* because people need not be in management positions to be leaders. Depending on the situation, all employees of the organization can act as leaders. Any time a person influences the behavior of others, regardless of the reason, that person is demonstrating leadership. For example, a sport management intern might have special skills using a computer software program to create complex video presentations. When that intern assists the controller or director, she or he is taking the lead during that time. Conversely, when employees in an organization rely on others for direction or guidance, those others are acting as leaders even if they are not in official decision-making positions. As dynamic and often complex structures, organizations in the sport industry require managers who are skilled in both management and leadership.

Like management, leadership is also conceptualized as an interactive process. The primary goal of leadership is to exert influence on individual and group behaviors toward the leader's goals, the organization's goals, or both. Although the terms *manager* and *leader* are sometimes used interchangeably, the two concepts are not the same. When people function as managers, they are primarily focused on efficiency and *doing things right*. When people function as leaders, they are concerned with effectiveness and *doing the right things*. Differences between management and leadership are further elaborated in table 5.4, which shows that managers cope with complexity in the workplace and that leaders cope with change.

Based on the distinction between managers and leaders, it is important for sport leaders to recognize the characteristics of effective leaders and determine which characteristics are present (or can be developed) within the human resources of their sport entity.

Greenleaf (2002) indicated that servant leadership may be the most effective form of leadership in today's society:

> The servant-leader is a servant first. [Servant leadership] begins with the natural feeling that one wants to serve. The best test is: do those served grow as persons: do they, while being served, become healthier, wiser, freer, more autonomous, more likely themselves to become servants? Then conscious choice brings one to inspire to serve. (p. 27)

According to Chelladurai and Kerwin (2017), sport organizations may provide a unique context for servant leaders to flourish, because many leaders enter the sport industry to serve and enrich the lives of athletes. Table 5.5 outlines the characteristics of successful servant leaders.

Table 5.4 Comparative Summary of the Management–Leadership Dichotomy

Management (coping with complexity)	Leadership (coping with change)
Planning and budgeting—Setting goals for the future, establishing procedures for achieving the goals, and allocating adequate resources to effectively achieve the goals	*Setting a direction*—Developing a vision of the future and strategies for producing the changes needed to achieve the vision
Organizing and staffing—Creating an organizational structure for accomplishing the plan, staffing the organization with qualified workers, delegating responsibility for carrying out the plans, and constructing a system to monitor implementation	*Aligning people*—Communicating the new direction to those who can create coalitions that understand the vision and are committed to its achievement
Controlling and problem solving—Monitoring results in some detail, both formally and informally, by means of reports, meetings, and other tools; identifying deviations; and planning and organizing to solve the problems	*Motivating and inspiring*—Keeping people moving in the same direction, despite confronting major obstacles, by appealing to basic but often untapped human needs, values, and emotions

Adapted from Kotter (1990).

Table 5.5   Characteristics of Successful Servant Leaders

Listening	Being committed to intently hearing others and reflecting on things that go unsaid
Empathy	Respecting people for their unique experiences, characters, and perspectives
Healing	Possessing increased potential to heal the self and heal relationships with and between others
Awareness	Being mindful of what is going on in the organization, between subordinates, and within one's self
Persuasion	Creating consensus around decisions rather than leading through coercion
Conceptualization	Seeing the big picture and planning beyond the day-to-day operations
Foresight	Learning from the past and using that knowledge to shape decisions for the future
Stewardship	Being committed to serving the needs of others
Commitment to growth of people	Seeing the intrinsic value of workers beyond their task-based contributions to the organization
Building community	Effectively building a sense of common identity among all stakeholders within an organization

Data from Spears (2010).

Sport management scholars conceptualize leadership and managerial behaviors as a unified concept. Soucie (1994), for example, suggested that management and leadership are qualitatively different and that each complements the other, resulting in more effective and efficient sport managers. Quarterman (1998) provided further support for this notion when he noted in his study that NCAA conference commissioners used both management and leadership skills depending on the given situation.

Contingency Theory of Leadership

As noted previously, leaders differ from managers in their ability to cope with change. When dealing with change, it is important for sport leaders to examine themselves, their followers, and the leadership context. Specifically, Fiedler's (1963) **contingency theory of leadership** suggests the most effective style of leadership is dependent on the situation or context. In this theory, leadership is multidimensional in that it includes the leaders' traits, power or influence, and goals; their followers' expectations and values; and the **leadership context** defined by organizational complexity and task uncertainty. The following subsections provide details for each of these elements of the contingency theory of leadership. Figure 5.2

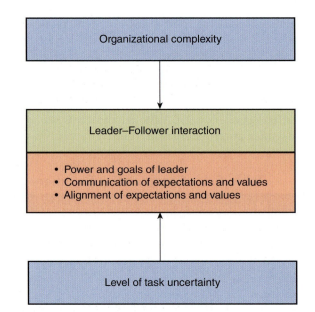

Figure 5.2   The interactive process associated with the contingency theory of leadership.
Adapted from Lorsch (2010).

illustrates the connection between each element and highlights the interaction that occurs between them during the leadership process.

---

contingency theory of leadership—Theory that recognizes there is no one best way to lead an organization; rather, effective leadership is dependent on the internal and external environment.
leadership context—The culture or condition in which individuals lead their organization or group.

Leaders

Within contingency theory, leaders are responsible for introducing and managing change. For leaders to be successful, they must possess some form of power over their followers to ensure buy-in and commitment to change. Whether this power comes in the form of charisma, superior knowledge or experience, or an individual's position in the organizational hierarchy, it provides a leader with the ability to influence the actions of followers toward personal and organizational goals. The leader's goal is to influence others to follow him or her on a certain path (designated by the leader) that ultimately leads to the end-state goal. For instance, the commissioner of the NBA strives to create change (goal) toward diversity and racial equality (end-state goal) within the NBA head office. The commissioner uses his place in the organizational hierarchy (position power) and legal expertise (legitimate power) to lead his followers through this change. Further description of sources of power will appear later in this chapter.

Followers

An important element within Fiedler's (1963) contingency theory is the interactive relationship between leaders and followers. Followers (or subordinates) are a vital component to the change process; however, they are often overlooked in favor of a leader-centered focus. Specifically, alignment between the followers' expectations and values and the leader's goals significantly influences the effectiveness of the change process. Specifically, within our example regarding the hypothetical diversity-change initiative within the NBA, the executive group within each NBA team (i.e., the followers) would have expectations of what diversity in the NBA should look like and personal values associated with how the change process should unfold. As such, for effective change to occur around the end-state goal of racial equality, the commissioner must actively align his goals and power with each executive group member's expectations and values. This may become a tall task for leaders when organizations have many layers with multiple leader–follower dyads. This potential complexity highlights the essential elements of communication and alignment within the leadership process.

Context

Within the leadership context, contingency theory (Fiedler, 1963) suggests that organizational complexity and task uncertainty will guide the leadership style that is most appropriate (and effective) when it comes to coping with change. Organizational complexity relates to the degree to which strategic management is adopted within an organization and can be influenced by the size of the organization or group within which leaders and followers operate and the location of the workspace. In terms of size, the larger the organization, the larger the number of leader and follower goals and expectations to strategically manage. Specifically, in a large sport organization such as FIFA, the president and executive officer would have to coordinate efforts with thousands of followers within their member associations to effect change. Following the tenets of contingency theory, the president must ensure that expectations and values of each member association are communicated and align with the leader's goals. This becomes more complex when a leader examines the location of FIFA and must coordinate, for example, member associations across the globe. Thus, the larger the organization and the greater the distance between a leader and their followers, the harder it is for leaders to match their power and goals with each follower's values and expectations. As such, larger sport organizations may require multiple leaders with complementary power and change goals to coordinate multiple followers.

Task uncertainty is a contextual factor that influences leaders' abilities to cope with change in their sport organizations. As noted by Fiedler (1963), tasks can range from routine and repetitive (certain) to innovative, novel, and nonrepetitive (uncertain), thus describing the level of uncertainty within a task. Implicit in this distinction is an analysis of the leadership style that may appropriately lead followers through change. For example, on the one hand, a foreman within the front lines of Nike's manufacturing division may be required to lead employees through a shift in production line techniques. This change process requires motivating followers directly connected to a very routine and certain daily task. In this case, a more directive leadership style may be appropriate, where followers are expecting guidance and structure and employees have little (if any) input in planning and decision making.

On the other hand, when a marketing manager with adidas asks her subordinates for a new and creative marketing strategy to target girls and women in their new fall marketing campaign, the leader may find a more participative leadership style most effective. This would involve the marketing manager seeking employee involvement in the planning and decision making of the campaign. With task

---

organizational complexity—The degree to which strategic management is adopted within an organization.
task uncertainty—Tasks that have never been done before or are accompanied by many unknown factors to be managed.
participative leadership style—Leaders seek employee involvement in project planning and decision making.

Kirsten Britton

Courtesy of Kirsten Britton, College of the Holy Cross.

Professional Profile

Title: Associate director of athletics for facilities, operations, and events, College of the Holy Cross

Education: BS (psychology), Providence College; MS (athletic administration), Springfield College

As the associate athletic director with primary responsibilities of providing leadership and oversight to the facilities, operations, and events staff, Kirsten Britton focuses on providing an optimal athletic experience for all student-athletes and fans at the College of the Holy Cross. Her leadership skills are in high demand because she is responsible for overseeing the construction of the largest athletic facilities project undertaken by the college, the US$95 million renovation and expansion of the Hart Center. Britton developed her leadership skills early in her career. After completing her master's degree and an internship at the University of Albany, she began her career as the assistant director of event management at Boston College. As a result of her success in that demanding role, Britton became the assistant director of athletics for event management at the University of Connecticut. In that role, she provided leadership, planning, and event management for 24 varsity sport programs. She also served in the role of the tournament director for the NCAA women's basketball first and second rounds in Storrs, Connecticut, and provided all operational logistics for the UConn women's basketball Final Four appearances in 2013, 2014, and 2015. The following is a snapshot of her development, education, duties, and insights as a leader in the sport industry.

What was your career path?

I received my bachelor's degree from Providence College in 2003 in psychology. After graduation, I went to Springfield College to pursue a master's degree in Athletic Administration and graduated in 2008. One of my graduate degree requirements was to complete an internship working full time in our chosen field of interest. In 2006, I applied and accepted an internship in the University of Albany athletic department focusing on marketing, tickets and event management. While

uncertainty, followers may expect flexibility and autonomy, which would promote innovation and creativity through change.

As a sport leader, it is imperative that the workplace context be assessed to determine which leadership style is most appropriate for the situation. The next section details the full range of leadership model and highlights effective leader behaviors attached to leadership theory.

Leadership Styles

Over the years, several approaches to the study of leadership have been developed. Among the most common approaches are theories that attempt to explain why some people are good leaders and others are not and models that represent observed patterns of effective leadership that can be learned. Leadership approaches have identified specific traits

working at Albany, I discovered my passion for event management and facilities and realized that was the area I wanted to pursue at the beginning of my career at a Division I institution. In 2007 I accepted an internship position in the Boston College athletic department specializing in event management and athletic operations. I worked tirelessly in my position to gain operations and facilities experience and was also fortunate to meet many fantastic individuals who have become great mentors to me throughout my career. At the end of that ten-month internship, I was offered a full-time position at BC as the Assistant Director of Event Management and I worked in that position until 2012. I next accepted a position as the Director of Event Management at the University of Connecticut and I worked there for four years. I was promoted to Assistant Director of Athletics – Event Management in 2015 at UConn. In February 2016, I began my current position as Associate Director of Athletics – Facilities, Operations & Events at the College of the Holy Cross. I am currently managing the US$95 million Hart Center expansion and renovation project and provide leadership and oversight for all athletic facilities, game operations, and outside events.

What characteristics must a person have to be successful in your job?

To be successful you must pay attention to detail and have strong organization and communication skills. There are a lot of events and facilities to plan for and maintain, so keeping preventative maintenance plans updated and prepared is essential. We all work best as part of a team, and everyone must be communicated with and be held accountable for their areas for us all to be successful with regard to event management.

Which websites, online tools, or resources do you frequently use or refer to?

First, CEFMA [Collegiate Event Facility Management Association] a subgroup of NACDA [National Association of College Directors of Athletics] has a great forum for members to share information and assist one another with questions that pertain to our area. Also, the NCS4 [National Center for Spectator Sports Safety and Security] is another great organization that has fantastic resources regarding event security management. The group develops best practice standards for our industry that many of us use and implement on a daily basis. Finally, Women Leaders in College Sports is also a great resource system. It offers subject circles that create dialogue and also provides networking as well as mentoring. The group also presents valuable personal development institutes.

What do you consider to be the biggest future challenge in your job or industry?

Creating a game day experience that exceeds the experience of our fans watching from home. It is imperative that we always strive to ensure our fans enjoy coming to games and that we provide the best atmosphere possible. This is in addition to ensuring that we provide the best game day experience possible for our student-athletes. Also, controlling expectations, especially when you are working for universities/colleges with smaller athletic budgets.

and characteristics held by leaders (e.g., honesty, integrity, self-confidence, cognitive abilities), behaviors assumed by leaders (i.e., **behaviors centered on tasks**, **behaviors centered on employees**, or behaviors centered on both tasks and employees), and leadership based on situations (i.e., as discussed in the previous section, where different situations call for different leadership styles). The following paragraphs focus on specific leadership behaviors outlined in the full range of leadership model. This model includes transactional, laissez-faire, and **transformational leader** behaviors. As you progress in your sport management curriculum and study leadership in more depth, you will discover additional leadership theories and models (see the work of Welty Peachey, Damon, Zhou, and Burton [2015] for a full review of leadership in sport management). You will also learn that some leader behaviors overlap categories

---

behaviors centered on tasks—Primarily concerned with the technical or formal aspects of jobs and considering followers primarily as the means for accomplishing the organization's goals.

behaviors centered on employees—Primarily concerned with interpersonal relations, meeting personal needs of followers, and accommodating personality differences among followers.

transformational leader—Leader who recognizes a need for change, creates a vision to inspire followers through change, and works through change with followers.

and defy neat classifications. Nonetheless, a brief discussion of this model will provide you with a basic understanding of current thought regarding leadership in organizations.

Full Range of Leadership Model

Bass and Avolio (1994) developed the full range of leadership model based on research investigations of a variety of leader behaviors. An overview of this model, which includes transactional, laissez-faire, and transformational leader behaviors, is presented in table 5.6. As shown in this table, the transactional leadership style implies an exchange between leaders and followers whereby they agree on the types of performances that will lead to reward or punishment for followers (Bass & Riggio, 2006). Transactional leadership includes three types of reinforcement behaviors: contingent reward, active management by exception, and passive management by exception. In contingent reward, leaders attempt to be clear about their expectations of followers. When followers' performances are satisfactory, leaders can provide rewards, such as praise or an increase in pay. When followers' performances are unsatisfactory, leaders can respond with notification of the inadequacies and, ideally, with additional clarification. Management by exception (MBE) is a more negative approach. Adherents to this leadership style ascribe

to the "if it ain't broke, don't fix it" philosophy (Bass & Riggio, 2006, p. 4). MBE-active leaders keep track of followers' performances. When followers make mistakes, the leaders take corrective action. MBE-passive leaders do not monitor followers' performances. Rather, they wait passively and make corrections only when mistakes occur.

The second leadership style in table 5.6 is characterized as nontransactional. The nontransactional approach is actually not a leadership style, because the people who use this approach are extremely passive and avoid all forms of leadership. They neither monitor nor correct their followers. Consequently, this style is the least effective.

As shown in table 5.6, the third type of leader behavior is the transformational style (Yukl, 2012). Transformational leaders practice the four *I*s: idealized influence, inspirational motivation, intellectual stimulation, and individualized consideration (Avolio, Waldman, & Yammarino, 1991). They are trustworthy, encouraging, risk taking, and considerate. They raise their followers' consciousness about the importance of outcomes and explain how followers can reach those outcomes by placing organizational interests ahead of self-interests.

Although most leaders engage in the full range of leadership styles, they do so to differing degrees. Many studies in a variety of organizations have

Table 5.6   Brief Overview of the Full Range of Leadership Model

Leadership behaviors	Transactional style
Contingent reward	Gives followers a clear understanding of what is expected of them; arranges rewards for satisfactory performance
Management by exception (active)	Monitors followers' performances and takes corrective action when mistakes are observed
Management by exception (passive)	Waits for mistakes to be made and then corrects them
	Nontransactional style
Laissez-faire	Avoids leadership; is inactive
	Transformational style
Idealized influence	Serves as a good role model; can be trusted to do the right thing
Inspirational motivation	Encourages the optimism and enthusiasm of followers
Intellectual stimulation	Encourages followers to consider new ways of looking at old methods and problems
Individualized consideration	Gives personal attention to followers; listens to them; serves as a coach or mentor

Adapted from Bass (1985); Bass and Avolio (1994).

suggested that the leaders who were most effective used the transformational style most frequently, the transactional style occasionally, and the nontransactional (laissez-faire) style rarely, if at all (Bass & Avolio, 1994; Bass & Riggio, 2006). Within sport management, scholars have been most interested in studying transformational leadership, which serves as an indication of the importance placed on this style of leadership within sport organizations (Welty Peachey et al., 2015).

No matter the leadership style, one of the most challenging areas that you will encounter in your first management position is exercising authority over subordinates, especially your former colleagues. On the one hand, most often, newly promoted managers must distance themselves from their former colleagues and friends and thus contend with being lonely at the top (well, not really the top, but closer to the top than before being promoted). On the other hand, the promotion brings the rewards of elevated status, higher salary, and additional opportunities to make important contributions to the organization as well as to subordinates. Specifically, promotion brings the opportunity to lead through (and cope with) change.

Multilevel Approach to Leadership

Following a review of 40 years of leadership research in sport management, Welty Peachey and colleagues (2015) proposed a multilevel conceptual model (figure 5.3) to enhance understanding of leadership in sport organizations with a focus on leadership as

> a multilevel (person, dyad, group, collective) leader-follower interaction process that occurs in a particular situation (context) where a leader (e.g., superior, supervisor) and followers (e.g., subordinates, direct reports) share a purpose (vision, mission) and jointly accomplish things (e.g., goals, objectives, tasks) willingly (e.g., without coercion). (Yammarino, 2013, p. 150)

Within their proposed model, Welty Peachey and colleagues (2015) examine how leadership may have an influence and operate differently in the context of sport. As an example, when describing individual characteristics that have an influence on a leader, this model includes consideration of a leader's experiences as a participant in sports and how this may affect the development of his or her leadership skills. These sport participation experiences influence the lived experience of the leader at the individual level of the leadership process. At the group level, coaches and athletes also influence the leadership process. Finally, at the organization/collective level, fans and alumni, governance by leagues (e.g., MLS or NCAA), and organizational culture influence the leadership process in sport organizations. The multilevel conceptual model of leadership in sport management has yet to be evaluated, but by presenting this work,

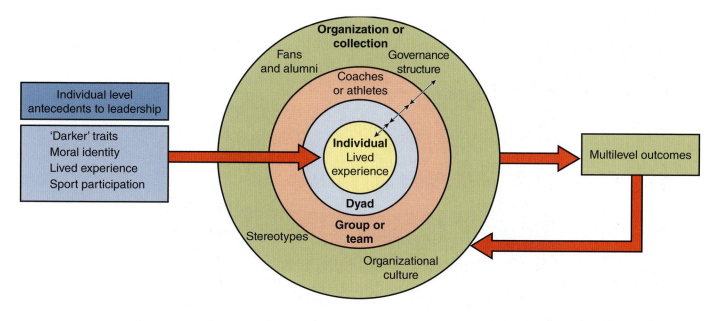

Figure 5.3 Multilevel approach to leadership.

Reprinted, by permission, from J. Welty Peachey et al., 2015, "Forty years of leadership research in sport management: A review, synthesis, and conceptual framework," *Journal of Sport Management* 29(4): 570-587.

Dual Development of Road Running Sport in Taiwan

Kong-Ting Yeh
National Taiwan Sport University, Taiwan

Road running is a simple and easy exercise that has various benefits. One running activity, the marathon, is a popular Olympic event. Currently, road running events are very popular globally, and many cities host international road running events. Such events attract tens of thousands of participants, including elite runners. These events generate economic and other benefits for the host cities, organizers, and stakeholders (Eagleman & Krohn, 2012).

Over the last decade, road running has become an increasingly popular sporting activity in Taiwan, and it has become a fashionable sport to be involved in (Chang, 2014; Lanning, 2016). In 2014, there were 521 events, and one year later this had grown to 740 events hosted around Taiwan (Runner's Plaza, n.d.). The number of participants in these events ranged from 5,000 to 100,000. The event organizers are diverse and include government sectors, nonprofit running organizations, and private companies.

Despite the numerous events in 2014 and 2015, participant demand seemed to be far greater than what the events suppliers offered. Prospective participants must register as soon as possible to secure their places because there are limited spots for many events. Events capacities are often met soon after online registration opens, sometimes within 30 minutes!

It is believed that low registration fees (US$20 on average per event) and awards (prize money up to US$60,000 for the fastest runner or record breaker, T-shirts, running supplies, and other products) motivate Taiwanese and international runners to take part in the Taiwanese events (Chu, 2016). Ironically, the monetary rewards associated with the Taiwanese running events draw international elite runners (especially from Africa) who stay in Taiwan for lengthy periods to attend various road running events; they then share the money with their agents (Apple Daily, 2014; Liberty Times News, 2016).

Although participation numbers are high, Taiwanese elite runners are not the fastest. For example, female Taiwanese runners placed 57th, 56th, 53rd, 77th, and 100th in the 1996, 2004, 2008, 2012, and 2016 Olympic Games, respectively. Although some argue that the participation of outstanding international athletes may motivate Taiwanese runners to improve their performances, others note that it may discourage them because they are not as likely to win. These factors affect the development of road running in Taiwan.

Road races are very popular in Taiwan. The New Taipei City Wan Jin Shi Marathon is recognized by the International Association of Athletics Federations (IAAF) as one of its gold label racing events.

Courtesy of Tsu-Lin YEH.

Welty Peachey and colleagues (2015) hope scholars in the field will begin to examine the proposed relationships to contribute to a better understanding of the leadership process in sport management.

Decision Making, Authority, and Power

Leaders and managers are consistently required to make important decisions for the welfare of the organization and its employees. In most cases, strategy decisions—big and small—involve change on some level within a sport organization. In the following sections, we introduce the steps involved in decision making and discuss the concepts of authority and power.

Decision Making

Decision making involves a series of steps. Although researchers may disagree on the number of steps, they agree on the essence of these steps. For the purposes of our discussion, we present the following six steps:

1. *Defining or framing the problem.* What is the problem or issue that requires a decision? Does the manager fully understand all that is involved in addressing this problem? For example, if an organization is going through a change process (e.g., rebranding), managers must be able to explain the need for change to employees.

2. *Identifying criteria for decision.* What criteria must be considered before making the decision? For example, is time of the essence in making rebranding decisions? Has there been a resistance to change by personnel in the past? Are other stakeholders involved in this decision (e.g., board of directors, international committees, sponsors, participants)? How can rebranding increase participant or consumer awareness of the organization?

3. *Developing and evaluating alternatives.* For every problem or issue, various alternatives may be available. Alternatives can include adjusting the mission of the organization. Answer questions regarding which logos and visual designs should represent the rebranding initiatives. Should an adjustment or realignment of organizational values be made?

Community and Youth Sport

Marlene A. Dixon
Jennifer E. McGarry
Justin Evanovich

LEARNING OBJECTIVES

- Define and distinguish between community sport and youth sport.
- Identify sectors and key providers of sport opportunities at the community and youth levels.
- Identify and explain challenges regarding access to community and youth sport.
- Explain key challenges in managing youth and community sport and propose possible solutions for those challenges.
- Differentiate among the outcomes and goals associated with various community and youth sport offerings and the related management implications.
- Identify the social media influences and career opportunities available within youth and community sport.

KEY TERMS

access
community sport
equity
multisport organization (MSO)
national regulatory association
nonprofit sport organizations
professional human resource management (HRM) model
quality of life
social capital
sport-based youth development (SBYD) model
sport league
sport tournament
youth sport

1844
Young Men's Christian Association founded

1858
Ladies Christian Association founded (YWCA first used in 1866)

1888
Amateur Athletic Union formed

1898
Canadian Amateur Athletic Union formed

1906
Federated Boys Clubs in Boston formed; later renamed Boys and Girls Clubs of America

1914
Police Athletic League began in New York City

1929
Pop Warner football began

1939
Little League Baseball began

1961
Fitness and Amateur Sport Act passed in Canada

1964
American Youth Soccer Organization founded

1978
Amateur Sports Act of 1978 adopted by the U.S. Congress

Many people around the world have participated in sport in their communities as children or as adults or perhaps throughout their lives. As a result, participants may tend to think that their experiences are similar to the experiences of most participants in other localities in North America or around the world. In so doing, they may take for granted the unique organizational and structural challenges surrounding the management of community and youth sport. This chapter introduces the history of community and youth sport in North America as well as its current forms. It also presents an overview of some of the operational, strategic, and sociocultural challenges and opportunities inherent in the design, delivery, and future direction of community and youth sport.

Origins of Community Sport

The history of sport in North America is difficult to condense because it varies widely by place of residence, ability, religion, gender identity, social class, race, ethnicity, sexual identity, and family background. In other words, not everyone's experience in sport was the same. But some general trends in this sport history can help us understand the place of community sport in our society and the way that community sport is organized and delivered today.

In North America, sport and games were part of communities and cultures long before the arrival of Europeans. Emerging histories of native communities in North America showed rich and varied traditions of sport and physical contests. The contests ranged from the races, wrestling, and rites-of-passage contests of the North American Dene and Inuit peoples, to moose-skin ball of the Athapaskan women, to perhaps the most influential game, lacrosse, among the Iroquoian, Algonquian, Sioux, Chickasaw, Choctaw,

and Cherokee nations (Morrow & Wamsley, 2005). In Mexico, the Aztecs, Mayans, Mixtecs, and Zapotecs enjoyed the ballgame *ulama*, which resembled volleyball (Villanueva & Luevano, 2016). In native communities, sport and contests often served the purposes of training youth for adult experiences; displaying the strength, skill, and prowess of community members; or celebrating the culture and religion of the community. Although in some cases much of the original meaning and symbolism of community sport from these native peoples has been lost or redefined, there are still examples (e.g., Mexican *charreria*, bullfighting) that have remained popular despite European and American influences. Indigenous people's sport activities have had an influence on the structure, form, and meaning of community sport in North America.

Before the 1800s, European North Americans rarely engaged in physical contests that could be labeled as sports as we know them today. Much time was spent simply surviving and establishing new towns, cities, and industries. The folk games played at this time were usually simple and had no written rules; they were legitimated by custom and often changed to fit the circumstances of play (e.g., space or time available). In rural North America during the early 1800s, these games often sparked contests between citizens or towns that formed the basis of early sport experiences. For example, fishing, hunting, snowshoeing, rowing, archery, throwing, running, and rail-splitting were activities that could be contested between men, often serving as a source of pride and identity for the family or village (Morrow & Wamsley, 2005). And, in Mexico, women participated as well, and even exclusively, in games such as the arihueta race, which involved running and throwing a hoop (Villanueva & Luevano, 2016).

At the same time, a sport fraternity of sorts emerged in urban centers such as New York, Philadel-

---

community sport—Organized physical activity that is based in community, school, and local sport organizations.

2002
Canadian Centre for Ethics in Sport released a report specifically addressing issues in youth sport

2006
U.S. Olympic Committee created Multi-Sport Organizations Council

2013
First Lady Michelle Obama launched *Let's Move!* Active Schools program

2016
U.S. Olympic Committee American Development Model unveiled

Lillehammer, Norway, hosted the second Winter Youth Olympic Games

1981
National Alliance for Youth Sports founded

2003
International Alliance for Youth Sports established

2009
President Barack Obama established White House Office of Olympic, Paralympic, and Youth Sport

2015
The Aspen Institute Report released *Sport for All, Play for Life: A Playbook to Get Every Kid in the Game*

2018
Summer Youth Olympic Games held in Buenos Aires, Argentina

phia, Montreal, and Toronto where men would gather to play sports and wager on billiards, horse racing, prize fighting, or footraces. For example, the Great Race of 1835 offered a prize of $1,000 to anyone who could run 10 miles in less than an hour. More than 20,000 spectators watched as one man, Henry Stannard, a farmer from Connecticut, finished in 59 minutes and 48 seconds. In Canada, curling contests, races, and hunting contests between fur traders and frontiersman thrived in local taverns and military garrisons (Morrow & Wamsley, 2005). The races and spectacles continued across the continent, but sport remained largely unorganized and unregulated.

In the early 1800s, however, voluntary sport clubs emerged for sports such as curling, rowing, cycling, snowshoeing, quoits, cricket, track and field, and baseball. These clubs were mostly the domain of upper- and middle-class men who could afford the time and membership dues required to belong to the sport clubs. **Access** was limited. Contests were arranged first within clubs for the benefit of the club members and then later between clubs. The sponsoring club provided the rules, the facilities, the prize money, and the social events surrounding the contests. For example, the Montreal Curling Club, established by the Scots in 1807, organized the first curling contests in North America exclusively for the benefit of its 20 elite citizens (Morrow & Wamsley, 2005).

The Montreal Snowshoe Club, the Montreal Bicycle Club, and the Montreal Lacrosse Club also served as important clubs for the early foundation of regulated amateur sport in Canada. In the United States, the New York Athletic Club (established in 1850) built the first cinder track and sponsored the first national amateur track and field championship in 1876. This club also sponsored the first national amateur championships for swimming (1877),

boxing (1878), and wrestling (1878). The various sport clubs in the United States and Canada represented the beginning of a larger sport movement in the countries that spread both in type of sports offered and its delivery and governance. As sport clubs expanded, battles ensued over who would provide and regulate community sport and who would define its guiding principles.

In the early 1900s, sport and physical activity continued to grow. In the United States, under President

Lacrosse, a North American sport dating back several centuries, has witnessed a significant resurgence in popularity among young people.
Courtesy of Paul M. Pedersen.

---

access—The ability, right, or permission to approach, enter, or use; admittance.

Theodore Roosevelt, local, state, and national funding was committed to the growth of parks and recreation facilities and spaces, and the Playground Association of America (which eventually became the National Parks and Recreation Association) was born. At this time, parks and recreation activities were more focused on play and leisure rather than on organized sport. Sport was in the domain of nonprofit and commercial clubs, schools, and the AAU, which represented the United States in international competition. After World War II and during ensuing decades, much debate occurred about America's lack of prominence in international sport, which led to the passage of the Amateur Sports Act in 1978 and the creation of national sport governing bodies (e.g., USA Swimming, USA Track and Field). These governing bodies were tasked with sport development in the United States, and they govern U.S. representation in international sport, but they do not necessarily have enforcement powers to become the sole sport providers or governors of amateur sport within the country.

In Mexico, during the second half of the 19th century, urban community sport evolved and became characterized by the government's involvement in the organization and promotion of both physical education and sport (Coelho e Silva, Figueiredo, Elferink-Gemser, & Malina, 2016). In postrevolution Mexico (1900-1917), leaders viewed the introduction of community-based sports as a means to bring citizens together "to create a sense of ethnic, social, and national unity that had not previously existed" (Brewster, 2004, p. 230). From there the Physical Education School and the General Directorate of Physical Education were created under the Secretariat of Public Education, and sport governance continued to become more formalized. In 1923, the Mexican Olympic Committee (COM) was created and the country participated in the Olympic Games for the first time in Paris in 1924. In 1933, the Mexican Sports Confederation (CODEME) was established to create policies for federated sports (Coelho e Silva et al., 2016).

In Canada, the governance of community sport took a slightly different route. The formation of the CAAU in 1898 gave Canada a unified structure for the regulation of 17 amateur sports. The CAAU began by investigating violations of the Canadian Amateur Code, taking action against the sport organizations that violated the code, and encouraging participants to abide by the expectations of amateur athletes (Howell, 2001). This body also "vowed to advance and improve all sports among amateurs and stated

an even loftier goal, that is, to encourage systematic physical exercise and education in Canada" (Morrow & Wamsley, 2005, p. 76). In 1909, the CAAU became known as the AAU. The AAU, along with the passage of the Fitness and Amateur Sport Act of 1961, kept Canada's sport and recreation systems more coordinated and unified than those in the United States. Thus, in Canada, sport is delivered on a local level but typically is coordinated under the auspices of the national governing body (i.e., a **national regulatory association**).

This history of North American sport in the 19th and 20th centuries has highlighted the emergence of different community sport systems in Canada, Mexico, and the United States. In Mexico, physical education in schools has taken on primary importance in the sport involvement of youth, and in poorer areas it is even more essential given fewer opportunities for elite youth sport participation (Simon, Rodriguez de Leon, Hernandez, Larrinaga, & Guadarrama, 2002). In the United States, public schools have seen shifting priorities and resulting budget cuts that limit sport opportunities. Many parks and recreation centers have adopted sport programming, but debate continues to this day about whether sport is complementary or contradictory to the mission and goals of parks and recreation, which often creates ongoing tension over the meaning and purpose of public recreation centers. This debate is not evident in Canada or in most other countries in the world. Furthermore, because no single body governs U.S. amateur sport, sport structures and systems vary widely across states, cities, and local communities. In Canada and Mexico, although sport is seemingly more uniform and coordinated, some sport organizations struggle for more control and voice in their local sport governance. Today, community sport in North America is a widely varying experience that offers challenges and opportunities to sport managers.

Youth Sport History

As Americans began to understand the effect of children's social interactions and activities on their development, organized sport emerged as a means to facilitate friendships and provide learning experiences transferrable to life outside these activities. Since the late 19th century, when the YMCA began offering boys competitive sport opportunities (Marten, 2008), sport has been a part of the landscape for children. The Boys Clubs also began in the 1800s with a mis-

---

national regulatory association—A national sport governing body that makes eligibility and playing rules and sponsors competition according to its rules.

sion of providing safe spaces for boys to play. The charter was expanded in 1990 to represent its current participants as the Boys and Girls Clubs, reflecting an equity approach. The Young Women's Christian Association (YWCA) began in 1866, although sport programming today is found only in a few of the YWCA facilities (Murphy, 2005). It is important to note that the responsibility to provide all youth with access to sport and recreation opportunities is under the purview of YMCAs, whereas the YWCA's mandate focuses on human rights, empowerment and economic advancement for women and girls, and health and safety for women and girls.

Other notable beginnings include the PAL, Pop Warner football, the CYO, and Little League. The PAL, created in 1914 in New York City, had the goal of providing safe places to play for children who lived in the city. Pop Warner football, started in 1929, is still the only youth football organization that requires participants to maintain academic standards. The CYO commenced in 1930, followed by Little League Baseball (1939) and Little League Softball (1974). The Canadian Royal Legion began in the 1940s with the Foster Fathers Program for boys left fatherless by World War II. The program originated as an effort to teach boys leadership skills through sport. This philosophy, as evidenced by the focus on boys in these original youth sport organizations, is supported by Howard Chudacoff's (2007) history of children at play in the United States. The historian traces the origins and evolution of community-based youth sport from the male-centered model aimed at building character and preparing young boys and men for their futures in the workplace. Over time, community-based youth sport has evolved to include more girls, particularly after the passage of Title IX in 1972 and its enforcement beginning in the 1980s. In the United States, approximately 20 million children of both genders between the ages of 5 and 14 "play sports, either organized or casual, during a given year, and it is estimated that 10-12 million play sports regularly or frequently" (Coakley, 2016, p. 84).

In Mexico, youth sport organization and participation have grown considerably since the 1980s. Mexicans operate under the assumption that most children should be able to participate. There has also been increased interest in developing Mexican national teams that was not present in the mid- to late 20th century (Coelho e Silva et al., 2016). The National Sports Commission (CONADE) was formed in 1988 as a replacement for the Mexican Sport Confederation under the supervision of the secretariat of public education. From there, in 2004, the commission was decentralized and became known as the National Commission of Physical Culture and Sports. In 2015, as noted by Coelho e Silva and colleagues, this office created guidelines for quality programs in youth sport. Currently, the percentages of Mexican youth between the ages of 10 and 18 who participate in sports are at 58 percent for males and 36 percent for females. These percentages are for organized sports and thus do not reflect the large numbers of Mexican youth who participate in self-organized games such as street *futbol* (Siegel, Cumming, Pena Reyes, Cardenas Barahona, & Malina, 2013).

Organized youth sport has a broad definition in North America that ranges from the community organizations highlighted earlier to interscholastic and club programs. The variations on sport that exist at town, region, state or province, and national levels are grounded in both the philosophy and the financial situation of the specific location. Shortly after the turn of the century, the Canadian Centre for Ethics in Sport (2002) released a report that specifically addressed issues in youth sport. The results included discussion that the increasing economic influence of youth sport, particularly at the club level of competition, and the "Americanization of sport" (p. 1) were leading youth sport away from its beginnings to educate children and build leaders and turning it into a source of revenue and entertainment. With the growing privatization and specialization of organized youth sport that continues throughout North America (Coakley, 2016), some community-based teams and leagues are finding themselves with fewer participants from which to draw. Furthermore, there is more media attention and publicity about elite youth athletes than about the participants in community-based programs.

Consider a recent development in youth basketball in the United States that speaks to issues of commercialization. The NCAA stepped into the youth arena because of its concern that school-based basketball was not as essential to children as it once was. The club system had taken over the role of developing young basketball players; according to the NCAA, it was missing the educational and fair play aspects that the organization believes are necessary. As a result, the NCAA announced an initiative to provide more structure to the club system, although a second aspect of the initiative is to identify and develop elite players who could eventually play at NCAA institutions. Given the NCAA's track record with commercialization and academic integrity, scholars and critics have suggested that the United States should consider a national governing body for amateur basketball in the

---

equity—Something that is perceived as fair and just.
youth sport—Organized physical activity for children and adolescents offered through schools, community organizations, or national sport organizations.

spirit of the FIBA (Lee & McFarlin, 2015) rather than have the organization that is most served to benefit financially from the club system (i.e., the NCAA) be involved with its governance.

The NCAA's role in amateur basketball is but one example of the ongoing tension in youth sport design and delivery in North America. In youth sport, many questions remain strongly debated: Should the focus be education or elite sport development? Who should govern youth sport? Who has access to the various sport opportunities? Remember that throughout the history of North American sport, not everyone has agreed on the purpose or process of youth sport, which continues to present significant challenges to sport managers in this context.

Definition of Community Sport

In defining community sport, we take a broad approach wherein it is conceptualized as organized physical activity that is based in community, school, and local sport organizations. Thus, this definition—drawn from work by Stewart, Nicholson, Smith, and Westerbeek (2004)—encompasses both recreational and competitive sport but does not include exercise and fitness facilities or programs. Further, community sport may, but does not necessarily have to, culminate

in high-performance sport that takes place at the college, professional, Olympic, national, or international level. The sidebar Sampling of Community Sport Organizations in North America provides examples of community sport organizations mentioned throughout this chapter.

Emphasis on the Participant

In professional sport, management concerns are often focused on people as spectators and consumers of sport as entertainment. In contrast, the emphasis in community sport is on people as participants. Therefore, management concerns revolve around continuing to attract new participants and keeping them involved in the programs as well as the types of programs or sports offered, the time and place of activities, the organization and delivery of programs, and cost and pricing considerations. Concern for the financial performance of the organization coincides with a focus on high-quality service as well as sport development. By keeping participant needs and wants central, managers can ensure the short- and long-term viability of their organizations. In terms of youth community sport, these needs and wants include participation and education on the rules and strategies of the game as well as the related social and ethical development of the children (Harvey, Kirk, & O'Donovan, 2014).

Sampling of Community Sport Organizations in North America

Amateur Athletic Union	Playworks
American Softball Association	Police Athletic League
Blaze Sports America	Pop Warner football and cheerleading
Boys and Girls Clubs of America	Sugar and Spikes Softball Club
Catholic Youth Organization	United States Field Hockey Futures
Fitzgerald Youth Sports Institute	United States Swimming
Girls on the Run (GOTR)	United States Tennis Association
GoGirlGo!	United States Volleyball Association
Husky Sport	United States Youth Soccer
International Alliance for Youth Sports	Up2Us Sports
Little League Baseball and Softball	U.S. Olympic Committee
Local Government Recreation Departments	USRowing
National Alliance for Youth Sports	Women's Sports Foundation
National Council of Youth Sport	YMCA

Benefits of Sport Participation

Numerous benefits are associated with sport participation. Some of these positive aspects include physical and health outcomes, improved family well-being, a sense of community, and increased social capital for families and other groups.

Quality of Life

The physical benefits of sport participation include increased cardiovascular health, decreased stress, and increased functioning of the musculoskeletal system (Eime, Young, Harvey, Charity, & Payne, 2013). One benefit of sport participation for children is that it helps maintain a healthy weight. Sport participation can also reduce weight in obese children (Conrad, 2016).

In addition, people who participate in recreation and sport report better concentration, task persistence, disposition, and analytical ability. These gains can lead to higher work productivity and lower absenteeism. People also report psychological benefits of participation such as increased self-esteem and social belonging (Dixon, 2009). Children, in particular, benefit from being physically active through sport. Physical activity improves psychological health and helps cognitive, physical, social, and emotional development. Sport participation and physical activity can delay the onset of many chronic diseases (Conrad, 2016). Overall, there is general agreement that sport participation can positively affect a person's quality of life and that childhood physical activity through sport increases the likelihood of maintaining an active lifestyle as an adult.

Note, however, that these benefits are not experienced universally or to the same degree across all groups. Sabo and Veliz (2016) published their most recent report with the WSF revealing that a gender gap continues to be present in youth sport participation and that the percentage of girls from both urban and rural communities participating in sport is disproportionate to that of boys. In addition, the data show that interest in being physically active in sport and exercise results not from biological inheritance but rather from the opportunity and encouragement of influential people in a child's life. The WSF report and subsequent research also revealed that physical education classes, which are indicative of other sport and exercise participation, are even further unequal based on gender and geography. That is, many schools no longer require physical education classes, and one in five schools does not offer physical education classes at all. School location and gender strongly influence access to physical education in that urban girls, rural girls, and low-income boys and girls are underrepresented in school physical education classes. On a more positive note, girls have expanded their participation to include a larger variety of sports and activities than boys, although boys' sports more often fall under the umbrella of school or community sports. Last, according to the data, girls have a shorter time frame in which to participate than boys do. Girls typically start organized sport later (i.e., age 7.4 compared with 6.8 for boys) and exit sooner, usually during middle school (i.e., between the ages of 12 and 14), and are not represented as broadly in competitive sports, which tend to be the sports that have the highest levels of physical activity. Sabo and Veliz (2016) have published reports about gender in youth sport that demonstrate that youth are still leaving organized sports in high numbers, particularly girls, children of color, and low-income children, and multiplier effects are in play when any or all of those identities intersect.

Family Life

Benefits of sport participation extend beyond the individual to include improved family well-being. Families report a greater sense of belonging and increased bonds through sport and recreation participation (Wood, Giles-Corti, Zubrick, & Bulsara, 2013). Many parents report enjoyment from participating in recreational activities with their children, in coaching their children's sport teams, or in attending sport events with their families (Dixon, 2009). Children's athletic participation was associated with higher levels of family satisfaction (Sabo & Veliz, 2016). Increasingly, however, sport participation is becoming a challenge for families and sometimes can create tensions when family members do not agree on the level or type of sport participation appropriate for the children or the family (Graham, Dixon, & Hazen-Swan, 2016).

Sense of Community and Social Capital

Finally, sport participation can create a sense of community and create social capital for families and other groups of people (Putnam, 2000). Social capital can be defined as a "contextual characteristic that describes patterns of civic engagement, trust, and mutual obligation among individuals" (Cuskelly, Hoye, & Auld, 2006, p. 8). People who participate in sport together and those who volunteer together to deliver a community sport program develop social

---

quality of life—The degree of well-being felt by an individual or a group of people.

social capital—Contextual characteristics of communities that describe how people develop trust and social ties; also described as the glue that holds communities together.

Next, volunteers often need to undergo training and development to understand the organization's goals, policies, and procedures and to become competent and successful in their volunteer duties. Much training is focused on volunteer coaches because they are often at the forefront of sport delivery, and participant experience in sport largely depends on the quality of coaching (Newman, Ortega, Lower, & Paluta, 2016). If children do not enjoy their sport experiences, they are unlikely to continue to participate. Coach training should include ethical standards, proper child safety (if coaching children), education in the sport coached (e.g., techniques and tactics), and education in motivation and behavior management (Newman et al., 2016).

Quality HRM is essential to community sport delivery. Although volunteers need guidelines and training to ensure a quality experience for themselves and the participants, community sport managers must also ensure that volunteers enjoy the experience and see it as valuable and worthwhile. Procedure should not be taught at the expense of experience.

Adult Community Sport Offerings

Community sport opportunities in North America are often provided through three basic structures: classes, leagues, and tournaments. Classes are instructional sessions that enhance the skill or fitness level of the participants. For example, people may want to participate in golf classes (individual or group) to enhance their golf skills for recreational or competitive play.

Leagues are organized forms of ongoing competition in a sport. They may be as simple as a few teams at a community recreation center that play each other on a rotating basis or as complex as a professional sport league (e.g., the Pacific Baseball

Bill Wise

Courtesy of Bill Wise.

Professional Profile

Title: Family activities minister, Central Baptist Church, College Station, Texas

Education: BA (journalism), Texas A&M University; MA (Christian education), Southwestern Baptist Theological Seminary

Bill Wise was born and raised in Houston, Texas. After he completed his bachelor's degree, he worked for six years as a special events supervisor at Missouri City Parks and Recreation in Missouri City, Texas. He then transitioned to Christian ministry, and for the next 10 years served as the recreation minister at Houston's First Baptist Church in Houston. Since 2009, he has served as the family activities minister at Central Baptist Church in College Station. He oversees all athletic, recreation, and church-wide programs and events. He also oversees the Central Sports program that includes soccer, flag football, basketball, and cheerleading, which reaches over 1,100 youth. Bill's passion is to see youth and adults impacted by the gospel through sports and recreation. During his tenure in this position, Wise completed his master's in Christian education. The following is a snapshot of his development, education, duties, and insights as a leader in the sport industry.

What was your career path?

As compared to a traditional career, the path to ministry is not a career path or trajectory. Rather, it is a calling. Specifically, I was called to ministry in 1998 and it took over a year to prepare for what lay ahead in my ministry efforts. Based upon my prior experience in sports and recreation, I was considered for my position as Family Activities Minister.

League in Mexico, the NFL in the United States, or the Canadian Hockey League). Leagues define the playing season, rules, and participant eligibility and usually provide a system to determine a champion. Although usually thought of in terms of team sports (e.g., soccer, basketball, hockey), leagues can also be formed for primarily individual sports (e.g., golf, tennis, archery).

Tournaments are organized forms of sport that usually extend over several days or weeks. They start with a large pool of participants and narrow to an eventual champion. Again, these can be as simple as a local three-on-three basketball charity fundraiser or as complex as the annual US Tennis Open Championships. For example, the United States Tennis Association (USTA) sponsors tournaments around the country nearly every weekend. The tournaments are managed and sponsored by local tennis clubs or facilities, but they are conducted under USTA rules and regulations.

Youth Sport Offerings

Community youth sport offerings and the rate at which children take advantage of those offerings vary by demographic factors (e.g., SES, race, and ethnicity), cognitive and behavioral factors (e.g., attitudes, family influences, beliefs, perceptions, social influences, sedentary behaviors), and community factors (e.g., general safety, built environment, availability of venues for sport, school-based sport) (National Council of Youth Sports, 2012). These factors are important to consider when planning, implementing, and managing youth sport. Organized activities affiliated with youth sport are typically structured as classes, instructional leagues, competitive leagues, and after-school programs.

Classes

Youth sport classes can be beginning sport instruction at facilities such as community recreation centers or

What characteristics must a person have to be successful in your job?

This context is a little different than some other jobs in sports. In order to be successful in this type of ministry, a person has to follow Jesus and understand how to communicate the values of Christian ministry through recreation and sport. Rather than relying on personal experience or knowledge, ministers are guided by faith.

Which websites, online tools, or resources do you frequently use or refer to?

Unfortunately, there are not many great websites for recreation ministry. I do visit Recreation Management (http://recmanagement.com), Christian Sports Recreation Ministers (http://csrm.org), and Texas Recreation and Park Society (http://traps.org). In addition, I subscribe to the online newsletters and magazines posted by these organizations.

What do you consider to be the biggest future challenge in your job or industry?

The biggest threat to any church or ministry is giving. The church relies on the hearts of others to give to the church and without these tithes there is no church. Since recreation ministry is a fringe ministry and does not provide a main service to the church, it will be one of the first to go if funds are unavailable. For example, we pulled out of a national sports partnership as it was costing the church too much money. Instead, we created our own programs and are able to do more for the leagues due to that independence. Although some church recreation programs see the local municipality, YMCA, and club teams as competition, I do not see it that way. We have great relationships with both the City of College Station and Bryan parks and recreation departments, so we are not threats to one another. While we offer some of the same sports, the leagues are different enough so that we are not in competition.

In regard to recreation as a whole, the biggest challenge is apathetic employees. I see this at the state level and nationwide in the next generation of recreation professionals who only want to work the standard 8:00 to 5:00 hours. The recreation professional provides programs, leagues, and events when the customer is not working. In recreation, the customers participate on evenings and weekends. If this trend does not change, there will not be jobs available because these services will be contracted out to nonprofit and commercial organizations and entities.

organizations such as the YMCA or YWCA. From a young age (even infancy in the case of swimming lessons), children can learn skills, rules, and strategies with an emphasis on enjoyment. The classes can be sport specific or address a variety of sports and emphasize development. For instance, the West Suburban YMCA in the Boston suburb of Newton, Massachusetts, offers a program called Super Sports for children ages 4 through 9. In the seven-week program, children play a different sport each week. Typically, the offerings include kickball, soccer, Wiffle ball, basketball, floor hockey, flag football, and an occasional game of dodgeball or capture the flag; these activities facilitate children's learning of sports while maintaining a fun environment.

Instructional Leagues

The goal of instructional leagues is to provide information and knowledge to children as they begin to play sports or are introduced to new sports. Youth sport programs build basic motor skills (e.g., eye–hand coordination, footwork, balance) and provide children with positive instruction in the basic skills, rules, and strategies associated with a specific sport. Children are also provided with the opportunity to scrimmage or play the sport to put into practice

what they have learned. At the younger levels, most leagues have at least an instructional component. Others are strictly instructional with no scores or standings being kept.

In Burbank, California, for example, the city recreation department provides instructional children's leagues for several sports (e.g., soccer, baseball, softball, volleyball, flag football). The philosophy of the offerings and instruction is based in several national models. The City of Burbank is a member of NAYS, which adheres to the provision of positive and safe sports and activities for children. The city does this through its application of the NAYS national standards for youth sports to its coaches, officials, administrators, and young athletes. In addition, the parents of participants complete the Parents Association for Youth Sports (PAYS) orientation program to assist them in understanding how sport plays a role in the development of their children. Specifically, Burbank's softball league offers noncompetitive tee ball divisions for kindergarten through grade 2 and then transitions into competitive leagues for grades 3 through 8. The instructional league provides motor skill and fundamental development and concludes the season with its annual jamboree, during which children participate in a parade and skill events to highlight what they have learned during their season.

Competitive Leagues

After children enter third grade in Burbank, for example, they transition into competitive spring and fall leagues guided by Amateur Softball Association (ASA) standards and rules. Children can continue in the competitive leagues until they graduate from high school and enter adult leagues. These ASA national standards and rules provide the structure for a positive environment with quality instruction that adds the competitive aspect of standings and the opportunity to enter the ASA district sport tournament and progress to a national championship. The ASA has more than 90 national championships, starting with fast pitch for ages 10 and under. Annually, more than 40,000 players from children to adults participate in ASA national championships.

Similar to the ASA model, other competitive sports progress from the local level to national championship events. The United States Volleyball Association (USVBA) sponsors junior leagues for children 10 years of age and under. For younger children, more emphasis is given to instruction and development; for older children, the emphasis shifts

Children can learn basic movement and athletic skills through various youth sport organizations, classes, and leagues.

Courtesy of Paul M. Pedersen.

sport tournament—A competition that involves a relatively large number of competitors; it can be offered over a set period at a single venue or can be a set of matches or competitions that culminate in a single champion.

to competition. Teams play at local and regional tournaments. Based on finishes at those events, they can qualify for national tournaments and even the Junior Olympic Championships. USVBA also sponsors outdoor leagues (e.g., Junior Beach Programs) and a Junior Beach Tour. Other examples of youth club sport opportunities include the United States Field Hockey Futures, the Amateur Athletic Union (e.g., track and field, basketball, gymnastics), and United States Swimming. The YOG are relative newcomers in international youth sport competition. It hosted its inaugural event in Singapore in 2010; this was followed by events in Innsbruck (2012), Nanjing (2014), Lillehammer (2016), Buenos Aires (2018), and Lausanne (2020).

After-School Programs

Historically, after-school programs have been viewed as beneficial to children for the personal enjoyment that they experience, the safety and supervision provided, the academic enrichment and improvement in social skills that may occur, and the emphasis on physical health and fitness (Afterschool Alliance, 2015). The hours immediately after school ends are considered a crucial time in the development of children, but the number of children in the United States in kindergarten through grade 12 who are in after-school programs of any kind has grown 60 percent in the last 10 years, with close to 4 million children enrolled (Afterschool Alliance, 2014). The challenge is that as many as 19.4 million parents indicated that they would enroll their children in quality after-school programs if those existed in their neighborhoods. Typically, younger children are more likely to be enrolled in after-school programs than older ones; as many as 66 percent of participants are in kindergarten through grade 5. The number drops to 15 percent for grades 6 through 8. Furthermore, as many as 11 percent of children in kindergarten through grade 5 are identified as taking care of themselves after school with no adults present. In particular, African American and Hispanic youth spend more time unsupervised than other children do, so the demand for after-school programs is much higher for those families.

In the United States, public schools provide the largest number of general after-school programs. YMCAs and Boys and Girls Clubs are within the top five of providers of after-school programs even when sports are not specified in the rankings. For example, the YMCA of Greater Toronto offers after-school programs for children in kindergarten through grade 8 at more than 125 facilities across the metro area, making it the largest provider of after-school programs and care for children in Canada. Through these programs, children receive affordable after-school care centered on healthy character development and

The Youth Olympic Games (YOG) are relative newcomers in the international youth sport competition. Here, a gold medalist in cross-country skiing shows off her medal at the Lillehammer 2016 YOG.

Courtesy of Paul M. Pedersen.

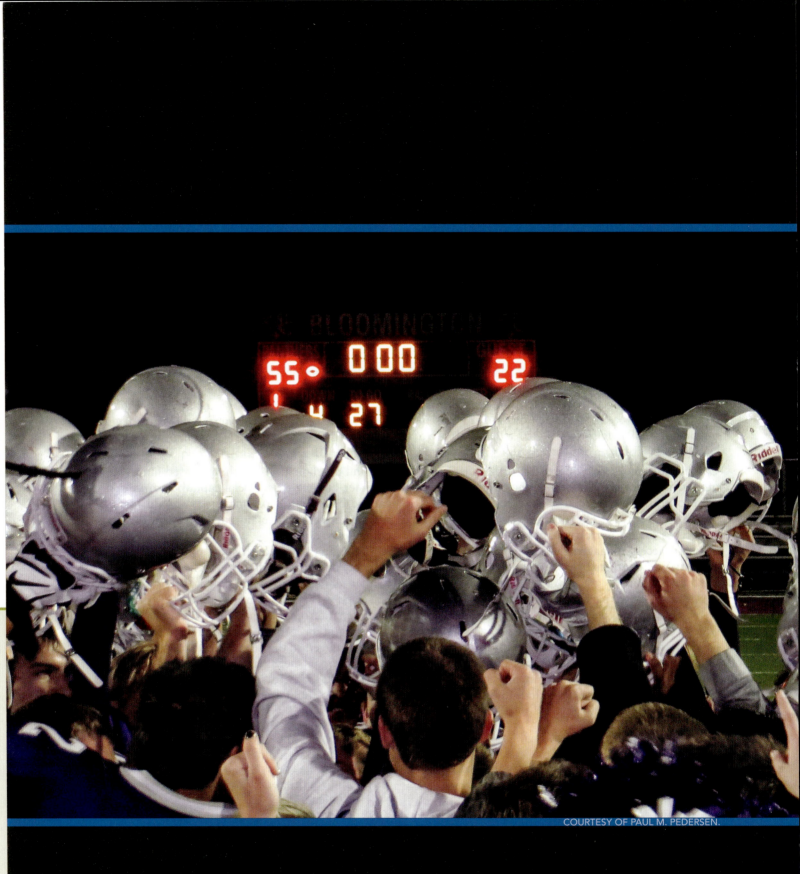

Interscholastic Athletics

Eric W. Forsyth
Tywan G. Martin
Warren A. Whisenant

LEARNING OBJECTIVES

- Identify the historical and governance foundations of interscholastic athletics.
- Explain the differing critical views of the role that interscholastic athletics plays in society.
- Discuss the operational differences between public and private schools.
- Identify careers available in interscholastic sports at the national, state, district, and local levels.
- Explain the unique and similar issues that face athletic directors at private schools and public schools.
- Discuss the associations related to interscholastic athletics at the national and state levels.
- Identify critical issues facing athletic administrators in their day-to-day duties.

KEY TERMS

athletic administrator

athletic director (AD)

centralized organizational structure

decentralized organizational structure

interscholastic athletics

interscholastic sport governance

National Federation of State High School (NFHS) Associations

National Interscholastic Athletic Administrators Association (NIAAA)

private schools

public schools

state athletic or activity associations

1888
Massachusetts established the Interscholastic Football Association

1904
Georgia became the first state to establish a high school athletic association

1921
Midwest Federation of State High School Associations founded

1971
National Conference of High School Directors of Athletics established

1974
Interscholastic Athletic Administration magazine launched

1977
National Interscholastic Athletic Administrators Association (NIAAA) formed

1979
Minnesota Adapted Athletics Association founded the first high school athletic conference for students with disabilities

1981
National Federation Interscholastic Coaches Association formed

1982
National High School Sports Hall of Fame established

1996
American Association of Adapted Sports Programs founded, first interscholastic athletics governing body for students with physical or visual impairments

Becky Oakes named first female president of the National Federation of State High School Associations (NFHS)

Interscholastic athletics is a segment within the sport industry that seems to draw the least amount of attention within the realm of sport management studies and academia. Scholars tend to focus their research toward collegiate and professional sport. Students entering the profession also tend to envision themselves as key players within an NCAA Division I athletic department, working in the front office of a professional sport team, or even working as an agent negotiating multimillion dollar contracts. The attention toward those segments is understandable considering the dominant national media exposure of the professional and collegiate segments within the sport industry provided by cable outlets such as Fox Sports and ESPN. If the lead story on *SportsCenter* dealt with a rift between the Bulldogs' athletic director and head football coach, viewers might expect to see a story involving Mississippi State University, not DeSoto County High School in Florida. A story concerning the job security of the head coach of the Cowboys would draw attention to Dallas, not LaBelle High School in Hendry County, Florida. The many issues facing interscholastic administrators seldom draw widespread attention or interest.

Although the national media may not cover high school athletics, this segment of the sport industry should not be overlooked in terms of growth, career opportunities, and economic impact. Lockard and Wolf (2012) suggested that the employment opportunities within sport and entertainment were expected to grow roughly 16 percent from 2010 to 2020, thereby exceeding the growth rate of many other occupations. A significant portion of that growth will occur in the more than 24,000 athletic departments at the high school level in public and commercial sec-

tors. As a business segment, interscholastic athletics contributes over US$15 billion to the sport industry in the United States and employs more than 300,000 coaches and administrators.

The potential influence interscholastic athletic administrators have over the lives of young adults can be significant. Over 7.8 million of the 15 million high school students (52 percent) who attended public schools during the fall of 2016 participated in athletics. As such, interscholastic administrators have a deep responsibility and obligation to meet a wide range of needs to their most important stakeholders, the youth of America. For many kids, the way their schools' athletic programs are managed and delivered will shape their perceptions about success and failure, organizational fairness, and other social norms. Although sport management professionals at both collegiate and professional levels are typically tasked with delivering a quality entertainment product for their fan base, interscholastic athletic administrators play an important role in the educational and social development of the students who are involved with their school's athletic program. High school athletics also plays a role in the community by providing sport entertainment and serving as a prominent source of community well-being.

Arrival of Interscholastic Athletics

The first intercollegiate athletic competition can be traced back to August 3, 1852, when Harvard and Yale matched their crew teams on the waters of Lake Winnipesaukee in New Hampshire. The details of the first interscholastic athletic competition are less

---

interscholastic athletics—Sport offerings whereby boys and girls can participate in athletics at the high school level.

2005
Athletic participation in high school athletics topped 7 million for the first time

2009
NIAAA established the Quality Program Award

2011
Interscholastic athletic contests banned by the NCAA from being televised on school- or conference-owned TV networks

2013
NFHS partnered with PlayOn! Sports to develop a high school sports network

2017
Mike Blackburn became the new executive director of the NIAAA

2008
NFHS developed its National High School Spirit of Sport Award

2010
Bob Gardner named the fifth executive director of the NFHS

2012
NIAAA launched national public service announcement campaign with NFHS

2015
NIAAA partnered with Sideline Access and introduced the NIAAA National High School Sports app

certain. But students from various public and private high schools in Massachusetts formed the Interscholastic Football Association in 1888. As such, it may well have been among those Boston-area schools that the first interscholastic athletic competition occurred. At the turn of the century, interscholastic sport had become the largest sector in the entire sport enterprise. No other level of sport has as many participants, sport teams, or athletic programs as interscholastic sport does. In addition, each school and each state provides an array of sporting options to meet the interests of their students. Both traditional sports and niche sports are offered across the country.

List of the Most Popular School-Sponsored Sports for Both Boys and Girls

Traditional Sports

Baseball	Golf	Tennis
Basketball	Soccer	Track and field
Competitive spirit squads	Softball	Volleyball
Cross country	Swimming and diving	Wrestling
Football		

Niche Sports

Adapted floor hockey	Field hockey	Orienteering
Alpine skiing	Flag football	Power lifting
Badminton	Gymnastics	Riflery
Bowling	Heptathlon	Rodeo
Canoeing	Ice hockey	Sailing
Crew	Indoor track and field	Skiing
Dance and drill team	Judo	Snowboarding
Decathlon	Kayaking	Synchronized swimming
Equestrian	Lacrosse	Water polo

Table 7.1 State Associations and the Year Each Joined the NFHS

Association	Year	Association	Year
Alabama	1924	Montana	1934
Alaska	1956	Nebraska	1924
Arizona	1925	Nevada	1939
Arkansas	1924	New Hampshire	1945
California	1940	New Jersey	1942
Colorado	1924	New Mexico	1932
Connecticut	1926	New York	1926
Delaware	1945	North Carolina	1949
D.C.	1958	North Dakota	1923
Florida	1926	Ohio	1924
Georgia	1929	Oklahoma	1924
Hawaii	1957	Oregon	1931
Idaho	1926	Pennsylvania	1924
Illinois	1920	Rhode Island	1952
Indiana	1924	South Carolina	1947
Iowa	1920	South Dakota	1923
Kansas	1923	Tennessee	1925
Kentucky	1941	Texas	1969
Louisiana	1925	Utah	1927
Maine	1939	Vermont	1945
Maryland	1946	Virginia	1948
Massachusetts	1944	Washington	1936
Michigan	1920	West Virginia	1925
Minnesota	1923	Wisconsin	1920
Mississippi	1924	Wyoming	1936
Missouri	1926		

Value of Interscholastic Athletic Programs

According to the NFHS (2016d) three central premises indicate the value of offering interscholastic activities: (1) Athletics support the academic mission of schools, (2) athletics are inherently educational, and (3) athletics foster success in later life. Many of the supporters of high school sport draw on these attributes to promote the importance of athletics in the educational mission of public and private schools.

Professional Profile

Title: Athletics director, director of athletic facilities, aquatics director, Ransom Everglades School, Coconut Grove, Florida

Education: BA (international finance and marketing), University of Miami, Florida

Courtesy of Ransom Everglades School.

The Ransom Everglades School was established in 1903 along the shores of Biscayne Bay. Located on two campuses, Ransom Everglades is a coeducational college preparatory school for grades 6 through 12. Athletics plays an integral role in the student's educational process; 93 percent of the 1,075 students participate in at least one of the school's 76 teams. In addition to the high level of student involvement, 90 percent of the school's teams are coached by faculty members. Andy De Angulo's primary role at Ransom is as the school's athletic director. The following is a snapshot of his development, education, duties, and insights as a leader in the sport industry.

What was your career path?

After college and a brief stint at a marketing and public relations firm, I switched my focus to coaching, which had been my passion for years. I began a club swim team, Miami Swimming, in 1998, which I currently own and operate as its CEO and head coach. The club started with 25 swimmers and now has over 200 swimmers. The team soon after relocated to the Ransom Everglades campus to help rebuild their aquatics program, which had a rich history but had not seen success for a few years. In the fall of 1999, I became head varsity swim coach. I also became the assistant athletic director and served in that role the next 17 years. During that time frame, the department grew to become a premier athletic program in Miami-Dade County and the state of Florida. I assumed the role of AD in 2016.

What characteristics must a person have to be successful in your job?

As an athletic director, [I] work with coaches, student-athletes, and parents who are on various programs and [I] preach one message: *team*. In this role, you need to lead by example and work as a team. To be successful as an AD, you have to understand that the coaches and staff are not your employees but rather your *teammates*. This ideal will bring out the positive characteristics that are required to be successful in your job: care, ethics, compassion, dedication, reliability, willingness to give of yourself for the betterment of others, passion, adaptability.

Which websites, online tools, or resources do you frequently use or refer to?

Many resources are available online for athletic directors to work with information. Some of the websites we use include: FHSAA.org, *Athletic Business Journal*, NFHS.org, Arbiter, LeagueMinder, HUDL, NAIS, SAIS, FIAAA. [We also monitor our internal website] for information and to remain current with certifications, officials, opponents, and transportation. There are also many additional online tools and resources that become personal preferences that work for communication to teams and parents, organizational tools, video sharing, etcetera.

What do you consider to be the biggest future challenge in your job or industry?

The explosion of club sports and outside coaching has had a major impact on high school sports. This has caused a change in culture of having multisport high school athletes and [we have] seen a spike in specialization. The issue of specialization has caused an increase in injuries caused by overuse and extended hours on fields, courts, and tracks. This will be a future challenge moving forward as many young student-athletes are looking for the next scholarship and working to be the next superstar in their sport.

Transgender Athletes

In February 2017, Mack Beggs won the Texas High School 6A 110-pound weight class division in girls wrestling. Beggs is a transgender athlete who is transitioning from female to male. Beggs wanted to compete against the boys during the wrestling season, but he was denied because he was born a female. The University Interscholastic League (UIL) policy states that individuals must compete according to the gender at birth; therefore, Beggs needed to compete with the girls. Some shared concerns that Beggs had an unfair advantage against other female wrestlers because he was taking testosterone treatments. Beggs was allowed to compete because the testosterone treatments were considered a valid medical use. Pending Texas legislation could disqualify transgender student-athletes from UIL-sponsored competition in the future.

nity and encouragement to grow intellectually, physically, emotionally, and socially in order to assume a responsible role in today's ever-changing world. Students, teachers, parents, and the community will work collaboratively so that all students will achieve a quality education.

The school's enrollment was approximately 1,100 students (55 percent girls and 45 percent boys). The athletic department at the school fielded six football teams each fall. Three teams were for seventh-grade boys who practiced in the morning before school. The other three teams were for eighth-grade boys who practiced in the afternoons after school. Each team

Administrators in interscholastic athletics often encounter ethical issues that require their decision making. Examples include making decisions regarding the offering of sports, scheduling of games, balancing of academics and athletics, allocating of fair usage of fields and facilities, and maintaining consistency between the athletic program and the mission of the school.

Courtesy of Paul M. Pedersen.

had a roster of approximately 45 boys. No teams cut players, so all boys who wanted to play could be on a team. For the girls, the major fall sport was volleyball. The school had one girls' volleyball team that had a roster of 12 girls. More than 200 girls tried out for the team each fall.

For chapter-specific learning activities, visit the web study guide at
www.HumanKinetics.com/ContemporarySportManagement.

Summary

This chapter has provided an overview of interscholastic athletics, which is one of the largest, but relatively understudied, segments of the sport industry. From a human development and sociological perspective, high school athletics affects 50 percent of all high school students. As a segment of the sport industry, interscholastic athletics contributes billions of dollars to the U.S. economy and provides full-time and part-time jobs for more than half a million people. School-sponsored athletic programs shape or influence, in some form, the lives of more than 14 million people (e.g., students, family members, coaches, administrators) in the United States. Although supporters and detractors may have differing views of the role that interscholastic athletics should play in the educational process, both would agree that athletics are tightly woven into the culture and society of the United States.

Review Questions

1. In what year did high school sport governance begin? Why was a governing body needed?

2. How has the passage of Title IX affected participation rates in high school sport?

3. What are the major operational differences between public school and private school athletic departments?

4. In relation to other levels of sport competition, where do interscholastic athletics rank in size and scope?

5. What are some of the underlying factors that caused interscholastic sport to become part of the educational system?

6. What are some of the perceived benefits of student participation in interscholastic sport programs?

7. How are career paths similar and different at the national, state, district, and local levels?

8. What are some of the ways the media (e.g., social media, sports broadcasts) have affected interscholastic athletics? What future changes do you see in terms of the media's influence at the high school level?

9. Which of the listed issues facing interscholastic athletics do you consider the most pressing or important? Explain your answer.

Intercollegiate Athletics

Ellen J. Staurowsky
Robertha Abney
Nicholas M. Watanabe

LEARNING OBJECTIVES

- Define *intercollegiate athletics*.

- Demonstrate an understanding of the events surrounding the development of intercollegiate athletics.

- Describe the purposes of intercollegiate athletic governance organizations.

- Identify key administrative personnel within intercollegiate athletic departments.

- Identify the roles and responsibilities of personnel working in intercollegiate athletic departments.

- Discuss several current challenges and social media issues facing intercollegiate athletic administrators.

- Identify key associations, organizations, and publications related to intercollegiate athletics.

KEY TERMS

academic progress rate (APR)
Equity in Athletics Disclosure Act (EADA)
historically Black colleges and universities
licensing royalty
outsource
Power Five
senior woman administrator (SWA)
tribal colleges and universities (TCUs)
ticket operations
ticket scalping

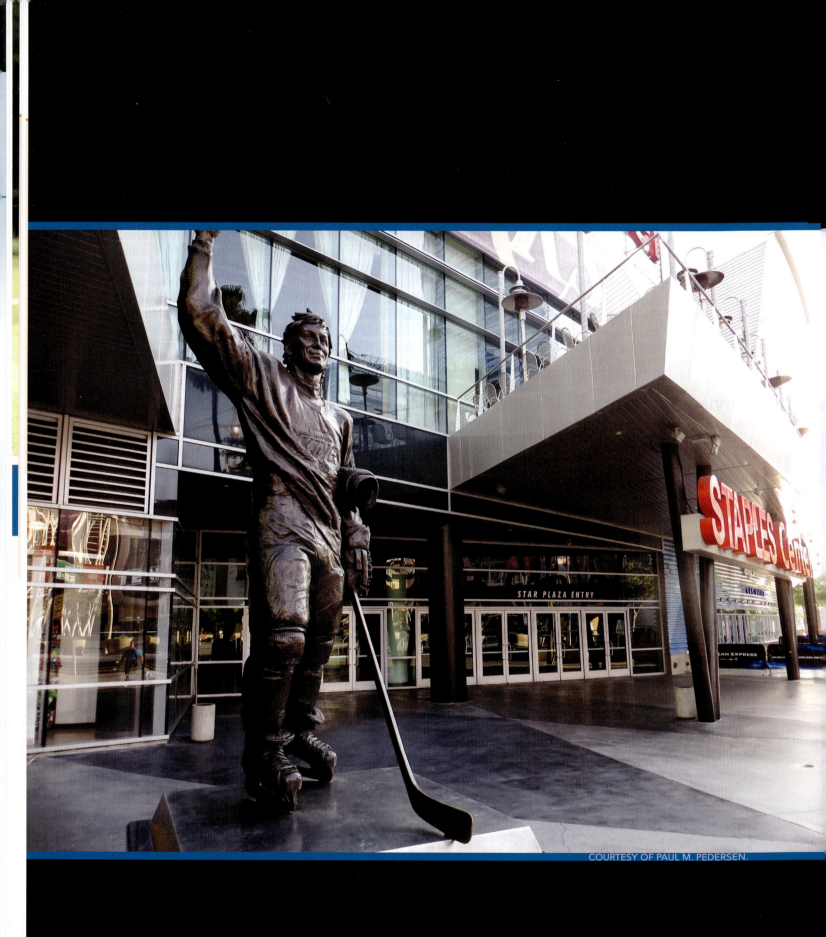

9

Professional Sport

Jacqueline McDowell
Amy Chan Hyung Kim
Natasha T. Brison

LEARNING OBJECTIVES

- Define, explain, and discuss the development of professional sport.
- Describe the unique facets of professional sport including its governance and the labor–management relationship on which professional team sports depend.
- Document the significance of the relationship between media, including new and social media, and professional sport.
- Describe the major revenue sources for a professional sport team.
- Identify the types of employment opportunities available in this segment of the sport industry.
- Apply ethical reasoning and critical thinking skills to issues in professional sport.

KEY TERMS

collective bargaining
governance
labor
league think
LED (light-emitting diode) signage
local television contracts
luxury tax
management
salary caps
sponsorship
virtual reality
virtual signage

Sport Management and Marketing Agencies

Catherine Lahey
Jezali Lubenetski
Danielle Smith

LEARNING OBJECTIVES

- Describe the inception, evolution, and mainstreaming of sport management and marketing agencies.

- Explain the role, scope, and influence of sport management and marketing agencies as they relate to the business of sport.

- Differentiate between the types of agencies to determine which are most appropriate for particular tasks and assignments.

- Appraise career opportunities associated with sport management and marketing agencies.

- Examine the critical skills needed and ethical issues associated with the work of agencies in the sport industry.

- Detail the key challenges facing agencies in the sport industry in the second decade of the 21st century.

KEY TERMS

client	in-house group	strategic planning
entitlement	inventory	turnkey program
gatekeepers	ROI analysis	venue
grassroots programs	stakeholder	

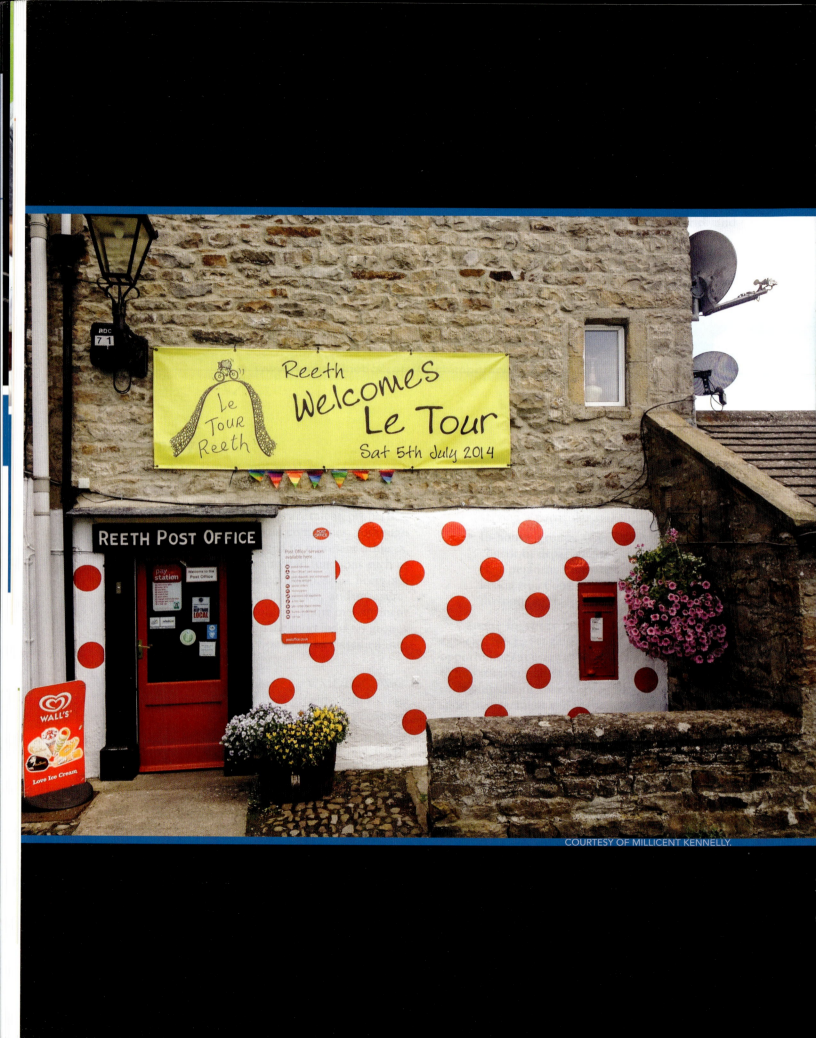

Sport Tourism

Heather Gibson
Sheranne Fairley
Millicent Kennelly

LEARNING OBJECTIVES

- Explain tourism and the tourism industry.
- Describe the intersection between sport and tourism.
- Distinguish among the three types (i.e., active, event, and nostalgia) of sport tourism.
- Discuss the sociocultural, economic, and environmental effects of sport tourism.
- Detail issues in sport tourism that involve critical thinking, ethical decision making, and technological (e.g., social media) application.
- Understand the basic premises of sustainability and how sustainable development relates to sport tourism.

KEY TERMS

casuals
destination image
destination marketing organization (DMO)
displacement effect
hallmark event
leverage
mega event
seasonality
small-scale sport event
sports commission
synergy
time switchers

1897
First Boston Marathon held

1912
Inaugural Calgary Stampede held

1939
National Baseball Hall of Fame dedicated

1963
Pro Football Hall of Fame opened

1975
First general assembly of World Tourism Organization held in Madrid, Spain

1978
First Ironman Triathlon held

1987
First National Senior Olympic Games held in St. Louis, Missouri

1992
National Association of Sports Commissions founded

1997
ESPN Wide World of Sports Complex (originally called Disney's Wide World of Sports) opened

2001
First World Conference on Sport and Tourism held in Barcelona, Spain

Sport tourism is one of the fastest growing sectors in the global tourism industry. In 2014, there were 25.65 million sport-related visitors in the United States who spent an estimated US$8.96 billion (Schumacher, 2015). In researching event sport tourism, specifically world championships, and multisport events, Sportcal (2016) found that 83 events generated more than US$3 billion in direct economic impact across 38 countries and attracted over 2 million international tourists.

Sport-related travel dates back centuries. The Greeks traveled to take part in the ancient Olympic Games from as early as 900 BCE, and the Romans regularly staged popular sport competitions that drew large crowds of spectators from various localities. In recent years, the term *sport tourism* has become widely used to describe sport-related travel and has gradually become a specialized sector of the sport and tourism industries. Sport tourism, as defined by Gibson (1998), encompasses three main types of travel and sport participation:

1. Active sport tourism: a trip in which the tourist takes part in a sport such as golf
2. Event sport tourism: a trip in which the tourist watches a sport event such as the Super Bowl
3. Nostalgia sport tourism: a trip in which the tourist visits a sport-themed attraction such as the Baseball Hall of Fame in Cooperstown, New York

The purpose of this chapter is to explore the relationship between sport and tourism, examine the three types of sport tourism, and recognize some of the environmental, economic, and sociocultural effects of sport tourism within a framework of sustainable development. The intent is to provide future sport managers with an understanding of the mutually beneficial relationship between sport and tourism and to present some of the issues related to this growing industry.

Tourism and the Tourism Industry

In the first decade of the 21st century, sometimes referred to as "the lost decade" by economists and tourism professionals, the tourism industry experienced some rocky times. Economic uncertainty; the terrorist attacks of September 11, 2001; the bombing of a nightclub in Bali (Indonesia); the SARS outbreak in Asia and Canada; and the swine flu epidemic in 2009 all affected the confidence of the traveling public. Despite the increased risks associated with travel, people have been travelling in even greater numbers. In 2016, the World Tourism Organization (UNWTO) reported that international tourism generated US$1,220 billion and the number of international visitors increased by 4.4 percent compared to the previous year (World Tourism Organization, 2016).

The enormous size of the tourism industry is partly attributed to the range of services and products associated with it, from airlines to rental cars, cruise ships to bus tours, campsites to five-star resorts, and theme parks to national parks. Indeed, Goeldner and Ritchie (2011) proposed that conceptions of tourism must include four components:

1. Tourists
2. Businesses that provide goods and services for tourists
3. The government in a tourist destination
4. The host community or the people who live in the tourist destination

The chapter authors wish to thank Ashley Schroeder, University of Florida, for her contribution to the Social Media and Sport Tourism sidebar.

2006
FIFA World Cup hosted in Germany

2008
Beijing Olympic and Paralympic Summer Games held

2010
First FIFA World Cup hosted on the African continent by South Africa

2012
London Olympic and Paralympic Summer Games held

2013
SportsTravel noted sport-related travel annually generates over 47 million room nights

2014
Sochi Olympic and Paralympic Winter Games held; Brazil hosted FIFA World Cup

2015
England and Wales hosted the Rugby World Cup

Sportcal estimated a sport tourism impact of over US$3 billion from 83 sport events hosted globally in 2015

2016
Olympic and Paralympic Summer Games held in Rio de Janeiro, Brazil

2017
FIS Alpine World Ski Championships held in St. Moritz, Switzerland; 165,000 spectators attended and more than 1,300 volunteers assisted

The tourism industry encompasses a wide range of traveler types including leisure travelers, business travelers, and those visiting friends and relatives. The sport tourist is one of many traveler types. There are three main types of sport tourism (active, event, and nostalgia), each of which is covered in the next sections.

Active Sport Tourism

Active sport tourism is travel to take part in sport. Some of the recent trends that might explain the increased popularity of active sport vacations are increased awareness of health and social benefits of physical activity, the burgeoning popularity of nontraditional sports and participatory sport events, and increased provision and awareness of active sport vacation options. A review of some of the specific types of active sport tourism illustrates the growth in opportunities for the active sport tourist.

Adventure Tourism

Active sport tourism includes activities such as skiing, mountain biking, and hiking, which can also be classified as adventure tourism. The Adventure Travel Trade Association (ATTA) noted that a trip may be classified as an adventure trip if it involves two of the following three elements: "(1) interaction with nature or (2) interaction with culture or (3) a physical activity" (ATTA, The George Washington University, & Vital Wave Consulting, 2011, p. 5). Adventure tourism is gaining in popularity. According to ATTA and colleagues, more than one-fourth of travelers engage in adventure activities while on vacation, and the adventure tourism industry is worth US$89 billion.

Some travelers seek hard adventure, whereas others seek soft adventure. Soft adventure activities include camping, canoeing, and wildlife viewing, and mountain biking, whitewater rafting, and hang

gliding are examples of hard adventure. Schneider and Vogt (2012) suggest that personality type influences the type of adventure tourism a person seeks. Both hard and soft adventurers seek thrill and new experiences, but they differ in the degree of arousal and novelty sought.

Amateur Sport Events

Amateur sport events are included in active tourism and event sport tourism (Kaplanidou & Gibson,

Opening ceremonies of the 2016 Invictus Games in Orlando, Florida.
Courtesy of Richard Shipway.

Sport Marketing

Ketra L. Armstrong
Patrick Walsh
Windy Dees

LEARNING OBJECTIVES

- Obtain a working definition of sport marketing.

- Identify the unique aspects (i.e., challenges and opportunities) of marketing sport.

- Recognize the importance of embracing a structured (strategic and tactical) approach to marketing.

- Understand the process of developing a marketing plan and the 10 steps contained therein.

- Discuss the influence of technology (social and digital media) on sport marketing success.

- Understand the role of research in effective marketing.

- Understand ethics and apply them to sport marketing.

- Engage in critical thinking to address challenges confronted by sport marketers.

KEY TERMS

ambush marketing
branding
external factors
internal factors
marketing mix
marketing plans
marketing research
market segmentation
place
product life cycle
promotions mix
sport marketing
sport sponsorship
SWOT analysis

Sport Consumer Behavior

Andrea N. Geurin
Cara Wright
James J. Zhang

LEARNING OBJECTIVES

- Identify key motives for sport participation, spectatorship, and sport product purchases.

- Define consumer perception and its application for the sport industry.

- Describe the components of consumers' attitudes toward sport.

- Differentiate between consumer involvement and identification.

- Explain ways in which groups can influence the consumption behaviors of individuals.

- Discuss the process of consumer decision making in sport and identify key organizational operations or perspectives that influence the consumer decision making in various sport product categories and service contexts.

- Identify situational factors that can influence the decision-making process.

- Explain how new media offerings and social media opportunities contribute to sport consumers' behavior.

- Define ethical marketing practices, apply ethical reasoning and critical thinking skills, and identify ethical and problematic areas related to sport consumer behavior.

KEY TERMS

aspirational reference group

cognitive dissonance

consumer demand

diversion

eustress

extrinsic rewards

intrinsic rewards

market segment

need recognition

service quality

situational influence

target market

user-generated branding

COURTESY OF PAUL M. PEDERSEN.

Communication in the Sport Industry

G. Clayton Stoldt
Stephen W. Dittmore
Paul M. Pedersen

LEARNING OBJECTIVES

- Describe how communication theory contributes to an understanding of communication in sport.

- Distinguish the key aspects of the field based on the strategic sport communication model (SSCM).

- Explain how communication technology, including the powerful influence of social media, affects the sport industry.

- Describe how media relations and community relations professionals serve their sport organizations.

- Identify ethical issues associated with aspects of and careers in sport communication.

- Explain how critical thinking skills relate to effective sport communication.

KEY TERMS

community relations
effects
over-the-top (OTT) delivery
sport communication
sport ephemeral social media
sport print communication
sport public relations
sport social media
strategic sport communication model (SSCM)

1883
New York World created first newspaper sports department

1895
New York Journal became first newspaper to publish an entire sports section

1939
First televised MLB broadcast on NBC: Cincinnati Reds versus Brooklyn Dodgers

1954
NCAA issued their first public relations manual for intercollegiate athletics

First issue of *Sports Illustrated* published

1957
College Sports Information Directors of America founded

1961
ABC's *Wide World of Sports* debuted

1963
Instant replay first used at Army versus Navy football game

1970
Monday Night Football launched on ABC; *MNF* moved to ESPN in 2006

1979
ESPN launched

1985
First all-sports radio station debuted in Denver

Sport communication is one of the most prominent and exciting aspects of sport management. Sport media personalities such as James Brown, Al Michaels, Rachel Nichols, and Scott Van Pelt are as recognizable as the coaches and athletes they cover. Fans often look with envy at sport public relations professionals who are hard at work in some of the best seats in the house: the press box or press row. Further, technological advancements are allowing sport consumers to interact with the organizations and athletes that they support and with one another in myriad ways. It is little wonder that so many sport management students are highly interested in communication.

In this chapter, you will learn how sport communication is defined and understood using communication theory. You will also be introduced to a model that portrays the various facets of the practical and academic aspects of the field (Pedersen, 2015). You will see why effective interpersonal and organizational communication is critical to success in the field. You will learn about the various forms of sport media and how sport organizations deal with the media and other key publics in their communities. You will see how technological advancements are changing the field, and you will be introduced to some of the key ethical issues confronting communication specialists in sport management.

Communication is such an integral part of our lives that it is easy to overlook how complex and pervasive it really is. In sport settings, communication includes everything from a conversation between an event manager and a volunteer regarding the logistics of hospitality to the release of new information through social media to the presentation of a live event on television. Conceptualizing something so multidimensional is challenging, but Pedersen, Miloch, Laucella, and Fielding (2007) offered a helpful definition. They described **sport communication** as "a process by which people in sport, in a sport setting or through a sport endeavor, share symbols as they create meaning through interaction" (p. 196).

As you will see in the following section, a number of communication theories and concepts influenced the development of this brief definition. Each has important implications for students and practitioners.

Theoretical Framework of Sport Communication

Numerous communication models, from basic to sophisticated, have been developed to help explain how we communicate. An examination of the theory base reveals five key concepts: communication genres, context, process, elements, and effects.

Genres

Communication researchers use a variety of approaches in studying their subject matter. Scholars (e.g., Littlejohn & Foss, 2011) work to synthesize and organize the various approaches. For instance, some of the approaches categorized by Littlejohn and Foss and other scholars over the years have ranged in focus from the individual (e.g., how people learn, why they behave as they do) and the societal (e.g., how social systems function) to the critical (e.g., how inequality is manifested) and the interpretive (e.g., how meaning is discovered). Students who pursue in-depth study in sport communication will become familiar with these theories. Sport-focused publications such as *Communication and Sport* (Billings, Butterworth, & Turman, 2018) can introduce students to sport communication

---

sport communication—A process by which people in sport, in a sport setting or through a sport endeavor, share symbols as they create meaning through interaction.

Timeline

1991
The National (daily sports newspaper) folded

1998
Street & Smith's SportsBusiness Journal launched

2006
Journal of Sports Media launched

2007
iPhone debuted, spurred the rise of numerous mobile sport applications

2008
International Journal of Sport Communication launched

2013
Communication and Sport launched

2016
ESPN subscriber losses exceeded 10 million households over five-year period

2017
Lexi Thompson lost a major championship (ANA Inspiration) when assessed a penalty after a viewer emailed the LPGA about incorrect ball placement by the golfer

Female Athletic Media Relations Executive (FAME) rebranded as WoSIDA (Women Sports Information Directors of America)

The Australian Womensport and Recreation Association (AWRA) rebranded as Women Sport Australia Inc. (WSA)

2018
NBC paid US$963 million for the TV rights to the XXIII Olympic Winter Games

Formula One (F1) returned to ESPN with a new U.S. television rights deal for the broadcast of F1 events and programming on ABC, ESPN, and ESPN2

---

theories and concepts. The key point for now is that no single approach to studying communication can adequately address the subject. By recognizing the varied approaches to communication, students can position themselves for better understanding.

Context

Just as there are multiple approaches to studying communication, there are many contexts in which communication occurs. Common contexts for communication include interpersonal, group, organizational, and mass mediated. Interpersonal communication occurs between two people (e.g., ticket taker greets a fan). Group communication takes place among three or more people (e.g., focus group interview). Some communication scholars differentiate between small groups and large groups because the dynamics vary based on the number of people involved. Organizational communication occurs both internally (e.g., meetings, memos) and externally (e.g., news releases, website). Mass-mediated communication takes place when information is shared with large audiences through print, electronic, or new media channels. Each context is relevant in sport management, and prospective sport managers should build knowledge and develop competencies in each.

Process

Sport communication is a process. This process involves multiple participants, the sharing of symbols in some form or another, and resultant interactions that are meaningful for those involved. In many exchanges, the related dynamics are multiple and varied. For example, a sport organization tweets information about a roster change to its large group of followers. Some will see the tweet, whereas others will not. Some will understand the full context of the roster announcement. Others may ignore the message altogether. Some will react by liking the tweet; others may retweet with additional commentary, thus extending the message's reach to others.

The process becomes particularly complex in mass communication settings. Although mass media commonly provide timely and accurate information, mistakes sometimes occur. In some instances, legitimate media outlets make errors such as when an inaccurate newspaper story was published about the New England Patriots filming their opponents' practice before Super Bowl XXXVI. In other situations, misinformation may be deliberately spread, such as when an impostor news site falsely reported the death of former pro basketball player Lamar Odom; the story was then widely shared on social media. As evident, the communication process often involves high stakes. A necessary step in understanding the process is to examine the different elements involved and effects that may occur.

Elements

The value of communication models is that they help us understand that process. Most people do so by identifying the elements involved in the process. The following are the most basic components as portrayed in a model developed by Lasswell (1948):

- Sender
- Message
- Channel through which the message is delivered
- Receiver

Using this model, the communication source could be a speaker at a community relations event, the author of a new company policy, or the writer

foundation on which the updated **strategic sport communication model (SSCM)** (Pedersen, Laucella, Kian, & Geurin, 2017) is built.

Strategic Sport Communication Model

The SSCM provides a framework that shows how the dynamics of communication and the various settings for communication come together in sport. The model, depicted in figure 14.1, has four primary elements. One element is the sport communication process, which is displayed twice to emphasize that the process, elements, and effects described in the previous section pervade all the settings within the field. The other key elements are the personal and organizational communication in sport component, the mediated communication in sport component, and the sport communication services and support

component. Note that these key elements (i.e., components in the model) are related and often overlap (Pedersen, 2013, 2015). The arrows pointing to and from component I denote that the types and forms of communication in the central component influence the forms of communication in components II and III, and vice versa.

Personal and Organizational Communication in Sport

Component I in the SSCM includes the various forms of personal communication and organizational communication in sport. Each is considered in the following paragraphs.

Personal Sport Communication

Personal communication includes intrapersonal, interpersonal, and small-group communication. The prefix *intra* means "within," so intrapersonal com-

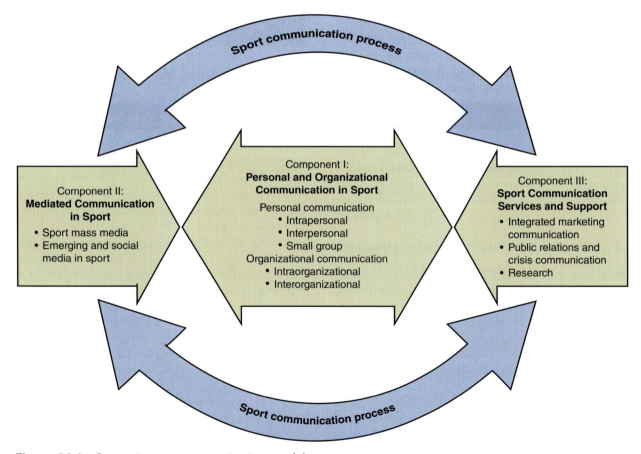

Figure 14.1   Strategic sport communication model.

Reprinted, by permission, from P.M. Pedersen, P.C. Laucella, E.T.M. Kian, and A.N. Geurin, 2017, *Strategic sport communication* (2nd ed.) (Champaign, IL: Human Kinetics), 95.

---

strategic sport communication model (SSCM)—Depicts the dynamics of communication and the various settings in which communication occurs in sport.

munication is a person's internal communication. The prefix *inter* means "between," so interpersonal communication is the exchange of messages between two people. Intrapersonal communication is so prevalent that it is arguably the most common type of communication. By definition it is private, but many people choose to share their thoughts via social media (e.g., Snapchat, Twitter) and other Internet sites (e.g., personal blogs). Although intrapersonal communication in sport is generally kept private, an exception is mediated intrapersonal communication, which is "internal communication revealed through some form of media—for example, a sport industry executive typing out a Facebook post that reveals her or his thoughts. Instances of mediated intrapersonal communication abound and are often revealed on social media platforms" (Pedersen et al., 2017, p. 96).

Interpersonal communication typically occurs between a couple of individuals in a close setting and may be verbal, nonverbal (e.g., facial cues), unmediated (e.g., exchanging information through notes, face-to-face interactions), or mediated (e.g., engaging in telephone conversations, email or social media correspondence, text messages). Thus, this form of communication "incorporates the varied social media that are now an essential part of our communication lives" (DeVito, 2017, p. xv). Mediated interpersonal communication in sport often involves social media interactions (e.g., communicating back-and-forth on a social media platform) and parasocial interactions. According to Abeza and colleagues (2014), parasocial interaction is "how media users develop a sense of relationships with media personae. As viewers continue to view media personalities, they develop bonds of intimacy, which resemble interpersonal social interaction but differ as is mediated" (p. 304).

Small-group communication occurs in settings of three or more people. Although more people are involved, the means for small-group communication are identical to those for interpersonal communication. Small-group communication is also like interpersonal communication in that the communication has a shared purpose and the people involved influence one another in the process. It is more complex, of course, because more people are involved. The varying degrees to which people in the group engage in communication and the differing ways they respond can make group communication extremely complex.

The following example incorporates each of the three types of personal sport communication. A university athletic director believes her department should deepen its understanding of its fan base. She engages in an internal dialogue (i.e., intrapersonal communication) regarding the various approaches the department may take to address the issue. After she identifies a few ideas, she shares them with the department's marketing director through an email message (i.e., interpersonal communication). The director replies that he will share the ideas with his staff members at their next meeting and will follow up with feedback after the meeting ends. The staff meeting (i.e., group communication) provides a forum for a discussion of the relative merits of the ideas. As a result, the best idea—a mixed methods fan research plan involving focus groups and surveys—is prioritized for development. The marketing director then shares the staff's plan with the athletic director for final approval.

Organizational Sport Communication

The three types of personal communication (i.e., intrapersonal, interpersonal, and small group) may occur in either an intraorganizational or an interorganizational setting. Intraorganizational communication occurs within a sport organization setting, and interorganizational communication occurs when members of a sport organization interact with those outside the organization. As with personal communication, the intra- or interorganizational communication in sport may be unmediated or mediated. For example, as noted by Pedersen and colleagues (2017), "*mediated* interorganizational sport communication involves activities such as a sport organization (e.g., team) using email or social media to communicate with another entity (e.g., sponsorship group)" (p. 98).

The example in the previous section was of intraorganizational communication in its various forms. To carry that example to its next step, the marketing department plans three focus group discussions involving different groups of fans. As the organizational representative leading the groups asks fans how they evaluate their experiences attending games and what they think of some possible initiatives to improve the fan experience, they are engaging in interorganizational communication. That is, they are communicating with people outside their organization.

Communication Skills

The most basic personal and organizational communication skills that you need to develop are your writing and speaking abilities. To write effectively, you must be able to track down information, organize it, and record it in a way that interests and informs readers. Sentences must be grammatically correct, wording must be succinct, and ideas must flow from one point to another. Speaking effectively also entails

Olympians David Wise and Alex Ferreira answer questions from the media in South Korea after winning gold and silver medals, respectively, in the freestyle skiing halfpipe at the 2018 Olympic Winter Games. In addition to interacting with the media, the freestyle skiers can interact with various stakeholders (e.g., fans, sponsors) through social media, such as their individual @mrDavidWise and @Alex_Ferreira3 Twitter accounts.

Courtesy of Paul M. Pedersen.

For example, the code stipulates that media relations personnel avoid public criticism of their colleagues and support their coaches and student-athletes when they refrain from commenting on a question posed by the media. Both tenets align with Kant's principle.

Another ethics-related issue relevant to media relations has to do with social media and student-athletes. Some coaches ban their student-athletes from using social media, especially Twitter, so they do not have to worry about inappropriate comments becoming public. But is such a ban an unethical violation of individual freedom? Athletes often make headlines with inappropriate tweets, but it is difficult to reconcile social media bans with the notion of building leaders, which is a commonly cited goal of athletic participation. Many institutions that do not ban athletes from using social media now monitor social media communications.

Ethical Issues in Community Relations

Community relations professionals also confront ethical issues. The notion of stewardship is particularly relevant when it comes to raising funds for charitable partners. An ESPN *Outside the Lines* investigation of 115 athlete charities found that 74 percent failed to meet commonly accepted standards for nonprofit organizations (Lavigne, 2013). In some instances, charitable foundations established by athletes failed to make any donations to the causes they purportedly supported despite generating revenue through fundraising events. The ethical, not to mention legal, dimensions of being a good steward when soliciting support for charitable ventures is one that is relevant to individual athletes and larger organizations, particularly in a field as high profile as sport.

For chapter-specific learning activities, visit the web study guide at **www.HumanKinetics.com/ContemporarySportManagement**.

Summary

Communication is a core skill required of all sport managers, and it presents an exciting array of career options for prospective professionals. As noted earlier in the chapter, sport communication is defined as a process in which people share symbols in and through sport endeavors and settings and create meaning through their interactions. The strategic sport communication model depicts both the dynamic sport communication process and the various settings in which sport communication occurs. The components of the SSCM include personal and organizational communication, sport media, and sport communication services and support.

Personal communication may occur on an intrapersonal, interpersonal, or small-group basis. It includes both intraorganizational communication (i.e., within the organization) and interorganizational communication (i.e., between organizational representatives and external constituents).

The many forms of sport media range from print to electronic to new media. The print media include sports sections in newspapers and sports magazines and books. The electronic media encompass sport on television, on radio, and in the movies. New media include sport on the Internet and as communicated through other relatively recent technological innovations. The Internet is particularly powerful because it provides opportunities to reach constituents directly, instantaneously, and interactively.

Social media are a particularly powerful form of engagement.

Sport communication services and support include advertising and public relations. The latter topic received considerable attention in this chapter. Sport media relations professionals disseminate information to the public through the mass media or through organizational websites. They also manage additional media requests, service the media during games or events, and manage records and statistics. Sport community relations professionals generate goodwill for their organizations. They coordinate organizational participation in charitable endeavors, fundraisers that benefit various nonprofits, and public appearances by managers and players. By carefully executing these activities, they enhance their communities and the reputations of their organizations within their communities.

A variety of ethical issues are associated with sport communication. These range from protecting people's privacy to allowing for give and take in communication with key publics. Strong critical thinking skills are also important for sport communicators because they face a rapidly evolving communication environment. New technologies, accompanied by more frequent demand for bottom-line results from communication programs, mean that future professionals will be required to process significant amounts of information, apply appropriate value judgments, and define prudent actions.

Review Questions

1. Why is communication a critical concern to all sport managers whether they are communication specialists or not?

2. What are the primary components of the SSCM? What kinds of career opportunities does the model encompass?

3. What linkages exist between the array of sport media you commonly use and those represented within the SSCM?

4. What skills and experiences are most important to sport communication professionals?

5. How have social media changed the way people relate to sport? What are the ramifications of these changes for sport communicators?

6. Describe the work of sport media relations professionals. What sorts of tasks are included in their job descriptions?

7. How would you describe some of the tasks performed by sport community relations professionals? How is the work of the Detroit Lions (discussed in this chapter) indicative of evolution in the field?

8. What are some of the common ethical issues facing sport public relations professionals?

9. What are some of the nontraditional forms of communication now being used by sport managers?

Finance and Economics in the Sport Industry

Timothy D. DeSchriver
Marion E. Hambrick
Daniel F. Mahony

LEARNING OBJECTIVES

- Explain the basic principles of economics and relate the theories of economics to the sport industry.

- Discuss the concept of economic impact analysis and its relationship to sport events and facilities.

- Describe the business structures of sport organizations.

- Identify the basic principles and tools of financial management and apply them to the sport industry.

- Recognize the basic elements of balance sheets and income statements for sport organizations.

- Identify the various professional and career opportunities in the sport industry that are related to economics and financial management.

- Understand the influence of social media and the importance of ethics and critical thinking skills in the areas of sport finance and economics.

KEY TERMS

demand	market shortage
economic interaction	market surplus
law of demand	scarcity
law of supply	sport economic impact studies
market equilibrium	supply

1966
Naming rights granted for Busch Memorial Stadium in St. Louis

1967
30-second Super Bowl ad cost US$42,500 on CBS and US$37,500 on NBC (the only time the game was broadcast on two networks); in 2017, the cost of some spots was more than US$5 million

1971
NFL New England Patriots Stadium became Schaefer Field in US$150,000 deal with Schaefer Brewing Company

1973
Buffalo Bills Stadium became Rich Stadium in US$1.5 million deal with Rich Foods

1985
The Olympic Partner Programme created

1990s
Approximately 170 new professional sport teams and 13 new leagues formed during decade of U.S. economic expansion

2002
YES Network, a joint venture between MLB's New York Yankees and the NBA's New Jersey Nets, established

2004
NHL lockout resulted in cancellation of 2004-05 season when CBA expired; NHL and NHL Players Association ratified a new CBA with a salary cap

2009
Real Madrid paid Manchester United a record US$131 million transfer fee for Cristiano Ronaldo

2010
Meadowlands Stadium built for US$1.6 billion; was the most expensive stadium built, surpassing the record set previously by the US$1.5 billion Yankee Stadium

Sport is one of the most diverse industries in the business world. It is composed of subindustries such as professional sports, collegiate athletics, event and facility management, health and fitness, youth sports, and sporting goods. This diversity increases the difficulty of measuring the overall economic size of the industry. For example, should the sale of outdoor equipment be considered sport spending? Should the money that Capital One spends to be an official sponsor of a college football bowl game be considered sport spending?

One unfortunate result of the lack of an exact definition of the sport industry is that research results on the size of the sport industry fluctuate greatly. Although no empirical measurement of the overall size of the sport industry has been completed for two decades, there have been several wide-ranging estimations. For example, the size of the global sport industry has been estimated at US$151 billion by PricewaterhouseCoopers (Cave, 2015), US$700 billion by A.T. Kearney (2014), and US$1.5 trillion by Plunkett Research (n.d.). From the large differences in these estimates, it is apparent that these groups used much different definitions for what is considered sport.

Although the U.S. Census Bureau does not estimate the overall size of the sport industry, historically it did provide some financial information on the size of specific sectors within the sport industry through the online publication of its Economic Snapshot (see table 15.1). For example, in 2014, approximately US$2.53 billion was spent at skiing facilities such as Winter Park Resort in Colorado and Camelback Ski Area in Pennsylvania. The most recent numbers also revealed that the skiing industry employed more than 75,000 full-time workers (U.S. Census Bureau, 2016). The SFIA reported that Americans spent more than US$84.3 billion on the purchase of sporting goods and equipment in 2014 (SFIA, 2015). Although the actual dollar amount that can be attributed to the sport industry might be debatable, available estimates make it clear that sport contributes a great deal to the U.S. and global economies.

Table 15.1   Economic Activity of Selected Sport Industry Sectors

Sport industry subsector	2014 sales level (US$)	2014 full-time employees
Skiing facilities	$2.53 billion	75,036
Golf courses and country clubs	$21.22 billion	293,862
Fitness and recreational sport facilities	$26.67 billion	637,182
Professional sport teams and clubs	$26.30 billion	68,884
Racetracks (horse and dog)	$7.24 billion	45,125
Agents and managers for artists, athletes, and public figures	$6.67 billion	20,089

Adapted from U.S. Census Bureau 2016.

2011
NBA experienced its fourth-ever lockout as owners and players debated issues surrounding revenue sharing and salary caps

2012
London spent £8.9 billion on the Olympics games; nearly £3.0 billion was for operational expenses

2013
Destination Marketing Association International released a sports module for its event-impact calculator

2014
Premier League's Wayne Rooney signed a contract extension with Manchester United for £85 million through 2019

2015
Boxing match between Floyd Mayweather and Manny Pacquiao generated more than US$400 million in pay-per-view revenue

2016
IPL brand valuation increased for ninth straight year, estimated at US$4.16 billion

2017
NFL salary cap established at US$167 million for the 2017 season

Total player salaries for the 2017 season ranged from the Dodgers (US$244 million) to the Brewers (US$68 million) with the World Series champions, the Astros, at US$133 million

2018
Final year of Carlos Tevez's record-setting US$41 million annual contract with Shanghai Shenhua of the Chinese Super League

Fox and the NFL agree to a five-year, US$3-billion deal for *Thursday Night Football*

Recognition of the growth and possible contraction of the sport industry leads to a discussion of economic and financial concepts. This chapter presents basic principles of economics and financial management, addresses the relationship between these economic and financial principles and the sport industry, and discusses career opportunities related to the financial management of the sport industry.

Current Financial Situation of U.S. Professional Sport

One segment of the sport industry that has seen tremendous growth over the past decade is professional sport. For example, in 2015, the NFL had operating revenues of approximately US$12.2 billion, and the league's teams produced an average operating income of more than US$26 million (Ozanian, 2016a). Throughout the last decade, major professional men's sport leagues have seen their revenues increase more than 10 percent annually. Despite this growth in revenue, economic challenges remain.

For example, MLB has seen a widening gap between the high- and low-revenue teams. In 2016, *Forbes* magazine estimated the New York Yankees generated more than US$516 million, making the club the highest revenue team in MLB. In the same year, the Tampa Bay Rays ranked last in revenue with only US$193 million ("The Business," 2016). This imbalance is an economic concern because all MLB teams, regardless of revenue, compete for the same players. The current revenue disparity makes it difficult for teams that have older stadiums or are in small markets, such as the Tampa Bay Rays and Pittsburgh Pirates, to acquire the best players and be competitive on the field. In the long run, this dispar-

ity may lead to a decrease in overall fan interest in MLB, particularly for fans of teams that consistently perform poorly.

To deal with this problem, most professional leagues attempt to equalize the differences in team revenues through revenue sharing. For example, the four major professional men's leagues in North America (i.e., NBA, MLB, NFL, and NHL) share revenues from national television rights fees and merchandise sales. Therefore, although an NFL team such as the New York Giants might be more popular than the Cincinnati Bengals, both receive the same amount of money from the NFL's US$7.1 billion annual television deals, which are the league's largest source of revenue (Novy-Williams, 2016). Revenue sharing equalizes team revenues and allows teams in smaller markets (e.g., the Green Bay Packers) to compete financially with big-market teams. This equalization is important for professional sport leagues because professional teams within a single league must simultaneously compete and cooperate with each other. Although teams attempt to beat each other on the field, team managers must cooperate to ensure financial success for all. If some teams struggle financially, the entire league could decline.

As you might have already noticed, professional men's sport leagues rely heavily on the media. For example, teams in the NFL generate more money from their national and local media deals than they do from gate receipts. Table 15.2 shows the amount of money some professional leagues and college events generate from media rights. Although most major professional men's sport leagues have seen media and other revenue sources grow substantially over the past decade, this increase has not guaranteed overall profitability. Both revenues and costs determine the profits of a business; the following

Table 15.2   Select U.S. Sports Television Rights Deals

Property	Networks	Annual average (US$)	Length
NFL	CBS, Fox, ESPN, NBC	$5.18 billion	2013-2022
NBA	ABC, ESPN, TNT	$2.66 billion	2016-2025
MLB	Fox, TBS, ESPN	$1.55 billion	2014-2021
NHL	NBC	$187.5 million	2011-2021
NASCAR	Fox, NBC	$820 million	2015-2024
NCAA Basketball Tournament	CBS	$770 million	2011-2024
College Football Playoff	ESPN	$470 million	2015-2026

equation can be used to calculate the profit level for a sport organization:

$$profit = total\ revenues - total\ costs$$

Although MLB has seen tremendous growth in revenue over the past decade, owners still claim to be losing money. They base this claim on cost increases in areas such as team payroll, travel expenses, and coaching and staff salaries. Although many have questioned the accuracy of statements by league and team officials regarding the number of franchises experiencing revenue loss, some teams in major professional sport leagues are clearly not profitable because revenue growth has not kept up with the large increases in team operating costs. Specifically, team owners have been unable to control their spending on players. The average player salary in MLB was US$4.51 million for the 2017 season, which is an increase of 1.6 percent from 2016 (Associated Press, 2017). In comparison, the average player salary just 10 years earlier was US$2.94 million (CBS Sports, n.d.). Thirty-six MLB players had contracts that paid at least US$20 million for the 2017 season; some of the noteworthy salaries belonged to Clayton Kershaw (US$33 million), Zack Greinke (US$32 million), and David Price (US$30 million) (Associated Press, 2017).

In the NHL, team owners have faced difficulty in controlling player salaries. This problem led to substantial losses for teams that had not been able to increase their revenues. The situation became a crisis in the fall of 2012. In an attempt to change the economic system in the league, the owners agreed to lock out the players before the start of the 2012-13 season. The club owners and the players' union (National Hockey League Players Association [NHLPA]) were unable to agree on a new economic

Economic Cycles and the Sport Industry

All economies experience cyclical changes. For example, the world economy fell into a recession in early 2008. This recession brought higher unemployment rates and lower sales of consumer goods such as automobiles and computers. Historically, most sport economists believed that the sport industry was recession proof because sales of sport-related products have not fallen during past recessions. This steady demand is most likely due to the need for people, even in bad economic times, to engage in leisure and recreational activities. Also, sport has been considered a relatively inexpensive and affordable type of leisure. However, several sport organizations faced financial distress in the 2008-09 global recession. For example, the Arena Football League (AFL) discontinued operations for the 2009 season in part due to financial difficulties as a result of the recession. If the sport industry is no longer recession proof, the reasons most often cited are the increases in ticket prices and sport teams' increasing reliance on revenues from corporate sponsorship, advertising, and luxury suite sales. Although some sectors of the sport industry were affected in the short term by the 2008 recession, it appears that they have recovered and are prospering once again.

Single-Entity Structure

As discussed throughout this book, the sport industry is unique in a variety of areas. One example is the use of the single-entity structure in professional sport. Although professional sport teams are all members of a particular league and often share certain revenue sources (e.g., television revenue) and expenses (e.g., league marketing), each team is generally operated as a separate business. But some sport leagues (e.g., MLS) have chosen to operate as a single-entity structure. The advantage of using the single-entity structure is that the league members can work together more efficiently and make decisions that focus more on what is good for the league than what is good for an individual team. In addition, the league can set limits for player salaries in a way that would be illegal if the league were not using the single-entity structure. The long-term success of the single-entity structure is still unknown, but it has become popular for certain sport leagues.

system until January 2013. More than two months of games were lost. After finally agreeing on a new CBA, a shortened 48-game schedule was played in 2013. The NHL has since rebounded from this lockout. The league experienced increased profitability in the 2015-16 season with an average operating income of US$15 million (similar to the previous season). This newfound stability resulted from the 2013 CBA, a 12-year CDN$5.23 billion media contract with Rogers Communications, and a US$600 million partnership with Major League Baseball Advanced Media (Ozanian, 2016b).

NFL and NBA owners have negotiated agreements with players through the collective bargaining process, which helps control salaries through the imposition of team and individual player salary caps. For example, the NBA has an individual player salary cap that limits the maximum amount an individual player may earn. Exceptions to this include the work stoppage in the NBA and the lockout in the NFL, both of which occurred at the beginning of this decade. For the NFL and NBA, the amount of money that owners spend on players' salaries is based on the revenues that the teams produce. Therefore, player salaries will increase only if teams are generating additional revenue. This arrangement reduces the likelihood that NBA and NFL owners will become as financially stressed as some professional sport leagues and teams. Team profitability is also more consistent in the NBA and NFL.

Current Financial Situation of U.S. College Athletics

Rising costs are also an important issue in collegiate athletics. Most collegiate athletic programs, even at the NCAA Division I level, do not produce enough revenue to cover their costs. A study of the finances in collegiate athletics found that only 24 Division I FBS athletic departments had revenues that exceeded costs; in many cases, this profit occurred only because the university provided institutional resources to the athletic department. Furthermore, the percentage of schools at which costs exceed revenues is even greater at the FCS and Division II and III levels (Burnsed, 2015).

Many athletic departments face a difficult financial future as costs increase in areas such as team travel, recruiting, equipment, coaches' salaries, and grants-in-aid. Some colleges and universities have also seen their costs increase as they increase opportunities for women. In response to the financial pressure from rising costs in all areas of collegiate athletics spending, some athletic departments have eliminated sport teams and reduced scholarships. For example, in 2016, the University of Tulsa eliminated men's golf (Ringler, 2016) and St. Cloud State University eliminated tennis, women's skiing, men's cross country, and men's track and field (Walsh, 2016). The University of North Dakota cut baseball and considered the elimination of soccer, softball, swimming and diving, and tennis (Wade Rupard Forum News Service, 2016).

Rising costs have also placed additional emphasis on the need to increase revenue. Athletic administrators have turned to private donations, corporate sponsorships, television, and merchandising for additional revenue. At the Division I level, athletic administrators have used television rights fees and ticket sales to help their financial situations. Within the past decade, schools such as Texas A&M University and the University of Oklahoma have expanded their football stadiums. In 2016, The Ohio State University (OSU) and the University of Tennessee at Knoxville announced stadium expansion plans to increase ticket sales revenue and meet spectator demand. OSU generates US$6.5 million in ticket revenue from one home game at its 108,000-seat stadium and an additional US$650,000 in concessions and parking revenue (Savitz, 2014). However, not all institutions can find additional revenue sources so easily. Many athletic departments rely on student fees and other forms of institutional support to avoid large budget deficits. Even Division I institutions apply this remedy, and it has become increasingly common at lower-division levels in the NCAA and at National Association of Intercollegiate Athletics (NAIA) schools where other revenue sources are limited.

The largest single source of revenue in collegiate athletics is the annual men's basketball championship. In 2016, the NCAA signed an eight-year US$8.8 billion contract extension with CBS Sports and Turner to televise three weeks of men's basketball in March. This represents more than 90 percent of the revenue generated by the NCAA. The amount marks an increase from the average US$770 million agreed to in 2011 and gives CBS Sports and Turner media rights through 2032 (NCAA, 2016). Division I universities have been pleased with this relationship because more than 75 percent of this money is distributed to them from the NCAA. This additional revenue has aided big-time college athletic departments as they attempt to pay for their growing expenses, but most programs will likely continue to experience annual deficits.

Another change affecting collegiate athletics is the formation of the Power Five conferences (the ACC, Big Ten Conference, Big 12 Conference, Pac-12 Conference, and SEC). As noted by Bennett (2014), the conferences have received permission from the NCAA Division I board of directors to make more autonomous decisions regarding player benefits such as stipends and insurance as well as rules regarding staffing, recruiting, and training. This decision helped circumvent a threat by the five conferences to leave the NCAA and form a separate governing body. While some lauded the change, teams from the remaining conferences and other critics believed the new alignment could increase the existing gaps in revenues and athletic performances between Power Five teams and the 75 programs outside of these five conferences.

Economics of Sport

The word *economics* intimidates many people. For some, it brings back memories of studying how intangible items (e.g., widgets) are produced and sold. But this example is far from the whole story.

Economics is one of the few academic disciplines that can be applied to almost any human action. Within the field of sport management, economics can help us understand issues such as the price consumers pay for a pair of shoes in a sporting goods store, the escalating salaries of NBA players, and the decision made by a student-athlete to leave college early and play professionally.

Definition of Economics

The economics of sport can be defined as the study of how people within the sport industry deal with scarcity. This statement leads to the obvious question, What is scarcity? Scarcity is present in the world today because resources are insufficient to meet the wants and needs of society. For example, a fitness center might want 100 machines available to its members. Unfortunately, because of the scarce resources available to center management, the club might only be able to provide 75 machines. Economics helps determine how the fitness center management will decide to distribute its scarce resources not only for machines but also for staff salaries, rent, utilities, and office supplies.

Scarcity is an important issue in sport management because all managers encounter it. Managers have a maximum quantity of resources available for their use. Even the ultra-rich Los Angeles Dodgers in MLB have a limited amount of resources that they are willing to devote to players' salaries. The most successful managers are those who make the best use of limited resources. Although the fact that the Dodgers have the most resources gives them a greater probability of winning the World Series, it does not guarantee a championship. Indeed, the team has not won the World Series since 1988. Their management must make wise decisions about how to allocate resources to be successful.

The limited resources available to managers are used to produce goods and services that are then sold to consumers. Goods are tangible products (e.g., football cleats, tennis balls, bicycles), and services are intangible products (e.g., marketing advice, business consulting, financial planning). Goods and services are exchanged through the economic interaction of individuals and organizations. For example, the purchase of a new set of golf clubs at a store is an economic interaction. One product of value, golf clubs, is exchanged for another product of value, cash. Note that not all economic interactions involve cash. For example, a business might provide free equipment (e.g., computers, tables) or services (e.g., shuttle

---

scarcity—The basic economic problem facing all institutions, including sport. A sport product is considered scarce if people want more of the product than is freely available for consumption.

economic interaction—The exchange of one product of value for another product of value.

support, medical personnel) to an event organizer in exchange for advertising space on the event T-shirt.

Transactions such as those just described occur in markets, which can be defined as arrangements by which economic exchanges among people or business occur. A market could be an actual physical location such as a hockey arena or a sports memorabilia store. It could also be an intangible idea such as an online secondary ticket market or the market for players in the WNBA. For teams such as the Indiana Fever and the Connecticut Sun, a market exists in which players are bought and sold, but it does not have an actual physical location. These markets are the core of economic activity. Without markets, the exchange of goods and services could not occur.

Economics has been traditionally separated into two areas of study: macroeconomics and microeconomics. For the sport manager, the principles of microeconomics have the most effect on the day-to-day operations of the organization. Therefore, the following section will examine that area of study within economics.

Microeconomics and the Sport Industry

Microeconomics is the study of the behavior of individual businesses and households (Keat, Young, & Erfle, 2014). It uses economic theories to explain specific industries such as sport and recreation, agriculture, and telecommunications. Scholars within the field of microeconomics study variables such as price, revenue, costs, and profits for individual industries and organizations. For example, microeconomics helps to explain why you might walk into two sporting goods stores and see different prices for the same tennis racket model.

Supply–Demand Model

Microeconomists often use models to explain the behavior of producers and consumers. These models are simplified descriptions of how markets operate. A market comprises two fundamental aspects: demand and supply. The supply–demand model is the most widely used and most powerful model in economics. As you will see, an accurate supply–demand model can provide information on the amount of a product or service that consumers are willing to buy at various prices, the amount that suppliers are willing to produce at various prices, and the final price that consumers will pay.

We will begin by discussing demand. **Demand** is the relationship between the price of a product and the amount of the product that consumers are willing to buy. The amount that consumers are willing to buy at various prices is the quantity demanded. In general, consumers will demand less of a product as its price increases, and they will demand more of a product as its price falls. This relationship is known as the **law of demand**. Demand can be shown through a table or a graph. Let's use the example of a hypothetical market for bicycles. Table 15.3 shows the quantity of bicycles demanded by consumers at different price levels. Figure 15.1 illustrates the same relationship graphically. As you can see, the demand curve slopes downward, and this will always be the case because of the law of demand.

The other side of the supply–demand model is supply. **Supply** is the relationship between the price of a product and the amount of the product that suppliers are willing to produce and sell. The amount that suppliers are willing to produce and sell at various prices is the quantity supplied. Overall, suppliers will increase production as the price of the product

Table 15.3 Demand Schedule for Bicycles

Price	Quantity demanded
$1,600	4,000
$1,400	6,000
$1,200	8,000
$1,000	10,000
$800	12,000
$600	14,000
$400	16,000

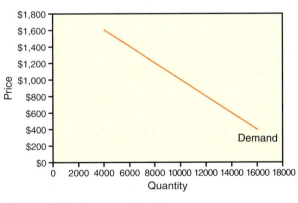

Figure 15.1 Demand for bicycles.

---

demand—The relationship between the price of a product and the amount of the product that consumers are willing to buy.

law of demand—Consumers will demand less of a product as its price increases and more of a product as its price falls.

supply—The relationship between the price of a product and the amount of the product suppliers are willing to produce and sell.

increases and decrease production as the price falls. This relationship is referred to as the **law of supply**. Like demand, supply can be represented in both tabular and graphic forms. Let's continue with the bicycle example. Table 15.4 shows the number of bicycles supplied by businesses in the market at various prices, and figure 15.2 presents the information in graphic form. Note that the supply curve will generally have this upward-sloping shape. Again, this relationship occurs because suppliers will increase production as the price that they can charge for their product increases.

The last phase of the supply–demand model is to determine **market equilibrium**. By analyzing tables 15.3 and 15.4, you can determine that at a price of $1,000, consumers are willing to buy 10,000 bicycles and suppliers are willing to produce and sell 10,000 bicycles. Thus, this point would be the market equilibrium. Graphically, the intersection of the supply and demand curves represents market equilibrium. As shown in figure 15.3, when the supply and demand

Table 15.4 Supply Schedule for Bicycles

Price	Quantity supplied
$1,600	16,000
$1,400	14,000
$1,200	12,000
$1,000	10,000
$800	8,000
$600	6,000
$400	4,000

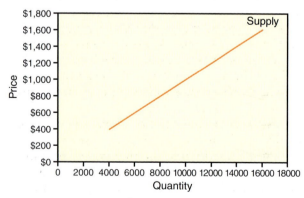

Figure 15.2 Supply for bicycles.

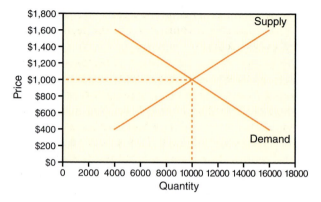

Figure 15.3 Market equilibrium for bicycles.

curves intersect, the equilibrium price is $1,000 and the quantity is 10,000 bicycles.

You might wonder what would happen if the price of bicycles was $600. Notice that at a price of $1,400, consumers are willing to buy 6,000 bicycles and suppliers are willing to sell 14,000 bicycles. Under these circumstances, the market is not in equilibrium. We would refer to this situation as a **market surplus** because producers are willing to sell more bicycles than consumers are willing to buy. Conversely, a **market shortage** occurs when consumers are willing to buy more bicycles than suppliers are willing to produce and sell. This condition would occur if the price was $600.

As you can see, the supply–demand model is a powerful tool in microeconomics. The model helps us determine the quantity of a product demanded and supplied at various prices and the equilibrium price and quantity. In addition, it can show whether the market is in a state of surplus or shortage.

Economic Impact of Sport Events and Facilities

With the growth of the sport industry, major sport events seem to take place every week. Although these events bring enjoyment to a community, they can also bring a substantial amount of economic activity. Community leaders believe that events such as the Olympic Games and Paralympic Games, the Super Bowl, and the NCAA Final Four will stimulate their local economies because of increased spending by out-of-town visitors. This spending will, in turn, increase local tax revenues and produce jobs (Howard & Crompton, 2004). Although major events such as those mentioned might produce a significant amount

---

law of supply—Suppliers will increase production as the price of the product increases and decrease production as the price falls.
market equilibrium—The price at which the quantity demanded equals the quantity supplied.
market surplus—A price at which the supplied quantity of a product is greater than the demanded quantity.
market shortage—A price at which the demanded quantity of a product is greater than the supplied quantity.

of money for a local economy, smaller events such as road races, soccer tournaments, and festivals can also increase economic activity.

Sport economic impact studies are estimates of the change in the net economic activity in a community that occurs because of the spending attributed to a specific sport event or facility (Turco & Kelsey, 1992). These studies are helpful in measuring the increase in revenues, tax dollars, and jobs attributable to a sport event or facility. For example, the Phoenix, Arizona, area hosted the 2015 NFL Super Bowl. A study conducted by the W.P. Carey School of Business at Arizona State University estimated the overall economic impact of the Super Bowl to be US$720 million (Corbett, 2015).

Researchers conduct economic impact studies by collecting information on the spending patterns of visitors to a sport event or facility. A researcher might distribute survey instruments to event spectators in person or online to determine how much they spent on items such as hotels, rental cars, food, game tickets, and merchandise. These data are then used to determine the overall new economic activity. Most often, researchers use computer software packages such as RIMS II (Regional Input–Output Modeling System) and IMPLAN (Impact Analysis for Planning) to calculate the final economic impact.

Experts disagree about the potential of sport events and facilities to generate economic activity. A study completed by the Maryland Department of Fiscal Services concluded that M&T Bank Stadium, home of the NFL's Baltimore Ravens, generates only about US$33 million per year in economic benefits for the state of Maryland. In addition, the stadium produced only 534 additional full-time jobs for the state. In comparison with other projects in the state, the new job creation was small. For example, Maryland's Sunny Day Fund for economic development cost taxpayers US$32.5 million and produced 5,200 full-time jobs (Zimmerman, 1997). Proponents of the public financing of sport facilities argue that the facilities and teams generate intrinsic benefits for a community that cannot be measured in monetary terms. Unlike the Ravens, the Sunny Day Fund cannot produce a Super Bowl–winning team.

As you can see, economic impact analysis is an important topic in the economics of sport. Economic impact studies have received a significant amount of media attention because civic leaders and team owners have used them to justify public funding for new sport facilities. Any economic impact study is only as good as the methods used to generate its results. Educated readers should always ask two questions when reading the results of an economic impact study:

1. Who conducted the research?
2. How was the research conducted?

Unfortunately, economic impact studies can be manipulated to generate a variety of results. A proponent of a new facility or event might greatly overestimate the economic impact, but a critic of the same facility might underestimate the economic impact. For example, a spokesperson for the NFL stated that economic impact studies for Super Bowl 50 in Santa Clara, California, ranged from US$800 million to "a couple hundred million dollars" (McInerney, 2016). For Super Bowl XLIII, a study done by PricewaterhouseCoopers estimated the direct spending impact of that event in Tampa to be about US$150 million ("Study," 2009). This finding is in stark contrast to a study completed by economist Philip Porter on the economic impact of the last Super Bowl hosted by Tampa in 2001. At that time, Porter estimated the impact of the Super Bowl to be around zero (Porter, 2001). The two sides might be using the same statistical information, but they are analyzing it in very different ways.

Overview of Financial Management

Generally, the functions of financial management fall into two broad areas—determining what to do with current financial resources (i.e., money) and determining how to procure additional financial resources. For example, in a given year, the NFL's Cleveland Browns might earn a profit of US$20 million. The question for the financial manager is what the Browns should do with that money. The franchise owners could decide to use the money to sign a high-priced free agent, renovate their practice facility, or increase the salaries of current employees. They could also decide to invest the money or distribute it among themselves.

Even after the organization decides how to use the money, the financial manager must choose the method for distributing the money. For example, if the Browns decide to spend the money on a free agent, they still must structure the player's contract, which would involve a number of financial decisions.

---

sport economic impact studies—Analyses of how expenditures on sport teams, events, or facilities economically affect a specific geographic region.

Olympic and Paralympic Winter Games Economic Impact: The Case of Sochi 2014

Victor Timchenko
Herzen State Pedagogical University of Russia, Saint Petersburg

The XXII Olympic Winter Games and XI Paralympic Winter Games were held in 2014 in Sochi, which is in the Krasnodar region of Russia. The Sochi Olympic Organizing Committee, in their final report, declared it to be a "unique and successful Games, giving a positive impression to competitors, guests and global television audience, and achieving a lasting legacy for Sochi, for Russia and for the Olympic and Paralympic Movement" (The Organizing Committee of the XXII Olympic Winter Games and XI Paralympic Winter Games of 2014 in Sochi, 2014, vol. 3, p. 142). The strategic aims of the Sochi Olympic Organizing Committee were tightly connected with the federal targeted program for development in the city of Sochi and in the Krasnodar region as an all-season mountain resort.

The entire project budget was US$46.4 billion, 60 percent of which came from business and 40 percent of which came from the state. The IOC contributed US$833 million to the Sochi 2014 Olympic Winter Games and received a return of more than US$53 million from the operational profit. From the budget US$8.5 billion was used for the Olympic venues and organizational purposes; US$21 billion was used for regional transport, power supply, and telecommuni-

cation infrastructure; and US$15.5 billion was used for development of Sochi and the Krasnodar region.

There are many legacies from Sochi 2014. First, most of the Olympic venues have been used for sport, cultural, and social events post-Games. For example, the new Sochi Park became the most attractive amusement place for tourists, and the new Russian International Olympic University (RIOU) in Sochi successfully provides educational programs for sport managers. The RIOU also has a special grant program in association with the Potanin Fund to support international students and professors. Sochi has also used these venues to successfully host other international sport mega-events.

Second, the city of Sochi and the Krasnodar region have benefited from improvements to various infrastructures. In terms of transportation, there are 367 kilometers (228 miles) of new roads and bridges, 200 kilometers (124 miles) of new railways with 54 bridges and 22 tunnels, and a new seaport. Further improvements to important infrastructure include 480 kilometers (298 miles) of low-pressure gas pipelines, two new thermal power plants and one gas power plant, three new sewage treatment plants, 550 kilometers (342 miles) of high-voltage power lines,

The financial manager would have to determine the difference in cost between giving the player a large signing bonus up front or structuring the deal in such a way that the player would receive most of the contract money in the future. Choosing what to spend the money on and how to spend it has significant long- and short-term implications for the team. For example, a team that loads much of the contract onto later years might face financial difficulties when it is paying the player more while he is likely to be less productive and may be generating less fan interest. In addition, the team could have more difficulty trading the player because of the large amount of money that it still owes him. These challenges have been faced by teams such as the New York Yankees and the Los Angeles Lakers when Alex Rodriguez and Kobe Bryant were playing out the final years of their contracts.

Although the example of the Browns described earlier may generate an interesting discussion, few sport organizations have the luxury of deciding how to spend excess money. Because many sport organizations were struggling financially well before the financial crisis in 2008 (Howard & Crompton, 2004) and continue to struggle, two of the key roles of the financial manager are determining how much money the organization will need to meet long-term obligations and how they will procure those funds. Although most involved with sport immediately think of selling tickets or merchandise as ways to increase available funds, many other means have potential. For example, good investments can produce significant income. Also, a few sport teams have sold stock in their organizations to raise funds, and many leagues have collected large fees from expansion

Sochi Olympic Park in Russia has been used to host other sport and cultural events.
Courtesy of Victor Timchenko.

and a new water and wastewater treatment plant. There are also 60 new educational, cultural, and health facilities and 25,000 additional hotel rooms in 56 new hotels.

Third, the Sochi 2014 project created close to 690,000 new jobs (50,000 full time), which during the Games contributed to the lowest level of unemployment in Russia at 0.17 percent. Business activity in Sochi increased 178.8 percent from 2005 to 2010 and outpaced the average country rate up to 2016. The average monthly salary in Sochi also increased 200 percent from 2007 to 2015.

Finally, Sochi has benefited from increases in tourism. The 2014 Games provided an opportunity for Sochi to transition from a regional summer resort to a year-round resort. The number of foreign tourists to Sochi grew by more than 2.5 times from 2005. The Sochi airport served 3.1 million passengers in 2014, and more than 6.5 million tourists visited Sochi in 2016 (8.3 percent growth from 2015). Hotels achieved 99 percent occupancy during the summer and 80 percent in the winter. Furthermore, the average revenue per room went up 41 percent from 2015.

teams. Teams can also get significant support from corporate sponsors and nonprofit organizations, such as college athletic departments, which rely heavily on individual donors.

Financial Statements

To allow internal and external parties to monitor its financial situation, a sport organization develops financial statements on a regular basis. The limited scope of this chapter does not permit discussion of all the details included in financial statements and all the ways in which one might examine those statements to understand an organization's current financial situation. It does, however, give an overview of the major financial statements and the useful information they provide.

Balance Sheet

Figure 15.4 is the balance sheet for a fictional professional football team, the Springfield Stars. In this example, the Stars are co-owned by Robert Goldstein and Connie Shumake. Connie owns 60 percent of the team, and Robert owns the remaining 40 percent. The balance sheet reflects the financial condition of the organization on a particular date. Although the balance sheet is generally reported at the end of a given financial period (e.g., the end of a year), a financial manager could generate a balance sheet any time such information is needed. The balance sheet includes three categories: assets, liabilities, and owners' equity. Assets are the financial resources of the company and include current and long-term assets. Current assets are generally cash and items that are expected to be converted into cash within the next year; these will be used to meet current obligations. Long-term assets are items that are not expected to be turned into cash during the next year such as land, buildings, and equipment. The initial price of each item is recorded, and some items are reduced as their values decline (i.e., depreciation). Long-term assets also include long-term investments, such as government bonds, that will not be converted to cash for a number of years.

Liabilities are obligations to pay money or provide goods or services to another entity. Current liabilities are those that are due to be paid in the next year, and long-term liabilities are those that are due sometime after the current year. The owners' equity is Connie's and Robert's shares of the resources of the business. It includes both the money that they have personally put into the company (i.e., paid in capital) and their earnings from the Stars that they have chosen to leave in the company (i.e., retained earnings). As you can see in figure 15.4, total assets are equal to liabilities plus owners' equity. This relationship is always true. Logically, all the resources (i.e., assets) either belong to the owners (i.e., owners' equity) or are owed to other entities (i.e., liabilities).

Income Statement

In figure 15.5, you will see the income statement for the Springfield Stars. The income statement provides the financial results of the organization's operations over a specific period. As with the balance sheet, the income statement is often reported at the end of a year but can be generated at any point and for any period. For many people, the income statement is the most important financial statement because it presents the organization's bottom line (i.e., the net profit or net loss). Although developing a complete understanding of the organization's financial situation requires a thorough examination of all the financial statements, the bottom line gives the user a quick assessment of the organization and its success in achieving the primary goal of profit-oriented companies, which is profitability.

The income statement includes two categories— revenue and expenses. Revenue is the inflow of value (not cash) to the business. Revenue is recorded when the good or service is delivered to a customer, not when the cash is received for that transaction. For example, when the NHL's New York Rangers sell a ticket to a December hockey game in July, the revenue from that sale is not recognized until the game is played in December. Likewise, if a customer receives a ticket for the December game but does not pay for the ticket until January, the revenue is recognized in December, not when the cash is received in January.

At the top of the income statement for the Stars is the organization's operating income. This figure represents the amount of revenue generated by the Stars from the team's main business. Note that some other revenue items (e.g., interest income) appear toward the bottom of the income statement. These items are separate from operating income because most financial analysts are more concerned with revenue from the company's main business, which is generally more useful for predicting future revenue.

The expenses are generally broken up into four categories: direct expenses (or cost of sales), operating expenses, other expenses, and income tax expense. Again, the income statement is more useful to analysts if the expenses are reported in this way. Direct expenses are expenses that can be directly matched to the main sources of revenue. For example, the cost of sales for a sporting goods company is the total cost to produce or manufacture all the items sold during the year. You will note that there are no direct expenses on the income statement for the Springfield Stars. Although it is relatively easy to tie the cost of a pair of shoes to the revenue produced from selling those shoes, it is not practical to directly tie the costs of a sport team to the revenue that is generated. Operating expenses are other normal business expenses, such as salaries, rent, and utilities, that cannot be directly matched to specific revenue items. Other expenses are those that occur outside normal business operations for a given company. Items such as interest expense and unusual losses are often recorded here. For example, if the Stars lost $500,000 in a lawsuit, the company would report that loss under other expenses. Finally, income tax expense is the amount that the company pays to the Internal Revenue Service (IRS), the state, or the city related to the profits for the year. After subtracting all the expenses from all the revenue, the income statement provides the user with the net income (or loss) at the bottom of the statement; this number is, literally, the bottom line.

While the financial statements for nonprofit sport organizations are very similar, there are a couple of differences. Although there are no owners, these organizations will have assets that are greater than their liabilities; these are referred to as net assets rather than owner's equity. Although the organizational goals can vary, nonprofit organizations want to have sufficient resources in net assets to provide for long-term financial stability. In addition, nonprofit organizations are not focused on making a profit, so they do not use this term; however, they do have a bottom line that is computed as revenue minus

Springfield Stars Balance Sheet (in thousands)

March 31, 2018

Assets

Current assets

Cash and cash equivalents	$33,365,586
Marketable securities	58,132,669
Other short-term investments	95,558,465
Accounts receivable	3,213,175
Notes receivable	5,678,695
Prepaid expenses	2,616,407
Other current assets	5,900,586
Total current assets	**$204,465,583**

Long-term assets

Land	$52,495,823
Facilities	45,895,631
Equipment	1,689,954
Long-term investments	6,028,318
Total long-term assets	**$106,109,726**
Total assets	$310,575,309

Liabilities

Current liabilities

Accounts payable	$19,714,620
Deferred revenue	28,610,372
Ticket refunds payable	150,908
Long-term debt, current portion	14,365,096
Deferred compensations, current portion	16,209,896
Total current liabilities	**$79,050,892**

Long-term liabilities

Long-term debt, noncurrent	$75,000,000
Deferred compensation, noncurrent	48,850,057
Total long-term liabilities	**$123,850,057**
Total liabilities	$202,900,949

Owners' equity

Paid-in-capital, Connie Shumake	$30,000,000
Paid-in-capital, Robert Goldstein	20,000,000
Retained earnings, Connie Shumake	34,604,616
Retained earnings, Robert Goldstein	23,069,744
Total owners' equity	**$107,674,360**
Total liabilities and owners' equity	$310,575,309

Figure 15.4 Springfield Stars balance sheet.

Springfield Stars Income Statement

For the period ending March 31, 2018

Revenue from operations

National television	$95,425,375
Road games	13,919,710
Other NFL revenue	15,075,968
Home games	30,451,440
Private box revenue	12,289,395
Marketing and sponsorships	37,789,075
Local media	7,721,250
Concessions and parking	5,932,282
Miscellaneous	3,393,293
Total revenue from operations	$221,997,788

Operating expenses

Salaries	$115,868,020
Team expenses	37,233,957
Marketing expenses	4,854,095
Operations and maintenance	13,838,354
General and administrative	25,883,773
Total operating expenses	$197,678,199
Net operating income	$24,319,589

Other income (expenses)

Interest and dividend income	$6,231,027
Interest expense	(859,333)
Gain (loss) on sale of assets	3,253,365
Net taxable income	$32,944,648
Income tax expense	12,100,000
Net income	$20,844,648

Figure 15.5   Springfield Stars income statement.

expenses. Overall, if you understand the financial statements of a for-profit organization, you should be able to understand the financial statements of a nonprofit organization, even though some of the terminology will be different.

Sources of Revenue and Expenses for Sport Organizations

Organizations in the sport industry have various types of revenue and expenses depending on the type of organization. In this section, we briefly discuss some of the business types in the sport industry and examine some sources of revenue and expenses in those businesses.

Types of Sport Organizations

As previously discussed (and illustrated in the CSM Sport Industry Sectors Model in chapter 1), sport organizations can take many forms and have varied goals. Some organizations are geared toward encouraging sport participation. These include youth sport organizations, community recreation programs, and high school sports. Other organizations seek to make a profit by providing participation opportunities not offered by nonprofit organizations (or by providing better opportunities than those offered by nonprofits). These include sport organizations that rent their facilities to participants (e.g., bowling alleys, health clubs), organizations that seek to train people (e.g., those that provide personal trainers, others who provide lessons in a sport), and organizations that provide the equipment necessary to participate in a certain sport (i.e., sporting goods companies).

Many companies focus more on sport spectators. These include professional sports (e.g., WNBA, NASCAR, PGA Tour) and big-time college sports. Although these organizations receive a large portion of the money generated by sport spectators, other entities also benefit from sport spectating, including independent sport facilities that host sporting events, the sport media that bring sport events and information related to sport events to the consumer (e.g., television, radio, newspapers, magazines, the Internet), and companies that sell products licensed by these professional and college sport organizations. The diversity of the sport industry produces a variety of revenue and expense sources. The next two sections focus on types and aspects of revenue and expenses that are unique in the sport industry.

Sources of Revenue

Some of the sources of revenue unique to sport are items related to game attendance (e.g., concessions, personal seat licenses, luxury suite rentals, athletic department donations), media rights, sponsorships,

and licensed merchandise. Although tickets are generally the major source of revenue related to event attendance, this is not always true for sport events. The total price of attendance is often much greater than the cost of the ticket. Consider the following:

- Most sport organizations charge fans an additional fee for parking during the event.
- Fans typically spend money on concessions at the stadium, and many fans consider this to be an important part of the game experience. Some sport teams and facilities maintain complete control over the concessions at the stadium, but others prefer to hire companies with expertise in handling concessions. In the latter case, the contract outlines how these organizations share the profits from concessions.
- Some professional and college sport teams now charge fans for personal seat licenses (PSLs) that give them the right to buy a particular seat. For example, a fan may buy a 10-year PSL for US$10,000. The fan must then pay for season tickets each year for the next 10 years. If the season ticket price is US$1,000 per year, the fan will end up paying US$20,000 over 10 years to watch games from that seat.
- A fan who wants a more exclusive setting for watching games might decide to rent a luxury suite or pay for a club seat. As with the PSL, the fan must still buy tickets for the game after paying the cost of renting the

For sport organizations around the world, fans are a vital revenue source.

Courtesy of Paul M. Pedersen.

luxury suite. For example, the NBA Brooklyn Nets' luxury suites at the Barclays Center have an average annual lease price of around US$260,000, and the 11 special suites in "The Vault" cost an average of US$550,000. These are still a bargain compared to some of the luxury suite prices; the Yankees' suites cost more than US$800,000, and Madison Square Garden suites are more than US$1 million. Single-event luxury suite rentals can also be very high; for example, suites for the Super Bowl have been leased for US$500,000. An average price for an NFL club seat is generally more than US$2,000, and some cost more than twice that.

College sport fans often donate money to an athletic department so that they can buy better seats or, in some cases, so they can buy any seat. For example, a college sport fan might have to donate US$4,000 each year for the right to buy two US$400 season tickets. In this case, the fan is paying US$4,800 for two season tickets. At the Division I FBS level, donations to college athletic departments have increased from 5 percent to about 21 percent of total athletic department revenue over the last four decades (Fulks, 2015).

Because of the increasing cost of attending games, many sport spectators watch or listen to games at home. This large audience for sport beyond those who attend games means that many sport teams make a large percentage of their revenue from media contracts. For example, the NFL recently signed new television agreements that increased the average annual television revenue for the league from US$3.085 billion per year (2006 to 2013) to US$4.95 billion (2014 to 2021). The largest NFL agreement is the ESPN deal for *Monday Night Football* that averages US$1.9 billion per year. As noted earlier in the chapter, the NCAA's contract for the men's basketball tournament is a 14-year contract for US$10.8 billion, which is a nearly 37 percent increase over the prior record-setting contract. Because the tournament takes place on only 12 days, the NCAA receives an average of more than US$64 million per day for the broadcast rights. The college football playoff contract with ESPN, which also includes six associated bowls, pays US$5.64 billion over 12 years or US$470 million annually. In many cases, television networks make little or no money directly from the broadcast of sporting events. The networks believe, however, that broadcasting the games will be beneficial because they can use the broadcasts to promote other programming, and they believe they will benefit from a positive association with sport.

Corporations also seek to take advantage of positive associations with sport events, leagues, teams, and players. Spending by corporate sponsors in North America is more than US$20 billion, and about 70 percent of that goes to sport sponsorships. Companies invest heavily in sport sponsorship because they believe the association with sport organizations will create a positive image of their company and influence people to buy their products or services. The largest sums of money have generally been paid for naming rights of stadiums such as the US$400 million paid for Citi Field and the US$20 million per year for the Barclays Center.

Corporations also pay large amounts of money to athlete endorsers to promote their products and services. For example, Nike became the dominant force in the athletic footwear industry just as the career of its top endorser, Michael Jordan, was taking off. Nike, like other corporations, continues to sign large endorsement deals with athletes (e.g., NBA star LeBron James). Some of the most popular athletes make more money from endorsements than they do from the teams for which they play.

Also seeking to take advantage of the positive feelings that sport spectators have about teams and players are the sellers of licensed products. Once a rather small industry, sales of sport licensed products became big business during the 1980s. Although most people immediately think of players' jerseys and team hats, the licensed products industry includes a variety of items such as video games, blankets, framed pictures, and sport equipment. Although most of the money from these sales goes to the producers of the products, sport organizations receive a percentage of the sales revenue.

Sources of Expenses

Two critical sources of expenses for most sport organizations are the cost of sport facilities and the cost of salaries. Sport facilities can be extremely expensive. Most sport organizations try to persuade local communities to pay for stadiums, but many are finding that they have to pay at least part of the cost. This arrangement results in long-term payments that can affect the financial stability of the organization for many years. Sport facilities are also costly to maintain, particularly large open-air facilities that might not be used for much of the year but must be maintained year-round. In addition, sport facilities tend to become obsolete fairly quickly. If an organization has to make payments for 30 years, it could end up

Mitch Moser

Professional Profile

Title: Deputy director of athletics/resource development and management/CFO, Duke University Athletics

Education: BA (business administration and speech communication), Concordia-Moorhead College; MA (sports administration and facility management), Ohio University

Courtesy of Duke University Sports Information.

Mitch Moser began his career in collegiate athletic administration in 1992 when he was hired as the ticket manager at Rice University. In 1997, he accepted the same position at Duke University. Moser later assumed the dual role of Duke's business manager and ticket manager in 1998. Since that time, he has taken on additional roles including administrative responsibilities for game operations, facilities, IT, band, and cheer. Moser has received a series of promotions including associate athletic director/CFO in 2001, senior associate athletic director/CFO in 2012, deputy director of athletics/CFO in 2014, and deputy director of athletics/resource development and management/CFO in 2016. He is now responsible for resource acquisition and resource management and for marketing and sales of new premium areas in Blue Devil Tower and Cameron Indoor Stadium. The following is a snapshot of his development, education, duties, and insights as a leader in the sport industry.

What was your career path?

I'm not sure that there is a specific path for getting to where I am today. Before going to graduate school at Ohio U, I had a background in business planning and experience with finance and statistics. And, my first [job] in collegiate athletics was in the ticket office at Rice University, which also gave me an opportunity to gain experience and help with various aspects of the business operation. I do believe that it is important to have some type of business and/or finance background and an advanced degree of some sort, either an MBA or MSA.

What characteristics must a person have to be successful in your job?

In my opinion, it is important for a person on this career path to possess characteristics [such as] great attention to detail, ability to plan and organize, good communication skills (oral and written), and the ability to gain consensus in establishing priorities.

Which websites, online tools, or resources do you frequently use or refer to?

Other than the NCAA and ACC finance websites that contain budgets and distribution information, there aren't any general websites that serve as resources.

What do you consider to be the biggest future challenge in your job or industry?

Continuing to grow our resource base in order to compete and continue to provide the best student-athlete experience possible. The industry has gone through a pretty massive amount of change with conference realignment and will continue to morph and change with the advent of television contracts and conference channels. Being able to anticipate changes in the industry and position our institution and department appropriately is probably the biggest future challenge from the perspective of a CFO.

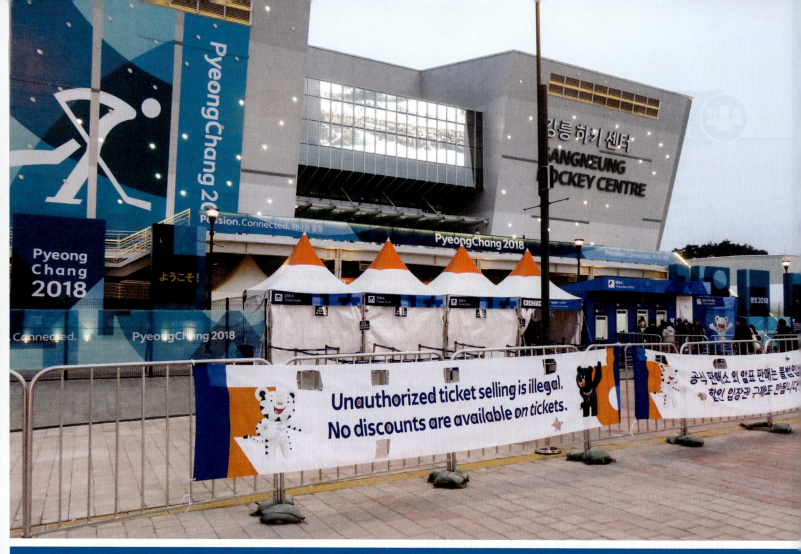

Countries, such as South Korea, have been willing to spend billions of dollars to host mega sporting events such as the 2018 Olympic and Paralympic Winter Games. One major aspect of the hosting expense is the construction of new lodging structures and sport facilities, such as the estimated US$90 million spent for the Gangneung Hockey Centre. While the new 10,000-seat facility was originally going to be dismantled after the 2018 Olympic and Paralympic Winter Games, the host city (Gangneung, South Korea) decided to keep the facility open for ice hockey, concerts, and other events.

Courtesy of Paul M. Pedersen.

As discussed throughout the chapter, the world of professional sports represents big business in terms of revenue generated by star athletes and the salary and endorsement contracts they receive. When potentially controversial activities such as athlete activism arise, how should sport organizations address these actions and athletes? Should players be rewarded for their efforts or punished for their beliefs and behaviors? What financial ramifications should they and the organizations they represent incur? What responsibilities do sport organizations have when handling these issues?

For chapter-specific learning activities, visit the web study guide at
www.HumanKinetics.com/ContemporarySportManagement.

Summary

This chapter introduces the basic concepts of economics and finance. Sport economics is the study of how people within the sport industry deal with scarcity. Ideas such as supply, demand, and market equilibrium are important for sport businesses such as professional teams, sporting goods manufacturers, and sport facility operators.

Financial management is the application of skills in the manipulation, use, and control of funds. Students need to have a thorough understanding of financial information available through financial statements. Balance sheets and income statements contain a plethora of data that are vital to the successful management of a sport organization. Sport managers must also have knowledge of the different types of revenues and costs that are present for sport organizations.

Review Questions

1. What does the term *economic impact* mean? Provide an example of how it can be used in sport.

2. How would you construct the supply and demand curves from table 15.5 to show the supply and demand for golf clubs?

3. From the table, how would you determine the market equilibrium price and quantity for golf clubs? What would happen if the price level were $250?

4. What are the different types of business structures in the sport industry? Give examples of each.

5. What is the main purpose of each type of financial statement discussed in the chapter?

6. What useful information does each financial statement provide?

7. What are the major sources of revenue and expenses in the sport industry? How are they different from or similar to sources of revenue and expenses of nonsport organizations?

8. What types of positions are available in financial management in the sport industry?

Table 15.5   Supply and Demand for Golf Clubs

Price	Quantity demanded	Quantity supplied
$500	30	180
$400	60	160
$300	90	140
$200	120	120
$100	150	80
$50	180	20

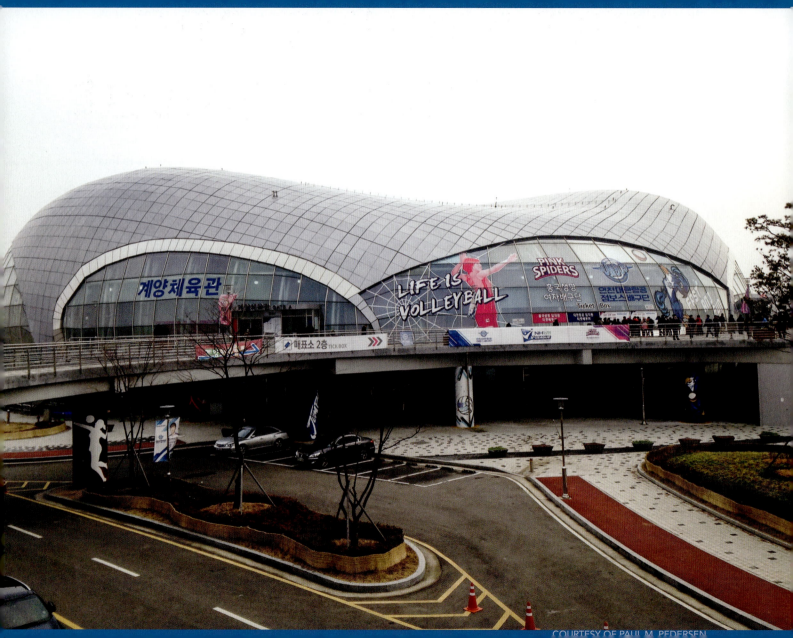

Sport Facility and Event Management

Brianna L. Newland
Stacey A. Hall
Amanda L. Paule-Koba

LEARNING OBJECTIVES

- Distinguish between the various types of venues that hold sport and entertainment events.
- Recognize the key steps that are necessary to effectively manage a facility.
- Identify the differences between public assembly facilities and those managed by private companies.
- Discuss the similarities and differences between event and facility management.
- Gain an understanding of the positions available in the field of event and facility management.
- Demonstrate an understanding of the procedures, principles, ethical practices, and current trends in planning and managing an event or facility.
- Recognize the importance of crowd management and identify critical elements for a proper crowd management plan.
- Identify similarities and differences in staging participant and spectator sport events.
- Use critical thinking skills to describe several major problems currently facing facility and event managers.

KEY TERMS

boilerplate contract
booking
command center
cost analysis
documentation
exercises

floor diagram
floor plan
Gantt chart
privatization
run sheet
settlement

tax-exempt bonds
vulnerability
work breakdown structure (WBS)
work order

1863
First covered skating rink in Canada opened in Halifax

1879
The first Madison Square Garden opened

1912
Fenway Park opened

1914
Wrigley Field opened

1931
Maple Leaf Gardens opened in Toronto

1959
First Daytona 500 held at Daytona International Speedway

1965
Astroturf developed and first used in the Houston Astrodome, which opened in 1965

1989
California earthquake caused 10-day interruption in A's versus Giants World Series

1999
Columbus Crew stadium, the first soccer-specific stadium in the United States, opened

2000
Pacific Bell Park (now AT&T Park) opened; it was the first privately funded MLB stadium built since 1962

2005
Ski Dubai, the world's largest indoor snow park, opened

The number of sport and event facilities built, renovated, or approved for construction around the world has increased dramatically over the past decade. For example, in the United States, there are eight major facilities with capacities over 10,000 that opened or were projected to open in 2017 or later. The estimated cost for these stadiums was nearly US$4.4 billion. This surge in construction is by no means specific to the United States. Brazil spent US$3.6 billion on the construction and renovations of stadiums for the 2014 World Cup and US$4.6 billion for the Olympic and Paralympic Games. Given the extensive price tag associated with construction, there has been backlash in the media and from community members who are not supportive of spending public money on these projects. In addition, the Oxford Olympics Study 2016 found that Russia spent US$21.9 billion to deliver the 2014 Olympic and Paralympic Winter Games in Sochi, which is US$19.4 billion more than Salt Lake City spent to host the events in 2002 (Flyvbjerg, Stewart, & Budzier, 2016). Although there were claims of corruption surrounding the financing of the event, Russian president Vladimir Putin maintained that the inflated prices were due to the honest mistakes of investors and that the actual figure that the government contributed was significantly lower (Myers, 2014). Regardless, the spending received criticism because it occurred amid a slow economy in Russia.

Although some publicly constructed stadiums have been successful, other professional teams in the United States have had trouble securing the necessary financing to complete their mega projects. One such example was the proposed US$1.2 billion Chargers Stadium for the NFL's San Diego franchise.

In November 2016, San Diegans voted down the initiative to fund a new football stadium for the Chargers (Brandt, 2016). The mayor and others opposed to the project stated financial concerns as a primary reason for not supporting the initiative. The franchise had hoped to stay in San Diego County, but instead were forced to move to Los Angeles. They now play in the 27,000-seat StubHub Center—a Major League Soccer venue—for the next three seasons (2017-2019).

A model example of a public–private partnership is the funding formula established for the Mercedes-Benz Stadium in Atlanta, Georgia. The Georgia World Congress Center Authority owns the stadium, and the Atlanta Falcons and the NFL operate the venue under a 30-year agreement. They contributed US$800 million to US$1 billion (70 to 80 percent of construction costs), including any cost overruns, toward stadium construction. The city of Atlanta and Fulton County contributed US$200 million (20 to 30 percent of the cost) through a hotel and motel tax paid by visitors (Mercedes-Benz Stadium, 2016).

Sport facilities provide students from a variety of majors, including sport management, with careers in planning, designing, and constructing facilities (Sawyer, 2013) and opportunities to work with facility operations, schedule events, oversee facility finances, equip facilities with TV and video connections, supervise maintenance and custodial services, conduct facility marketing and promotions, engage in event merchandising, and direct risk-management services. The distinction between sport and entertainment has blurred to the point that sport and entertainment events are more similar than they are

2009
New US$1.5 billion
MLB Yankee Stadium
opened

2013
Terrorist attack with two
homemade bombs at Boston
Marathon killed three and
injured more than 260

2016
TriHabitat, the world's first and only self-
contained endurance sports racing and
training venue, was conceived

Record college football crowd of 156,990
attended game between Tennessee and
Virginia Tech at Bristol Motor Speedway

2018
U.S. Bank Stadium
in Minneapolis
hosted Super
Bowl LII (Eagles
over Patriots) and
Summer X Games

2008
Beijing National Stadium
(Bird's Nest) opened; it
was the world's largest
steel structure

Washington Nationals
opened the first green
stadium in the United
States

2010
Stampede at
Makhulong Stadium
in South Africa
injured 15 fans
before World Cup

2015
The first day/night cricket test match was
played between Australia and New Zealand
at the Adelaide Oval in Australia

Series of coordinated terrorist attacks in
Paris included a suicide bomber trying to
gain entry to the Stade de France while
the French national soccer team played an
exhibition match against Germany

2017
NFL Atlanta Falcons and MLS
Atlanta United FC opened their
new home, Mercedes-Benz
Stadium, at an estimated cost of
US$1.4 billion; it had the largest
circular video board in the world

different. The competencies required to manage the facilities that host the events are comparable. Students who develop the right skill sets position themselves to work in these areas of the sport industry.

Overview of Facility Management

Types of sport and entertainment facilities are as diverse as the events that they host (see table 16.1). Some are single-purpose facilities that are used specifically for one sport or activity. One example is the New York Mets' Citi Field (although the facility sometimes hosts concerts). Bowling alleys, golf courses, motorsport tracks, skate parks, swimming pools, and water parks are other examples of single-purpose facilities. Other facilities are built for specialized events, but they might not be considered single-purpose facilities because they host other types of events. For example, TriHabitat is a newly conceived endurance sports racing and training venue that not only supports the three disciplines of triathlon (swim, bike, run) but also includes a lodge and conference center, a pavilion that can host music events, five separate stadiums for spectators, and a marina. The facility can host triathlon events, music and work events, and single-sport swimming, cycling, and running events.

Other facilities, called multipurpose facilities, host a variety of events such as concerts, truck pulls, motocross races, home and garden shows, and recreational vehicle shows. These facilities might also be home to intercollegiate and professional sport competitions. For example, Levi's Stadium (home to the NFL's San Francisco 49ers), named by *Street & Smith's SportsBusiness Journal* as the sports facility of the year in 2015, hosted the NCAA Pac-12 Championship, the NCAA Foster Farms Bowl, the NHL Outdoor Stadium Series, WrestleMania 31, Monster Jam, Monster Energy Supercross, Coldplay: A Head Full of Dreams Tour, the Beer and Bacon Classic, and Super Bowl 50.

Many types of events were originally held in large outdoor stadiums going as far back as the chariot races in ancient Rome. In recent years, many stadiums

Table 16.1   Types of Sport Facilities

Type of facility	Examples
Single purpose	Softball complex, bowling alley, large stadium (e.g., Lambeau Field in Green Bay, Wisconsin)
Single purpose, specialized	Ice arena
Multipurpose	Large stadium (e.g., Mercedes-Benz Stadium in Atlanta), high school field house
Nontraditional	Skateboard park, convertible indoor–outdoor facility

With a 2019 opening, the new US$200 million-plus headquarters for the International Olympic Committee (IOC) in Lausanne, Switzerland, houses the 600 IOC staffers in the various IOC departments.
Courtesy of Paul M. Pedersen.

and large arenas, some of which are covered, have been built as sport organizations have attempted to improve their facilities to increase their chances of success. With the growing popularity of sports, stadium capacities have increased a great deal. In the United States, two of the largest stadiums in the world are home to collegiate football teams. The University of Michigan's stadium (The Big House) was built in 1927. The stadium's original capacity was 72,000, but it has since been increased to 109,901. Penn State University's Beaver Stadium has a slightly smaller capacity at 106,572. In addition, six other collegiate football teams (Ohio State, Texas A&M, Tennessee, Louisiana State, Alabama, and Texas) have stadium capacities over 100,000. Stadium capacities have increased at the international level as well. The original seating capacity of San Siro in Milan, Italy, was 10,000 when it was built in 1926. Its capacity has

since been expanded to 80,018. Rungrado May Day Stadium in Pyongyang, North Korea, built in 1989, is the largest stadium in the world and has a seating capacity of 150,000. The second largest stadium in the world is Salt Lake Stadium in Kolkata, India, with a capacity of 120,000.

Not all sport and entertainment facilities are restricted to spaces that are roofed and walled. Golf courses, ski areas, and amusement parks are classified as sport and entertainment facilities. In addition, not all facilities have seating for large numbers of spectators. For example, a fitness center does not have seating areas but instead has activity spaces that include cardiovascular equipment, free weights, fitness machines, jogging tracks, racquetball courts, and swimming pools. In some situations, the mission of a facility is broad, and it incorporates many sports or activities. For example, a multipurpose high school gymnasium might be designed for interscholastic sport practices and competition, physical education classes, school plays, and graduation ceremonies. This same concept holds true for facilities such as gymnasiums on college campuses.

Regardless of the size or type of the facility or the kinds of events that it hosts, one factor remains consistent: To maintain a safe and enjoyable environment, proper management of the facility and events is crucial. During the past 20 years, many sport and entertainment facilities have turned to private companies to handle their management tasks. **Privatization** is the term used to describe this move from public to private management. Either private owners or municipalities still own the facilities, but they outsource (the process of subcontracting services to an independent contractor) the management of their facilities to professionals who specialize in facility management (Steinbach, 2004).

The trend toward privatization began with U.S. professional team facilities and spread to intercollegiate facilities, the minor professional leagues, and sport and entertainment facilities in other countries. Some high schools and municipal recreation centers in the United States have also privatized. Often, the owners of private sport and entertainment venues and the managers of public facilities are not prepared to engage in the facility management business. In such cases, poor management can lead to less-than-optimal operational efficiency, and venue operations become a drain on financial resources. In most of these cases, gross operating expenses exceed gross revenue, causing the facilities to operate at a deficit. This has led to reductions in services and the elimination of events, which in turn has led to privatization (Ammon, Southall, & Nagel, 2016). SMG is an example of a global entertainment and convention venue management company that oversees many professional and collegiate event and facility operations.

Despite the efforts to privatize sport venues, many owners depend on the state and local governments to issue **tax-exempt bonds** to finance construction projects, thereby lowering the organization's debt. To provide funding to sport organizations for capital projects, governments typically raise taxes. For example, in San Diego, voters had an option to increase hotel room taxes from 12.5 percent to 16.5 percent to help fund the proposed US$1.8 billion Chargers stadium project (Schrotenboer, 2016). The vote did not pass in San Diego, but many professional sport teams rely on this method to finance stadiums. This issue is heavily debated; many people argue that

for-profit sport entities should fund their own enterprises and public resources should be funneled to programs and infrastructure that support the greater community. Although a professional sport team does provide the community with a source of civic pride, many are single-entity facilities that fail to offer community programming or events outside the sport season.

Facility Management

The number of managers in a facility, as well as their specific titles and duties, varies depending on the size and purpose of the facility. Consequently, those interested in working in facility management need to read job descriptions carefully to determine the precise duties associated with specific job titles. In the sections that follow, we describe several management positions and their accompanying responsibilities with the caveat that specific situations may differ. In general, however, three positions that exist in most facilities are the facility director, the operations manager, and the event coordinator.

The *facility director* (also called the facility manager, general manager of the facility, or the chief executive officer) has overall responsibility for the entire facility. This person is mainly responsible for the creation and proper administration of the facility's standard operating procedures.

The *operations manager* reports directly to the facility director and is responsible for all personnel, procedures, and activities related to the facility. This manager has a variety of duties such as defining the roles, responsibilities, and authority of facility staff; recruiting personnel to coordinate the various areas of the facility; coordinating personnel, policies and procedures, and activities within the facility; evaluating facility operations; and making recommendations to the facility director.

The *event coordinator*, who also reports to the facility director, is responsible for managing individual events held in the facility. These events can vary from concerts to ice shows and from political rallies to sport events. The event coordinator's responsibilities usually include transporting, assembling, erecting, and storing equipment; establishing a control system for venue and equipment logistics; recruiting, training, and supervising specific personnel; assisting in maintaining venues and equipment during the event; facilitating ticketing and ticket distribution at venue sites; and evaluating venue and equipment operations.

---

privatization—Moving the management of facilities from the public sector to private companies or organizations.

tax-exempt bonds—Owners of professional sport franchises receive subsidies from local, state, and federal taxpayers when the stadium is financed with government bonds. These bonds are issued at below-market interest rates and are paid for by the exemption of the bonds' interest income.

The Spyros Louis Olympic Complex in Athens, Greece

Dimitra Papadimitriou
  University of Patras, Greece

The Athens Olympic Stadium, Spyros Louis, or OAKA, is part of a large complex of sport facilities located in the municipality of Marousi, Greece. The stadium was originally built in 1982 and named after Spyros Louis, the inaugural 1896 Athens Olympics marathon winner.

The stadium has hosted several major events in athletics including the 1982 European Championships, the 1987 UEFA Cup Winners' Cup Final, the 1991 Mediterranean Games, two football finals for the UEFA Champions League (1994, 2007), and the 1997 World Championships. A unique event in this stadium was the 2005 Acropolis Rally, the first-ever Federation Internationale de l'Automobile World Rally event that was staged in a stadium. The stadium has also been used extensively to host major pop and rock music concerts (e.g., Madonna, U2, Pyx Lax, the Red Hot Chili Peppers, Bon Jovi).

After extensive renovations, the stadium hosted the opening and the closing ceremonies of the 2004 Olympic Games, Olympic athletic events, and the final of the Olympic football tournament. One of its landmark features is the roof, which was designed by world-renowned Spanish architect Santiago Calatrava. OAKA is owned by the Greek state and run by an independent nonprofit organization that is largely subsidized by the state. A board of directors that consists of nine members appointed by the government is responsible for running the stadium along with the executive director and 158 largely underskilled employees. Many important sport services are located in the facility or are part of the stadium's organizational structure such as the National Anti-Doping Agency, the National Sport Research Center, and the specialized labs for ergo-physiology, biochemistry, and sport medicine that support national teams in different sports.

In recent years, OAKA has been used extensively by local football clubs (i.e., Panathinaikos, AEK); however, they had no choice but to end the stadium usage deals due to the economic crisis. This left behind damages to the facility from fan riots and added to the stadium's mounting debt. Today the complex faces profound financial problems as it depends largely on state support, which is in a free fall. There has been a 65-percent drop in public subsidies between 2011 and 2016 because of the effects of the five-year government economic crisis. In the same vein, key former users of the stadium (i.e., clubs) face their own difficulties in convincing owners to spend money to attract football and basketball teams back to the stadium for games and events.

OAKA leadership has made some efforts to develop new areas of the market relevant to sport participation and tourism, with quality programs for families and tourists. For example, the development of two new Olympic-themed museums within OAKA could open up the sport tourism market, but even these have been delayed due to lack of resources.

The Athens Olympic Stadium, Spyros Louis, now faces a battle for survival and threats for privatization.

Courtesy of Stella Leivadi.

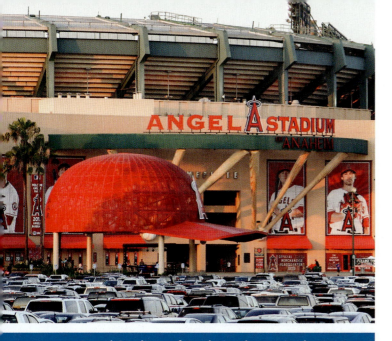

Angel Stadium of Anaheim, home to the MLB Los Angeles Angels, has a seating capacity of over 45,477. While the stadium, which is owned by the city of Anaheim, California, was renovated as a single-purpose (baseball) facility, in the offseason it hosts a variety of other activities (e.g., weddings, business meetings). Before the MLB season started, in 2018 the facility hosted motorcycle racing and monster truck events.

Courtesy of Paul M. Pedersen.

Event Management

Every event is a product, an outcome, and an occurrence. An event occurs in a specific year and month, on a specific date, and at a specific place. All preparation must be completed before the event begins, and the pressure for perfection in event management is high. Many students think that obtaining a 90 percent (A) grade for academic work constitutes excellent performance. But if you are managing an event for 70,000 people and the satisfaction level is 90 percent, you will have 7,000 unhappy patrons. Having 7,000 unhappy patrons could be disastrous for an organization due to word of mouth and social media. Therefore, event managers need to make every effort to ensure all patrons have an enjoyable experience.

Events come in many shapes and sizes, from a small corporate 5K run to the New York City Marathon, from an 18-hole community golf tournament fundraiser to the Masters, from a Little League Baseball game to the World Series. Event management includes the planning, coordinating, staging, and evaluating of an event. Most events have similar components, regardless of their scope.

Planning for an event involves setting goals and determining the best course of action to achieve the goals that were set forth by the event managers. It also involves creating a plan to ensure that the process leading up to the event and the event itself run smoothly. Whether the event is a small golf tournament or the NFL Super Bowl, the planning of many components is crucial to its success. The components involved depend on the nature of the event, the time, the place, and the clientele. For example, a ticket to an event such as the Super Bowl is a prized possession, so serious attention is paid to the ticket design. Likewise, think of the preparation of the stadium maintenance crew for an NFL playoff game. Events like NCAA postseason championships present unique challenges because teams do not know where they will play until a few days before the competition. In addition, event managers must also consider the unique challenges for participation events. For example, the director of an Ironman triathlon event must plan a 140.6-mile (226.3 kilometer) course that includes a 2.4-mile (3.9 kilometer) swim, 112-mile (180.2 kilometer) bike, and 26.2-mile (42.2 kilometer) run. Not only does the race director need to consider logistics for each stage of the race, but she or he must also coordinate the traffic on the bike and run courses because it is nearly impossible to shut down 138 miles (222 kilometers) of road.

Event Management Personnel

Because of the varied nature of events, no two events will have identical organizational structures. Many elements, however, are common across the industry of event management. Figure 16.1 shows a typical event management personnel structure for a moderately large (2,000-3,000 participants) sporting event. As you study the figure, you will notice that the executive director is at the top of the hierarchy, division managers are in the second tier, and the remaining positions are primarily coordinators. For the sake of brevity, we will discuss only four of the positions identified in this figure: executive director, operations division manager, security coordinator, and public relations, marketing, and hospitality division managers.

- *Executive director.* The executive director is responsible for the overall administration of the event. Some of the responsibilities include developing operational and strategic plans, preparing the financial statements and budgets for approval, anticipating problems, and implementing solutions. The director is responsible for hiring and recruiting division managers and coordinators and defining their roles, responsibilities, and authority. The director also needs to provide administrative support for division managers and coordinators in the overall planning for each area. The executive director also

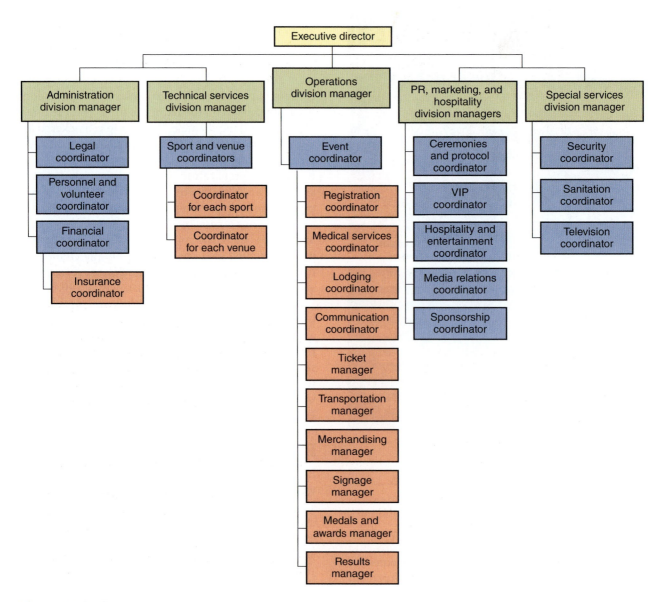

Figure 16.1   Event management structure.

must prepare an event manual with guiding principles, policies and procedures, and so on. The manual should clearly define the roles, responsibilities, and authority of each division manager and facilitate communication among the divisions. The director assumes responsibility for organizational duties not specifically assigned to division managers or coordinators; approves overall plans, strategies, and budgets; and monitors financial and human resources (e.g., budget, revenue, expenditures, staff, volunteers). Ultimately, the director is accountable for all aspects of the event.

• *Operations division manager.* The operations division manager is responsible for all personnel, procedures, and activities contained in the operations division. These items include registration, lodging, medical services, communications, merchandising and concessions, transportation, signage, medals and awards, and results. This person clearly defines the roles, responsibilities, and authority of each coordinator and manager while recruiting personnel to coordinate each operations area; helps coordinators and managers complete their assigned tasks; assists them in the overall planning for each area; coordinates personnel, policies and procedures, and activities within the operations division; and facilitates communication among all operations coordinators and managers and among other division personnel as needed. The operations division manager communicates with other division managers while supervising

Alicia Greco-Walker

Professional Profile

Courtesy of University of Delaware Athletic Department.

Title: Associate athletic director for events and operations, University of Delaware Department of Athletics

Education: BS (sport management) and MEd (higher education), University of Delaware

Following a key internship with the New York Mets as a site manager and Fantasy Camp representative, Alicia Greco-Walker landed a job at Octagon as an event coordinator for corporate events and hospitality. She then returned to her alma mater, the University of Delaware, for graduate education and to pursue a career in collegiate athletics. Greco-Walker served as a graduate assistant in athletic operations, and this position led to a full-time job as the assistant athletic director for facilities and operations. In January 2014, Greco-Walker became the associate athletic director for event operations and continues to serve in that role today. She manages all aspects of the intercollegiate athletic operations including day-to-day operations of all 21 intercollegiate programs as well as planning and logistics of events. She is also involved with event scheduling, operational and event budgeting, and athletic facility management. The following is a snapshot of her development, education, duties, and insights as a leader in the sport industry.

What was your career path?

Early in my career, I was eager to learn as much as I could about the industry. I never shied away from work or new experiences that would broaden the scope of my knowledge. This approach meant a lot of hours, late nights, and weekends, but I knew this was the career path I wanted to take and that the experiences would only strengthen my portfolio for the future. I had the opportunity to return to the University of Delaware, where I had completed my undergraduate degree, for a graduate assistantship. This afforded me the opportunity to pursue a master's degree while also getting pertinent experience working in the athletic department. While in this role, the woman I was working for left to take another opportunity, so I filled the role in an interim capacity. When the job was posted, I applied for it and the rest is history!

What characteristics must a person have to be successful in your job?

I would have to say the ability to be prepared for anything. Things can get hectic quickly, and having to work in the 11th hour as much as I do has helped me deal with tough situations. Staying organized is also critical. I keep a calendar of weekly events and divide responsibilities amongst the staff on my team. I am also very careful when planning and assigning the different tasks necessary to complete the event. Fortunately, I have a great staff and a number of volunteers for support.

Which websites, online tools, or resources do you frequently use or refer to?

Since I entered the sports industry, I've loved reading *Street & Smith's SportsBusiness Journal*. They highlight stories that span such a broad scope of the industry but are so applicable to collegiate athletics. Topics like facilities, technology, and fan engagement are cornerstones to professional and collegiate sport. It's truly an insightful resource that has helped with idea generation and philosophical approach.

What do you consider to be the biggest future challenge in your job or industry?

The rate at which technology is advancing has a major impact on our events and the fan experience. Our ability to keep up with those changes at the same rate at which they are happening has been challenging. These leaps in technology impact our customers from the ticketing process to their ability to know and get around our venues.

personnel and approving policies. Finally, the person in this position evaluates the operations division and makes recommendations to the executive director, to whom he or she reports directly.

• *Security coordinator.* The security coordinator works with multiagency representatives within a command group structure to ensure a safe and secure event. The command group is composed of individuals from the following areas: facility management, law enforcement, emergency management, fire and hazmat, and emergency medical services. These key stakeholders are involved in the risk assessment process prior to event day and are responsible for developing risk management, emergency, and evacuation plans. In addition, the security coordinator must collaborate with any outsourced security vendors to ensure staff are adequately trained and familiar with the venue specifics.

• *Public relations, marketing, and hospitality division managers.* The public relations, marketing, and hospitality division managers work at the direction of the executive director in all matters pertaining to public relations (PR), marketing, and hospitality. These people are responsible for personnel, procedures, and activities contained in their respective divisions including (but not limited to) ceremonies and protocol, sponsorship, VIP services, media and PR, and hospitality entertainment. They recruit personnel to coordinate each activity and help staff complete assigned tasks and responsibilities. While coordinating personnel, policies, procedures, and activities within these divisions, these managers also assist other divisions with their respective PR, marketing, and hospitality needs. These managers develop, implement, and manage the overall event marketing plan and facilitate communications among personnel in other divisions as needed. These managers report directly to the executive director. In addition, they will evaluate the PR, marketing, and hospitality divisions and make recommendations.

An effective organizational structure facilitates effective event planning. All events, from a local tennis tournament to the Wimbledon Championships, need effective event management plans. A management plan should include six basic steps: scheduling, negotiating, coordinating, staging, cleaning up, and evaluating. The executive or facility director is ultimately responsible for developing this plan.

Preevent Tasks

The major tasks to be done before the event are scheduling the event, negotiating the details with the organization involved, and coordinating the management of every aspect of the event.

Scheduling the Event

There are two perspectives to consider when scheduling the event. The first is from the perspective of the facility. Scheduling an event entails a reservation process in which events are planned according to the philosophy of the facility. Because most facilities maintain a profit-oriented philosophy, a facility director tries to schedule the largest possible number of events without overburdening the facility or employees. The second perspective of scheduling is that of the event promoter or event director. In this case, the event promoter or director secures a venue based on the needs of the event itself. Because the event promoter or director also maintains a profit-oriented philosophy, he or she will book a venue that provides the best location and amenities to serve the demands of the event. Securing and contracting one specific event or attraction is known as **booking** an event.

Scheduling may involve difficult decisions about what events are acceptable to the directors and management of the facility and what facility will best fit the needs of the event for the event promoter or director. For example, a boxing match or a mixed martial arts competition might be considered too controversial for some constituents or might be distasteful to owners or managers, but they might produce a large profit from significant ticket sales and the accompanying concession and merchandise revenues. The facility builds its reputation on how its directors handle such conflicts. If the event promoter or director is attempting to schedule a controversial or risky event with apprehensive facility leaders, preparing for conflicts by developing a cost–benefit analysis and a risk-management plan can assist in negotiating and securing venues.

Negotiating the Event

After making the decision to schedule the event, the facility director (or his or her representative) negotiates the terms of the contract with the event promoter or director. Most facilities use a **boilerplate contract** that addresses the specific terms (e.g., cost of facility, division of revenue) agreed on by the facility and the promoter. This type of document uses standard language and a fill-in-the-blank format (similar to most apartment leases) to describe the various clauses in the contract. Normally, a prearranged and negotiated percentage, known as a split, is used to divide the various sources of revenue (e.g., sale of tickets, merchandise, concessions, parking) between the pro-

---

booking—Securing and contracting one specific sport or entertainment event.
boilerplate contract—A generic document that uses standard language and a fill-in-the-blank format to outline expectations between parties.

Hurricane Threatens Event

An unexpected hurricane made its way up the East Coast and left a great deal of damage in its wake. A long-distance triathlon was scheduled for the Sunday following the Thursday-night hurricane. When the event director toured the 112-mile (180 kilometer) bike course on Friday morning, it was apparent that some of the washed-out roads would not be in any condition for use by Sunday. The event director did not have the permits to use any other roads, and it was too late to determine a new bike route and secure the new permits. Fortunately, the swimming and running courses were not as damaged, and that portion of the race could proceed as planned.

The event director gathered her staff and discussed moving forward with the event. Their company had just taken over ownership of the race, so cancelling the first year was out of the question. The team discussed the consequences of shortening the bike leg. Would participants be angered? Would it hurt their reputation? The team discussed all options and their subsequent consequences to determine how the event should proceed. They had 2,300 athletes and 1,200 volunteers, 15 key sponsors, and a number of city stakeholders to consider. What would you do?

Here is the play-by-play of what the event team decided:

1. They gathered the crisis management team and started their action plan. They were confident that the race could proceed with a shortened 50-mile (80 kilometer) bike course.

2. They secured the participant registration lists from the website database and divided the contact information into groups: email and phone. IT people sent email blasts to everyone with a known address and notified them of the problem. All professional athletes were called and informed of the status of the course and given the opportunity to race a different course.

3. All members of the crisis management team were responsible for calling the sponsors. In addition, they created and printed flyers. As people came to the registration counters, they received flyers indicating the course change and what to expect on the course due to the damage from the storm.

4. Athletes were granted permission to set up bike trainers near transition to ride in place to accumulate the entire 112 miles (180 kilometers) necessary for the iron distance.

5. People who requested refunds were given transfer waivers to different races owned by the organization and were assigned reference numbers. All refunds were granted with a transfer only.

6. Staff members were instructed to deal with complaints right away and to be up front and honest; all messages on the team's phones were to be returned immediately.

7. The logistics team did a final sweep of the course to ensure no one was in danger due to storm damage.

8. The event began on Sunday morning at 8:00 a.m., and all participants completed the event safely.

moter and the facility. These financial negotiations are critical factors in establishing the cost of an event. If the amount is too high, additional negotiations ensue to determine which costs to adjust and which splits to modify. When a reasonable split is not found between two sides, it is possible that the facility director or the event promoter or director will walk away from the negotiation.

Coordinating the Event

After completing the preliminary negotiations with the event promoter or director and calculating the cost analysis, the event coordinator sits down and studies all aspects of the event. This person is responsible for providing specific venue and equipment needs as requested by the promoter or director or appropriate representatives. An event coordinator needs to transport, assemble, erect, and store equipment while establishing procedures and guidelines for the rental, purchase, storage, and transportation of venue equipment. Depending on the type of facility, the event promoter or director might be required to secure additional equipment. For example, an event promoter or director hosting a marathon might

---

cost analysis—A systematic process used to provide an estimation of the revenue and expenses of an event.

secure a community pavilion to stage the finish line festivities and sound equipment and fencing to use at the pavilion. The event director, not the facility, is responsible for all the equipment rentals required for the event. Securing a warehouse area for equipment storage and distribution and establishing a control system for venue and equipment logistics (e.g., inventory management, storage, transportation of equipment) are crucial steps in the process. After completing these tasks, the event coordinator works with the facility director to recruit and hire event personnel who will assist in maintaining the venues and equipment during the event. The event coordinator then trains and supervises these personnel.

In the facility, the event coordinator designs a **work order** for all employees to follow. The work order is the game plan for the event. It documents all requirements discussed with the promoter or director or other company representative. Anything not documented will be the responsibility of the event coordinator. The work order also defines the time required to do each assigned task. The event promoter or director will also design a work order for event staff. In addition, the promoter or director will create a **work breakdown structure (WBS)** and a **Gantt chart** to assist him or her in managing the event. The WBS breaks the event tasks down into manageable parts and assigns specific resources to those tasks. The Gantt chart provides a visual illustration of the tasks in a bar chart.

Staging the Event

After much planning and anticipation, the day of the event arrives. To ensure the event runs smoothly, the event director will create **run sheets**, **floor plans**, and **floor diagrams**. The run sheet lays out the timing of the event, and the floor plans illustrate where equipment must be placed in the venue. The floor diagrams represent how event participants will move through the venue. For large events such as concerts and ice shows, an entire day (sometimes the day prior) is usually allowed for load-in and setup of event equipment. For a small event such as a local golf tournament, the event coordinator ensures that items such as the longest-drive and closest-to-the-pin markers are in place, that each group has received its caddy or electric cart, and that refreshments, award tables, and portable toilets are properly located.

Run sheets, floor plans, and floor diagrams will all be necessary for all events, but their detail will vary with the scope of the event.

For larger events such as men's football games, many planning elements come into play. For example, when television crews are on campus for a prime-time game, they must have everything they need to carry out their broadcast. At a minimum level, this involves ensuring that crews have access to the stadium at least a day in advance. During the 2016 football season, ESPN's *GameDay* was on the campus of The Ohio State University (OSU) for the show's weekly television broadcast. Due to the hype surrounding the game and the implications of the match up (opponents were ranked 2 and 3 in the nation), ESPN extended the broadcast to 5 hours instead of their normal 2 hours. The plan was for the broadcast to be outside from 7:00 to 10:45 a.m. and then to move inside the stadium. In addition to the on-air talent, ESPN reportedly had 90 staffers working *GameDay* and an additional 175 staff members there for the game. These staffers were to assist the director, Derek Mobley, and producer, Bill Bonnell, on the production of the game, which featured additional cameras, including eight pylon cameras to show images from the goal line, sideline, and backline; super slow motion cameras to provide precise images; and an above the stadium camera for the aerial shots (Volner, 2016). Event managers at OSU had to work with all these people to produce a quality broadcast and event.

Providing a safe and enjoyable event for spectators requires substantial security planning well in advance of the event. Event managers must consider event risks and develop plans in collaboration with local response agencies, including alcohol policies inside the venue. Promoting a safe event also requires adequate staff training to implement policies and procedures while balancing a customer friendly experience.

Security

Delivering a safe and secure event is a priority for event management. As the profile of sporting events increases, so does the level of risk. Sport event threats may be intentional (i.e., terrorism, hooliganism, vandalism) or unintentional (i.e., logistical failure, inclement weather), and they have the potential to affect spectators, participants, and sponsors. It is

---

work order—A document that details all the requirements of an event.

work breakdown structure (WBS)—A document that divides event tasks into smaller, manageable tasks.

Gantt chart—A bar chart that displays the various tasks and the timeline in which they must be completed.

run sheet—A detailed schedule of the timing and sequence of the event elements.

floor plan—An illustration of where equipment or items are placed in the event venue.

floor diagram—An illustration of how event attendees will move through a venue.

therefore imperative for management to develop and implement an effective security system (Hall, Cooper, Marciani, & McGee, 2012). The event security coordinator will collaborate with the command group (as previously discussed) to develop plans and conduct necessary training and exercise initiatives. First, a risk assessment will be conducted to identify relevant threats and **vulnerabilities** so appropriate plans, policies, procedures, and protective measures can be implemented. Essential facility plans include an emergency response plan (including incident response and evacuation procedures) and a business continuity and recovery plan. An event operation plan will also be developed to include policies for the following areas: alcohol, communications, credentialing, emergency medical services, fan conduct, missing person, parking, prohibited items, tailgate, ticket-taking, search, and seating. Protective measures to be considered include the use of closed-circuit television, adequate facility lighting, law enforcement presence at entry points, facility lockdown prior to events, scheduled vendor deliveries, staff background checks and use of photo credentials, briefing and debriefing event meetings, and use of certified security providers (if outsourced). Staff training and **exercises** will be conducted that address basic awareness (suspicious behavior or criminal activity), crowd control methods, and emergency or evacuation procedures. Once training is completed, management should conduct exercises to test plans, ensure staff awareness of roles and responsibilities, and identify any resource gaps (Schwarz, Hall, & Shibli, 2015).

Seating arrangements at an event or facility as well as the flow of the crowd into and out of an event or facility are both of particular importance to those in charge of event and facility operations. Many facilities in the United States use reserved seats for events. This policy has not always been in place in sport stadiums around the world. Standing-room areas or terraces were permitted in many European stadiums until the late 1980s. In April 1989, thousands of soccer fans flocked to Hillsborough Stadium in Sheffield, England, to watch the Football Association Cup semifinal between Liverpool and Nottingham Forest. Too many fans were allowed into an already-full terrace at one end of the stadium. In the resulting crush, 96 Liverpool fans were killed and many others were seriously injured. Reserved seating is now required for the Premier League and Champion League levels of British soccer, although standing room is still allowed in the lower divisions (Merrick, 2016).

With a reserved ticket, a spectator is assigned a specific seat, in a specific row, in a specific section at the event. With the use of trained ushers and an effective crowd control plan, few problems occur at events with this type of seating. Other types of seating are not as easy to manage. General admission (GA) seating is a first-come, first-served process that sometimes causes fans to line up outside for hours before the facility opens in the hope of gaining that prestigious front-row seat. Festival seating is a type of GA seating, but it is a misnomer because no actual seats exist. Festival seating allows spectators to crowd together standing shoulder to shoulder in open floor space. Although promoters can sell more tickets by using festival seating rather than reserved or GA seating, it is a potentially deadly arrangement that continues to be a controversial topic in event management.

Event security issues may include terrorism, fan violence, inclement weather, crowd control, fraudulent tickets, and vandalism. The following are some of the fatal incidents that have occurred at entertainment events around the world:

- May 1964, Lima, Peru: 318 people were killed and 500 injured in riots at National Stadium after Argentina beat Peru in an Olympic qualifying match.
- December 1979, Cincinnati, Ohio: 11 people were killed in a crush to get into a concert by The Who.
- January 1991, Salt Lake City, Utah: Three teenagers were killed when the crowd at an AC/DC concert rushed the stage.
- May 1999, Minsk, Belarus: 53 people were killed when a crowd fleeing a severe rainstorm during a downtown rock concert and beer festival stampeded in an underground passage.
- July 2000, Copenhagen, Denmark: Eight people were killed in a crush of fans trying to get closer to Pearl Jam at an outdoor concert.
- February 2003, Chicago, Illinois: 21 people died at a Chicago nightclub when guests stampeded to the exits after a security guard used pepper spray to break up a fight.
- February 2003, West Warwick, Rhode Island: 100 people died after pyrotechnics ignited flammable foam lining the walls of the venue during a Great White concert.
- July 2003, Moscow, Russia: 17 people were killed when two explosions went off at a

---

vulnerability—Any exploitable facility security deficiency.

exercises—Focused practice activities that place staff members in simulated incident scenarios and require them to function in the capacity expected of them in a real-world event.

rock festival. Reports were that two suicide bombers set off the blasts in the crowd at the entrance to the festival when security guards prevented them from entering the gates.

- April 2008, Quito, Ecuador: 15 people died after pyrotechnics, lit by a band member, ignited a nightclub hosting a rock concert.
- June 2010, Johannesburg, South Africa: Although not fatal, a stampede before a warm-up World Cup soccer match injured 15 fans.
- July 2010, Duisburg, Germany: A crowd disaster at the Love Parade music festival caused the death of 21 people from suffocation. Approximately 500 more were injured.

- February 2012, Port Said, Egypt: 74 people were killed and 250 were injured when spectators at a soccer match broke onto the pitch and attacked players and rival fans.
- April 2013, Boston, Massachusetts: Two bombs went off near the finish line of the Boston Marathon. Three spectators died and over 260 additional people were injured.
- July 2013, Nabire, Indonesia: 18 people died and over three dozen more were injured in a brawl and the ensuing stadium stampede after a boxing match in the Kota Lama Sport Stadium.
- September 2015, Mecca, Saudi Arabia: A crush and stampede caused more than 2,000

Staging a Spectacular World-Class Mega Event: The 2022 FIFA World Cup in Qatar

The 2022 FIFA World Cup has suffered a great deal of criticism due to the perceived corruption and human rights issues related to the migrant workers hired to build the necessary infrastructure for the World Cup. More than 2.1 million people working in Qatar are foreigners who must be sponsored to work in the country. This is a law known as the "kafala system." Under Qatar law, the employee must be sponsored by a Qatari citizen to work in the country. Workers must ask permission of the sponsor to change jobs or to obtain an exit visa to leave the country (which are often not granted). The working and living conditions are harrowing. Workers endure hours in the blazing heat, receive low pay, and live in squalid accommodations. It has been reported that more than 2,575 workers have died in the construction of the World Cup stadiums (Human Rights Watch, 2017). Due to increased world pressure from human rights groups, Qatar's emir recently abolished the kafala system, but many criticize that the new law removes the word *sponsorship* but leaves the same basic system in place (BBC News, 2016).

Whether this mega event can be successful is certainly up for debate. To stage this particular World Cup, planners must consider the severe heat, strict Qatar laws (e.g., regarding how women should dress and alcohol consumption), and other factors that will affect spectators, fans, and tourists. To combat the heat, the World Cup was rescheduled to Novem-

ber and December, but temperatures can still reach the mid-90s. The schedule change is controversial because it will interfere with the regular-season schedules of domestic leagues around the world.

Although alcohol and sports go together in other parts of the world, Qatar has announced that it plans to ban the public consumption of alcohol during the tournament in streets, public squares, and the stadiums. The secretary general of the Supreme Committee for Delivery and Legacy, Al-Thawadi, noted: "I am personally against the provision of alcohol in stadiums and public places based on our values and our traditions and our culture." He went on to explain that those who wish to consume alcohol can still do so in "specific and faraway places from the public squares," although where these places will be is unclear (Payne, 2016). The penalties for breaking the law are severe and include immediate arrest, hefty fines, deportation, and imprisonment (Payne, 2016). Alcohol bans in stadiums are nothing new; they are often used to help curb violence. However, alcohol has always been a part of World Cup culture. For example, Brazil relaxed its ban on alcohol in stadiums during the 2014 World Cup. How will the stiffness of Qatar's restrictions on public consumption of alcohol affect the atmosphere of the Cup? In addition, what will FIFA do about key alcohol sponsors such as Anheuser-Busch?

deaths of pilgrims during the annual Hajj pilgrimage.

- October 2017, Las Vegas, Nevada: A lone shooter opened fire on a country music festival, killing 59 people and wounding over 500.

Customer Service

Tod Leiweke, the COO of the NFL, says that for any sport or entertainment event to be a success, facility and event managers must concentrate on three fundamentals: brand, audience, and experience (Yoshida, 2017). The brand is the venue, the audience comprises all those people driven by a passion for the product (the event) and the service that accompanies it, and the experience is the relationship between the attendee and the event itself (Yoshida, 2017). Customer service, guest relations, and fan and participant services are terms used to describe the relationship between the event (or facility) management and the people who attend the event.

The event attendees, whether spectators or active participants, are the fuel that the sport and entertainment industry relies on. Without attendees, there would be neither events nor facilities to house them. But the guests who attend sport and entertainment events are products of a society that has come to expect immediate results or instant gratification. Everyone knows that most businesses must have repeat customers to be profitable. In the same way, event managers depend on repeat customers to produce a profit. Thus, to guarantee repeat customers, event and facility managers must listen to their guests and respond effectively to their concerns. These managers must not only understand the role of the consumer experience but also establish which consumers will be satisfied with the core product (the event) and ancillary services in order to ensure the attendee will return (Yoshida, 2017).

To enhance this process, sport organizations can use social media to gauge what consumers are saying about their events and their experiences at the facility. In many instances, topics include congestion at the event, ease of parking and entering the location, and other experiences at the facility. By taking a proactive approach to monitoring feedback, sport organizations can ensure that they develop loyal consumers who will maximize word-of-mouth initiatives.

Alcohol Policies

A potential liability exists if intoxicated patrons create dangerous situations for themselves and others. Some people argue that revenue generated from alcohol sales is worth the risk, and some facilities would find it difficult to generate a profit without alcohol sales. Others have determined that the increased revenue produced by selling alcohol does not outweigh the liabilities. Even at college stadiums, administrators have found ways to serve alcohol in enclosed

Social Media and Sport Facility and Event Management

With the evolution of social media, sport managers have the opportunity to enhance their efficiency in many areas including facility and event management. The two-way communication offered in social media outlets such as Twitter enables managers to seek feedback from consumers who attend their events. In an article in *Street & Smith's SportsBusiness Journal*, Sutton (2012) explained that many top organizations outside of sports use social media to get feedback to enhance their operations. For example, he noted that companies such as Orbitz and Southwest have used Twitter to find complaints about their products. As a result, they have taken a proactive approach to correcting issues with their operations to build customer loyalty.

Sport organizations have the same ability to use social media to gauge their effectiveness in event- and facility-related areas. For example, when assessing the different elements of the stadium experience, sport organizations can hire a social media tracking service that gathers and provides evaluative feedback about what will improve the customer experience. In addition, facilities and events promoters and directors should hire a social media coordinator or intern to disseminate information about the event and facility experience. Many events have used this strategy to keep their event attendees informed of promotions, emergency details, and experiences. For example, WrestleMania, the WWE annual event, used social media to solicit fan-submitted pictures with signs indicating how far people traveled to the event, and they made a video using the photos. CEO Vince McMahon joined Twitter days prior to WrestleMania 29 and used the hashtag #BigReveal to keep followers engaged and excited about the event. The use of social media is not only necessary to inform event attendees but also to enable cocreation of event experiences.

spaces such as suites because it is a desirable element for consumers. Although the controversy continues, alcohol probably will continue to be a part of many sporting events, and facility managers must continue to devise tactics to reduce the risks created by alcohol consumption. Best practices for alcohol management are presented below (Filce, Hall, & Phillips, 2016):

- *Policy and training.* Develop an alcohol management plan that addresses admission policy and detection of alcohol products entering the stadium, restrictions on sales and marketing, and public awareness of stadium alcohol policies. Event staff should be trained through a certified alcohol management program such as Training for Intervention Procedures (TIPS) or Techniques for Effective Alcohol Management (TEAM).

- *Sales and marketing.* Consider time and quantity limits before, during, and after events and verify patrons' identification. For example, begin alcohol sales one hour prior to the event and end sales before event closure, and place a limit of the number of drinks that can be purchased at one time.

- *Tailgating.* Ensure that security officers monitor tailgate areas before and after games, and limit tailgating hours before and after the event.

- *Detection and enforcement.* Conduct gate searches for alcohol products, deny entry to visibly intoxicated fans, and enforce a no reentry policy. Consider implementing an anonymous text messaging system that fans can use to report problems to the command center. Enforce policies with ejection, revocation of season tickets, and termination of tailgating privileges.

Fan behavior at stadiums has become an increasing concern at all major sport venues. Leagues and teams often publish codes of conduct for spectators. Outrageous behavior and stadium fights are often videoed and posted on social media platforms. Unruly fans who cause disruptions at games are often ejected and sometimes arrested. Intoxicated fans are often reported by fellow attendees to stadium authorities, and drunk spectators are often asked to leave games or are denied access into the stadium. For certain offenses, season ticket holders can lose their seats if they or their guests are ejected.

Crowd Management

A facility or event manager needs a crowd management plan for every event. Whether the event is a small high school basketball tournament at a local YMCA or an NCAA Division I Softball Champion-

ship, managing the ingress and egress of spectators and any potential crowd control issues is crucial to the safety of patrons and the subsequent success of the event. Crowd management planning components to consider include the following:

- *Staff recruitment and training.* Event organizers must ensure they have adequate staff with appropriate skills. Factors to consider when determining staff requirements include anticipated attendance, number of events (single event versus multiple events), expertise required for specific roles, staff composition (outsourced, in-house, or volunteer), and relative threat intelligence. Industry standards for the number of security personnel needed vary from country to country. In the United States, the National Fire Protection Association standard for fire and safety protection applies to crowd management principles; it states that there should be one trained crowd management professional for every 250 spectators in any facility with a capacity of more than 250 people (Hall, 2013). Once management has decided on the appropriate number of staff, they must determine whether they will use in-house operations, hire an outside company, or recruit a volunteer workforce. Some facilities choose to use their own staff to conduct crowd control duties; with these in-house operations, management must develop a staff training protocol to ensure appropriate responses. Other facilities outsource crowd management services to independent contractors. Outsourcing might be cost-effective if leaders do not have the time to invest in recruiting, training, and managing a security team. Another option is the use of volunteers. Volunteers are often essential to events, especially mega events such as the Olympic and Paralympic Games. More than 50,000 volunteers were recruited for the Rio Olympics in 2016, and 70,000 volunteers were used in the London Olympics in 2012.

- *Emergency planning.* The intent of an emergency plan is to ensure that minor incidents do not become major incidents and that major incidents do not become fatal. Emergencies take many forms such as medical problems (e.g., life-threatening issues, minor injuries), severe weather (e.g., lightning, tornadoes), natural disasters (e.g., earthquakes, floods), fires, bomb threats, power losses, and terrorist activities. Managers must not only design and implement emergency plans but also practice them, because courts will ask for documentation about when the plans were practiced. Because of the terrorist threat, managers at several venues use practice sessions to test the ability of their emergency services during a

---

command center—A designated area where the command group (security team) controls the security functions by monitoring activities inside and outside the facility.

Whether the sport activity is held inside or outside, facility and event managers need to have a crowd management plan in place that involves staff recruitment and training, emergency planning, accessibility for spectators with disabilities, procedures for ejecting disruptive people, an efficient communication system, and effective information and directional signage.

Courtesy of Paul M. Pedersen.

mock attack. In the hope of helping a wide range of sport organizations prepare for a disaster, the National Center of Spectator Sports Safety and Security created a simulation software program called SportEvac that allows sport organizations to work through mock disaster situations. In addition to mimicking threat situations, the program allows facility managers to face a wide range of situations (e.g., full capacity stadium, emergency lights fail) to help prepare evacuation plans for stadiums (Department of Homeland Security, n.d.). In light of the 2013 terrorist bombing at the Boston Marathon and other threats and emergencies at sport facilities (e.g., detonated bomb outside Stade de France during the November 2015 Paris attacks), such training is essential.

• *Ensuring accessibility for spectators with disabilities.* An effective crowd control plan should address the procedures necessary to ensure facility accessibility for all citizens. Congress passed the Americans with Disabilities Act (ADA) in 1992. The ADA has had a major effect on the design of sport and entertainment venues. Sport and entertainment event managers must be familiar with the ADA because its various requirements pertain to facility features such as signage, restrooms, telephones, parking, and shower stalls. Furthermore, event managers must also develop plans for the evacuation of spectators with disabilities or special needs.

• *Procedures for ejecting disruptive people.* An effective crowd control must address the procedures necessary to eject disruptive, unruly, or intoxicated patrons. The ejection duties should be the responsibility of trained crowd control staff and, in some jurisdictions, police officers, sheriff's department personnel, or state troopers. These people must understand the concepts of the reasonably prudent person and excessive force, and they should understand that they might be sued for negligence if they eject patrons incorrectly. Ushers should not undertake these duties if they are not trained in crowd control procedures. Removing disruptive or intoxicated fans will provide a safer environment for the remaining spectators and help protect the facility or event manager from potential litigation (Ammon & Unruh, 2013).

• *An efficient communication system.* Communication is critical in ensuring spectator safety, enjoyment, and security. The use of a centralized area (command center) for representatives from each group involved in event management (e.g., law enforcement, maintenance, medical services, and security) will facilitate communication and improve decision making. The command center should be able to access the facility's public-address system, fire alarm system, turnstile system, and door access control. Incident reports are collected and analyzed at this site, and the appropriate event security personnel are notified to address any imminent crowd issues.

• *Effective signage.* Informational and directional signs build a support network between fans and facility management staff. Spectators appreciate being treated fairly and, if they are informed, they normally abide by facility directives pertaining to no-smoking sections, alcohol policies, and prohibited items. Directional signs have several important uses. As spectators approach the facility, road signs can indicate the correct exits and provide relevant parking information. Other signs serve to indicate the correct gate or portal and direct ticket-buying patrons to the box office. Signage will help facility patrons locate concession stands, first-aid rooms, telephones, and restrooms. Informational signs regarding prohibited items assist patrons in making decisions before entry (Ammon & Unruh, 2013).

Postevent Tasks

After the event, several additional items need to be completed. The postevent procedures include activities such as event cleanup, settlement, and evaluation of the event.

Event Cleanup

After the event is over and the attendees have filed out, the equipment used by the event is gathered up and put away or stored in trucks, and cleanup of the facility commences. Depending on the size of the event, an additional day might be set aside for the load-out, but most events will load out on the same day because venues often have other events scheduled. Cleanup will also involve inventorying the equipment to make sure nothing has wandered off and ensure everything is still in working order and safe for the next time it is used.

Evaluating the Event

Immediately after the event, the management team evaluates the process. Documentation of the entire process is critical not only for protection against subsequent litigation but also for reference in planning future events. Feedback stations, where event attendees can leave positive or negative feedback, can elicit helpful information. Event satisfaction surveys, observations from event and facility staff, and incident reports can also provide valuable information to the event manager. A security debrief is important after an event to analyze safety and security issues and develop recommendations for future events.

Critical Thinking in Sport Facility and Event Management

Many aspects of ethical and moral conduct involve consideration and debate of possible actions and outcomes. One feature of critical thinking is the systematic evaluation of various arguments and positions. These discussions help managers weigh possible alternatives and their requisite outcomes. For example, consider the following event and facility management scenario about transgender athletes. An event director received a call from an event participant who was in the process of undergoing her transformation from male to female. Because there were no set rules for transgender athletes, the participant wanted to know how she should register. The IOC and the NCAA have recently set policies for transgender athletes in competition. Some have debated that it is not fair for transitioning male athletes to compete as females, especially if their transformation is not complete. Others have argued that an athlete should compete

---

settlement—Reconciling the expenses and revenue of an event and dividing the profits according to a contracted arrangement.
documentation—Detailed records that describe an event.

in the category to which he or she identifies. Consider how you would handle this situation to ensure fair competition and inclusion at your running event.

Ethics in Sport Facility and Event Management

All employee-training programs should include a discussion of the role that professional ethics plays in facility and event management. Ethical behavior is not the sole province of employees. Most sport facilities have ethical standards by which patrons are expected to comply. For example, the Seattle Seahawks have created a code of conduct that is committed to creating a safe, comfortable, and enjoyable experience for guests at CenturyLink Field. To achieve this, their organization has created the following list of behaviors that are not acceptable under any circumstances:

- Behavior that is unruly, disruptive, or illegal in nature

- Over-intoxication or other signs of alcohol or substance impairment
- Foul or abusive language or obscene gestures
- Interference with the progress of the game (including throwing objects on the field)
- Failing to follow instructions of stadium personnel
- Verbal or physical harassment of home or opposing team fans
- Verbal or physical harassment of stadium guests and staff members
- Smoking, tobacco, or marijuana use on CenturyLink Field property
- Possession of outside alcohol inside the stadium

Fans who do not abide by these rules can be ejected from the stadium and have future ticket privileges revoked. Fans who are ejected because of violations of the Fan Code of Conduct are not allowed back into CenturyLink Field until they have taken a required four-hour, US$250 course (Seattle Seahawks, 2017).

For chapter-specific learning activities, visit the web study guide at
www.HumanKinetics.com/ContemporarySportManagement.

Summary

The FIFA World Cup, the Olympic Games, concerts, and high school track meets have two common denominators: They take place in some type of facility, and they are events. Given that they have these two traits, they must have people to manage them. Sport organizations can choose to manage events in-house or outsource them to private management companies. These private entities have been successful in raising the profit margins of many sport and public assembly facilities across the United States.

To ensure a successful event, facility directors must perform several important tasks, and they need to understand how these tasks relate to the successful completion of every event. Scheduling and booking an event begin the overall process, and a cost analysis is critical in these initial operations. After the facility director has decided that the event will be held, the necessary contracts need to be signed, and the event coordinator must create and communicate a work order to the others on the event management team.

Items such as seating arrangements, crowd management, alcohol policies, settlement, and event evaluation must be carried out for an event to be successful.

The number of facilities has grown significantly in recent years, and many of these facilities schedule sport and entertainment events with global implications. Worldwide terrorist attacks have changed the facility and event management industry dramatically. In addition, some areas of sport have downsized because of factors such as changes in the economy, corporate mergers, and business failures. Because of these trends, the future of facility and event management is not as clear as once imagined. Slower revenue growth has affected profit margins. This has had a domino effect on facility and event management that needs to be consistently monitored moving forward. In addition, sport organizations must also be aware of the ways that they can use technology to enhance the experience provided to customers who attend their events.

Review Questions

1. What is the nearest major single-purpose facility in your area? List the personnel who would be involved in the management at this type of facility.

2. What are some of the nearby multipurpose facilities in your area? How would the management of these facilities differ from the single-purpose facility you identified in the previous question?

3. Currently, several companies privately manage more than 300 facilities nationally and internationally. What are some of the companies near you?

4. In reference to the previous question, why would a facility choose to contract with one of these companies? What are the potential benefits of contracting with these companies?

5. What is the purpose of a work order or a WBS? Who compiles these and for what purpose?

6. Why do the management team members need to meet to evaluate the overall production after the event ends? Why should the team complete all the proper documentation at this meeting?

7. Why is employing trained people to reduce facility risks a less expensive alternative than reacting to potential disasters without such people?

8. Why is it important for sport event and facility managers to develop proper ethical guidelines and critical thinking skills?

9. What role can technology play in the event management process to ensure that consumers are enjoying their experience at the facility?

PART IV

Current Challenges in Sport Management

A critical step in the process of becoming a responsible and effective manager of sport enterprises is recognizing the significance of sport as a major social institution that is increasingly influenced by legal rulings, data analytics, global commerce, and research findings. The first three chapters in this section provide the foundation for understanding the challenges presented by legal, social, and international aspects of sport. An appreciation of these facets of sport will increase the likelihood that you will make wise managerial decisions within the context of the broad social and global environment in which sporting activities occur. The final two chapters of the book deal with analytics and research in the field of sport management.

Anita M. Moorman, R. Christopher Reynolds, and Amanda Siegrist address sport management's legal issues in chapter 17. The authors open their chapter with an introduction to the basic concepts of law. They then discuss the influence of the U.S. Constitution on sport management and the effects of federal legislation, specifically Title IX sexual violence guidelines regarding sexual harassment and sexual violence in intercollegiate athletics. The authors then examine state legal systems including tort law, negligence, premise liability, intentional torts, and contracts. They conclude the chapter with a discussion of legal challenges that await prospective sport managers. The professional featured in this chapter is Steven J. Silver, an associate with Pierce Atwood's Litigation Practice Group. This chapter's international profile sidebar by Richard Parrish (Edge Hill University, England) provides an introduction to sport law and policy in the United Kingdom.

Chapter 18 focuses on the role of sport sociology in the management of sporting activities. Nicole M. LaVoi, Mary Jo Kane, and Nancy Lough open with a discussion of the social significance of sport and then examine possible benefits of sport such as its ability to socialize participants and unify people. Next, the authors present several examples of the darker side of sport including sexism, homophobia and heterosexism, and racism. They conclude the chapter with a discussion of how sport can serve as a vehicle for social transformation and how you can apply your knowledge of sport sociology in the management of sport. Megan Kahn, the executive director of the Alliance of Women Coaches, is the sport industry professional profiled in this chapter. The international profile sidebar in this chapter is an essay on the sociological influences of sport and the media in Slovenia, the homeland of the sidebar author, Simon Ličen (Washington State University).

In chapter 19, Ceyda Mumcu, Sylvia Trendafilova, and Lucie Thibault first define international sport. The authors then analyze the international growth of sport and provide examples to illustrate this phenomenon: changes to the Olympic Games, expanded opportunities for women, the redefinition of international sport, increased recruitment and marketing efforts at the international level, and increased participation in international sport by countries with emerging economies. They also discuss governance, environmental sustainability, and gender issues related to international sport. Next, they discuss guidelines for international travel and the necessary skills for a successful career in international sport. Two sport industry professionals are featured in this chapter: Sheila N. Nguyen, the executive director of the Sports Environment Alliance, and Andrew Tinnish, the assistant general manager of the Toronto Blue Jays (MLB). This chapter's international profile sidebar by Rosa López de D'Amico (Universidad Pedagógica Experimental Libertador, Venezuela) examines curricular aspects of sport, physical activity, and physical education in Venezuela.

Chapter 20 is new to this edition of *Contemporary Sport Management*. Kevin Mongeon, David P. Hedlund, and Ryan Spalding examine the rise, influence, usefulness, and trends of sport analytics. They first discuss the sport analytics process and its various components and then apply this process to predictive analytics (e.g., the Pythagorean win percentage expectancy). The authors then examine sport analytics techniques. This is followed by an overview of sport analytics in practice in which the authors examine applications for managers, coaches, and sport businesses. Other topics covered are the influence of technology, the use and evaluation of metrics, and the knowledge areas, skills, and career opportunities in sport analytics. The professional profile is on Kyle Dubas, the assistant general manager of the Toronto Maple Leafs Hockey Club (NHL). Adam Karg (Deakin University, Australia) is the author of the chapter's international profile sidebar, which addresses how analytics can be used to build sport fan equity.

In chapter 21, Nola Agha, Jess C. Dixon, and Brendan Dwyer address research in sport management. The authors begin their examination of this topic by explaining what sport management research is and the various types of research conducted in this field. They then explain why sport managers need to understand research and address the features of what constitutes quality research. In addition to examining research-related ethical and critical thinking issues, the authors discuss major challenges in sport management research as well as the future of research conducted by sport managers. The professional profile is on Tracy Schoenadel, the senior vice president of SMG Insight, a global business-to-business and business-to-consumer firm that specializes in sport and sponsorship research and consulting. The international profile sidebar in this chapter examines alcohol sponsorship in the sport industry. Sarah Gee of the University of Windsor, Canada, and Guillaume Bodet of Université Claude Bernard Lyon 1, France, contributed this essay.

Before you complete additional sport management courses and enter the field, you are encouraged to become familiar with the topics and issues presented in the final section of the book. The first three chapters of this section provide you with a basic understanding of three current challenges (or opportunities) in sport management (i.e., law, sociology, and globalization), and the final two chapters give you a basic understanding of the concepts and usages of data analytics and research in the sport industry. The information provided in the research chapter, for example, has practical application as you complete your education and when you become a professional. Some of your instructors will require you to write research reports, because they know that when you become a professional one of your obligations to your employer, your employees, the consumers of your products, and the public will involve being familiar with the research in your field.

For More Information

Professional and Scholarly Associations, Institutes, and Organizations

- Academy of Legal Studies in Business (ALSB)
- Alliance of Women Coaches
- American Sociological Association (ASA)
- Association Femmes Mixité Sports
- Australia and New Zealand Sports Law Association (ANZSLA)
- Black Entertainment and Sports Lawyers Association (BESLA)
- Canadian Association for the Advancement of Women and Sport and Physical Activity (CAAWS)
- Center for the Study of Sport in Society
- Cerebral Palsy International Sports and Recreation Association (CPISRA)
- Court of Arbitration for Sport (CAS)
- European Paralympic Committee (EPC)
- European Women and Sport (EWS)
- Global Association of International Sports Federations (GAISF)
- International Association of Physical Education and Sport for Girls and Women (IAPESGW)
- International Association of Sports Law (IASL)
- International Committee of Sports for the Deaf (ICSD) and the Deaflympics
- International Cricket Council (ICC)
- International Paralympic Committee (IPC)
- International Working Group on Women and Sport (IWG)
- International World Games Association (IWGA)
- LA84 Foundation
- National Center for Catastrophic Sport Injury Research (NCCSIR)
- National Center on Health, Physical Activity and Disability (NCHPAD)
- National Sports Law Institute (NSLI)
- North American Society for the Sociology of Sport (NASSS)
- Professional Football Researchers Association (PFRA)
- Society of Health and Physical Educators (SHAPE America)
- Sport and Recreation Law Association (SRLA)
- Sport Business Research Network (SBRnet)
- Sport Dispute Resolution Centre of Canada
- Sport, Health and Physical Activity Research and Policy Center (SHARP)
- Sport Research Intelligence Sportive (SIRC)
- Sports Lawyers Association (SLA)

Statistics in Sports (section of the American Statistical Association)

STRI (formerly Sports Turf Research Institute)

Tucker Center for Research on Girls & Women in Sport

Womensport Australia (WSA)

WomenSport International (WSI)

Women's Sports and Fitness Foundation (WSFF)

Women's Sports Foundation (WSF)

Youth Olympic Games (YOG)

Select Professional and Scholarly Publications

Adapted Physical Activity Quarterly

American Business Law Journal

Berkeley Journal of Entertainment & Sports Law

Catalyst eNewsletter

Culture, Sport, Society

DePaul Journal of Sports Law & Contemporary Problems

Entertainment and Sports Law Journal

Entertainment and Sports Lawyer

European Journal for Sport and Society

Florida Entertainment, Art & Sport Law Journal

Harvard Journal of Sports & Entertainment Law

Human Relations

International Gambling Studies

International Journal of Computer Science in Sport

International Journal of Sports Science and Engineering

International Review for the Sociology of Sport

International Sports Law Journal

International Sports Studies

Journal of Business Research

Journal of ICHPER-SD (International Council for Health, Physical Education, Recreation, Sport & Dance)

Journal of Quantitative Analysis in Sports

Journal of Sport and Social Issues

Journal of Sport Behavior

Journal of Sports Analytics

Journal of Sports Law & Contemporary Problems

Journal of the International Society for Comparative Physical Education and Sport

Journal of the Legal Aspects of Sport

Legal Issues in College Athletics

Marquette Sports Law Review

Mississippi Sports Law Review

The Paralympian: The Official Magazine of the International Paralympic Committee

Qualitative Research in Sport, Exercise and Health

Quest

Research Quarterly for Exercise and Sport

Seton Hall Journal of Sports and Entertainment Law

Sex Roles: A Journal of Research

Soccer and Society

Sociology of Sport Journal

Sport, Education and Society

Sport in Society

The Sport Journal

The Sport Psychologist

Sports and Entertainment Litigation Reporter

Sports Facilities and the Law

Sports Law Forum at Fordham University School of Law

Sports Lawyer

The Sports Lawyers Journal

Sports, Parks and Recreation Law Reporter

Texas Review of Entertainment & Sports Law

University of Denver Sports & Entertainment Law Journal

University of Miami Entertainment and Sports Law Review

Villanova Sports and Entertainment Law Journal

Virginia Sports and Entertainment Law Journal

Willamette Sports Law Journal

Women in Sport and Physical Activity Journal

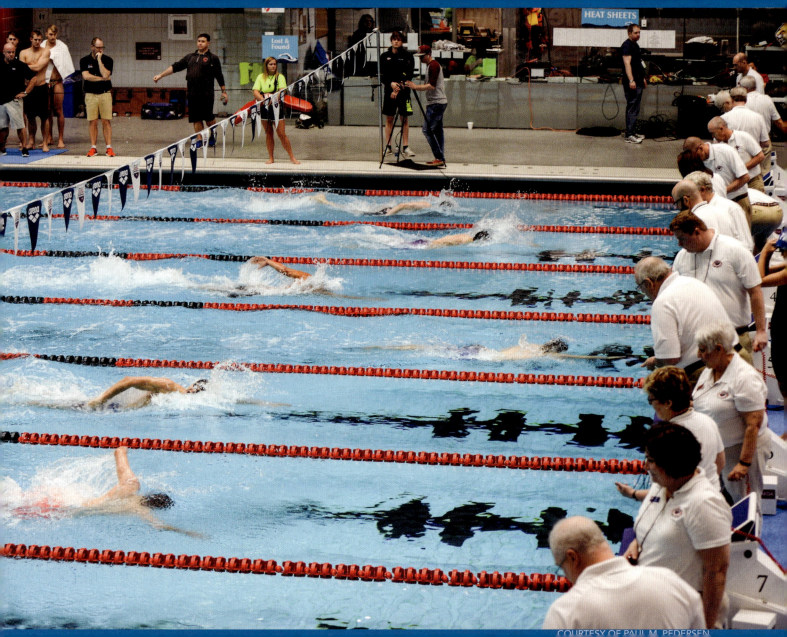

Legal Considerations in Sport Management

Anita M. Moorman
R. Christopher Reynolds
Amanda Siegrist

LEARNING OBJECTIVES

- Identify select legal issues affecting sport management stakeholders, operations, and organizations.

- Explain the American judicial system and its application to the sport industry.

- Identify situations involving the management or marketing of sport in which legal issues influence the decision-making process of those in leadership positions.

- Describe legal concepts in a sport context including federal law issues such as Title IX, state law issues such as premise liability, and the legal relationship between NCAA and its members and student-athletes.

- Discuss the fundamental elements of contract law and apply them in a sport management context.

- Engage in critical thinking and problem solving regarding how the law can influence sport management decisions.

- Apply systematic guidelines to ethical dilemmas involving legal concepts in sport.

KEY TERMS

acceptance	precedent
common law	proximate cause
consideration	stare decisis
constituencies	state action
due process	statutes
offer	tort

Sociological Aspects of Sport Management

Nicole M. LaVoi
Mary Jo Kane
Nancy Lough

LEARNING OBJECTIVES

- Define sport sociology and its importance for sport managers.
- Discuss the social and cultural significance of sport in our society.
- Identify positive and negative social effects of sport.
- Discuss significant research findings in sport sociology pertaining to sexism, racism, and homophobia.
- Discuss patterns of leadership in sport and media coverage patterns based on gender and race.
- Discuss race logic and stacking in sport.
- Discuss how homophobia affects athletes and sport practitioners.
- Discuss the effect that framing in sport media has on the value of women's sport or female athletes.
- Discuss how a lack of diversity in sport organizations affects operations and management.

KEY TERMS

empirical
gender roles
heterosexism
homophobia
race logic
role learning

social activism
socialization
sport sociology
stacking
Title IX

1926
Gertrude Ederle became the first woman to swim the English Channel

1936
Jesse Owens won four gold medals in athletics at the Berlin Olympic Games

1943
AAGPBL formed; disbanded in 1954

1957
Althea Gibson became the first African American woman to win the Wimbledon singles title and appear on a *Sports Illustrated* cover

1968
At the Olympic Games in Mexico City, Tommie Smith and John Carlos raised black-gloved fists on the medal stands

1977
Shirley Muldowney won the NHRA Top Fuel Championship

1999
Women's World Cup match between the United States and China drew 90,000 spectators at the Rose Bowl stadium

1997
Dee Kantner and Violet Palmer became the first female referees to officiate an NBA game

2008
NCAA prohibited member use of Native American mascots

2010
Super Bowl became the most viewed television program of all time in the United States

An important step in becoming a successful sport manager is gaining in-depth awareness of sport as a social, political, and economic activity that permeates our society and influences institutions and people in a variety of ways. To understand the complex dynamics of how and why people participate in sport and physical activity, you must have knowledge about individual behavior (e.g., psychological aspects such as motivation to participate) and the social context in which that behavior occurs. For nearly 40 years, the scientific investigation of the relationships and social worlds that people create, maintain, change, and contest in and through sport has been at the heart of an academic discipline called sport sociology.

The purpose of this chapter is to define sport sociology and highlight several domains of scholarly inquiry within this discipline. Attention is devoted to the areas where sport sociology and sport management intersect. Knowledge in this area can help you engage in social activism and address social challenges, especially as those challenges relate to real-world concerns such as racism, sexism, homophobia, and changing gender roles.

Given that sport is a significant part of many societies of the world, it is not surprising that scholars would be interested in studying its dimensions, scope, and influence. According to Coakley (2015), sport sociology is the subdiscipline of sociology that studies sports as social phenomena. Sport sociologists rely on sociological theories and concepts to examine institutions and organizations (e.g., the IOC), microsystems (e.g., women's professional basketball teams), or subcultures (e.g., sport gamblers). As part of their analyses, sport sociologists do not typically focus on the behavior of specific people. Instead, they examine the symbols, social patterns, structures, and organizations of groups that are actively engaged in sport and physical activity.

An underlying assumption of sport sociology is that sport is an important institution of the same magnitude as the family, the educational system, and our political structure. A fundamental goal of sport sociology is to describe the complex dynamics surrounding patterns of participation (e.g., the number of girls versus the number of boys involved in youth sports), social concerns (e.g., an overemphasis on winning that may lead to the use of steroids), and symbols (e.g., mascots) that make up this all-pervasive institution (Sage & Eitzen, 2016). Keep in mind that sport sociologists do far more than describe sport involvement by, for example, gathering data on how many people participate on an annual basis. They are ultimately concerned with understanding the social context in which this participation occurs and the meaning of sport as an influential social, political, and economic institution.

Social Significance of Sport

Did you ever wonder why local television newscasts describe their content as news, weather, and sports? Why not news, weather, and technology? Why do they not highlight education or literature? Have you ever wondered why so many families spend discretionary resources and time at youth sport events? Or why advertising rates during the NFL Super Bowl are so astronomical? The entry cost for some 30-second ads for the 2016 Super Bowl reached US$5 million or roughly US$166,700 per second (Groden, 2016). Perhaps it is because sport influences almost every aspect

---

sport sociology—The scientific investigation of relationships, social interactions, and culture that are created, maintained, changed, and contested in and through sport.

social activism—An intentional action with the goal of bringing about social change.

2012
For the first time, women competed in every sport on the program in the 2012 Olympic Games in London

2013
Lance Armstrong confessed to a decade of blood doping and the use of banned performance-enhancing substances; he was stripped of his seven consecutive Tour de France titles from 1999 to 2006

2014
WNBA Pride marketing campaign launched; WNBA was first league to recognize LGBTQ fans

2015
FIFA Women's World Cup became the most watched televised soccer match in U.S. history

2016
Simone Manuel became the first African American woman to win Olympic gold in swimming; U.S. Women's National Soccer team sues over pay discrimination

2017
Dakota Access Pipeline (DAPL) protesters arrested after climbing rafters and unfurling an anti-DAPL banner during an NFL game at U.S. Bank Stadium in Minneapolis

San Francisco 49ers hire Katie Sowers, the second woman hired by an NFL team as a full-time coach, and the first publicly out player or coach to participate in a regular-season NFL game

2018
MLB's Cleveland Indians announce the Native American caricature—the Chief Wahoo symbol—would be removed from the team's jerseys starting in 2019

In response to the demands of the USOC, the entire USA Gymnastics board of directors resigned as a result of the sexual abuse scandal

of our lives. Undeniably, billions of corporate and personal dollars are spent annually on sport-related products and services. In 2014, US$84.3 billion was spent on sporting goods, apparel, footwear, fitness equipment, and licensed sport merchandise (Jacobs, 2015), which demonstrates that the sport industry has an enormous economic effect on U.S. society.

Another way the significance of sport is highlighted is to see how individual acts and governance often come to symbolize broader social concerns. Some examples of this include racism (e.g., in 2016, NFL player Colin Kaepernick kneeled during the national anthem to bring awareness to racism in the US), sexism (e.g., the public debate on whether female professional soccer players should get equal pay), and criminal behavior (e.g., NFL's handling of sexual and domestic violence perpetuated by some players in the league). These examples clearly indicate

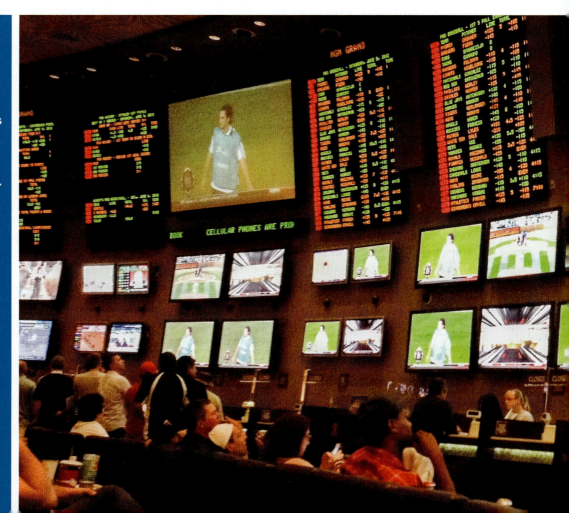

Rather than examining the behavior of specific people, sport sociologists examine institutions, organizations, and subcultures. The sociological aspects and prevalence of legal and illegal gambling in sports are examined by some sport sociologists.

Courtesy of Paul M. Pedersen.

that sport holds a prominent place in our society and that the consumption, valuation, and participation of sports have potential for positive and negative outcomes and consequences. Sport can be a place where sexism, racism, homophobia, and violence occur and are perpetuated. Keep in mind, however, that sport also has incredible potential to serve as a vehicle for positive youth development and social change.

Benefits of Sport

Clearly, sport shapes and maintains many social values that are held in high regard such as hard work and fair play, self-discipline, sacrifice, and commitment to oneself and others. Many researchers over time have documented that sport participation can lead to greater health and well-being as well as social, emotional, moral, physical, and psychological development. In short, sport has the *potential* to contribute to the positive development and stability of individuals and society.

Sport as a Socializing Agent

The socialization process refers to the various ways in which a society's dominant values, attitudes, and beliefs are passed down from generation to generation. Socialization also pertains to the process of starting, continuing, changing, and discontinuing sports as well as the effect of sport participation on the individual player (Coakley, 2015). Children learn from coaches, parents, teachers, peers, and siblings about what is normative, important, valued, and expected in a sport context, which helps them construct meaning of their experiences. In addition, what and who are portrayed in the sport media communicate values and attitudes to consumers and spectators about what is important.

Sport as a Unifier

Sport can bring people together by giving them a sense of personal identity and fostering feelings of group membership and social identification (Sage & Eitzen, 2016). For example, many U.S. citizens must have felt unified around the 2016 Super Bowl, which was the third-most-viewed U.S. television program of all time with 111.9 million viewers (Sandomir, 2016). Sport accomplishes feelings of unity in a number of additional ways, from the individual level (e.g., an athlete who feels that she is part of something bigger than herself because she is a University of Minnesota Golden Gopher), to the regional level (e.g., when citizens and professional sport teams such as the Celtics, Bruins, and Red Sox banded together to raise money to help victims of the 2013 Boston Marathon bombing), to the national and international levels (e.g., the entire nation cheering for athletes in the Olympic Games). Few, if any, institutions can unite people the way sport does, largely because the popularity of sport cuts across social categories such as race and class.

Dark Side of Sport

Although sport can be unifying and have beneficial outcomes for individuals and society, involvement in sport does not bring only good things; it can also be exclusionary and divisive in terms of race, class, gender, age, ability, and sexual orientation and their complex intersections. For example, not all families can afford the rising pay-to-play fees of professionalized youth sport. Seats inside professional sport stadiums funded by public tax dollars are so expensive that only a small minority of people can afford to attend a game in the very stadium that they helped fund! Participation rates are lowest and the number of barriers to sport participation and physical activity are greatest for underserved girls—girls for whom geography, class, race, gender, and ethnicity intersect (Thul, LaVoi, Hazelwood, & Hussein, 2016). A change in cultural beliefs pertaining to impaired athletes is occurring. In early 2013, the U.S. Department of Education amended and released new guidelines for the Rehabilitation Act of 1973 that will help ensure equal access to school-based sports for disabled students. While this change is a move in the right direction, improvements in access and accommodation for impaired athletes have come slowly.

As is apparent, sport participation can have a darker side. This dark side of participation includes aspects such as sexual and emotional abuse of athletes, burnout, dropping out, steroid use, chronic injuries, and eating disorders. Anxiety, yet another issue in sport participation, can result from a win-at-all-costs philosophy that characterizes the pressure-cooker world of big-time athletics. Furthermore, the same inclination increasingly characterizes youth sport. Besides the concerns just listed, research findings from sport sociology highlight four areas of sport that reflect and contribute to some of the most troubling aspects of the United States as we move into the second decade of the 21st century: sexism, homophobia and heterosexism, and racism.

---

socialization—The process by which people learn and develop through social interactions and come to know the environment around them.

Sexism in Sport

In the wake of the modern feminist movement that began in the early 1970s, a number of women's roles expanded into areas traditionally occupied by men; the world of sport was no exception. As you learned in chapters 7 and 17, Title IX of the Education Amendments Act was passed in the United States in 1972. This landmark federal legislation prohibits sex discrimination in educational settings. Since its passage and implementation, enormous changes in the world of women's sports have taken place. For example, substantial gains have occurred in the number of sports offered, access to sport-related scholarships and facilities, and overall athletic budgets. However, although a record number of girls and women are participating in sports at all levels of competition, boys and men still outnumber their female counterparts and receive a disproportional amount of resources, and the number of women in positions of power in sport is stagnant (LaVoi, 2016). Sociologists argue these trends are due to maintenance of power hierarchies, organizational structure, policies, and societal beliefs that preserve sport as a space that is still primarily by, about, and for men (Cooky, Messner, & Hextrum, 2013).

Female Patterns of Sport Participation

With respect to sports offered on a nationwide basis, in 2014, the average number of teams (per college or university) that were available for women was 8.83—an all-time high. Compare that with 1972, when the average number was 2.5 sports per school (Acosta & Carpenter, 2014). The National Federation of State High School Associations (NFHS, 2017) reported more than 3 million girls (3,400,297), a record high, are now involved in interscholastic sports nationwide compared with only 298,000 before Title IX in 1972. And more than just participation rates have skyrocketed in the wake of Title IX; the number of fans is exploding as well. Consider women's college basketball, one of the most popular women's sports; 98.8 percent of member NCAA institutions have a women's basketball team. During the NCAA 2016 season, 11.4 million women's basketball fans in all three divisions broke attendance records (NCAA, 2016), which have increased for 30 consecutive years. The 2015 FIFA Women's World Cup, in which the United States beat Japan, set an all-time television viewership record at over 750 million, and the game became the most watched soccer match in the United States (FIFA, 2015). These statistics make it clear that

Nearly half a century after the passage of Title IX, record numbers of girls and women are participating in sports. Some of the sport participation opportunities can lead to professional careers, such as playing in the National Women's Soccer League.

Courtesy of Paul M. Pedersen.

because of Title IX, millions of girls and women are participating in and consuming a variety of sports at all levels in unprecedented numbers.

Resources Allocated to Female Collegiate Athletes

Although women have made enormous progress in sport, assuming they have attained equality would be a mistake. Consider the following examples. More than four decades after the passage of Title IX, women received 43 percent of the participation opportunities at intercollegiate level even though they represented 57 percent of all undergraduates nationwide (NCAA, 2014). Moreover, athletic budgets, salaries for coaches, and access to facilities are nowhere near an equitable ratio. These disparities not only put women's sports at a distinct disadvantage in building successful programs but also send a powerful message about which sports (and athletes) are considered the most valued and important.

Title IX—Federal legislation passed in 1972 that amended the 1964 Civil Rights Act and prohibited sex discrimination in educational settings.

A North American Perspective on International Sport

Ceyda Mumcu
Sylvia Trendafilova
Lucie Thibault

LEARNING OBJECTIVES

- Explain factors one might consider when defining international sport.
- Identify five key changes that have resulted in the expansion of international sport.
- Discuss three factors that have redefined international sport during the first quarter of the 21st century.
- Explain how advances in recruitment of athletes and marketing of teams and events have affected international sport.
- Identify nations with emerging economies that are attractive hosts for international sport competitions.
- Discuss the influence of governance on international sport.
- Discuss current issues that affect female athletes and sports internationally.
- Discuss current issues related to environmental sustainability and the Olympic Games.
- Identify skills, experiences, and competencies that help aspiring international sport managers prepare for the job market.

KEY TERMS

environmental sustainability
European Union (EU)
General Agreement on Tariffs and Trade (GATT)
International Olympic Committee (IOC)
International Paralympic Committee (IPC)
match fixing

North American Free Trade Agreement (NAFTA)
spot fixing
Title IX
Youth Olympic Games (YOG)

1896
First modern Olympic Games held in Athens, Greece

1903
First Tour de France held

1930
First British Empire Games (now Commonwealth Games) held in Hamilton, Ontario

1950
Inaugural Formula One World Championship held in Great Britain

1960
First Paralympic Summer Games held in Rome, Italy

1975
First International Cricket Council Cricket World Cup held

1976
First Paralympic Winter Games held in Örnsköldsvik, Sweden

1987
First Rugby Union World Cup held

1989
Hillsborough Stadium disaster claimed 96 lives during soccer match in England

During the latter part of the 20th century, a number of events, companies, teams, and personalities transcended the isolation and limitations of regional and national recognition to become international sport brands across a broad cross section of cultures, religions, and locations around the globe. International events in this category include America's Cup, the Solheim Cup, the Ryder Cup, the FIFA World Cup, the Tour de France, the Rugby World Cup, the **YOG**, FISU Universiades and University World Championships, and the Olympic and Paralympic Summer and Winter Games. Professional leagues such as the NBA, the English Premier League, and the International Premier League are also global brands. Similarly, athletic apparel and shoe companies (e.g., Nike, adidas, Puma) and sport teams (e.g., Manchester United, Real Madrid, New York Yankees) share a high degree of global brand recognition. Like actors and musicians, athletes such as Novak Djokovic, Lindsey Vonn, Inbee Park, Rory McIlroy, Stephen Curry, LeBron James, Lewis Hamilton, Serena Williams, Cristiano Ronaldo, Lionel Messi, Alexander Ovechkin, Sidney Crosby, Marta Empinotti, Usain Bolt, Alan Fonteles Cardoso Oliveira, Michael Phelps, Maria Sharapova, Carli Lloyd, and Simone Biles have reached near-cult status. This chapter provides snapshots of people, organizations, and historical events that have shaped and will continue to shape the international sport industry in the first quarter of the 21st century, and this will give you a better understanding of the ever-changing and expanding dimensions of international sport. This chapter also emphasizes special skills and competencies that will prepare you to be a new sport management professional in international sport.

What Is International Sport?

We consider two factors in determining whether a sport is international: (1) the context in which an individual, organization, or event operates within the global sport enterprise and (2) the degree to which, or the regularity with which, action by an individual, organization, or event focuses primarily on the global stage.

With respect to the context in which an organization operates, the Olympic and Paralympic Games, world championships (FIFA Men's and Women's World Cups), and major annual international events such as the Tour de France, the Ryder Cup, and the tennis Grand Slam are among the giants of international sport. The same is true for multinational sport product and service corporations such as Nike and adidas, sport marketing and representation agencies such as Octagon and IMG, and sport facility design and management firms such as Populous, Ellerbe Becket, AEG (Anschutz Entertainment Group), and Spectra by Comcast Spectacor.

Assessing the degree to which an organization is engaged in international sport can be more difficult, especially if it operates almost exclusively in one nation or is only occasionally involved with international athletes or clients. Examples of these types of organizations include U.S.-, European-, or Asian-based professional sport leagues. For example, the NBA, WNBA, MLB, NHL, and MLS have a wealth of talented players who originate from all continents of the world. These leagues broaden their regional or national bases through marketing, branding, and broadcasting events to international audiences. They also recruit and market international players in hopes

---

YOG—The Youth Olympic Games is an elite multisport event created by the IOC to provide competitive opportunities to 15- to 18-year-olds in 28 summer sports and 7 winter sports. The inaugural summer YOG took place in 2010 in Singapore, and Innsbruck hosted the inaugural winter YOG in 2012.

2017
Special Olympics World Winter Games held in Graz and Schladming, Austria

Erzurum, Turkey hosted the European Youth Olympic Winter Festival

Deals were reached for Paris and Los Angeles to host the 2024 and 2028 Olympic and Paralympic Games, respectively

2006
Inaugural World Baseball Classic held

2014
IOC changed the Olympic Games bidding process as part of the Agenda 2020

1991
First Women's FIFA World Cup held

2013
UEFA banned Turkish clubs, Fenerbahce and Besiktas, for three years from Champions League over match fixing

2015
Canada hosted the 7th FIFA Women's World Cup

2018
XXIII Olympic and Paralympic Winter Games held in PyeongChang, South Korea

With 12 city-based teams around the world (e.g., Seoul, Shanghai, London, Boston), the esports league, Overwatch League, held its first regular season

of gaining new international fans, start developmental leagues in various countries, and allow their athletes to play for their home countries during the Olympic Games or world championships. The creation of grand tours in the United States and China by some of the world's most famous soccer teams (e.g., Manchester United, Real Madrid, Liverpool, AC Milan, FC Barcelona) signals the recognition of the value of creating an international brand. We can examine international sport in several ways. To avoid confusion, this chapter addresses only the organizations, events, and governance structures with primary international functions.

Expansion of International Sport

During the last two decades, sport enjoyed unprecedented international growth mostly in first-world economies (i.e., North America, Western Europe, Australia, and parts of Asia). This growth is evident in the dramatic changes in the Olympic and Paralympic Games, the increased opportunities for women in sport, the redefinition of international sport, the extension of international recruitment and marketing efforts, and the introduction of countries from emerging economies, such as Brazil, Russia, India, China, and South Africa, as potential hosts for major global sport events.

Dramatic Changes in the Olympic Games

Between 1968 and 1984, several events occurred that produced lasting effects on the Olympic Games. Change began at the 1968 Mexico City Games with the compelling and symbolic Black Power salute on

the medal podium by American sprinters Tommie Smith and John Carlos. The Munich Summer Olympic Games of 1972 marked the birth of an international sport revolution. The West German government was eager to demonstrate its rebirth as a peaceful nation free of its dark past associated with

The Irish Open, sponsored in 2018 by Dubai Duty Free and the Rory Foundation, is one of the 47 tournaments in the European Tour Race to Dubai. The professional tournaments in the season-long Race to Dubai are held in 26 countries.

Courtesy of Paul M. Pedersen.

Despite numerous environmental initiatives, the Olympic Games continue to cause significant damage, and making the Olympic Games sustainable will not come easy. Different cities and countries have different environmental needs and priorities and different systems of collaboration among governing authorities and environmental organizations. Under the current IOC structure for bidding and planning of the Olympic Games, it is extremely difficult to achieve sustainable Games. The key is for each OCOG to find the best way to engage a variety of stakeholders and to do their best to improve the environment in which the Games are held. Furthermore, the way sustainability in the Olympic Games is currently planned, implemented, and monitored does not hold the IOC and the OCOGs accountable for any environmental damage or neglect of environmentally sensitive areas. Despite specific guidelines provided by the IOC, adherence to those guidelines is rather rare. The outcome is often a negative effect on the ecosystem. Decisions related to sustainability are complex and need to be addressed at all levels of sport, not just the Olympic Games, as the movement toward environmental awareness continues to grow.

Gender Inequality in International Sports

Female athletes have made tremendous gains in international sports since the inception of the Olympic Games. When Pierre de Coubertin founded the IOC in 1894, women were excluded from the Olympic Movement and its Games. Female athletes officially participated in Olympic Games for the first time in 1924. In 1994, the IOC expressed their commitment to gender equality in their Olympic Charter, and since then, women's participation has become more prevalent. The 2012 London Olympic Games were called "the women's Olympics" due to three milestones: (1) the highest percentage of female athletes to date in the Games, (2) female Olympians participating in every sport, and (3) all participating nations having a female Olympian on their roster. In the 2016 Rio Olympic Games, 45 percent of the participating athletes were women, which was a new record.

Although the increase in participation is encouraging, we are far from gender equality in international sport, and female athletes still face many issues. Some of the issues discussed in this section are IFs' unequal treatment of women's sports, trivializing representations of women's sports in the media, and sex testing.

Challenges to Women's Sport Participation

Some cultures and religions impose obstacles to women's sport participation. Countries with strong patriarchal views do not approve of women's participation in sports. For example, Rafaela Silva, a Brazilian female Olympian in judo, noted "Everyone criticized me. They said judo wasn't for me. I was an embarrassment to my family" (Russell, 2016, para. 5). Similarly, female athletes from Muslim countries such as Afghanistan and Saudi Arabia face great adversity from their home countries. IFs' leadership is instrumental in changing these views and providing opportunities to women all around the world as these sport organizations strive to achieve peace and social development through sport.

In the 21st century, IFs stated their commitment to gender equality. FIFA's mandate is "to develop football everywhere and for all" (FIFA, 2014a, para. 1), and their mission is to develop women's soccer, provide financial support, and create opportunities for women to become involved in soccer (FIFA, n.d.). Although FIFA commits to developing soccer for women and girls around the world, some of its actions are contradictory to its mission. In 2011, Iran's national women's soccer team was not allowed to play at an Olympic qualifier against Jordan due to FIFA's hijab ban, which was lifted in 2012. Similar to FIFA, FIBA, the Fédération Internationale de Volleyball, the Fédération Internationale de Natation, and the International Boxing Association have restrictions on competition attire. Currently, FIBA and other IFs are testing the use of conservative competition uniforms for safety concerns and are expected to make changes to regulations that prevent or limit the participation of Muslim women.

In 85 years of senior-level Men's World Cup history, not once had men's soccer players played on artificial turf. All games for the 2015 FIFA Women's World Cup event were played on artificial turf while Men's World Cup games are played on natural grass. As a result, a coalition of women's soccer stars unsuccessfully filed a lawsuit against FIFA for gender discrimination. Players' complaints were that artificial turf becomes hotter and is more dangerous than natural grass. However, FIFA argued that artificial turf offers a good playing surface and all stadium pitches in Canada met the requirements of the FIFA Quality Programme (FIFA, 2014b).

The discrepancy in the prize money given to the participating teams and winners of the Men's and Women's World Cups is another example of gender inequality. In 2014, the German men's national team was awarded US$35 million for winning the World Cup in Brazil, and the total prize money given out was US$576 million. In 2015, the U.S. women's national team collected US$2 million for the same accomplishment, and the total prize money for the tournament was US$15 million (Galanis, 2015). The Women's World Cup is a newer event than the Men's World Cup, but the astonishing all-time record television viewership of over 750 million around the world proves the global success of the women's event, and the gap in prize money should be smaller. FIFA's unequal treatment of women diminishes the image of women's football and the athletes.

Media Representation of Women's Sport

The media marginalize women's sports through gender marking, which is labeling a sport event as a women's event but not stating a gender for the men's event (e.g., Women's World Cup versus FIFA World Cup). Gender marking of women's sport events insinuates that men's sport events are the mainstream events and women's sport events are substandard and the other (Lough & Mumcu, 2015). In addition, the media trivialize female athletes' accomplishments by focusing on their attractiveness, making familial references, and infantilizing them by referring to them as girls. Recent examples from the 2016 Rio Olympic Games are media outlets calling Simone Biles the next Usain Bolt, as if men were the only competitors capable of high levels of athletic performance; crediting the success of Hungarian swimmer Katinka Hosszu to her husband and coach in the stands by stating "and there is the man responsible"; and announcing American Olympic medal winner Corey Cogdell-Unrein as the wife of a Chicago Bears' lineman without even mentioning her name (Bates, 2016).

Sex Testing in Women's Sport

In order to ensure fair competition, the IOC introduced sex testing in 1968. Only female athletes, however, are subject to the testing, and since 1999, sex testing has only been conducted when the sex of an athlete is questionable. The test allows relentless scrutiny of female athletes and includes chromosome analysis, ultrasound, MRI, a gynecological exam, and blood testing for testosterone levels.

In 2009, South African runner Caster Semenya underwent sex testing. Her natural testosterone level was found to be higher than the threshold set by the IOC and the IAAF for female athletes. Therefore, hormone therapy was recommended to reduce the testosterone levels below the threshold so she could compete (IAAF, 2011). After being cleared, Semenya competed in the 2012 London Olympic Games and won a silver medal.

Another athlete who was recently subjected to sex testing was Dutee Chand from India who described the testing process as mortifying (Padawer, 2016). Chand was banned from racing due to her natural testosterone levels. She took her case to the CAS. The CAS ruled in favor of Chand based on the lack of conclusive scientific evidence proving a competitive advantage for women with naturally high testosterone levels. The CAS concluded that IAAF's policy requiring women athletes to undergo hormone therapy to change their natural bodies was unjustifiably discriminatory (Padawer, 2016). As a result, Dutee Chand was able to participate in the 2016 Rio Olympic Games.

Another gender inequality created by FIFA was the use of artificial turf at the 2015 Women's World Cup.

Courtesy of Paul M. Pedersen.

Guidelines for Future International Sport Management Leaders

In this section, we present guidelines to help you consider traveling beyond the borders of your country. You may choose to take advantage of study-abroad programs offered by numerous colleges and universities, or you may work in an international setting after your studies. Developing skills suited for international work as well as networking with key colleagues working across the globe are imperative to a successful career in international sport.

Studying Abroad

If you are interested in studying abroad, visit your college's or university's international office or talk to your professors to find out about the opportunities available. When you travel abroad, it is important for you to find out as much as you can about the country or countries you will visit. Understanding the languages spoken, the culture, the customs and traditions, the currency used, daily life, the weather, characteristics of the people, the geography and history, the dominant economic activities, the major cities, and the current news is imperative before you travel. Potential sources for this information are the U.S. State Department (https://travel.state.gov/content/passports/en/country.html) and the World Factbook of the Central Intelligence Agency (https://www.cia.gov/library/publications/the-world-factbook/). These websites provide important up-to-date information on the major features of all countries. You can also consult the country's handbook on the International Student Exchange Program's (ISEP) website. ISEP is one of the largest study-abroad organizations that connects students with academic programs across the world.

You must also understand the visa requirements and the regulations for visiting, studying, or working in another country. In addition, health and safety are extremely important to understand and may require some advance planning (e.g., immunizations and vaccinations, obtaining health insurance, locating your home country's embassy or consulate). It is also a great idea to photocopy (or have an electronic copy of) your travel documents and provide these and an itinerary of your travel plans to your family members. If you lose your passport, having a copy of the document in a secure location may facilitate its replacement.

Important Skills for International Sport Management

In international settings where people with diverse backgrounds work together, avoiding ethnocentric behavior is essential to conducting business successfully. Ethnocentrism refers to evaluating other cultures based on your own culture and assuming

Volunteer and Internship Programs in International Sport

Hosting and organizing international mega events would be impossible without the support of volunteers and interns, because they perform many of the day-to-day activities during the events. For the 2016 Rio Olympic and Paralympic Games, the organizing committee received more than 240,000 applications for 70,000 volunteer positions. Similarly, there were more than 150,000 volunteer applicants for the 2017 Confederation Cup and the 2018 FIFA World Cup in Russia, and 30 percent of those applicants were from abroad.

You can gain invaluable experience by volunteering or interning at international sport events. FIFA's volunteer program and the organizing committees of Olympic and Paralympic Games, for example, provide information on how to apply to be a volunteer, what qualifications and skills are needed, and how the interview process will be undertaken. Keep in mind that volunteer applications are accepted well before the event (often two years prior to the games). Internships at sport events and IFs are also available. If you plan to study abroad, you can investigate the professional teams, IFs, and national and regional sport organizations in the area. You should also research internship opportunities in the country. A potential resource for internship positions is Global Sports Jobs (www.globalsportsjobs.com), which lists open full-time and part-time jobs and internship positions in the sport industry.

Over 16,000 volunteers, including several sport management students, signed up to work the 2018 Olympic and Paralympic Winter Games. Volunteers were placed at various venues throughout the event, including at the Alpensia Biathlon Centre in PyeongChang, South Korea, which hosted the women's biathlon relay.

Courtesy of Paul M. Pedersen.

your own culture is superior. In addition, refusing to adapt to a culture and insisting that your way of doing things is the only correct approach can result in loss of business opportunities. As an international sport manager, you need to be respectful of existing hierarchies established by various cultural and religious practices and rituals.

An international sport manager also needs to be patient and must be able to listen. You might be told that your colleagues from other countries understand English better than they do. You might obtain the services of an interpreter who, as it turns out, cannot or will not convey the nuances of key oral exchanges. Consequently, in international business and sport, being able to communicate in the language of the

country in which you are doing business, even at a rudimentary level, can provide an invaluable advantage over the competition.

A basic knowledge of how a sport operates internationally, how the specific rules of the game are applied, how the sport is structured, and where the locus of power resides with sport (politically as well as on the field of play) and knowledge of primary trade treaties and agreements, such as the **General Agreement on Tariffs and Trade (GATT)** and **NAFTA**, and understanding rules and regulations can enhance your marketability. Additionally, understanding of trends in licensing, marketing, promotion, event management, and contracts is also helpful.

General Agreement on Tariffs and Trade (GATT)—An agreement negotiated in 1947 among 23 countries, including the United States, to increase international trade by reducing tariffs and other trade barriers.

NAFTA—A 1994 agreement reached by the United States, Canada, and Mexico that instituted a schedule for the phasing out of tariffs and eliminated a variety of fees and other hindrances to encourage free trade among the three countries.

Andrew Tinnish

Courtesy of Andrew Tinnish.

Professional Profile

Title: Assistant general manager, Toronto Blue Jays (MLB)

Education: BRECL (recreation and leisure studies) and BSM (sport management), Brock University, Canada

Andrew Tinnish has been the assistant general manager for MLB's Toronto Blue Jays since 2012. Tinnish is responsible for three critical areas of club operations: (1) roster construction, (2) international scouting in Latin America, and (3) the arbitration process. The following is a snapshot of his development, education, duties, and insights as a leader in the sport industry.

What was your career path?

I started working as an intern in 2001. Interning for the club was a logical progression for me given my background as an elite baseball player and my passion for all aspects of the sport. I was initially hired in the front office and then became area scout and was promoted to scouting director in 2009.

What characteristics must a person have to be successful in your job?

Characteristics required for the position include strong communication and interpersonal skills and the ability to build and maintain relationships with numerous stakeholders such as players and prospects, agents, scouts, coaches, and other staff. Trust and negotiation skills are also vital to all aspects of the job. I handle major league player contracts, free agents, arbitrations, and negotiations with international players.

Another skill acquired over time and probably the toughest part of any baseball job is evaluating, projecting, and predicting what a 16-year-old baseball prospect is going to look like in 5 to

Networking

Success in the international sport and the business sphere is predicated on personal contact and friendships. Attending meetings of national sport federations, professional sport-related associations, and other conferences and symposia helps maintain and expand your network of professional contacts. Time availability, relevance to your professional interests, and financial resources are important factors to consider when choosing the associations or conferences and trade shows (e.g., China International Sporting Goods Show, Seoul International Sports and Leisure Industry Show) that you want to attend. Volunteering at a major international sport event, conference, or trade show is an effective way to gain access to the field and to network.

Critical Thinking in International Sport

The symbiotic relationship among media, sponsors, and powerful sport organizations often results in a Western-centric approach to international sports. Cricket is one of the most popular sports around the world, but its governing body—the International Cricket Council (ICC)—and its international events are not well-publicized in North America. To

10 years. International scouting involves the investment of a lot of money. We will sign players for seven-figure contracts. In order for me to feel comfortable with those contracts, I need to have a lot of questions answered about these prospects. It's not just about what I see on the field on a given day, it's about our scouting reports, personality and aptitude tests, the player's performance, and how we have him ranked compared to his peers. It's about putting a lot of pieces together.

Language skills are also important, and I rely heavily on my staff to translate while I learn to speak Spanish. I travel extensively, spending between 160 and 180 days on the road. I travel mostly to the Dominican Republic and Venezuela and to a lesser extent to Mexico, Panama, and other Latin American countries.

Which websites, online tools, or resources do you frequently use or refer to?

I regularly consult the following online sources for my job: MLB Trade Rumors (www.mlbtraderumors.com), Fangraphs (www.fangraphs.com), and Baseball America (www.baseballamerica.com), but I have to admit that the first thing I check when I get on my phone is Twitter; I check Twitter at least 15 to 20 times a day if not more. I follow major national beat writers such as Jon Heyman, Buster Olney, Jon Paul Morosi, and Joel Sherman. I also follow sportswriters who focus on the Toronto Blue Jays and major league and minor league players as well as prospects. In this information age, you really have to keep up to date; it is such a fast-changing industry.

What do you consider to be the biggest future challenge in your job or industry?

The importance of remaining competitive on the field is one of the biggest challenges in baseball. As the Toronto Blue Jays are considered a large-market team, they do not benefit from the competitive balance system set up by MLB where clubs located in the bottom 10 in revenue and bottom 10 in market size get a round A or round B draft pick. As well, with new rules on signing international talent, clubs benefiting from the competitive balance system can spend between US$500,000 and US$1 million additional money to acquire international players. These rules are in place to ensure an even, level playing field; however, for the Toronto Blue Jays, it means the club has to work hard to identify key prospects sooner, develop relationships with these individuals, and make sure these prospects understand what the club has to offer beyond financial compensation. I feel strongly that Canada's and Toronto's diversity are attractive features for international prospects.

generate financial gain and expand their markets, media and sponsors are drawn to the IOC, FIFA, and well-established North American and European professional leagues (e.g., NBA, MLB, and EPL). Developing countries and their sport leagues as well as other sport governing bodies around the world do not receive the same attention, and they mostly go unnoticed by many in North America. As a result, it is important for individuals within western countries to be curious of sports in developing countries and their participation in international sports. Finally, when reading news or viewing media programming, it is important for the audience to appreciate the content from multiple perspectives, consider the local context and culture, and critically analyze the information presented because of different interest groups and power differentials. This may require seeking some additional knowledge to learn more about the specific country.

Ethics in International Sport

In the media, we are bombarded with multiple examples of illegal, immoral, and corrupt practices in sport such as drug use and doping, cheating, match fixing, spectator hooliganism and violence, questionable decisions that favor personal profits, and commer-

Social Media and a North American Perspective on International Sport

Traditional media have been critical for the operations of large-scale sport events and organizations. They provide an important source of revenue and much-needed visibility to international audiences.

With the introduction of new media, the potential to reach even more spectators and to engage them actively in sport events have grown exponentially. Digital and social media coverage of the Olympic and Paralympic Games was officially introduced for Beijing 2008. Digital and social media coverage greatly increased at the London 2012 Olympic and Paralympic Games. Some observers coined London the "Twitter Games," given that "during the 17 days of the Olympics, there were 82.6 million social media comments about the Games, its athletes, and its sporting events" (Dowling, 2012, para. 6). Thornton (2012, para. 21) explained that "the media is forging on to new screens well outside the living room." Social media allow organizers and athletes to directly connect with fans.

In response to this increasing social media presence, the IOC had to develop social media, blogging, and Internet guidelines. These guidelines not only regulated the behaviors of athletes and accredited personnel during the 2012 London Olympic Games, but they also referred to Rule 40 and served to protect the IOC's sponsors and partners. Guidelines encouraged social media and blogging activity at the Games as long as it was not for commercial or advertising purposes, and they restricted athletes', coaches', and officials' social media use. These guidelines have been met with resistance from many athletes who felt they were being censored by the IOC (Whiteside, 2012). In 2015, the IOC relaxed Rule 40 to allow generic advertising featuring Olympians during the Games. However, this amendment came with strict timelines and approvals, leading to implications experienced during the Rio 2016 Olympic Games (IOC, 2015).

Social media coverage was central to the Rio 2016 Olympic and Paralympic Games. For example, 187 million tweets resulted in 75 million impressions, 277 million people had 1.5 billion interactions on Facebook, and 131 million users had 916 interactions on Instagram (Cohen, 2016). In addition, digital media was a prevalent choice for viewership. According to the NBC Sports media release (2016), "NBC Olympics' digital coverage set event records with 3.3 billion total streaming minutes, 2.71 billion live streaming minutes, and 100 million unique users." The Rio Olympic Games were called the "mobile device Games" because 80 percent of the audience was expected to watch the Olympic Games from mobile devices (Powell, 2016). For large-scale sport events, social and digital media are increasingly playing a central role in reaching and engaging even greater global audiences than those reached by traditional media.

cial interests that take precedence over athletes' and participants' welfare. Several high-profile athletes and sport team members have been featured in the media because they took part in immoral or illegal activities within or outside of sport; examples include Tiger Woods, Lance Armstrong, Maria Sharapova, Oscar Pistorius, Lionel Messi, Phil Mickelson, and numerous athletes involved in match fixing, **spot fixing**, and betting issues in IPL cricket.

Athletes are not the only ones involved in illegal, immoral, and corrupt activities in sport. Leaders, coaches, and officials have also been active in questionable practices; examples include the corruption and bribery scandal involving Sepp Blatter and a number of his peers through the FIFA's bidding process for the 2018 and 2022 World Cup events; Union Cycliste Internationale's role in concealing the doping scandal of their star athlete, Lance Armstrong; and Russian doping officials ensuring clean doping results for their athletes by substituting samples through deceitful practices. There are many more cases; the extent to which IF leaders are facing questionable

spot fixing—An illegal activity in sport that involves betting on aspects of a game (that are not related to the final outcome of the game) that are fixed such as the timing of the first throw-in in football (soccer) or the timing of a ball's wide delivery in cricket; often associated with cricket, football, and rugby.

practices, unethical behaviors, and illegal activities is surprising.

Given the prevalence of immoral, illegal, and corrupt practices in sport, how can we make sure sport and leisure remain positive, constructive, inclusive, enjoyable, and beneficial for all? What solutions can we propose to cure sport of these issues and problems? As future sport management leaders, you must understand the good, the bad, and the ugly of sport and work to protect sport for all participants. Working with stakeholders and involving them in the decision-making process and in the development of policies that directly affect the quality of their participation in sport may certainly contribute to ensuring ethical practices in sport.

For chapter-specific learning activities, visit the web study guide at www.HumanKinetics.com/ContemporarySportManagement.

Summary

Organizations, events, and governance structures are deemed to be international if they are involved in the global context on a regular basis or as one of their primary functions. Current issues in international sport include concerns associated with governance, gender equity, environmental sustainability, and corruption. To be successful internationally, aspiring sport managers must have the appropriate skills and knowledge, open minds and cultural sensitivity, strong communication skills, and business etiquette. The future of international sport will occur in a world that is becoming smaller because of technology, a global community that is aware of social and ethical concerns that can be addressed through sport, and a world citizenry that possesses a heightened commitment to environmental concerns related to reducing the negative impact on the environment. Career opportunities in international sport will expand for people who are oriented to the global marketplace and possess the ability to integrate new technologies including the effective use of social media.

Review Questions

1. What is the definition of international sport? What factors are considered in determining whether a sport fits this definition?

2. Name three factors that served to redefine international sport. What was the effect of each?

3. What five key changes over the past few decades have contributed to the expansion of international sport? How have they done so?

4. How have advances in the recruitment of athletes and a focus on more globalized marketing affected international sport?

5. Name some of the emerging economies that are becoming attractive hosts for international competitions. What makes them attractive?

6. Identify the various stakeholders, policy experts, and governing bodies that are involved in the staging of environmentally sustainable Olympic Games. Elaborate on the efforts the IOC has put forward to address sustainability within the Olympic Movement.

7. What are some of the current issues that affect female athletes and women's sports in international sport?

8. What skills, experiences, and competencies would help aspiring international sport managers prepare for the job market?

Analytics in the Sport Industry

Kevin Mongeon
David P. Hedlund
Ryan Spalding

LEARNING OBJECTIVES

- Explain the sport analytics process and discuss each component in various contexts.
- Discuss how analytics are used in player acquisitions, coaching, and sport business, and identify emerging trends.
- Discuss the role of technology in enabling the rapid growth of sport analytics.
- Understand how metrics are derived and learn how to evaluate their effectiveness.
- Identify various knowledge areas, skills, and career opportunities in sport analytics.
- Identify sport analytics techniques and technologies.
- Discuss the history and potential effect of sport analytics.
- Identify the areas affected by sport analytics.

KEY TERMS

analysis
Bayes' rule
data management
decision making
dynamic ticket pricing
measurement
metrics
prediction

probability
quantitative
regression
statistics
tracking technology
variables
variable ticket pricing

Applications for Sport Business

The previous discussions showcased how analytics are valuable tools that inform managerial decision making in player and team management. Although it is well-known that managers and coaches use analytics to increase their teams' chances of winning, sport organizations also implement their own or third-party analytics into management, marketing, ticketing, sales, and other important business processes. As the prevalence of analytics in on-field decision making has increased, so too has the use of analytics off the field.

The use of analytics to optimize the functional areas of business (e.g., marketing, finance, management) is not unique to the sport industry. Well-known businesses have implemented analytics to improve their supply chain management (e.g., Walmart), customer loyalty and service (e.g., Harrah's), pricing (e.g., Progressive), product quality (e.g., Honda), financial performance (e.g., Verizon), and research and development (e.g., Amazon) (Davenport & Harris, 2007). Within sport management, analytics-based approaches are largely concentrated in marketing, specifically as it relates to ticketing, customer relationship management, and fan engagement.

Sport ticket prices were traditionally fixed. Teams set ticket prices at the beginning of the season based on traditional economic factors (e.g., population, income, substitutes, team quality). Prices varied by the quality of the seat (e.g., seat location), and a given seat had the same price for every game throughout the season. In the early 1990s, improved technology enabled teams to collect and analyze more detailed ticket sales data such as whether sales varied based on the day of week and the quality of opponents. Shortly thereafter, teams began implementing variable and dynamic ticket pricing strategies to increase revenue. Under variable ticket pricing, teams vary ticket prices based on various factors (e.g., quality of opponent, day of the week) but do not alter the set ticket price (which is generally determined prior to the beginning of the season). Under dynamic ticket pricing, teams continually alter the set ticket price in response to changes in demand. Variable ticket prices are fixed in time, whereas dynamic ticket prices are not. Most major North American professional sport teams use variable or dynamic ticket pricing strategies.

The 2017 Boston Red Sox ticket pricing strategy provides a good illustration of a variable ticket pricing strategy. Ticket prices are grouped into five tiers; the lowest-priced tickets range from US$30 in tier 1 to US$10 in tier 5, and the highest-priced tickets range from US$189 in tier 1 to US$111 in tier 5. Based on the results from their analytical models, the games that fall in the tier 1 category are the home opener and games against the New York Yankees and the Chicago Cubs. The tier 5 games are on weekday nights against teams such as the Oakland A's, the Pittsburgh Pirates, and the Baltimore Orioles.

Variable ticket pricing allows teams to increase revenue through the introduction of new and important factors into the ticket demand equation. However, variable ticket pricing is limited to variables that are known before the ticket price was set, most often prior to the start of the season. Dynamic ticket pricing that continually alters the set ticket price can account for a host of other factors that vary within a season such as recent team play, recent opponent play, the importance of the game, the weather, and the emergence of star players.

During the 2009 MLB season, the San Francisco Giants experimented with dynamic ticket pricing with 2,000 of its lower-quality seats. The team adjusted prices each day based on factors such as whether the team was on a winning streak and the starting pitcher for that day. The result was an additional 25,000 tickets sold and US$500,000 generated. The following year, all Giants single-game tickets were dynamically priced, which led to a 6 percent increase in revenue (Brustein, 2010). The NFL permitted teams to dynamically set ticket prices at the start of the 2015 season. During the first few games of the season, the 24 teams that implemented a dynamic pricing strategy collectively earned millions of dollars in incremental revenue (Kaplan, 2015). The use of dynamic ticket pricing is now widespread, and its practice is estimated to have led to a 60 percent increase in sales volume and a 98 percent increase in sales revenue in 2014 (Turnkey Intelligence, 2015).

In addition to using variable and dynamic ticket pricing, many sport organizations have begun to examine their relationships with fans; because the organization is better able to track and manage relationships with frequent patrons, they often look at season ticket holders. With the proliferation of customer data collection, teams have expanded their business analytics practices to include customer relationship management (CRM) that examines customers' purchase histories to increase customer retention and future sales. Many sport organizations offer rewards programs; when fans make purchases at the stadium and online through official vendors, they can use a rewards program card to earn discounts. In return, the organization can collect demographic

---

dynamic ticket pricing—The process of altering the price of a ticket in response to changes in demand.

data on its customers and track their spending habits.

The front office staff of the NBA's Orlando Magic is regularly recognized as one of the most sophisticated users of business analytics. Based on the team's recent use of analytics, they continually have one of the highest season ticket renewal rates in the NBA despite the team's low ranking in the league standings. The Magic first used a predictive renewal model in the 2010-11 season, and they partnered with SAS, a leader in business analytics software, for the start of the 2011-12 season (Charski, 2013). One of their first major initiatives was to collect data. To do so, they connected the credit card data of those who bought tickets to concessions and merchandise purchases. The data were analyzed to develop estimates of the likelihood that a customer would renew season tickets. The Magic then targeted customers differently based on their likelihood of renewal. They also analyzed the data to develop personalized marketing programs to enhance the fan experience. For example, customers who purchased a specific player's jersey would receive invitations to events that player was attending.

The next phase of business analytics for sport teams involves the active design of experiments rather than post-hoc analysis. In other words, sport organizations design multiple types of advertising and marketing and then test the different messages with different types of consumers to determine which messages are most effective. For example, sport organizations can create targeted marketing messages (e.g., go to the game because of a bobblehead giveaway versus go to the game because of a T-shirt giveaway) for different consumer groups and compare the click-through or response rates to identify the most effective message.

Other analytical tools available to sport organizations include Google Analytics and Google Trends. Google Analytics is the leading web analytics service, and it allows businesses to track views of their

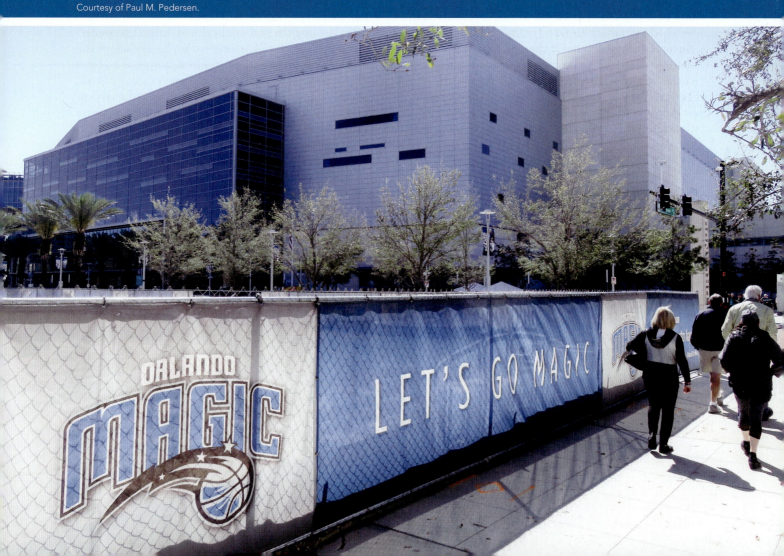

Due in no small part to their sophisticated use of analytics, the Orlando Magic have continually had one of the NBA's highest season ticket renewal rates. The Magic play their homes games at the Amway Center, shown here.

Courtesy of Paul M. Pedersen.

Social Media and Sport Analytics

One of the biggest challenges of social media marketing in the sport industry is to evaluate its effectiveness beyond a tally of the number of followers, likes, or shares. One company working in this area is MVPindex, which uses analytics to rank and measure social media content in sports. MVPindex tracks 30,000 athletes and 5,000 teams across more than 40 sports and catalogs mentions, references, comments, and other relevant data. Clients spend between US$50,000 and US$100,000 per year for up-to-the-minute custom dashboard analysis of their social media measurements such as how they are being mentioned and by whom and the extent of their reach. From the data collected, comparisons can be made within categories such as a particular sport or city, specific business categories, or among teams and athletes. For example, MVPindex used its algorithms and analysis to determine that the value of social media for the Chicago Blackhawks during a recent season was US$5.7 million, which was the highest in the NHL (Spanberg, 2016). The Blackhawks can use this information to evaluate the financial effectiveness of their various social media initiatives for the team and for sponsors to identify what type of campaign, post, or tweet was the most successful and how best to refine strategies moving forward.

websites and includes information such as whether the visitor has previously been to the website, the site that directed the visitor to the page, and much more. This information can be combined with different marketing and communication strategies or into existing CRM models. Google Trends, which counts word searches across time and locations, can be used to evaluate interest in the team and players throughout the season. If the organization observes increased fan interest in a player, its marketing efforts can reflect that increased interest. For example, if an NFL team observes that search traffic for the team is low during the off-season but peaks in the two weeks preceding the draft, the team might concentrate its off-season ticket sales advertising to the two weeks prior to the draft.

In addition to website analytics, teams are also using a variety of social media platforms (e.g., Snapchat, Facebook, Twitter, Instagram) to directly connect and engage with fans. Social media analytics have also become popular in the last few years. In general, the social media analytics packages record real-time consumer responses to team actions; therefore, they have the potential to greatly enhance data-driven marketing decisions through decreased response times. However, the data collected from social media are frequently difficult to understand in their raw form because the potential value is difficult to understand in a tweet, a video posted on Facebook, or the image in an Instagram post. For example, if a social media user posts an image, it is extremely difficult, at this point in time, for most computerized analytics programs to draw out any words or meaning, because the text is embedded in the image itself. Only human beings or advanced technology (e.g., optical character recognition [OCR] software) are capable of reading words posted as images. Until social media data can be more easily extracted, cleaned, and analyzed, their potential will remain unrealized without large armies of staff scouring each and every post.

For chapter-specific learning activities, visit the web study guide at
www.HumanKinetics.com/ContemporarySportManagement.

Summary

Sport analytics involves three steps: collecting data, analyzing data, and communicating results. The growth in sport analytics can largely be attributed to advances in technology that have enabled data to be collected and analyzed efficiently. Sport analytics relies on analytical models that find patterns in data to describe or predict an event or outcome.

Sport contests are complex systems with outcomes determined by numerous factors. Regression is a useful technique to analyze sport contests because it can measure the effect of numerous factors on a game outcome or goal outcomes. Bayes' rule is another useful technique available to sport analytics experts. Bayes' rule is a formula used to calculate conditional probabilities, and it can provide accurate predictions of uncertain outcomes such as game outcomes. Sport analytics has applications for management, coaching, and the business aspects of sport organizations. Moving forward, many successes on and off the field are likely to be attributed to the use of analytics.

Review Questions

1. Define sport analytics in one sentence. Do you think it is important for sport organizations to use sport analytics in their operations?

2. What are the three steps of the sport analytics process? Briefly describe each step.

3. What is the Pythagorean win expectancy model, and how is it useful?

4. What skills and software knowledge are expected of people working in sport analytics?

5. Describe a few of the more recent analytics-driven player performance metrics. How are these metrics an improvement over traditional player statistics?

6. How can general managers determine the appropriate salary for a potential free agent?

7. What is the difference between variable and dynamic ticket pricing? Give an example of each.

8. Imagine you work in the marketing and sales department of your favorite sport team. What data would you want to collect on season ticket holders to improve renewal rates?

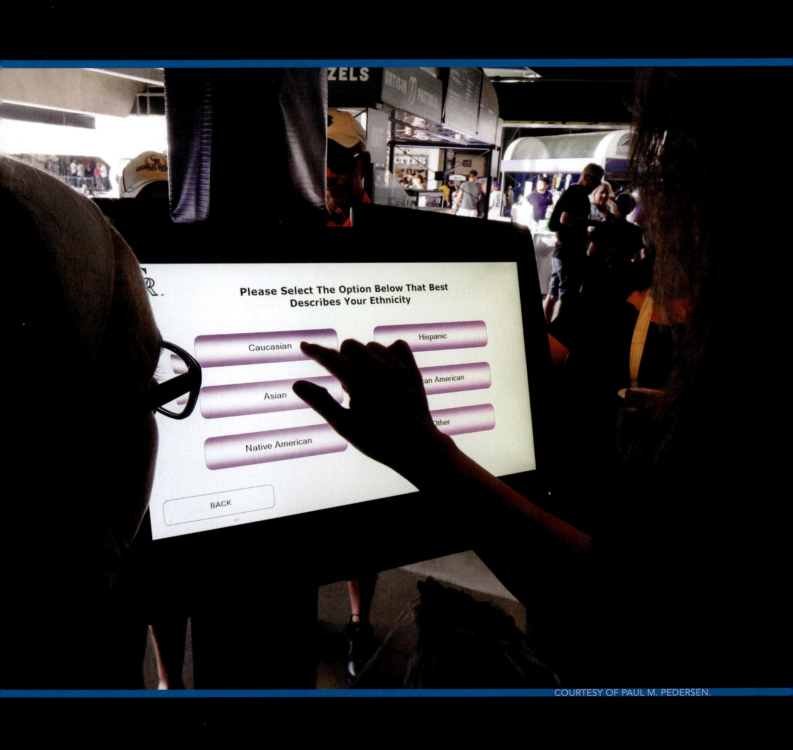

Sport Management Research

Nola Agha
Jess C. Dixon
Brendan Dwyer

LEARNING OBJECTIVES

- Define research and describe why it is important to sport management students and sport organizations.

- Recognize the value of asking and answering research questions in sport management.

- Identify, summarize, and explain different ways of conducting sport management research.

- Know where to locate and how to access various types of sport management research.

- Critique and assess the quality of research in all its various forms.

- Attain a thirst for knowledge.

- Identify sport management careers that require sound research skills.

KEY TERMS

anonymity
concept
confidentiality
qualitative data
quantitative data
reliability
research design
social science
theory
validity

1968
SPSS released

1973
Sport Information Resource Centre incorporated

1974
SPORTDiscus, an important database in the field, launched

1977
Journal of Sport and Social Issues published its first issue

1981
QSR NVivo (qualitative research software) released

1993
R (open source statistical software) released

1994
ESPN Sports Poll began
Street & Smith's SportsBusiness Daily launched

1996
SportBusiness International started
Sports Business Research Network founded

2000
International Journal of Sport Management and *Journal of Sports Economics* launched

Interest in research has paralleled the growth of the sport industry and sport management educational programs around the world. This interest has occurred because people in business and education understand that research can inform managerial decisions, uncover solutions to managerial problems, improve organizational effectiveness and efficiency, point out inequalities in sport leadership or participation, and help sport management continue to develop a relevant body of knowledge.

Regardless of the area that you are studying or your career aspirations, understanding research is critically important. Progressive sport organizations want to find out about the latest trends, evaluate whether their customers are satisfied, update their policies, attract new participants, provide data to sponsors and partners, and stay ahead of their competitors. Increasingly, these sport organizations are looking to sport management graduates for expertise in information searches, feasibility studies, program evaluations, marketing studies, and economic impact studies, to name a few.

Even if you do not expect research to be a major component of your future career, you need to be able to understand, evaluate, and use research when solving problems and making professional decisions. This chapter introduces key concepts and various types of research conducted in the sport management field. It also provides you with a foundation for becoming a responsible producer and consumer of research so you can become a more informed decision maker. To develop your skills further, you should seek out courses in research methods at your institution.

What Is Sport Management Research?

At the monthly department meeting, the president of the local professional soccer team indicated a need to sell more tickets. Brainstorming ensued, and four employees of the franchise offered the following:

1. "Let me research some ideas," responded the intern majoring in sport management. A quick Google search for "how to sell more tickets" had 127 million results and more than 600,000 videos that included compelling titles such as "4 Ways to Sell More Tickets With Zero Budget" and "10 Ways to Double Your Ticket Sales in 2016."

2. "I remember seeing an infographic in *Street & Smith's SportsBusiness Journal* about the most popular promotional giveaways; let me research what it was," offered the director of marketing.

3. The director of sales said, "I'll ask our business analyst to examine the renewal rates for season ticket holders and see if we can find some patterns. If there's nothing there, we can hire a consultant to research trends in ticketing."

4. "Research in *Sport, Business and Management: An International Journal* analyzed soccer attendance and found that star players and games with rivals are associated with higher attendance," suggested the director of operations.

The word *research* in each of these examples carries a different connotation. In the first example, research indicated a search for information or facts. In the second example, research was carried out to locate and summarize data from a table, figure, or chart that was published in a trade publication. In the third case, research was used more expansively to describe a process by which an employee or hired consultant analyzes data, computes statistics, and writes a report on the findings. In the last case, research referred to the scientific process used by

2004
Google Scholar launched

2008
Journal of Issues in Intercollegiate Athletics and Journal of Intercollegiate Sport launched

2011
Sport, Business and Management: An International Journal launched

2001
Wikipedia founded

2006
International Journal of Sport Finance launched

2009
Journal of Venue and Event Management, International Journal of Sport Policy and Politics, and Journal of Applied Sport Management launched

2015
Journal of Global Sport Management published its first issue

researchers to systematically gather data and analyze facts, develop new conclusions, and publish those findings in scientific journals.

We commonly use the word research to mean all of these tasks, and in each case, important information is being gathered to help make decisions, develop strategies, and enhance organizational operations. As illustrated in table 21.1, these cases represent a hierarchy of rigor in which the most simplistic form

of research can be completed in a few minutes and the most complex form can take weeks or months to complete. The fourth example illustrates what academics commonly refer to as *research*. According to Merriam-Webster (Research, n.d., para. 2), this type of research is "studious inquiry or examination; *especially*: investigation or experimentation aimed at the discovery and interpretation of facts, revision of accepted theories or laws in the light of new facts, or

Table 21.1   Examples and Sources of Research

Definition of research (from Merriam-Webster)	How this type of research might be conducted	Examples of sources for this type of information
"The activity of getting information about a subject" (n.d., para. 2)	Perform Internet searches or ask Google, Siri, or Cortana.	Wikipedia, web pages, blogs, Twitter feeds, and so forth
"Careful or diligent search" (n.d., para. 1)	Read magazines or trade publications in your field of study.	*Athletic Administration* *Athletic Business* *Athletics Management* *Coach and Athletic Director* *NCAA News* *PanStadia & Arena Management* *SportBusiness International* *Sporting Goods Business* *Sporting News* *The Sports Business Exchange* *Sportsnet* *SportsPro* *SportTechie* *Street & Smith's SportsBusiness Daily* *Street & Smith's SportsBusiness Journal* *Team Insight* *Venues Today*

> continued

Table 21.1 > *continued*

Definition of research (from Merriam-Webster)	How this type of research might be conducted	Examples of sources for this type of information
"Careful study that is done to find and report new knowledge about something"	An employee or an external firm collects data, analyzes it using statistics, and summarizes the findings; this is also called applied research, analytics, or business intelligence.	Primarily studies published in the form of reports that are carried out by a firm's internal employees or external agencies such as Ipsos, Kantar, Millward Brown, Nielsen, Repucom, Scarborough, Simmons Research, Sponsorship Research International, Sports Business Research Network, SportsEconomics, and Turnkey Sports & Entertainment
"Investigation or experimentation aimed at the discovery and interpretation of facts, revision of accepted theories or laws in the light of new facts, or practical application of such new or revised theories or laws" (n.d., para. 2)	Similar to previous item, but with the added use of existing concepts, theories, and frameworks. It also builds off of previous academic research. It can be applied or theoretical.	Thousands of academic research journals. Reputable examples in sport management include the following: *Communication & Sport* *European Sport Management Quarterly* *International Journal of Sport Communication* *International Journal of Sport Finance* *International Journal of Sport Management* *International Journal of Sport Management and Marketing* *International Journal of Sport Policy and Politics* *International Journal of Sports Marketing and Sponsorship* *Journal of Applied Sport Management* *Journal of Contemporary Athletics* *Journal of Intercollegiate Sport* *Journal of Issues in Intercollegiate Athletics* *Journal of Legal Aspects of Sport* *Journal of Sport and Tourism* *Journal of Sport Management* *Journal of Sports Economics* *Journal of Sports Media* *Journal of Venue and Event Management* *Sport, Business and Management* *Sport Management International Journal* *Sport Management Review* *Sport Marketing Quarterly*

practical application of such new or revised theories or laws." The following section explains this type of research in more detail.

Types of Sport Management Research

When you hear research defined in the context of science, you might associate it with experiments done in exercise physiology laboratories where subjects' heart rates are monitored to determine their fitness levels. This experiment-based laboratory science is known as natural science, and it has a long historical tradition in physical education and kinesiology programs in university settings. Conversely, social science includes areas such as sport sociology, sport psychology, and sport management. In general, a social science approach to sport is concerned with individuals, groups, and organizations in real-life situations (Creswell, 2014). This type of research is published in journals geared toward the academic community (e.g., *Journal of Sport Management*, *Sport Management Review*, *Sport Marketing Quarterly*, *European Sport Management Quarterly*) whose readership is made up almost exclusively of professors, researchers, and students in institutions of higher learning.

Given the premium that is placed on information and analytics in decision making, many firms have established their own internal research departments dedicated to collecting, analyzing, and explaining data. This includes firms in ticketing, concessions, security, player development, recruiting, social media, sponsorship, fantasy sports, esports, merchandise, media, marketing, and professional teams. Some internal analytics divisions have been so successful that they spun off into separate, independent ventures. For instance, the New England Patriots of the NFL converted its analytics division into the firm KAGR. This analytics firm was so successful that it created a joint venture with college sports outsourcing expert Learfield to create KLEAR Intel, which provides data analysis for college athletic programs (Smith, 2016). Smaller firms, or those that lack in-house expertise or full-time research staff, often hire the services of an external research firm. There are thousands of firms that specialize in sport and sport-related research. For example, a sporting event seeking an economic impact study might contact SportsEconomics, Sportsimpacts, or Conventions, Sports and Leisure International (CSL). A team seeking to understand fan behavior might retain Turnkey Sports and Entertainment, Simmons Research, or Luker on Trends.

Although scientific research is easy to identify because it is published in academic research journals and consulting-based research is easy to identify because it comes from professional service firms (see table 21.1) and is often published in reports, it is more difficult to identify the quality of facts, information, and research found via other sources.

Many sport practitioners tend to rely on trade publications for information (see table 21.1 for an abbreviated list of sport management-related trade publications). These publications typically include articles written by journalists or sport professionals for the benefit of other professionals working in the field. Written in lay terms, these articles commonly highlight best practices for managing sport teams, programs, facilities, events, and the like as well as trends in the sport industry. Although some of these articles report on research conducted by sport managers working in the field, not all of these studies would stand up to scientific scrutiny. Moreover, although some trade publications, such as *Street & Smith's SportsBusiness Journal*, feature articles written by academics, they are not vetted through the same review process as academic journal articles, so readers should be cautious when basing decisions on the findings published in these outlets.

The most caution should be exercised when conducting research that is based on a web search. Consider that nearly 90 percent of 18-year-olds rely on social media sites for their news, yet "four in 10 high-school aged students trusted the headline above a photo on a photo-sharing site as a fact, despite not having any information about where the photo was taken" (Hoover, 2016, para. 8). Because the Internet is full of easily searchable information, it is incredibly important to evaluate the credibility of the source, the data, and the analysis and quality of the information. This is especially necessary in the context of click-baiting sites that are designed to look official (e.g., "The Top 10 Ways to Sell Tickets") or for sites such as Wikipedia that are crowd-sourced and are rarely verified for accuracy.

Why Sport Managers Need to Understand Research

Students who aspire to careers in the sport industry sometimes undervalue research because they assume that it is not practical and is conducted primarily

---

social science—The branch of science that investigates society, institutions, and social relationships.

Tracy Schoenadel

Courtesy of Tracy Schoenadel, SMG Insight.

Professional Profile

Title: Senior vice president, SMG Insight

Education: BS, MS, EdD, ABD, West Virginia University

SMG Insight is a global research and consulting services firm that specializes in sports and sponsorship. Tracy Schoenadel is responsible for business development, meeting with clients from teams and leagues, and managing staff across the United States, the United Kingdom, and India. SMG Insight collects quantitative and qualitative data on consumers and media using a variety of proprietary tools. On the consumer side, it runs BrandIndex, which collects 8,000 surveys daily to track public perception of 7,500 brands including 17 sports and 60 events. The media side entails in-broadcast, TV news, social media, digital, press, and online measurement of earned media from sponsorship exposure. Schoenadel has worked on NBA and MLB sponsorship evaluations, a NASCAR branding study, and a Women's Tennis Professionals/Association of Tennis Professionals evaluation of international audiences. Schoenadel spends the majority of her time working with and through people either managing her talented staff or in customer and client interaction. It is no surprise, then, that her favorite part of her job is interacting with clients and solving their problems through research. The following is a snapshot of her development, education, duties, and insights as a leader in the sport industry.

in colleges and universities. It is often not until you have served in a management position that you fully appreciate the importance of research in assisting with the managerial role. Now is the best time to begin developing an understanding of why research is critical to sport managers who want to stay current in their respective fields.

Decisions Are Data Driven

In 2014, the NFL's San Francisco 49ers simultaneously opened a new home (Levi's Stadium) and launched a mobile app designed to allow in-stadium fans to order concessions from their seats. The team and Centerplate, the stadium's concessionaire, projected 15,000 to 20,000 orders for the first season with the majority of users opting for express pickup instead of in-seat delivery. By the end of the season, data revealed over 17,000 orders for in-seat delivery alone and another 13,650 for express pickup (Muret, 2015b). The findings allowed the team to develop a specific promotion for in-seat concession sales for the team's second season.

This data-driven approach is not unique to Centerplate or the 49ers. Every major concessionaire, ticketing firm, and media company now dedicates entire departments to the gathering and analysis of research data. Amy Cross, the vice president of Digital Innovation and IT Strategy at concessionaire Aramark, reported that its clients are asking for information on where fans are sitting compared to where they are purchasing concessions and at what time during the game (Muret, 2015a). The technology director at concessionaire Delaware North Sportservice reported that the firm collects data on a wide variety of transactions including product stock keeping units (SKUs), transaction times, and method of pay to optimize beverage sizes and retail revenue. Levy Restaurants, a competitor of Centerplate, launched a wholly owned subsidiary called E15 to collect data, analyze them, and help its clients drive revenue. The

What was your career path?

In 1992, I began working in media/advertising directly after graduate school. Although there were many requests for sponsorship insight and data, little existed. I focused more on sport media valuation, realizing that sponsorship values are driven by media. In 1995, I moved to NYC for my first job in sponsorship research at SRi/ISL as a senior research project director and moved to the Interpublic Group of Companies in 1997. From 1999 to 2007, I served as the executive director of the ESPN Sports Poll, and during this time I was also an adjunct professor at New York University. I then accepted a position at the University of Massachusetts Isenberg School of Management to run the McCormack Center for Research. I returned full-time to the practitioner side at Kantar Media in 2013. In the summer of 2015, I was hired to my current position running the North American offices for SMG Insight as senior vice president.

What characteristics must a person have to be successful in your job?

It is essential to have a research background. However, I believe the most successful skill and experience I have is in media and advertising. My time working in advertising and media at the beginning of my career was the most important factor in my growth. Without that experience, I would have never learned how to evaluate sport-related media.

Which websites, online tools, or resources do you frequently use or refer to?

My focus is generally on *Street & Smith's SportsBusiness Journal*, *Street & Smith's SportsBusiness Daily*, and *Advertising Age*. I learn more from working in NYC and client relationships than I do from publications.

What do you consider to be the biggest future challenge in your job or industry?

The changing media landscape, especially the focus on social media, is a current challenge. Social media is measurable, but it is very young. It is important that the tools to quantify social media are accurate and widespread. To do this, boutique shops need the power of a full-service research firm behind them. SMG Insight has this with its joint venture with YouGov.

company recently discovered that winning on the field can increase the amount spent per person on concessions, and losing can have the opposite effect (Muret, 2015a).

Having sound intuition and a wealth of experience is useful, but if Centerplate had not collected transactional data for the 49ers, adjustments for the second season would have been based on faulty assumptions, potentially leading to risky and expensive mistakes. In a world where more than 2.5 quintillion (i.e., 2.5 followed by 18 zeros) bytes of data are produced daily (IBM, n.d.), decisions are increasingly data-driven, and there is no place for managerial decisions based on gut feeling or trial and error.

Research Helps Make Better Decisions

In 2012, the SEC began discussing how each school could upgrade its stadium with more Wi-Fi connec-

tivity to increase the fan experience at football games. In 2013, the conference hired Sporting Innovations to conduct surveys of over 26,000 fans who had attended a game. To its surprise, connectivity was a low priority for the majority of fans, and short concession lines and clean bathrooms were the highest priorities. In response to this research, 12 of the 14 SEC schools added more points of concession and digital menu boards, eight schools added bathroom attendants and more bathrooms, and eight schools upgraded their in-stadium connectivity (Smith, 2014).

From this example, it is clear that managers make better decisions through research. While an athletic director could spend US$5 million to $10 million to modernize the Wi-Fi infrastructure, a smaller investment in more concession stands and bathrooms led to a larger increase in overall fan satisfaction at the stadium. Regardless of whether the findings obtained from research confirm or challenge our assumptions, they will help us make better decisions. Thus, sport managers increasingly rely on research before investing financial, human, and other types of resources into new or ongoing projects. They want to avoid the costly errors that can occur when decisions are based on false or unfounded assumptions. Effective sport managers want assurances that their decisions will help them achieve desired goals based on evidence that has been carefully collected, analyzed, and interpreted.

Research Keeps You Current

The results of the SEC survey indicated that in-stadium connectivity was a lower priority overall, but a deeper analysis of the data provided more insight. Text messaging ranked 37th in importance among premium seating ticket holders, 21st among general seating ticket holders, and 2nd among students (Smith, 2014). These findings illustrate why nearly two-thirds of the schools still opted to invest in the digital upgrade. Although current ticket holders have a lower preference for connectivity, students with high demand for it will soon graduate and become consumers. If they had poor experiences as students, they may be less likely to purchase tickets once they have graduated. This example illustrates the importance of staying current. Times change, consumer demands evolve, and sport managers can be proactive by making appropriate changes in product, pricing, or services.

The field of sport management is no different from other professional areas. By applying research findings from human resources, leadership, marketing, organizational development, and countless other areas, the practicing sport manager has a much better chance of identifying and implementing sensible solutions to everyday managerial problems.

Key Features of Quality Research

As explained previously, not all research is of equal quality. There can be differences in the credibility of the source, the data, or the analysis. Remember the president who demanded more ticket sales? Four different options were presented from four different employees. Which of those kinds of research will help the team president make a better decision? As a sport manager, you do not always need a rigorous, scientific approach to research your problem. However, if you are able to understand the principles that define high-quality research, then you will always be able to use those skills in assessing the quality of

other research presented to you. The remainder of this section will help you understand the features that are common to high-quality research.

Specific Research Question

In management decision making, the starting point is to know what problem or issue you are trying to solve. For the president, the problem was low ticket sales. To translate the problem into potential solutions, a researcher must define what questions need to be answered. These are called research questions.

If you worked for the soccer team, what would you want to know before you could make a decision on how to allocate scarce resources to solving the problem? At the highest level, one might wonder, Why *aren't* people purchasing tickets? This simple question leads to many smaller ones, such as, Are tickets too expensive? Are people too busy to attend? Do they dislike the stadium or in-game experience? Is the product on the field not appealing?

You could also consider it from the opposite point of view: Why *are* people purchasing tickets? Are they fans of the team? Do they like the food, entertainment, atmosphere, or crowd energy? Do they like attending with friends, family, or both? What are other reasons they are more likely to attend?

Although these are great examples of high-level questions, there are many more specific questions we could ask that are based on our perspective of the problem. As we addressed earlier, in trying to determine how to sell more tickets, the three directors perceived the problem from the following different angles:

- The director of marketing imagined more promotions might incentivize increased attendance and could be wondering, Are fans more likely to attend if there is a promotional giveaway? Which promotional giveaways lead to the highest attendance gains?

- The director of sales thought it might be related to retention of season ticket holders and could be wondering, What makes season ticket holders renew from one season to the next? Are the tickets too expensive? What is the added value of being a season ticket holder over someone who purchases a single game ticket?

- The director of operations considered the issue from an economic lens by understanding what drives demand and could be wondering, Are fans less likely to attend if the game is being televised? Does the quality of the starting lineup matter? Does attendance decrease if one or more of the star players is injured? Does weather affect attendance?

By dividing the larger problem into more manageable pieces, a sport manager is able to understand that quality research begins by knowing the problem and identifying clear, specific avenues to solve it. A quality research question is specific, testable, and has not yet been answered.

Discipline-Specific Research

The different ways that the three directors approached the bigger research problem are aligned with their different backgrounds and training. In an academic setting these are called disciplines, and you can see them all around you through the different academic departments on campus and the different faculty members who teach courses in each discipline. Your sport sociology professor has had years of training in sociology, and your sport law professor has had equivalent training in law. In the case of ticket sales, the director of marketing is examining the problem from a marketing angle, and the director of operations is considering the issue in terms of demand, which comes from the discipline of economics.

Concepts and Theories

Researchers receive specialized training because each discipline is guided by theories, concepts, and approaches to creating knowledge. A **theory** is a possible explanation for why something occurs, and a **concept** is "a shared representation of an object, a property, or a behavior" (Jones, 2015, p. 91). A simple example of a concept is age. We define age by the number of times the earth revolves around the sun, and there is a broadly-shared understanding that each additional orbit increases our age by one unit. A concept can have a number of different definitions (perhaps there is a group of people who define age by the number of full moons that rise throughout your life), but the power of a concept is when there is a shared understanding that allows all researchers to use the same definition in their work.

Fandom is a common concept in sport management research. Imagine that study A defined a fan as any person who attended 12 or more games each year, but study B defined a fan as any person who purchased merchandise at least once in the last year. An FC Barcelona soccer fan living outside of Spain who watched every single game on television for the past 20 years would not be considered a fan in either of these studies. This is problematic, because neither definition of fandom captured someone who was, by all common definitions of the word, a fan. Equally problematic is that results of studies A and B cannot be compared and contrasted because they used different definitions of fandom. Thus, high-quality research will use previously established definitions of the concept of fandom, which allows results to be compared, contrasted, and extended into future research studies.

To illustrate how theories and concepts relate to the soccer team's ticket sales conundrum, let us

---

theory—A possible explanation for a phenomenon of interest to sport management researchers.

concept—A shared definition of the characteristics of an otherwise abstract word or idea.

Action Research Needed in Sport

As a consequence of being a practically oriented area of study, the sport management field is an ideal forum for what is commonly known as action research, which refers to generating knowledge about a social system while at the same time attempting to change it. In sport management circles, this activity involves solving problems that come directly from those who are or would like to be involved in sport. Although action research is not commonly used in sport management, interest in this research design is growing because it is a way of bringing study participants, practitioners, and researchers together to tackle problems of mutual concern (Frisby, Reid, Millar, & Hoeber, 2005). The overall goal of action research is to produce knowledge about how everyday experiences of people can be improved to promote social change and social justice (Reason & Bradbury, 2007). For example, we know that those living below the poverty line are much less likely to participate in sport because of the high costs of programs, apparel, and equipment. By collaborating with those living in poverty on all phases of the research process, community sport managers can identify barriers to participation and develop action strategies for overcoming them.

focus on the following question: Why *are* people purchasing tickets? Sport management scholars have spent decades trying to understand the concept of motivation—that is, the reasons people attend events as spectators. The first attempt to assess why people were motivated to attend events was called the Sport Fan Motivation Scale (Wann, 1995). A scale is a series of questions that, when used together, can fully measure and identify a concept. Later, authors attempted to create other scales that defined sport fan motivation and identified different sets of reasons; some of these were the same as the first, but some were different.

An employee of the soccer team with little knowledge of quality research might take a nonscientific approach to studying the problem of low ticket sales by creating a survey that is distributed to spectators before a game and asks the following question: Why did you come to the game today? Alternately, a multiple-choice question could be used to gather information about what motivated people to attend the game (e.g., (a) price, (b) convenience, and (c) to spend time with friends). But, as we can see from table 21.2, by not relying on existing definitions of concepts, a simplistic survey will miss many important points. Conversely, a scientific approach to answering this question would rely on one of the scientifically validated and reliable scales to gather information about the fans of this particular team. Validity assesses how well measures capture the meaning of abstract concepts, and reliability refers to the consistency or dependability of measures. The more valid and reliable the methods are for collecting and analyzing data, the more confident you can be in the results that are derived from them.

Reliance on Questions That Have Been Previously Answered

Another benefit of dividing larger problems into smaller pieces is that it allows you to solve only the problems that have not been solved yet. In other words, many of the smaller questions from the director of operations about the effects of television, weather, winning records, and star players on consumer demand have already been answered. Sport economists have spent decades trying to understand the concept of attendance demand, that is, the factors that are associated with increased or decreased attendance. They have found that television broadcasts do not decrease attendance (Alavy, Gaskell, Leach, & Szymanski, 2010), better weather is associated with higher attendance (Meier, Konjer, & Leinwather, 2016), and star players are associated with higher attendance (DeSchriver, Rascher, & Shapiro, 2016). The team president who wants to sell more tickets does not need to dedicate scarce financial resources to study whether weather and television will affect ticket sales. Instead, the team can focus on solving only those questions that have not yet been answered and implementing solutions based on past research, such as finding a way to sign more star players.

How do we find out whether a question has already been answered? While enrolled in college, you will have access to many research databases through your library including SPORTDiscus, Business Source Complete, and EconLit. Google Scholar is an open-source Internet tool that can also be used to search for academic research. The process of reading scholarly research on a particular topic is called a literature review, and this enables a researcher to

Table 21.2   Different Definitions of Fan Motivation and the Scales Used to Measure the Concept

Authors	Scale	Reasons people consume sports as spectators
Wann (1995)	Sport Fan Motivation Scale	Eustress, self-esteem benefits, escape, entertainment, economic factors, aesthetic qualities, group affiliation, and family needs
Milne and McDonald (1999)	Motivations of the Sport Consumer	Risk-taking, stress reduction, aggression, affiliation, social facilitation, self-esteem, competition, achievement, skill mastery, aesthetics, value development, and self-actualization
Trail and James (2001)	Motivation Scale for Sport Consumption	Achievement, acquisition of knowledge, aesthetics, drama, escape, family, physical attractiveness of participants, the quality of the physical skill of the participants, and social interaction

validity—The degree to which measures capture the meaning of abstract concepts.
reliability—The consistency or dependability of measures of abstract concepts.

not only uncover what questions have already been answered but also to narrow their own research questions based on previously acquired knowledge. For example, if the director of marketing searched for previous research on the effects of promotions on ticket sales, there is research showing that promotions increase attendance for MLB games (McDonald & Rascher, 2000) and for NCAA women's basketball games (Trail & Kim, 2011). This suggests the need for a specific study related to the effect of promotions on soccer game attendance. A literature review also allows you to find useful concepts, theories, and scales that you can integrate into your own research projects as you produce more knowledge. Research databases also allow you to avoid research that is of questionable or unknown quality (which you might find in a general web search).

Thoughtful Research Design

When the director of sales suggested that staff review the renewal rates for season ticket holders, the implication was that some sort of vague search would occur. Perhaps staff could compare renewal rates with other information that the sales department might have on each ticket holder such as age, gender, household income, or number of years as a season ticket holder. This approach to the problem lacks a clear question and a systematic, scientific plan of action. Andrew, Pedersen, and McEvoy

(2011) defined a research design as a selected mode of inquiry or "the structure of the research project being implemented in order to answer the research questions" (p. 264). The choice of research design is determined by factors such as the purpose of the research, the research questions, the training and expertise of the researcher, available resources, and how the research will be used.

Table 21.3 lists common research designs in sport management research and examples of studies that have used those designs. Experimental designs expose groups to different treatments or interventions so the researcher can examine whether the treatment is causing a change in an outcome of interest. A cross-sectional research design analyzes a portion of the population through data collected from a survey or data obtained from an external source such as the U.S. Census Bureau, SportVu camera operators, or the NCAA Equity in Athletics Disclosure Act financial reporting system. Cross-sectional research is by far the most common design in sport management. Time-series research tracks variables over time to identify trends. Alternatively, a longitudinal design gathers data from the same person or sample group repeatedly over time.

Research questions are sometimes best answered by going out into the field and studying how sport is managed in a natural setting. Ethnography is one type of field research. The goal is often to understand the context or conditions that shape people's perspectives

Table 21.3 Examples of Research Designs

Type of research design	Example
Experimental	Cialdini et al. (1976) presented half of respondents with one set of facts and half with a different set of facts. The differences in their responses identified the behavioral fan response called BIRGing.
Cross-sectional (survey)	Two separate surveys were conducted by Tyler and Cobbs (2015) to identify and then confirm 11 elements that define a rivalry.
Time series	To determine the effect of labor strikes and lockouts on attendance, Schmidt and Berri (2004) collected yearly attendance data from the MLB between 1901 and 2000.
Longitudinal	In surveying 128 British athletes over three years, Reinboth and Duda (2006) found that sport environments marked by task orientation spur athlete well-being.
Ethnography	Hoeber and Kerwin (2013) explored the experience of being female sport fans through their interactions as fans.
Case study	Kelley, Harrolle, and Casper (2014) studied one NHL team to uncover consumer spending on tickets, merchandise, and food and beverage.

research design—A strategy or plan of action that links the research questions to the choice of research methods and the desired outcomes.

Alcohol Sponsorship of Sport: Carlsberg and EURO 2016

Sarah Gee
  University of Windsor, Canada
Guillaume Bodet
  Université Claude Bernard Lyon 1, France

Conducting research on sport and alcohol has its challenges. Part of the complexity is entangled with the nature of the relationship between alcohol (largely regarded as an unhealthy product linked with related harms) and sport (perceived as a healthy activity). Yet, most of us think nothing of enjoying a beer while watching sport or wearing a jersey of our favorite team that has the team's alcohol sponsor logo on it.

Laws that regulate alcohol sponsorship of sports events, teams, and athletes differ from one country to another. In many countries there are no, or very minimal, restrictions. However, France has one of the most eminent and controlling laws, *Loi Évin*, that prohibits alcohol sponsorship of cultural and sport events. This is significant considering that France hosted the EURO 2016 football tournament, and Carlsberg (a Danish beer brand) was the official beer sponsor of the tournament. This ensured exclusivity for Carlsberg as the only beer sold at the stadiums and in the fan zones, but *Loi Évin* restricted how Carlsberg advertised its brand during the event. We were interested in documenting the ways in which alcohol logos and images were associated with the tournament.

We visited stadiums and fan zones during the tournament and found that Carlsberg's visual presence at these venues was very different. At the stadiums, alcohol logos (in the form of billboards around the pitch) were not permitted. However, Carlsberg's promotional campaign, centered on the brand's "Probably . . . the best in the world" tagline and in the traditional Carlsberg-branded font and colors of green and white, was allowed. Arguably, this in itself created an association of the event with the brand if one was able to recognize the campaign and the colors. Alternatively, many of the fan zones contained a purpose-built Carlsberg bar as well as a number of drinks outlets cladded in the Carlsberg logo. Carlsberg also circulated maps of French cities with small Carlsberg logos representing the locations of pubs and bars that sold Carlsberg beer.

Digital media were not originally regulated by *Loi Évin* because the Internet was not a prominent outlet for sponsorship and advertising in 1991 when *Loi Évin* was established. In 2013, a court of appeal in France claimed that Facebook content edited by alcohol brands was considered to be publicity and consequently ruled that *Loi Évin* applied (no publicity linking alcohol and sports should be allowed). However, this law only applies to French versions of digital media; English versions of social media platforms offered Carlsberg multiple oppor-

of their experiences as sport organizers, volunteers, consumers, or sponsors. Case studies explore a person, process, event, team, or organization in depth over time using a variety of data collection methods (Jones, 2015).

Methods of Data Collection

We usually associate data with numbers or statistics, but sport managers rely on many different types of data. Data in the form of numbers are known as quantitative data, whereas data in the form of words, pictures, or actions are known as qualitative data. The choice of data depends on the research question and the research design. When investigators combine quantitative and qualitative data collection to answer their research questions, they are employing a mixed-methods approach.

The research method is the process by which the researcher obtains data. Surveys are one of the most common methods to obtain quantitative data. Other common methods are secondary data analysis, such as downloading data from Statistics Canada or the U.S. Census Bureau, and content analysis, which could involve calculating the frequency of positive and negative comments on an athlete's Twitter account. Common techniques for collecting qualitative data are interviews, focus groups, field observations, and content analyses. Each of these data collection methods has its advantages and disadvantages, but a skilled researcher selects the method of data collection to maximize the quality of the data and to most accurately answer the research question.

In trying to solve the problem of low ticket sales, the director of sales likely feels comfortable that

---

quantitative data—Data in the form of numbers.
qualitative data—Data in the form of words, pictures, or actions.

Carlsberg pop-up bar at the EURO 2016 fan zone in Lyon, France.
Courtesy of Sarah Gee.

tunities to promote its brand with the tournament globally. Using its official Twitter (@carlsberg) and Facebook feeds, Carlsberg circulated highlights of game footage showcasing its "Man of the Match" and "Goal of the Tournament" activations. Negotiating sport and alcohol sponsorship laws for digital media based on national boundaries is complex.

Digital alcohol-branded spaces and activities such as those employed by Carlsberg through its English social media accounts certainly evade the restrictions imposed by *Loi Évin*. However, they also facilitate fans' exposure to and engagement with alcohol-branded sport content within and beyond French borders.

the internal database of season ticket holders is of high quality. Conversely, if the director of marketing locates an article with results in an industry publication, it may not be clear where the data originated. Regardless of where data come from or how they are collected, a skilled researcher must be able to trust the data. Similarly, a skilled sport manager must ask important questions so that the data, and the results that emerge from them, can be trusted.

Safeguards for Quality

The type of research that builds from existing knowledge and relies on discipline-specific concepts and theories is generally found in academic settings. Those who publish research papers have spent years learning about various methodologies and statistical approaches for analyzing research data. Before an

academic research paper is published, it is reviewed anonymously by others with similar training to ensure that the concepts, theories, reliance on previous research, data collection, and analysis methods meet appropriate standards. This peer review process is the hallmark of academic research, and it is the single most important factor ensuring that research published in academic journals is of the highest quality and rigor with regard to research methods and data analysis.

In addition to adhering to a peer-review process, academic research is also considered the highest quality in terms of its adherence to ethical standards. Universities, hospitals, financial and government agencies, and companies, and the employees who work in them, are bound by laws that require strict accountability and protection for human subjects

Social Media and The Olympics

Second-screen viewership represents a threat to traditional sport broadcasting but also represents an opportunity to connect with sport fans through mobile applications and social media. The IOC's broadcast strategy for the 2016 Olympic Summer Games in Rio de Janeiro was a clear example of how a high-stakes media asset can embrace the ever-changing digital world. Viewership data from Global Web Index anticipated that 85 percent of likely Olympic viewers would use additional devices while they watched television. NBC Universal embraced this research and increased second-screen viewing opportunities. As a result, television viewership was down 9 percent from London 2012, but viewers streamed 2.71 billion minutes of coverage, and Twitter, Facebook, and Instagram saw huge interaction increases (Hutchinson, 2016). According to executive producer Jim Bell, "If we hadn't been on 11 linear channels and had massive digital distribution and had social engagement across the board and an app, people would be writing about that, saying we didn't embrace the new world. So we embraced the new world" (Holloway, 2016, para. 13). This represents an excellent example of how using research that tracks trends in behavior can lead to strategic organizational decisions.

to qualitative and mixed-methods research to avoid making faulty assumptions about future directions.

Current Challenges in Sport Management Research

Several major issues will affect sport management research as we head into the third decade of 21st century. Two of the most urgent are addressed in the following sections.

Judging the Quality of Research

Sport managers who lack adequate training face considerable challenges when interpreting research. Because of the information explosion that has accompanied the emergence of a knowledge-based economy, sport managers are bombarded with research from a variety of sources including mass media, social media (e.g., Twitter, Instagram), Internet sites, LinkedIn posts, blogs, SlideShares, trade publications, academic journals, consulting and governmental reports, workshops, and conference presentations as well as research done for their own organizations. Because research varies considerably in quality, sport managers must be able to make accurate evaluations of the research methods used and the data analysis techniques employed to judge whether the conclusions drawn and the recommendations made are reliable and credible. Here are some other questions worthy of consideration when assessing the quality of research:

- Are the purposes or research questions clearly stated?
- Who conducted the research, and what are their credentials?
- Who sponsored the research, and how will they benefit from it?
- What is the source of the research, and is a rigorous review process in place for ensuring its quality?
- Are the key concepts or variables under investigation clearly defined?
- If applicable, was relevant literature or background information provided?
- What are the limitations of the research design?
- Were the sources and methods used to collect data appropriate?
- Did the researcher consider ethical issues when conducting the research?
- Are conclusions and recommendations provided, and are they supported by the findings?

If it is not clear who conducted the research or what their credentials are, if few details are provided about the sample or research methods, and if no mention is made of the validity and reliability of the measures or indicators used, you should be highly suspicious of the claims being made. A systematic approach to research may have been used, but until you can verify that, you should critically question whether the conclusions and recommendations are justified and be hesitant about relying on the information when making decisions.

Knowing Where to Find the Answers You Seek

As we covered earlier in this chapter (table 21.1), the source of the research is an element to consider. Many people are suspicious of research reported over the Internet, and with good reason. As the Stanford History Education Group (2016) stated, "there are scores of websites pretending to be something they are not. Ordinary people once relied on publishers, editors, and subject matter experts to vet the information they consumed. But on the unregulated Internet, all bets are off" (p. 4). Although some websites contain research information that has been carefully monitored or reviewed, many do not. Readers often have difficulty determining whether information is credible because the source may not report adequate details regarding the research design or the qualifications of the researcher. As you have learned in this chapter, your university library offers access to databases of journals, articles, and reports that used sound research design and ethical guidelines.

Obtaining access to information becomes more challenging after you graduate, when access to scholarly research is no longer paid for through your tuition and available to you through your university library. Some institutions allow alumni access to libraries and library databases after graduation. However, outside of academic settings, sport managers are usually expected to pay for their own journal subscriptions. For instance, one-year electronic access to a single article published in some of the field's top journals could cost US$20 or more, and annual journal subscriptions could exceed US$100 depending on the mode of delivery (i.e., electronic versus print access). In an effort to combat this problem and make research findings more accessible to policymakers and practitioners who rely on them when enhancing sport, some researchers are being encouraged to publish their findings in open-access journals (e.g., *Journal of Issues in Intercollegiate Athletics*), and some universities encourage or require their faculty to post to open access repositories such as Digital Commons Network (which has a separate Sports Management Commons with sport-related research). Advocates of open access believe that such policies help ensure that research carried out with public funds is accessible to the same taxpayers who make the projects possible.

Future of Sport Management Research

More sport managerial issues will arise with the growth of the field, innovation, and technological progress. Changing technologies, environments, workforces, venues, and security measures and changing demographics of participants, fans, and spectators, along with a plethora of other factors, will influence sport and the ways in which it is managed. Sport scholars and practitioners foresee changes in media delivery, game management, and customer service to be at the forefront of concern. What issues and problems do you foresee? How will you solve these to the satisfaction of various stakeholders? What methods will you use to address your research questions?

An article published in the *Harvard Business Review* proclaimed that "data scientists" have the sexiest job of the 21st century (Davenport & Patil, 2012). Unfortunately, the demand for these positions is racing ahead of the supply of qualified talent to fill them, and the demand for these skills extends far beyond the front offices of professional sport teams. Companies such as Yahoo!, Facebook, Google, Amazon, Microsoft, eBay, LinkedIn, and Twitter are

As noted in this chapter (and illustrated in table 21.3), common research designs in sport management research are experimental, cross-sectional, time series, longitudinal, ethnography, and case study. Here, a sport management researcher, who is monitoring the data provided by a subject in an adjacent room, conducts an experimental design study on emotions and advertisements in the sport industry.

Courtesy of Paul M. Pedersen.

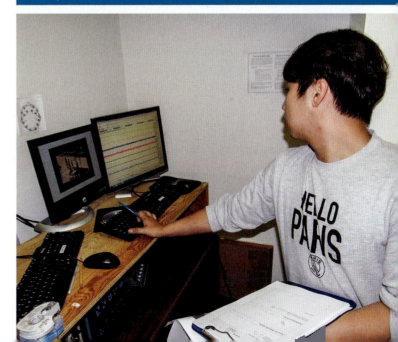

at the forefront of this revolution. As noted by Davenport and Patil, with any quality researcher, "the dominant trait among data scientists is an intense curiosity—a desire to go beneath the surface of a problem, find the questions at its heart, and distill them into a very clear set of hypotheses that can be tested" (p. 73). If research courses are not included as a core content area in your sport management curriculum, you would be well served to seek courses in research methods and quantitative and qualitative data analysis to prepare yourself for a future career in the knowledge economy.

For chapter-specific learning activities, visit the web study guide at **www.HumanKinetics.com/ContemporarySportManagement**.

Summary

In our information-based economy, sport managers who ask relevant and focused research questions and obtain valid and reliable answers through sound research practices will enhance their planning and improve the likelihood of achieving success on and off the playing field. The most successful sport managers will be those who use research to inform their decision making. Sport management research is available from a variety of sources, and each has its own strengths and weaknesses. Regardless of the source, sport managers need a solid foundation in research to be able to assess what types of information are credible and worthy of consideration.

Engaging in the research process can be a stimulating and rewarding experience. Besides learning about disciplinary research in your courses, you may also attend conferences, join academic societies or trade associations, and read articles in peer-reviewed journals and trade publications to stay on top of the latest concepts, theories, trends, and best practices. In addition, you can ask your professors about how to get involved in research as a volunteer or participant in their research projects. Doing so may lead you to consider graduate studies, where students are challenged to conduct their own research and contribute to the creation of new knowledge.

Review Questions

1. How can research affect managerial decision making in sports?

2. What are the features of high-quality research?

3. What are some of the differences between quantitative and qualitative data? Describe one common data collection technique for each.

4. Why is it important to consider ethical issues when conducting sport management research?

5. Do you agree that the need for expertise in sport management research will continue to grow in the future? Justify your argument.

6. What are some reputable sources, databases, or websites for accessing sport management research?

7. How can knowledge of sport management research and procedures provide you with a competitive advantage in the job market?

References

Chapter 1

Acosta, R.V., & Carpenter, L.J. (2014). *Women in intercollegiate sport—a longitudinal, national study: Thirty-seven year update 1977-2014*. Retrieved from www.acostacarpenter.org/2014%20Status%20of%20 Women%20in%20Intercollegiate%20Sport%20 -37%20Year%20Update%20-%201977-2014%20. pdf

Browne, M.N., & Keeley, S.M. (2018). *Asking the right questions: A guide to critical thinking* (12th ed.). Englewood Cliffs, NJ: Pearson/Prentice Hall.

Coakley, J. (2017). *Sports in society: Issues and controversies* (12th ed.). New York, NY: McGraw-Hill Education.

Danylchuk, K.E. (2011). Internationalizing ourselves: Realities, opportunities, and challenges. *Journal of Sport Management, 25*, 1-10.

Danylchuk, K.E., & Boucher, R. (2003). The future of sport management as an academic discipline. *International Journal of Sport Management, 4*, 281-300.

DeSensi, J.T., & Rosenberg, D. (2010). *Ethics and morality in sport management* (3rd ed.). Morgantown, WV: Fitness Information Technology.

Ennis, R.H. (2015). Critical thinking: A streamlined conception. In M. Davies & R. Barnett (Eds.), *The Palgrave handbook of critical thinking in higher education* (pp. 31-47). New York, NY: Palgrave Macmillan.

Environmental Protection Agency. (n.d.). Green sports. Retrieved from www.epa.gov/green-sports

Eschenfelder, M.J., & Li, M. (2007). *Economics of sport* (2nd ed.). Morgantown, WV: Fitness Information Technology.

Frank, R. (1984). Olympic myths and realities. *Arete: The Journal of Sport Literature, 1*(2), 155-161.

George Washington University. (n.d.). Sports philanthropy executive certificate. Retrieved from http://business.gwu.edu/programs/executive-education/professional-certificates/sports-philanthropy

Green Sports Alliance. (n.d.). About. Retrieved from http://greensportsalliance.org/about

Henry, E. (2017). *42 faith: The rest of the Jackie Robinson story*. Nashville, TN: Thomas Nelson.

Horch, H., & Schütte, N. (2003). Competencies of sport managers in German sport clubs and sport federations. *Managing Leisure, 8*, 70-84.

Isaacs, S. (1964). *Careers and opportunities in sport*. New York, NY: Dutton.

Jenny, S., Manning, R.D., Keiper, M.C., & Olrich, T.W. (2016). Virtual(ly) athletes: Where eSports fit within the definition of "sport." *Quest, 69*(1). Retrieved from www.tandfonline.com/doi/full/10.1080/00336297.20 16.1144517?scroll=top&needAccess=true

Josephson Institute of Ethics. (2016). *Making ethical decisions*. Retrieved from http://josephsoninstitute. org/blog/2016/08/18/making-ethical-decisions-six-pillars-character

Lapchick, R. (with Bulloch, T., Jr.) (2016). *The 2016 racial and gender report card: National Basketball Association*. Retrieved from www.tidesport.org/racial-and-gender-report-cards.html

Mahony, D.F. (2008). No one can whistle a symphony: Working together for sport management's future. *Journal of Sport Management, 22*, 1-10.

Malloy, D.C., & Zakus, D.H. (1995). Ethical decision making in sport administration: A theoretical inquiry into substance and form. *Journal of Sport Management, 9*, 36-58.

Markkula Center for Applied Ethics. (2009). *Making an ethical decision*. Retrieved from www.scu.edu/media/ ethics-center/resources/making.pdf

Mason, J.G., Higgins, C.R., & Wilkinson, O.J. (1981). Sports administration education 15 years later. *Athletic Purchasing and Facilities, 5*(1), 44-45.

McCullough, B.P., Pfahl, M.E., & Nguyen, S.N. (2016). The green waves of environmental sustainability in sport. *Sport in Society, 19*(7), 1040-1065.

Meek, A. (1997). An estimate of the size and supported economic activity of the sports industry in the United States. *Sport Marketing Quarterly, 6*(4), 15-21.

Mullin, B.J. (1980). Sport management: The nature and utility of the concept. *Arena Review, 4*(3), 1-11.

North American Society for Sport Management (NASSM). (n.d.). Academic programs. Retrieved from www.nassm.com/Programs/AcademicPrograms

Parks, J.B., Chopra, P.S., Quain, R.J., & Alguindigue, I.E. (1988). ExSport I: An expert system for sport management career counseling. *Journal of Research on Computing in Education, 21*, 196-209.

Parks, J.B., & Olafson, G.A. (1987). Sport management and a new journal. *Journal of Sport Management, 1*, 1-3.

Pedersen, P.M., Laucella, P.C., Kian, E.T.M., & Geurin, A.N. (2017). *Strategic sport communication* (2nd ed.). Champaign, IL: Human Kinetics.

Pitts, B.G., Fielding, L.W., & Miller, L.K. (1994). Industry segmentation theory and the sport industry: Developing a sport industry segmentation model. *Sport Marketing Quarterly, 3*(1), 15-24.

Pitts, B.G., & Stotlar, D.K. (2013). *Fundamentals of sport marketing* (4th ed.). Morgantown, WV: Fitness Information Technology.

Players in the esports space. (2017). *Street & Smith's SportsBusiness Journal, 19*(43), 18.

Rath, J. (2017, January 24). Tough Mudder is generating $100 million in revenue and is about to launch a TV show – here's how it began. *Business Insider.* Retrieved from www.businessinsider.com/how-tough-mudder-went-from-harvard-business-to-tv-show-on-sky-and-cbs-2017-1

Ross, S.R., & Parks, J.B. (2008). Sport management students' attitudes toward women: A challenge for educators. *Sport Management Education Journal, 2*, 1-18.

Sennaar, K. (2017, August 28). Artificial intelligence in sports – Current and future applications. *TechEmergence.* Retrieved from https://www.techemergence.com/artificial-intelligence-in-sports/

Sky Sports. (2016, October 21). Drone racing is coming to Sky Sports Mix. Retrieved from www.skysports.com/more-sports/other-sports/news/29877/10576444/drone-racing-is-coming-to-sky-sports-mix

Smith, M. (2016). Plugged in: Joni Smoller. *Street & Smith's SportsBusiness Journal, 19*(23), 3.

Snapshots from the esports market from intelligence firm Newzoo. (2017). *Street & Smith's SportsBusiness Journal, 19*(43), 19.

Sports market place directory. (2017). Amenia, NY: Grey House.

Thibault, L. (2012). Delivering sport in the global context. In L. Trenberth & D. Hassan (Eds.), *Managing sport business: An introduction* (pp. 231-246). London, England: Routledge.

Women's Sports Foundation. (2011). *Coaching—Do female athletes prefer male coaches? The Foundation position.* Retrieved from www.womenssportsfoundation.org/advocate/foundation-positions/equity-issues/female-athletes-prefer-male-coaches

Chapter 2

Asher, D. (2011). *Cracking the hidden job market.* New York, NY: Random House.

Bai, J., Larimer, S., & Riner, M.B. (2016). Cross-cultural pedagogy: Practical strategies for a successful interprofessional study abroad course. *Journal of the Scholarship of Teaching and Learning, 16*(3), 72-81.

Boitnott, J. (2015). *How to avoid getting taken in by the office gossip.* Retrieved from www.inc.com/john-boitnott/how-to-avoid-getting-taken-in-by-your-office-gossip.html

Brassie, P.S. (1989). Guidelines for programs preparing undergraduate and graduate students for careers in sport management. *Journal of Sport Management, 3*, 158-164.

Buchmeier, W., & Zieschang, K. (1992). *Sportökonomen in beruf und studium.* Schorndorf, Germany: Karl Hofmann.

CareerBuilder. (2016). *Number of employers using social media to screen candidates has increased 500 percent over the last decade.* Retrieved from www.careerbuilder.com/share/aboutus/pressreleasesdetail.aspx?ed=12%2F31%2F2016&id=pr945&sd=4%2F28%2F2016

Carney, C.G., & Wells, C.F. (1995). *Discover the career within you* (4th ed.). Pacific Grove, CA: Thomson Brooks/Cole.

Chelladurai, P. (2005). *Managing organizations for sport and physical activity: A systems perspective* (2nd ed.). Scottsdale, AZ: Holcomb Hathaway.

Cuneen, J., & Sidwell, M.J. (1994). *Sport management field experiences.* Morgantown, WV: Fitness Information Technology.

Cunningham, G.B. (2016). Diversity and inclusion in sport. In R. Hoye & M.M. Parent (Eds.), *The SAGE handbook of sport management* (pp. 309-322). Thousand Oaks, CA: Sage.

Dixon, M.A., Cunningham, G.B., Sagas, M., Turner, B.A., & Kent, A. (2005). Challenge is key: An investigation of affective organizational commitment in undergraduate interns. *Journal of Education for Business, 80*, 172-180.

Donaldson, L. (2001). *The contingency theory of organizations.* Thousand Oaks, CA: Sage.

Doyle, A. (2015). *What is the career planning process?* Retrieved from www.thebalance.com/what-is-the-career-planning-process-2063709

Duggan, T. (n.d.). *Work ethic, attitude and productivity.* Retrieved from http://smallbusiness.chron.com/work-ethics-attitude-productivity-10950.html

Gentile, D. (2010). *Teaching sport management: A practical guide.* Sudbury, MA: Jones and Bartlett.

Gower, R.K., & Mulvaney, M.A. (2012). *Making the most of your internship: A strategic approach.* Champaign, IL: Sagamore.

Harvey, T.R., & Drolet, B. (2004). *Building teams, building people* (2nd ed.). Lanham, MD: Scarecrow Education.

Higuera, V. (n.d.). *How to show professional maturity in the workplace.* Retrieved from www.ehow.com/

how_8459065_show-professional-maturity-workplace.html

Jobling, I., & Deane, J. (1996). Sport management in Australia. In J.-L. Chappelet & M.-H. Roukhadzé (Eds.), *Sport management: An international approach* (pp. 21-31). Lausanne, Switzerland: International Olympic Committee.

Kahle-Piasecki, L. (2011). Making a mentoring relationship work: What is required for organizational success. *Journal of Applied Business and Economics, 12*(1), 46-56.

Langford, B. (2016). *The etiquette edge: Modern manners for business success* (2nd ed.). New York, NY: AMACOM.

Lopiano, D., & Zotos, C. (2014). *The athletic directors' desk reference.* Champaign, IL: Human Kinetics.

McCullough, B.P., & Kellison, T.B. (2017). An introduction to environmental sustainability and sport. In B.P. McCullough & T.B. Kellison (Eds.), *Routledge handbook of sport and the environment* (pp. 3-10). New York, NY: Routledge.

Mitchell, M. (with Corr, J.). (1998). *The first five minutes: How to make a great first impression in any business situation.* New York, NY: Wiley.

National Association of Colleges and Employers (NACE). (2015). Percentage of students with internship experience climbs. Retrieved from www.naceweb.org/s10072015/internship-co-op-student-survey.aspx

National Association of Colleges and Employers (NACE). (2016). *Employers identify four "must have" career readiness competencies for college graduates.* Retrieved from www.naceweb.org/s04202016/four-career-readiness-competencies.aspx?terms=career%20readiness

National Association of Colleges and Employers (NACE). (n.d.). *Job outlook 2016: Attributes employers want to see on new college graduates' resumes.* Retrieved from www.naceweb.org/s11182015/employers-look-for-in-new-hires.aspx

Nonis, S., & Swift, C.O. (2001). An examination of the relationship between academic dishonesty and workplace dishonesty: A multi-campus investigation. *Journal of Education for Business, 77*(2), 69-77.

Parks, J.B. (executive producer), Harper, M.C. (writer), & Lopez, P.G. (director). (1994). *One person's struggle with gender-biased language: Part 1* [Videotape]. (Available from WBGU-TV, Bowling Green State University, Bowling Green, OH 43403.)

Peck, A., Hall, D., Cramp, C., Lawhead, J., Fehring, K., & Simpson, T. (2016). The co-curricular connection: The impact of experiences beyond the classroom on soft skills. *Journal of the National Association of Colleges and Employers, 76*(3), 30-34.

Pedersen, P.M., Osborne, B., Whisenant, W.A., & Lim, C. (2009). An examination of the perceptions of sexual harassment by newspaper sports journalists. *Journal of Sport Management, 23,* 335-360.

Pollak, L. (2017). *Millennials manage differently, and that's a good thing.* Retrieved from www.lindseypollak.com/millennial-managers-what-you-need-to-know/

Saunderson, R. (2012). Onboarding recognition. *Training, 49*(2), 60, 62.

Scheele, A. (2005). *Launch your career in college: Strategies for students, educators, and parents.* Westport, CT: Praeger.

Schütte, N. (2016). *Grundwissen sportmanagement.* Munich, Germany: utb.

Sukiennik, D., Bendat, W., & Raufman, L. (2008). *The career fitness program: Exercising your options* (9th ed.). Upper Saddle River, NJ: Pearson/Prentice Hall.

Williams, J. (2003). Sport management internship administration: Challenges and chances for collaboration. *NACE Journal, 63*(2), 28-32.

Zaharia, N., Kaburakis, A., & Pierce, D. (2016). US sport management programs in business schools: Trends and key issues. *Sport Management Education Journal, 10*(1), 13-28.

Zunker, V.G. (2009). *Career, work, and mental health: Integrating career & personal counseling.* Thousand Oaks, CA: Sage.

Chapter 3

Adelman, M.L. (1986). *A sporting time: New York City and the rise of modern athletics, 1820-70.* Urbana, IL: University of Illinois Press.

Badenhausen, K. (2017). Full list: The world's 50 most valuable sports teams 2017. *Forbes.* Retrieved from www.forbes.com/sites/kurtbadenhausen/2017/07/12/full-list-the-worlds-50-most-valuable-sports-teams-2017/#2f0503164a05

Betts, J.R. (1974). *America's sporting heritage 1850-1950.* Reading, MA: Addison-Wesley.

de Wilde, A., Seifried, C., & Adelman, M.L. (2010). The culture of history in sport management's foundation: The intellectual influence of Harvard Business School on four founding sport management scholars. *Quest, 62*(4), 406-422.

ESPN Films. (2013). *Nine for IX.* Retrieved from www.espn.com/espnw/w-in-action/nine-for-ix

Fielding, L.W., & Miller, L.K. (1998). The ABC trust: A chapter in the history of capitalism in the sporting goods industry. *Sport History Review, 29*(1), 44-58.

Katz, D. (2016). Mobile, millennials and (social) media: What the mean for sports content. *Street & Smith's SportsBusiness Journal.* Retrieved from www.sportsbusinessdaily.com/Journal/Issues/2016/06/20/Opinion/David-Katz.aspx

Lewis, G. (1973). World War I and the emergence of sport for the masses. *Maryland Historian, 4,* 109-122.

National Sporting Goods Association. (2015). *Sporting goods industry FAQ.* Retrieved from www.nsga.org/globalassets/research/public/sporting-goods-industry-faq---2015.pdf

Once upon a time: Turning back the pages of Spalding's first ledger. (1947). *Sporting Goods Dealer, 96,* 128-130.

O'Reilly, N., & Seguin, B. (2009). *Sport marketing: A Canadian perspective.* Toronto, Canada: Nelson.

Ozanian, M. (2017). The world's most valuable soccer teams 2017. *Forbes.* Retrieved from www.forbes.com/sites/mikeozanian/2017/06/06/the-worlds-most-valuable-soccer-teams-2017/#7fc2517877ea

Rader, B.G. (1984). *In its own image: How television has transformed sports.* New York, NY: Free Press.

Rader, B.G. (2009). *American sports: From the age of folk games to the age of televised sports* (6th ed.). Upper Saddle River, NJ: Prentice Hall.

Roberts, R., & Olsen, J. (1989). *Winning is the only thing: Sports in America since 1945.* Baltimore, MD: Johns Hopkins University Press.

Robinson, P.R. (1909). Trade prospects for 1909. *Sporting Goods Dealer, 20,* 31-32.

Seifried, C. (2014). A review of the North American Society for Sport Management and its foundational core: Mapping the influence of "history." *Journal of Management History, 20*(1), 81-98.

Smith, R.A. (1988). *Sports & freedom: The rise of college athletics.* New York, NY: Oxford University Press.

Spanberg, E. (2016). Placing values on social media engagement. *Street & Smith's SportsBusiness Journal.* Retrieved from www.sportsbusinessdaily.com/Journal/Issues/2016/02/22/In-Depth/Social-media.aspx?hl=Twitter%20Spanberg&sc=0

Sports and Fitness Industry Association (SFIA). (n.d.). Overview. Retrieved from www.sfia.org/about/overview

Chapter 4

Abeza, G., O'Reilly, N., & Reid, I. (2013). Relationship marketing and social media in sport. *International Journal of Sport Communication, 6,* 120-142.

Babiak, K. (2007). Determinants of interorganizational relationships: The case of a Canadian nonprofit sport organization. *Journal of Sport Management, 21,* 338-376.

Boucher, R.L. (1998). Toward achieving a focal point for sport management: A binocular perspective. *Journal of Sport Management, 12,* 76-85.

Byers, T., Slack, T., & Parent, M. (2012). *Key concepts in sport management.* London, England: Sage.

Carroll, A.B. (1999). Corporate social responsibility: Evolution of a definitional construct. *Business and Society, 38*(3), 268-295.

Caza, A. (2000). Context receptivity: Innovation in an amateur sport organization. *Journal of Sport Management, 14,* 227-242.

Colyer, S. (2000). Organizational culture in selected Western Australian sport organizations. *Journal of Sport Management, 14,* 321-341.

Comeaux, E. (2013). Rethinking academic reform and encouraging organizational innovation: Implications for stakeholder management in college sports. *Innovative Higher Education, 38*(4), 281-293.

Cousens, L., Babiak, K.M., & Slack, T. (2001). Adopting a relationship marketing paradigm: The case of the National Basketball Association. *International Journal of Sports Marketing and Sponsorship, 2,* 331-355.

Cunningham, G.B. (2006). Does structure make a difference? The effect of organizational structure on job satisfaction and organizational commitment. *International Journal of Sport Management, 7,* 327-346.

Daft, R.L. (2016). *Organization theory and design* (12th ed.). Boston, MA: Cengage Learning.

Damanpour, F., & Schneider, M. (2006). Phases of the adoption of innovation in organizations: Effects of environment, organization and top managers. *British Journal of Management, 17*(3), 215-236.

Drucker, P.F. (2002). The discipline of innovation. *Harvard Business Review, 80,* 95-104.

Edwards, A. (1999). Reflective practice in sport management. *Sport Management Review, 2,* 67-81.

Ferkins, L., & Shilbury, D. (2012). Good boards are strategic: What does that mean for sport governance? *Journal of Sport Management, 26,* 67-80.

Freeman, R.E. (2010). *Strategic management: A stakeholder approach.* New York, NY: Cambridge University Press.

Frisby, W. (2005). The good, the bad, and the ugly: Critical sport management research. *Journal of Sport Management, 19,* 1-12.

Frontiera, J. (2010). Leadership and organizational culture transformation in professional sport. *Journal of Leadership and Organizational Studies, 17*(1), 71-86.

Giroux, M., Pons, F., & Mourali, M. (2015). Is CSR important for all types of fans? The value of corporate social responsibility in sport. In L. Robinson Jr. (Ed.), *Marketing dynamism and sustainability: Things change, things stay the same . . .* (pp. 497-500). New York, NY: Springer International.

Greiner, L.E. (1972). Evolution and revolution as organizations grow. *Harvard Business Review, 50*(4), 37-46.

Harris, J.C. (1993). Using kinesiology: A comparison of applied veins in the subdisciplines. *Quest, 45*, 389-412.

Hoeber, L., Doherty, A., Hoeber, O., & Wolfe, R. (2015). The nature of innovation in community sport organizations. *European Sport Management Quarterly, 15*(5), 518-534.

Howell, J.M., & Boies, K. (2004). Champions of technological innovation: The influence of contextual knowledge, role orientation, idea generation, and idea promotion on champion emergence. *The Leadership Quarterly, 15*(1), 123-143.

Kane, G.C. (2017). The evolutionary implications of social media for organizational knowledge management. *Information and Organization, 27*(1), 37-46.

Kanter, R.M. (2008). Transforming giants. *Harvard Business Review, 86*(1), 43-52.

Milton-Smith, J. (2002). Ethics, the Olympics and the search for global values. *Journal of Business Ethics, 35*, 131-142.

Mintzberg, H. (1979). *The structuring of organizations.* Englewood Cliffs, NJ: Prentice Hall.

Miranda, F.J., Chamorro, A., Rubio, S., & Rodriguez, O. (2014). Professional sports teams on social networks: A comparative study employing the Facebook Assessment Index. *International Journal of Sport Communication, 7*, 74-89.

Olberding, D.J. (2003). Examining strategy content in U.S. Olympic sport organizations. *International Journal of Sport Management, 4*, 6-24.

Oliver, C. (1990). Determinants of interorganizational relationships: Integration and future directions. *Academy of Management Review, 15*, 241-265.

Papadimitriou, D. (2001). An exploratory examination of the prime beneficiary approach of organizational effectiveness: The case of elite athletes of Olympic and non-Olympic sports. *European Journal of Sport Management, 8*, 63-82.

Parent, M.M. (2008). Evolution and issue patterns for major-sport-event organizing committees and their stakeholders. *Journal of Sport Management, 22*(2), 135-164.

Parent, M.M. (2010). Decision making in major sport events over time: Parameters, drivers, and strategies. *Journal of Sport Management, 24*(3), 291-318.

Parent, M.M. (2015). The organizing committee's perspective. In M.M. Parent & J.-L. Chappelet (Eds.), *The Routledge handbook of sports event management* (pp. 43-64). London, England: Routledge.

Parent, M.M. (2016). The governance of the Olympic Games in Canada. *Sport in Society, 19*(6), 796-816. doi:10.1080/17430437.2015.1108652

Parent, M.M. (2017). Event management. In R. Hoye & M.M. Parent (Eds.), *The Sage handbook of sport management* (pp. 422-441). London, England: Sage.

Parent, M.M., & MacIntosh, E.W. (2013). Organizational culture evolution in temporary organizations: The case of the 2010 Olympic Winter Games. *Canadian Journal of Administrative Sciences, 30*(4), 223-237. doi:10.1002/CJAS.1262

Parent, M.M., Rouillard, C., & Leopkey, B. (2011). Issues and strategies pertaining to the Canadian governments' coordination efforts in relation to the 2010 Olympic Games. *European Sport Management Quarterly, 11*(4), 337-369. doi:10.1080/16184742.2011.599202

Parveen, F., Jaafar, N.E., & Ainin, S. (2016). Social media's impact on organizational performance and entrepreneurial orientation in organizations. *Management Decision, 54*(9), 2208-2234.

Pettigrew, A.M. (1987). Context and action in the transformation of the firm. *Journal of Management Studies, 24*, 649-670.

Pettigrew, A.M. (1990). Longitudinal field research on change: Theory and practice. *Organization Science, 1*, 267-292.

Pfahl, M. (2011). Strategic issues associated with the development of internal sustainability teams in sport organizations: A framework for action and sustainable environmental performance. *International Journal of Sport Management, Recreation, and Tourism, 6*(C), 37-61.

Polite, F.G., Waller, S., Spearman, L., & Trendafilova, S.A. (2012). Social accountability and responsibility in sport: An examination of the National Collegiate Athletic Association. *Sport Science Review, XX*(1-2), 111-135.

Porter, M.E. (2008). *On competition: Updated and expanded edition.* Boston, MA: Harvard Business School.

Porter, M.E., & Kramer, M.R. (2006). Strategy and society: The link between competitive advantage and corporate social responsibility. *Harvard Business Review, 84*(12), 78-92.

Price, G. (2016, August 8). Rio Olympics problems: 14 things that have gone wrong at the 2016 summer Games. *International Business Times.* Retrieved from www.ibtimes.com/rio-olympics-problems-14-things-have-gone-wrong-2016-summer-games-2398944

Quinn, R.E., & Cameron, K. (1983). Organizational life cycles and shifting criteria of effectiveness: Some preliminary evidence. *Management Science, 29*, 33-51.

Quinn, R.E., & Rohrbaugh, J. (1981). A competing values approach to organizational effectiveness. *Public Productivity Review, 5*(2), 122-140.

Sack, A.L., & Nadim, A. (2002). Strategic choices in a turbulent environment: A case study of Starter Corporation. *Journal of Sport Management, 16*, 36-53.

Schein, E.H. (1985). *Organizational culture and leadership.* San Francisco, CA: Jossey-Bass.

Sheth, H., & Babiak, K.M. (2010). Beyond the game: Perceptions and practices of corporate social responsibility in the professional sport industry. *Journal of Business Ethics, 91*(3), 433-450.

Shilbury, D., & Moore, K.A. (2006). A study of organizational effectiveness for national Olympic sporting organizations. *Nonprofit and Voluntary Sector Quarterly, 35*(1), 5-38.

Slack, T., & Parent, M.M. (2006). *Understanding sport organizations. The application of organization theory* (2nd ed.). Champaign, IL: Human Kinetics.

Stavros, C., Meng, M.D., Westberg, K., & Farrelly, F. (2014). Understanding fan motivation for interacting on social media. *Sport Management Review, 17*(4), 455-469.

Tainsky, S., & Babiak, K. (2011). Professional athletes and charitable foundations: An exploratory investigation. *International Journal of Sport Management and Marketing, 9*(3/4), 133-153.

Theodoraki, E.I. (2001). A conceptual framework for the study of structural configurations of organising committees for the Olympic Games (OCOGs). *European Journal for Sport Management, 8*, 106-124.

Thibault, L. (2009). The globalization of sport: An inconvenient truth. *Journal of Sport Management, 23*, 1-20.

Thibault, L., & Babiak, K. (2005). Organizational changes in Canada's sport system: Toward an athlete-centred approach. *European Sport Management Quarterly, 5*, 105-132.

Thibault, L., Slack, T., & Hinings, C.R. (1993). A framework for the analysis of strategy in nonprofit sport organizations. *Journal of Sport Management, 7*, 25-43.

Treem, J.W., & Leonardi, P.M. (2012). Social media use in organizations: Exploring the affordances of visibility, editability, persistence, and association. *Communication Yearbook, 36*, 143-189.

Turner, P.E., & Shilbury, D. (2010). The impact of emerging technology in sport broadcasting on the preconditions for interorganizational relationship formation in professional football. *Journal of Sport Management, 24*, 10-44.

Wolfe, R., Hoeber, L., & Babiak, K. (2002). Perceptions of the effectiveness of sport organisations: The case of intercollegiate athletics. *European Sport Management Quarterly, 2*, 135-156.

Wolfe, R., & Putler, D. (2002). How tight are the ties that bind stakeholder groups? *Organization Science, 13*, 64-80.

Wolfe, R., Wright, P.M., & Smart, D.L. (2006). Radical HRM innovation and competitive advantage: The moneyball story. *Human Resource Management, 45*(1), 111-145.

Yoshida, M., James, J.D., & Cronin, J.J. (2013). Sport event innovativeness: Conceptualization, measurement, and its impact on consumer behavior. *Sport Management Review, 16*(1), 68-84.

Zeigler, E.F. (1987). Sport management: Past, present, future. *Journal of Sport Management, 1*, 4-24.

Chapter 5

Apple Daily. (2014). *The expensive African runners—5 million NTDs earning for one game.* Retrieved from www.appledaily.com.tw/appledaily/article/sports/20141202/36241324

Avolio, B.J., Waldman, D.A., & Yammarino, F.J. (1991). Leading in the 1990s: The four I's of transformational leadership. *Journal of European Industrial Training, 15*, 9-16.

Bandura, A. (1977). *Social learning theory.* Englewood Cliffs, NJ: Prentice Hall.

Bass, B.M. (1985). *Leadership and performance beyond expectations.* New York, NY: Free Press.

Bass, B.M., & Avolio, B.J. (1994). *Improving organizational effectiveness through transformational leadership.* Thousand Oaks, CA: Sage.

Bass, B.M., & Riggio, R.E. (2006). *Transformational leadership* (2nd ed.). Mahwah, NJ: Lawrence Erlbaum Associates.

Brown, M.E., & Treviño, L.K. (2006). Ethical leadership: A review and future directions. *The Leadership Quarterly, 17*(6), 595-616.

Bruening, J.E., & Dixon, M.A. (2007). Work-family conflict in coaching II: Managing role conflict. *Journal of Sport Management, 21*, 471-496.

Carnevale, A.P., & Stone, S. (1994). Diversity: Beyond the golden rule. *Training & Development, 48*(10), 22-39.

Chang, F. (2014). *The capitalism of "road races": An initial observation in Taiwan.* Retrieved from https://twstreetcorner.org/2014/12/30/changfengyi

Chelladurai, P. (2014). *Managing organizations for sport and physical activity: A systems perspective* (4th ed.). Scottsdale, AZ: Holcomb Hathaway.

Chelladurai, P., & Kerwin, S. (2017). *Human resource management in sport and recreation* (3rd ed.). Champaign, IL: Human Kinetics.

Chu, L. (2016). *Race events in Taiwan.* Retrieved from www.taiwanngo.tw/files/15-1000-23879,c156-1.php?Lang=en

Cunningham, G.B. (2008). Creating and sustaining gender diversity in sport organizations. *Sex Roles, 58*(1-2), 136-145.

Cunningham, G.B. (2015). *Diversity and inclusion in sport organizations.* Scottsdale, AZ: Holcomb Hathaway.

Dixon, M.A., & Bruening, J.E. (2007). Work-family conflict in coaching I: A top-down perspective. *Journal of Sport Management, 21*, 377-406.

Doherty, A.J., & Chelladurai, P. (1999). Managing cultural diversity in sport organizations: A theoretical perspective. *Journal of Sport Management, 13*, 280-297.

Eagleman, A.N., & Krohn, B.D. (2012). Sponsorship awareness, attitudes, and purchase intentions of road race series participants. *Sport Marketing Quarterly, 21*, 210-220.

Fiedler, F.E. (1963). *A contingency model for the prediction of leadership effectiveness*. Champaign, IL: University of Illinois Press.

Fink, J.S., & Pastore, D.L. (1999). Diversity in sport? Utilizing the business literature to devise a comprehensive framework of diversity initiatives. *Quest, 51*(4), 310-327.

French, J.R.P., & Raven, B. (1959). Bases of social power. In D. Cartwright (Ed.), *Studies in social power* (pp. 150-167). Ann Arbor, MI: University of Michigan Press.

Greenleaf, R.K. (2002). *Servant-leadership: A journey into the nature of legitimate power and greatness*. Mahwah, NJ: Paulist Press.

Gulick, L., & Urwick, L. (1937). *Papers on the science of administration*. New York, NY: Institute of Public Administration.

Hersey, P., Blanchard, K.H., & Johnson, D.E. (2008). *Management of organizational behavior: Leading human resources* (9th ed.). Upper Saddle River, NJ: Prentice Hall.

Hums, M.A., Barr, C.A., & Gullion, L. (1999). The ethical issues confronting managers in the sport industry. *Journal of Business Ethics, 20*, 51-66.

Jones, G.R., & George, J.M. (2009). *Contemporary management* (6th ed.). Toronto, Canada: McGraw-Hill Ryerson.

Kane, G. (2014). Leadership theories. In J.F. Borland, G.M. Kane, & L.J. Burton (Eds.), *Sport leadership in the 21st century* (pp. 1-19). Burlington, MA: Jones & Bartlett.

Katz, R.L. (1974). Skills of an effective manager. *Harvard Business Review, 52*, 90-102.

Kihl, L.A. (2007). Moral codes, moral tensions, and hiding behind the rules: A snapshot of athletic administrators' practical morality. *Sport Management Review, 10*, 279-305.

Kotter, J.P. (1990). What leaders really do. *Harvard Business Review, 68*(3), 103-111.

Lanning, R. (2016). *Road races in Taiwan*. Retrieved from www.taiwanfun.com/north/taipei/articles/0409/0409Road.htm

Lapchick, R. (n.d.). *The racial and gender report card*. Retrieved from www.tidesport.org/reports.html

Lee, W., & Cunningham, G.B. (2015). A picture is worth a thousand words: The influence of signaling organizational reputation, and applicant race on attraction of sport organizations. *International Journal of Sport Management, 16*, 492-506.

Liberty Times News. (2016). *Kenya racers dominate Taiwanese marathon events and earn a lot*. Retrieved from http://news.ltn.com.tw/news/life/breakingnews/1885627

Lorsch, J.W. (2010). A contingency theory of leadership. In N. Nohria & R. Khurana (Eds.), *Handbook of leadership theory and practice* (pp. 411-429). Boston, MA: Harvard Business Press.

Lukes, S. (1974). *Power: A radical view*. London, England: Macmillan.

Matton, J.N., & Hernandez, C.M. (2004). A new study identifies the "makes and breaks" of diversity initiatives. *Journal of Organizational Excellence, 23*, 47-58.

Mayo, E. (1933). *The human problems of an industrial civilization*. New York, NY: MacMillan.

Melton, E.N., & Cunningham, G.B. (2014). Who are the champions? Using a multilevel model to examine perceptions of employee support for LGBT inclusion in sport organizations. *Journal of Sport Management, 28*, 189-206.

Quarterman, J. (1998). An assessment of the perception of management and leadership skills by intercollegiate athletics conference commissioners. *Journal of Sport Management, 12*, 146-164.

Robbins, S.P., & Judge, T.A. (2008). *Organizational behavior* (13th ed.). Upper Saddle River, NJ: Prentice Hall.

Runner's Plaza. (n.d.). Race events in Taiwan. Retrieved from www.taipeimarathon.org.tw/contest.aspx?lang=en-US

Sando, M. (2016). *Rooney Rule in reverse: Minority coaching hires have stalled*. Retrieved from www.espn.com/nfl/story/_/id/17101097/staggering-numbers-show-nfl-minority-coaching-failure-rooney-rule-tony-dungy

Schermerhorn, J.R., Hunt, J.G., & Osborn, R.N. (2008). *Organizational behavior* (10th ed.). Hoboken, NJ: Wiley.

Scott, W.R. (1987). The adolescence of institutional theory. *Administrative Science Quarterly, 32*, 493-511.

Soucie, D. (1994). Effective managerial leadership in sport organizations. *Journal of Sport Management, 8*, 1-13.

Spears, L.C. (2010). Character and servant leadership: Ten characteristics of effective, caring leaders. *The Journal of Virtues & Leadership, 1*(1), 25-30.

Staw, B.M. (1986). Organizational psychology and the pursuit of the happy/productive worker. *California Management Review, 2*, 40-53.

Taylor, F.W. (1911). *The principles of scientific management.* New York, NY: Harper.

Tesler, M. (2015, May 15). Does race matter in NFL rosters? *The Washington Post.* Retrieved from www.washingtonpost.com/news/monkey-cage/wp/2015/05/15/does-race-matter-in-nfl-rosters/?utm_term=.9c51d9b0e467

Welty Peachey, J.W., Damon, Z.J., Zhou, Y., & Burton, L.J. (2015). Forty years of leadership research in sport management: A review, synthesis, and conceptual framework. *Journal of Sport Management, 29,* 570-587.

Yammarino, F. (2013). Leadership: Past, present, and future. *Journal of Leadership & Organizational Studies, 20*(2), 149-155.

Yukl, G. (2012). *Leadership in organizations* (8th ed.). Upper Saddle River, NJ: Prentice Hall.

Chapter 6

Afterschool Alliance. (2014). *America after 3PM: Afterschool programs in demand.* Retrieved from www.afterschoolalliance.org/documents/AA3PM-2014/AA3PM_Key_Findings.pdf

Afterschool Alliance. (2015). *Evaluations backgrounder: A summary of formal evaluations of afterschool programs' impact on academics, behavior, safety and family life.* Retrieved from http://afterschoolalliance.org//documents/Evaluation_Backgrounder.pdf

Bartram, T., Hoye, R., & Cavanaugh, J.M. (2014). Special issue on human resource management in the NGO, volunteer and not-for-profit sector. *The International Journal of Human Resource Management, 25*(22), 3178-3180.

Brewster, K. (2004). Redeeming the "Indian": Sport and ethnicity in post-revolutionary Mexico. *Patterns of Prejudice, 38*(3), 213-231.

Canada survey of giving, volunteering and participating. (2012). Ottawa, Canada: Volunteer Canada. Available at www.vsi-isbc.org/eng/knowledge/nsgvp.cfm

Canadian Centre for Ethics in Sport. (2002). *Public opinion survey on youth and sport: Final report.* Ottawa, Canada: Decima Research.

Carpiano, R.M., & Hystad, P.W. (2011). "Sense of community belonging" in health surveys: What social capital is it measuring? *Health & Place, 17*(2), 606-617.

Chudacoff, H. (2007). *Children at play: An American history.* New York, NY: New York University Press.

Coakley, J. (2016). Youth sports in the United States. In K. Green & A. Smith (Eds.), *Routledge handbook of youth sport* (pp. 84-97). London, England: Routledge.

Coelho e Silva, M.J., Figueiredo, A.J., Elferink-Gemser, M.T., & Malina, R.M. (Eds.). (2016). *Youth sports: Participation, trainability and readiness* (2nd ed.). Coimbra, Portugal: Coimbra University Press.

Conrad, D. (2016). The Stanford sports to prevent obesity randomized trial (SPORT). In D. Conrad & A. White (Eds.), *Sports-based health interventions* (pp. 261-267). New York, NY: Springer.

Cuskelly, G., Hoye, R., & Auld, C. (2006). *Working with volunteers in sport: Theory and practice.* London, England: Routledge.

Dixon, M. (2009). From their perspective: A qualitative examination of physical activity and sport for working mothers. *Sport Management Review, 12,* 34-48.

Doherty, A., Misener, K., & Cuskelly, G. (2014). Toward a multidimensional framework of capacity in community sport clubs. *Nonprofit and Voluntary Sector Quarterly, 43*(2 suppl.), 124S-142S.

Eime, R.M., Young, J.A., Harvey, J.T., Charity, M.J., & Payne, W.R. (2013). A systematic review of the psychological and social benefits of participation in sport for children and adolescents: Informing development of a conceptual model of health through sport. *International Journal of Behavioral Nutrition and Physical Activity, 10.* Retrieved from https://ijbnpa.biomedcentral.com/articles/10.1186/1479-5868-10-135

Engelberg, T., Skinner, J., & Zakus, D. (2014). What does commitment mean to volunteers in youth sport organizations? *Sport in Society, 17*(1), 52-67.

Graham, J., Dixon, M.A., & Hazen-Swan, N. (2016). Coaching dads: Understanding managerial implications of fathering through sport. *Journal of Sport Management, 30,* 40-51.

Hartmann, D. (2008). *High school sports participation and educational attainment: Recognizing, assessing, and utilizing the relationship.* Retrieved from www.la84foundation.org/3ce/HighSchoolSportsParticipation.pdf

Harvey, S., Kirk, D., & O'Donovan, T.M. (2014). Sport education as a pedagogical application for ethical development in physical education and youth sport. *Sport, Education and Society, 19*(1), 41-62.

Howell, C.D. (2001). *Blood, sweat, and cheers: Sport and the making of modern Canada.* Toronto, Canada: University of Toronto Press.

Kidd, B. (2013). The Canadian state and sport: The dilemma of intervention. *Sport in Society, 16*(4), 362-371.

Lee, J., & McFarlin, J. (2015). A European solution to America's basketball problem: Reforming amateur basketball in the United States. *Journal of Sports & Entertainment Law, 6,* 95-158.

Lin, Y.C., Chalip, L., & Green, B.C. (2016). The essential role of sense of community in a youth sport program. *Leisure Sciences, 38*(5), 461-481.

Marten, J. (2008). A new view of the child: Children and youth in urban America, 1900–1920. *Romanian Journal of Population Studies, 1,* 67-81.

Morrow, D., & Wamsley, K. (2005). *Sport in Canada: A history.* Toronto, Canada: Oxford University Press.

Murphy, K.P. (2005). Hallelujah lads and lasses: Remaking the Salvation Army in America, 1880–1930; Making men, making class: The YMCA and working-men 1877–1930. *Labor, 2,* 112-114.

National Council of Youth Sports. (2012). *Congressional caucus on youth sports.* Retrieved from www.ncys.org/advocacy/congressional-caucus-youth-sports.php

Newman, T.J., Ortega, R.M., Lower, L.M., & Paluta, L.M. (2016). Informing priorities for coaching education: Perspectives from youth sport leaders. *International Journal of Sports Science & Coaching, 1*(3), 436-445.

Physical Activity Council. (2016). *2016 Physical Activity Council report.* Retrieved from www.physicalactivity-council.com/pdfs/current.pdf

Putnam, R. (2000). *Bowling alone: The collapse and revival of American community.* New York, NY: Simon & Schuster.

Sabo, D., & Veliz, P. (2016). Surveying youth sports in America: What we know and what it means for public policy. In M.A. Messner & M. Musto (Eds.), *Child's play: Sport in kids' worlds* (pp. 23-42). New Brunswick, NJ: Rutgers University Press.

Siegel, S.R., Cumming, S.P., Pena Reyes, M.E., Cardenas Barahona, E.E., & Malina, R.M. (2013). Characteristics of youth sport participants and non-participants in Mexico City. In P.T. Katmarzyk & M.J. Coelho-e-Silva (Eds.), *Growth and maturation in human biology and sports* (pp. 217-231). Coimbra, Portugal: Coimbra University Press.

Simon, E.S., Rodriguez de Leon, S.H., Hernandez, M.V., Larrinaga, E.G., & Guadarrama, J.N. (2002). Mexico: A cultural based sport for all with social inclusion. In L.P. DaCosta & A. Maragaya (Eds.), *Worldwide experiences and trends in sport for all* (pp. 661-674). Aachen, Germany: Meyer and Meyer Verlag.

Skirstad, R., Waddington, I., & Säfvenbom, R. (2012). Issues and problems in the organization of children's sport: A case study of Norway. *European Physical Education Review, 18*(3), 309-321. doi:10.1177/1356336X12450790

Stewart, B., Nicholson, M., Smith, A., & Westerbeek, H. (2004). *Australian sport: Better by design? The evolution of Australian sport policy.* London, England: Routledge.

Thibault, L., & Harvey, J. (Eds.). (2013). *Sport policy in Canada.* Ottawa, Canada: University of Ottawa Press.

United States Olympic Committee. (n.d.). Multi-sport organizations. Retrieved from www.teamusa.org/About-the-USOC/In-the-Community/Partner-Programs/Multi-Sport-Organizations.aspx

Villanueva, M.M., & Luevano, M.P. (2016). Women and sport in Mexico. In R. Lopez de D'Amico, T. Benn, & G. Pfister (Eds.), *Women and sport in Latin America* (pp. 144-157). London, England: Routledge.

Wood, L., Giles-Corti, B., Zubrick, S.R., & Bulsara, M.K. (2013). "Through the kids . . . we connected with our community": Children as catalysts of social capital. *Environment and Behavior, 45*(3), 344-368.

Chapter 7

Barney, J.B. (1991). Firm resources and sustained competitive advantage. *Journal of Management, 17,* 99-120.

Blackburn, M., Forsyth, E., Olson, J., & Whitehead, B. (2013). *NIAAA's guide to interscholastic athletic administration.* Champaign, IL: Human Kinetics.

Coakley, J. (2015). *Sports in society: Issues and controversies* (11th ed.). New York, NY: McGraw-Hill Higher Education.

Comstock, R.D., Currie, D.W., Pierpoint, L.A., Grubenhoff, J.A., & Fields, S.K. (2015). An evidence-based discussion of heading the ball and concussions in high school soccer. *The Journal of the American Medical Association Pediatrics, 169,* 831-837.

De Bosscher, V., De Knop, P., van Bottenburg, M., & Shibli, S. (2006). A conceptual framework for analysing sports policy factors leading to international sporting success. *European Sport Management Quarterly, 6,* 185-215.

Florida High School Athletic Association. (n.d.). *About the FHSSA.* Retrieved from www.fhsaa.org/about

Forsyth, E. (2012). Contemporary issues surrounding interscholastic sports: Finance issues. *Interscholastic Athletic Administration, 31*(1), 16-18.

Forsyth, E. (2013). Contemporary issues surrounding interscholastic sports: Parents issues. *Interscholastic Athletic Administration, 39*(3), 16-17.

Forsyth, E. (2016). *Current issues surrounding high school athletics: Survey report.* Indianapolis, IN: National Interscholastic Athletic Administrators Association.

Georgia High School Association. (n.d.). About us. Retrieved from www.ghsa.net/about-us

Golden, J. (2015). *Youth sports: Kids' athletics are in danger.* Retrieved from www.cnbc.com/2015/07/29/youth-sports-kids-athletics-are-in-danger.html

Griffin, P. (2015). *Developing policies for transgender students on high school teams.* Retrieved from www.nfhs.org/articles/developing-policies-for-transgender-students-on-high-school-teams/

Leibsohn, B. (2013). Analysis of the NCAA rule prohibiting a school- or conference-owned television. *Marquette Sports Law Review, 23*(2), 434-454.

Lincoln, A.E., Caswell, S.V., Almquist, J.L., Dunn, R.E., Norris, J.B., & Hinton, R.Y. (2011). Trends in concussion incidence in high school sports: A prospective 11-year study. *The American Journal of Sports Medicine, 39,* 958-963.

Lockard, C.B., & Wolf, M. (2012). Occupational employment projections to 2020. *Monthly Labor Review, January,* 84-108. Retrieved from www.bls.gov/opub/mlr/2012/01/art5full.pdf

Mullin, B.J., Hardy, S., & Sutton, W.A. (2014). *Sport marketing* (4th ed.). Champaign, IL: Human Kinetics.

National Federation of State High School Associations (NFHS). (2016a). *2015-16 high school athletics participation survey.* Indianapolis, IN: Author. Retrieved from www.nfhs.org/ParticipationStatistics/PDF/2015-16_Sports_Participation_Survey.pdf

National Federation of State High School Associations (NFHS). (2016b). *High school sports participation increases for 27th consecutive year.* Retrieved from www.nfhs.org/articles/high-school-sports-participation-increases-for-27th-consecutive-year

National Federation of State High School Associations (NFHS). (2016c). *NFHS handbook 2016–2017.* Indianapolis, IN: Author.

National Federation of State High School Associations (NFHS). (2016d). *The case for high school athletics.* Indianapolis, IN: Author. Retrieved from www.nfhs.org/articles/the-case-for-high-school-activities

National Interscholastic Athletic Administrators Association (NIAAA). (n.d.). NIAAA certification program. Retrieved from www.niaaa.org/niaaa-programs/niaaa-certification-program

Norlian, A. (2016). *Equality Virginia: VHSL transgender policy leading the south and nation.* Retrieved from www.nbc12.com/story/32114768/equality-virginia-vhsl-transgender-policy-leading-the-south-and-nation

Rosenthal, J.A., Foraker, R.E., Collins, C.L., & Comstock, R.D. (2014). National high school athlete concussion rates from 2005-2006 to 2011-2012. *The American Journal of Sports Medicine, 42,* 1710-1715.

Sage, G.H., & Eitzen, D.S. (2016). *Sociology of North American sport* (10th ed.). New York, NY: Oxford University Press.

Smith, M. (2013). PlayOn!, high school group planning national network. *Street & Smith's SportsBusiness Journal.* Retrieved from www.sportsbusinessdaily.com/Journal/Issues/2013/06/24/Media/High-school-TV.aspx

Truyens, J., De Bosscher, V., & Sotiriadou, P. (2016). An analysis of countries' organizational resources, capacities and resource configurations in athletics. *Journal of Sport Management, 30*(5), 566-585.

University Interscholastic League. (2017). *Character attitude responsibility ethics: Sportsmanship and UIL athletics.* Austin, TX: Author. Retrieved from www.uiltexas.org/files/athletics/manuals/sportsmanship-manual.pdf

Chapter 8

Big Ten history. (2015). Retrieved from www.bigten.org/trads/big10-trads.html

California Community College Athletic Association (CCCAA). (n.d.). *Commission on Athletics.* Retrieved from www.cccaasports.org/about/CCCAA.pdf

College Football Playoff (CFP). (n.d.). Overview. Retrieved from www.collegefootballplayoff.com/overview

Covitz, R. (2016, March 14). Attrition forces NAIA to consider changes to Division I basketball tournament format. *The Kansas City Star.* Retrieved from www.kansascity.com/sports/college/naia-tournament/article66008797.html

Crabtree, J. (2016). *The "social" science of recruiting.* Retrieved from www.espn.com/college-football/recruiting/story/_/id/14646545/social-media-becomes-powerful-aide-dangerous-connection-recruiting

Crowley, J. (2006). *In the arena: The NCAA's first century.* Indianapolis, IN: NCAA.

Dimaggio, A. (2014). *Why higher education should rid itself of college athletics.* Retrieved from www.counterpunch.org/2014/04/22/why-higher-education-should-rid-itself-of-college-athletics

Dodd, D. (2015). *C-USA to name Judy McLeod as first female FBS commissioner.* Retrieved from www.cbssports.com/college-football/news/c-usa-to-name-judy-macleod-as-first-female-fbs-commissioner

Doyle, P. (2016, September 17). Aresco says American Athletic Conference planning for possible defections to Big 12. *Hartford Courant.* Retrieved from www.courant.com/sports/uconn-huskies/hc-mike-aresco-09-18-20160917-story.html

ECAC Staff. (2016). Search for new ECAC president/CEO now underway. *ECACsports.org.* Retrieved from http://www.ecacsports.com/news/2016/8/29/gen_0829164816.aspx

Edes, G. (1922). *The annals of the Harvard class of 1852.* Cambridge, MA: Author.

Elejalde-Ruiz, A. (2016). Northwestern modifies handbook to treat football players like employees. *Chicago Tribune.* Retrieved from www.chicagotribune.com/business/ct-northwestern-handbook-nlrb-1012-biz-20161011-story.html

Epstein, T.L. (2012). Student-athlete: Regulation of student-athletes' social media use: A guide to avoiding NCAA sanctions and related litigation. *Mississippi Sports Law Review, 1*(1), 1-36.

Fortier, S. (2016, September 10). Boise State mounts a paper defense of its home turf. *The New York Times.* Retrieved from www.nytimes.com/2016/09/11/sports/ncaafootball/boise-state-mounts-a-paper-defense-of-its-home-turf.html?_r=0

Gaines, C. (2016). *Only 5% of Americans call NBA their favorite.* Retrieved from www.businessinsider.com/most-popular-sports-in-the-us-2016-3

Hanson, K.O., & Savage, M. (2012). *Ethics in college sport.* Retrieved from www.scu.edu/ethics/focus-areas/more/resources/ethics-in-college-sports

Hosick, M.B. (2011). *Equal opportunity knocks.* Retrieved from www.ncaa.com/news/ncaa/2011-02-02/equal-opportunity-knocks

Huma, R., & Staurowsky, E.J. (2013). *The $6 billion heist: Robbing college athletes under the guise of amateurism.* Retrieved from www.ncpanow.org/news/articles/the-6-billion-heist-robbing-college-athletes-under-the-guise-of-amateurism

Jackson, D.Z. (2016). *HBCUs unfairly penalized by NCAA academic and graduation standards.* Retrieved from http://theundefeated.com/features/hbcus-unfairly-penalized-by-ncaa-academic-and-graduation-standards

Koch, B. (2016). *Inside the search that brought Luke Fickell to UC.* Retrieved from www.gobearcats.com/sports/m-footbl/spec-rel/121416aab.html

Lavigne, P. (2016). *Rich get richer in college sports as poorer schools struggle to keep up.* Retrieved from www.espn.com/espn/otl/story/_/id/17447429/power-5-conference-schools-made-6-billion-last-year-gap-haves-nots-grows

Long, B., & Smith, J. (2016). The spirit soars: An interpretive inquiry of leadership, health and wellness, and culture in tribal college athletic departments. *Tribal College: Journal of American Indian Higher Education.* Retrieved from http://tribal853.rssing.com/chan-43933689/all_p2.html#item27

Lumpkin, A., Achen, R.M., & Heyland, S. (2015). Education, experiences, and advancement of athletics directors in NCAA member institutions. *Journal of Contemporary Athletics, 9,* 249-265.

McDonald, S. (2016). *Nearly 80 percent of the 2016 U.S. Olympic team has competed in college sports.* Retrieved from www.teamusa.org/News/2016/August/12/Nearly-80-Percent-Of-The-2016-US-Olympic-Team-Has-Competed-In-College-Sports

National Association for Intercollegiate Athletics (NAIA). (n.d.). About the NAIA. Retrieved from www.naia.org/ViewArticle.dbml?DB_OEM_ID=27900&ATCLID=205323019

National Christian College Athletic Association (NCCAA). (2016). *Why the NCCAA?* Retrieved from www.thenccaa.org/documents/2016/7/14/Why_the_NCCAA.pdf

National Christian College Athletic Association (NCCAA). (n.d.). About us. Retrieved from www.thenccaa.org/sports/2017/7/17/About_Us.aspx

National Collegiate Athletic Association (NCAA). (2016a). *2015 national college football attendance.* Retrieved from http://fs.ncaa.org/Docs/stats/football_records/Attendance/2015.pdf

National Collegiate Athletic Association (NCAA). (2016b). *NCAA Eligibility Center. 2016-2017 Guide for the college-bound student-athlete.* Indianapolis, IN: Author. Retrieved from www.ncaapublications.com/productdownloads/CBSA17.pdf

National Collegiate Athletic Association (NCAA). (n.d.-a). *Championships.* Retrieved from www.ncaa.org/championships

National Collegiate Athletic Association (NCAA). (n.d.-b). *Conference personnel.* Retrieved from http://web1.ncaa.org/rgdSearch/exec/displayResultsPercents

National Collegiate Athletic Association (NCAA). (n.d.-c). *Data summary.* Retrieved from http://web1.ncaa.org/rgdSearch/exec/main

National Collegiate Athletic Association (NCAA). (n.d.-d). *What is the NCAA?* Retrieved from www.ncaa.org/about/resources/media-center/ncaa-101/what-ncaa

National Junior College Athletic Association (NJCAA). (2016). *NJCAA handbook & casebook.* Retrieved from www.njcaa.org/member_colleges/handbook

NCAA Academic and Membership Affairs Staff. (2017). *NCAA Division I manual – 2017-2018.* Retrieved from http://www.ncaapublications.com/productdownloads/D118.pdf

NCAA v. Board of Regents. 468 U.S. 85, 88. (1984). Retrieved from https://supreme.justia.com/cases/federal/us/468/85/case.html

New, J. (2016). *An "epidemic" of academic fraud.* Retrieved from www.insidehighered.com/news/2016/07/08/more-dozen-athletic-programs-have-committed-academic-fraud-last-decade-more-likely

Nocera, J. (2016, September 18). Historically black schools pay the price for a football paycheck. *The New York Times.* Retrieved from www.nytimes.com/2016/09/19/sports/ncaafootball/historically-black-schools-pay-the-price-for-a-football-paycheck.html?_r=0

Northwest Athletic Conference (NWAC). (n.d.). About the NWAC. Retrieved from www.nwacsports.org/aboutus.php

Novy-Williams, E. (2017, January 3). The unraveling of college football starts with all these empty stadiums. *Bloomberg.* Retrieved from https://www.

bloomberg.com/news/features/2017-01-03/the-unravelling-of-college-football-starts-with-all-these-empty-stadiums

Our Three Divisions. (2016). Indianapolis, IN: National Collegiate Athletic Association. Retrieved from http://www.ncaa.org/about/resources/media-center/ncaa-101/our-three-divisions

Popp, N. (2015). Ticket sales in college athletics. *The NACDA report.* Retrieved from http://grfx.cstv.com/photos/schools/nacda/sports/nacda/auto_pdf/2014-15/misc_non_event/dec14.pdf

Reese, J. (2013). *Ticket operations and sales management.* Morgantown, WV: Fitness Information Technology.

Sack, A., & Staurowsky, E.J. (1998). *College athletes for hire: The evolution and legacy of the NCAA amateur myth.* Westport, CT: Praeger Press.

Santus, R. (2014). Colleges monitor, restrict athletes on social media. *American Journalism Review.* Retrieved from http://ajr.org/2014/03/26/social-media-monitoring-widespread-among-college-athletic-departments

Schwartz, A. (2013). *Illuminating the obscure: Accounting change looming at NCAA?* Retrieved from http://sportsgeekonomics.tumblr.com/post/53439422488/illuminating-the-obscure-accounting-change

Sherman, R. (2016). *The NCAA's new March Madness TV deal will make them a billion a year.* Retrieved from www.sbnation.com/college-basketball/2016/4/12/11415764/ncaa-tournament-tv-broadcast-rights-money-payout-cbs-turner

Sirota, D., & Perez, A. (2016). *College football: Public universities spend millions on stadiums, despite slim chance of a profit.* Retrieved from www.ibtimes.com/college-football-public-universities-spend-millions-stadiums-despite-slim-chance-2258669

SI Wire. (2015, January 30). College sports received a record $1.26 billion in donations in 2014. *Sports Illustrated.* Retrieved from www.si.com/college-football/2015/01/30/college-sports-record-1-billion-donations-2014

Smith, M. (2016). The evolution of IMG College. *Street & Smith's SportsBusiness Journal.* Retrieved from http://m.sportsbusinessdaily.com/Journal/Issues/2016/09/12/Colleges/IMG-College.aspx?

Smith, R. (1994). *Big-time football at Harvard 1905: The diary of Coach Bill Reid.* Urbana, IL: University of Illinois Press.

Snyder, M. (2016, October 8). Michigan football equipment manager set for first road game (finally). *Detroit Free Press.* Retrieved from www.freep.com/story/sports/college/university-michigan/wolverines/2016/10/08/michigan-football-road-game/91784166

Solomon, J. (2015). *College football attendance drops for fifth straight year, but at a slower rate.* Retrieved from www.cbssports.com/college-football/news/college-football-attendance-drops-for-fifth-straight-year-but-at-slower-rate

Solomon, J. (2016a). *SEC rakes in $527.4 million in first year of CFP and SEC network.* Retrieved from www.cbssports.com/college-football/news/sec-rakes-in-5274-million-in-first-year-of-cfp-and-sec-network

Solomon, J. (2016b). *Power Five conferences see revenue grow by 33 percent in one year.* Retrieved from www.cbssports.com/college-football/news/power-five-conferences-see-revenue-grow-by-33-percent-in-one-year

Staples, A. (2016). *The future of college sports media rights: How will deals evolve with the landscape?* Retrieved from www.campusrush.com/college-sports-media-rights-deals-punt-pass-pork-1692890873.html

Staurowsky, E.J. (2014). An analysis of Northwestern University's denial of rights and recognition of college football labor. *Journal of Intercollegiate Sport, 7*(2), 134-142.

Stensholt, J. (2017, August 25). Stanford v. Rice: The business of bringing American college football to Sydney. *Financial Review.* Retrieved from www.afr.com/business/sport/the-business-of-bringing-american-college-football-to-sydney-20170824-gy3e9a

Trahan, K. (2016). *Should Grambling State, Southern, and other HBCUs drop out of Division I football?* Retrieved from https://sports.vice.com/en_us/article/should-grambling-state-southern-hbcus-drop-division-i-football

U.S. Department of Education. (n.d.). What is an HBCU? Retrieved from https://sites.ed.gov/whhbcu/one-hundred-and-five-historically-black-colleges-and-universities/

Veneziano, J. (2002). *America's oldest intercollegiate athletic event.* Retrieved from www.hcs.harvard.edu/~harvcrew/Website/History/HY

Wells, Y. (2016, December). Convince others to be best in class when resources are limited. *CABMA Corner.* Retrieved from http://grfx.cstv.com/photos/schools/nacda/sports/cabma/auto_pdf/2016-17/misc_non_event/CABMACornerDec16.pdf

Whiteside, E., Hardin, M., & Ash, E. (2011). Good for society or good for business? Division I sports' information directors attitudes toward the commercialization of sports. *International Journal of Sport Communication, 4*, 473-491.

Wolverton, B., & Kambhampati, S. (2016, January 27). Colleges raised $1.2 billion in donations for sports in 2015. *The Chronicle of Higher Education.* Retrieved from www.chronicle.com/article/Colleges-Raised-12-Billion/235058

Wright, M.W., & Wilkerson, C. (2016). *SWAC commissioner discusses the ups and downs in the conference.* Retrieved from http://theundefeated.com/videos/

swac-commissioner-discusses-the-ups-and-downs-in-the-conference

Chapter 9

Badenhausen, K. (2016). Warriors, Chase Bank tie-up ranks among biggest stadium naming rights deals ever. *Forbes.* Retrieved from www.forbes.com/sites/kurtbadenhausen/2016/01/28/warriors-chase-tie-up-joins-ranks-of-biggest-stadium-naming-rights-deals/#328de8de344f

Brown, M. (2015). How MLB's 30 teams surpassed record $4.4 billion in player salaries. *Forbes.* Retrieved from www.forbes.com/sites/maurybrown/2015/12/21/how-mlbs-30-teams-surpassed-record-4-4-billion-in-player-salaries/#257a50655fca

Browne, L. (1992). *Girls of summer.* Toronto, Canada: HarperCollins.

Dietl, H., Lang, M., & Werner, S. (2010). The effect of luxury taxes on competitive balance, club profits, and social welfare in sports leagues. *International Journal of Sport Finance, 5*(1), 41-51.

Federal Base Ball Club of Baltimore, Inc. v. National League of Professional Base Ball Clubs, 259 U.S. 200 (1922).

Freedman, W. (1987). *Professional sports and antitrust.* New York, NY: Quorum.

Garcia, A. (2016). The ratings are in for Twitter's NFL stream. *CNN Money.* Retrieved from http://money.cnn.com/2016/09/16/technology/nfl-twitter-ratings-livestream

Gorman, J., & Calhoun, K. (1994). *The name of the game: The business of sports.* New York, NY: Wiley.

Harris, D. (1986). *The league: The rise and decline of the NFL.* New York, NY: Bantam.

Inoue, Y., Funk, D.C., Wann, D.L., Yoshida, M., & Nakazawa, M. (2015). Team identification and post-disaster social well-being: The mediating role of social support. *Group Dynamics: Theory, Research, and Practice, 19*(1), 31-44.

Kaniasty, K. (2012). Predicting social psychological well-being following trauma: The role of postdisaster social support. *Psychological Trauma: Theory, Research, Practice, and Policy, 4,* 22-33.

Mullin, B.J., Hardy, S., & Sutton, W.A. (2014). *Sport marketing* (4th ed.). Champaign, IL: Human Kinetics.

National Labor Relations Board. (n.d.). *National Labor Relations Act.* Retrieved from www.nlrb.gov/resources/national-labor-relations-act

Negro League Baseball. (2003). *Negro League Baseball: Timeline of events in professional black baseball.* Retrieved from www.negroleaguebaseball.com/timeline.html

Nightengale, B. (2016, April 4). 2016 MLB salaries: Royals way pays, while average salary hits $4.4 million. *USA Today.* Retrieved from www.usatoday.com/story/sports/mlb/2016/04/03/2016-mlb-salaries-payrolls/82592542

Ozanian, M., Badenhausen, K., & Settimi, C. (2016). The business of baseball. *Forbes.* Retrieved from www.forbes.com/teams/new-york-yankees

Pallotta, F., & Stelter, B. (2016). Super Bowl 50 audience is third largest in TV history. *CNN Money.* Retrieved from http://money.cnn.com/2016/02/08/media/super-bowl-50-ratings

Porter, M.E., & Kramer, M.R. (2011). Creating shared value. *Harvard Business Review, 89*(1/2), 62-77.

Reid, J. (2016, July 4). Kevin Durant agrees to 2-year, $54.3 million contract with Golden State Warriors. *The Times Picayune.* Retrieved from www.nola.com/pelicans/index.ssf/2016/07/kevin_durant_agrees_to_2-year.html

Roberts, R., & Olson, J. (1995). *Winning is the only thing: Sports in America since 1945.* Baltimore, MD: Johns Hopkins University Press.

Staudohar, P.D., & Mangan, J.A. (1991). *The business of professional sports.* Urbana, IL: University of Illinois Press.

Stefani, R. (2015). The interrelated back stories of Kenny Washington reintegrating the NFL in 1946 and Jackie Robinson integrating Major League Baseball in 1947. *The Sport Journal.* Retrieved from http://thesportjournal.org/article/the-interrelated-back-stories-of-kenny-washington-reintegrating-the-nfl-in-1946-and-jackie-robinson-integrating-major-league-baseball-in-1947

Chapter 10

16W Marketing. (n.d.). 16W Marketing, LLC. Retrieved from www.16wmktg.com

Belloni, M. (2016, March 30). Ari Emanuel and Patrick Whitesell unleashed: WME-IMG's strategy, IPO plans, China and the doubters. *The Hollywood Reporter.* Retrieved from www.hollywoodreporter.com/features/ari-emanuel-patrick-whitesell-unleashed-879003

Jensen, J.A., Spreyer, J., & Mishra, A. (2017). *Intercollegiate multimedia rights agreement report.* Chapel Hill, NC: Center for Research in Intercollegiate Athletics.

Kish, M. (2017). See how much your university gets from corporate sponsors. *Portland Business Journal,* March 15.

Smith, M., & Ourand, J. (2017). Learfield-IMG College merger: 'Anything you want in college'. *Street & Smith's SportsBusiness Journal, 20*(13), 1, 40-41.

WME/IMG. (n.d.-a). Careers. Retrieved from www. wmeimg.com/careers

WME/IMG. (n.d.-b). Expertise: Events. Retrieved from www.wmeimg.com/expertise/events

WME/IMG. (n.d.-c). Expertise: Brand strategy, activation, and licensing. Retrieved from www.wmeimg. com/expertise/brand

WME/IMG. (n.d.-d). Expertise: Media. Retrieved from www.wmeimg.com/expertise/media

Chapter 11

Adventure Travel Trade Association (ATTA), The George Washington University, & Vital Wave Consulting. (2011). *Adventure tourism development index, 2010 report*. Retrieved from www.adventuretravel. biz/wp-content/uploads/2011/07/atdi_2010_report .pdf

Agha, N., Fairley, S., & Gibson, H. (2012). Considering legacy as a multi-dimensional construct: The legacy of the Olympic Games. *Sport Management Review, 15*, 125-139.

BBC News. (2016). *Great Barrier Reef suffers worst bleaching on record, report says*. Retrieved from www. bbc.com/news/science-environment-38136165

Buning, R.J., Cole, Z., & McNamee, J. (2016). Visitor expenditure within a mountain bike event portfolio: Determinants, outcomes, and variations. *Journal of Sport & Tourism, 20*. Retrieved from www.tandfonline.com/doi/full/10.1080/14775085.2016.1239547

Chalip, L. (2004). Beyond economic impact: A general model for sport event leverage. In B. Ritchie & D. Adair (Eds.), *Sport tourism: Interrelationships, impacts and issues* (pp. 226-252). Clevedon, England: Channel View.

Crompton, J. (1995). Economic impact analysis of sports facilities and events: Eleven sources of misapplication. *Journal of Sport Management, 9*, 14-35.

Dawson, J., & Scott, D. (2013). Managing for climate change in the alpine ski sector. *Tourism Management, 35*, 244-254.

Doğan, H.Z. (1989). Forms of adjustment: Socio-cultural impacts of tourism. *Annals of Tourism Research, 16*, 216-236.

Fairley, S. (2003). In search of relived social experience: Group-based nostalgia sport tourism. *Journal of Sport Management, 17*, 284-304.

Fairley, S., Kellett, P., & Green, B.C. (2007). Volunteering abroad: Motives for travel to volunteer at the Athens Olympic Games. *Journal of Sport Management, 21*, 41-57.

Fairley, S., Ruhanen, L., & Lovegrove, H. (2015). On frozen ponds: The impact of climate change on hosting pond hockey tournaments. *Sport Management Review, 18*(4), 618-626.

Fourie, J., & Santana-Gallego, M. (2011). The impact of mega-sport events on tourist arrivals. *Tourism Management, 32*, 1364-1370.

Gibson, H. (1998). Sport tourism: A critical analysis of research. *Sport Management Review, 1*, 45-79.

Gibson, H., Kaplanidou, K., & Kang, S. (2012). Small-scale event sport tourism: A case study in sustainable tourism. *Sport Management Review, 15*, 160-170.

Goeldner, C., & Ritchie, J.R.B. (2011). *Tourism: Practices, principles, philosophies*. New York, NY: Wiley.

Goss, A. (2012, August 5). You can still grab a holiday bargain at home or abroad. *Sunday Times*, p. 10.

Great Barrier Reef Legacy. (n.d.). Retrieved from www. greatbarrierreeflegacy.org

Hodges, A., Rahmani, M., & Clouser, R. (2016). *Economic contributions of the University of Florida and related entities in 2014-15*. Retrieved from http:// fred.ifas.ufl.edu/media/fredifasufledu/news/docs/ Economic-Contributions-of-the-University-of-Florida-2014-15-5-26-16.pdf

Kaplanidou, K., & Gibson, H. (2010). Predicting behavioral intentions of active event sport tourists: The case of a small scale recurring sports event. *Journal of Sport & Tourism, 15*, 163-179.

Kennelly, M. (2017). "We've never measured it, but it brings in a lot of business": Participatory sport events and tourism. *International Journal of Contemporary Hospitality Management, 29*(3). Retrieved from http:// dx.doi.org/10.1108/IJCHM-10-2015-0541

KPMG. (2015). *KPMG on golf tourism growth trends*. Retrieved from http://static.golfbenchmark.com/ media/2/9/9/2/2992.pdf

Lewis, R. (2017). *The economic impact of the Florida sports industry: 2017 fact book*. Retrieved from www. flasports.com/wp-content/uploads/2017/01/2017-Economic-Impact-of-Sports.pdf

National Golf Foundation. (2016). *2015 golf participation in the U.S.—a slight dip tempered by strong positive indicators*. Retrieved from http://ngfdashboard. clubnewsmaker.org/Newsletter/1ll1udoge19?a=5&p =2389923&t=410871

Ong, T., & Musa, G. (2012). Examining the influences of experience, personality and attitude on scuba divers' underwater behavior: A structural equation model. *Tourism Management, 33*, 1521-1534.

Petyk, S. (2016, October 28). *What Florida can learn from the Great Allegheny Passage success. Bike the gap*. Presentation at the Celebration of Cycling, Gainesville, Florida.

Phillips, D. (2016, August 5). Thousands join anti-Olympic protest in Rio before Games begin. *The Washington Post*. Retrieved from www.washingtonpost.com/news/ worldviews/wp/2016/08/05/thousands-join-anti-olympic-protest-in-rio-before-games-begin/?utm_term=.45530cae74bb

Schneider, P., & Vogt, C. (2012). Applying the 3M model of personality and motivation to adventure travelers. *Journal of Travel Research, 51,* 704-716.

Schumacher, D.G. (2015). *National Association of Sports Commission's report on the sports travel industry.* Retrieved from www.sportscommissions.org/Portals/sportscommissions/Documents/About/STI_report_Oct_15.pdf

Soutar, D., & Lindén, O. (2000). The health and future of coral reef systems. *Ocean & Coastal Management, 43,* 657-688.

Sparvero, E., Trendafilova, S., & Chalip, L. (2005). *An alternative approach to environmental dispute resolution in sport contexts.* Paper presented at the 20th Annual Conference of the North American Society for Sport Management, Regina, Saskatchewan, Canada.

Spencer, J. (2017, May 17). Introduction to the Great Barrier Reef Marine Park and its management [lecture]. Townsville, Australia: Reef HQ.

Sportcal. (2016). *Global sports impact report 2016.* London, England: Sportcal.

Sun, Y., Rodriguez, A., Wu, J., & Chuang, S. (2013). Why hotel rooms were not full during a hallmark sporting event: The 2009 World Games experience. *Tourism Management, 36,* 469-479.

Tepper, T. (2014, August 28). How college football sacked the NBA and MLB. *Time.* Retrieved from http://time.com/money/3198130/college-football-popularity/

Wade, S. (2017). Olympic ghost town: Bills due, venues empty after Rio games. Retrieved from www.news.com.au/sport/olympics/olympic-ghost-town-bills-due-venues-empty-after-rio-games/news-story/bd3b0a794bc9ee55493826c4c5a0df32

Walker, M., Kaplanidou, K., Gibson, H., Thapa, B., Geldenhuys, S., & Coetzee, W. (2013). "Win in Africa, with Africa": Social responsibility, event image, and destination benefits. The case of the 2010 FIFA World Cup in South Africa. *Tourism Management, 34,* 80-90.

Wheeler, K., & Nauright, J. (2006). A global perspective on the environmental impact of golf. *Sport in Society, 9*(3), 427-443.

World Tourism Organization. (2016). *International tourist arrivals up 4% reach a record 1.2 billion in 2015.* Retrieved from http://media.unwto.org/press-release/2016-01-18/international-tourist-arrivals-4-reach-record-12-billion-2015

Chapter 12

Armstrong, K.L. (2002). An examination of the social psychology of Blacks' consumption of sport. *Journal of Sport Management, 16,* 267-288.

Armstrong, K.L. (2008). Consumers of color and the "culture" of sport attendance: Exploratory insights. *Sport Marketing Quarterly, 17,* 218-231.

Armstrong, K.L. (2013). Cultural essence and sport consumption: Marketing organizational charisma. *Innovative Marketing, 9*(1), 62-71.

Baker, L. (2016). *Under Armour leads Olympic marketing shake-up after "rule 40" changes.* Retrieved from www.reuters.com/article/us-olympics-rio-under-armour-insight-idUSKCN0ZF1NI

Barker, J. (2003). *The marketing book* (5th ed.). Burlington, MA: Butterworth-Heinemann.

Belk, R.W. (1995). Studies in the new consumer behavior. In D. Miller (Ed.), *Acknowledging consumption* (pp. 58-96). London, England: Routledge.

Brooks, C.M. (1994). *Sports marketing: Competitive business strategies for sports.* Englewood Cliffs, NJ: Prentice Hall.

Eagleman, A.M. (2011). Stereotypes of race and nationality: A qualitative analysis of sport magazine coverage of MLB players. *Journal of Sport Management, 25,* 156-168.

Fullerton, S., & Merz, G.R. (2008). The four domains of sports marketing: A conceptual framework. *Sport Marketing Quarterly, 17,* 90-108.

Grunig, J.E., & White, R. (1992). Communication, public relations and effective organizations. In J.E. Grunig (Ed.), *Excellence in public relations and communications management* (pp. 1-30). Hillsdale, NJ: Erlbaum.

Hall, M. (2002). Taking the sport out of sports. *Street & Smith's SportsBusiness Journal.* Retrieved from http://m.sportsbusinessdaily.com/Journal/Issues/2002/08/20020819/Opinion/Taking-The-Sport-Out-Of-Sports.aspx

Harwell, D. (2014, September 12). Women are pro football's most important demographic. Will they forgive the NFL? *The Washington Post.* Retrieved from www.washingtonpost.com/business/economy/women-are-pro-footballs-most-important-market-will-they-forgive-the-nfl/2014/09/12/d5ba8874-3a7f-11e4-9c9f-ebb47272e40e_story.html?utm_term=.6454206f4ee6

Kim, K., & Cheong, Y. (2011). The effects of athlete-endorsed advertising: The moderating role of athlete-audience ethnicity match. *Journal of Sport Management, 25,* 143-155.

Levitt, T. (1960). Marketing myopia. *Harvard Business Review, July-August*, 45-60.

Lombardo, J. (2011). New president aims to widen WNBA's fan base. *Street & Smith's SportsBusiness Journal, 14*(7), 10.

MacFadyen, L., Stead, M., & Hastings, G. (2003). Social marketing. In J. Barker (Ed.), *The marketing book* (5th ed., pp. 694-725). Burlington, MA: Butterworth-Heinemann.

McLeod, K. (1999). Authenticity within hip-hop and other cultures threatened with assimilation. *Journal of Communications, 49*(4), 134-150.

Meenaghan, T. (1991). The role of sponsorship in the marketing communications mix. *International Journal of Advertising, 10*(1), 35-47.

Midol, N. (1998). Rap and dialectical relations. Culture, subculture, power, and counter-powered. In R. Genevieve (Ed.), *Sport and postmodern times* (pp. 333-343). Albany, NY: State University of New York Press.

Mullin, B.J., Hardy, S., & Sutton, W.A. (2014). *Sport marketing* (4th ed.). Champaign, IL: Human Kinetics.

Nielsen. (2014). *Sports fans amplify the action across screen*. Retrieved from www.nielsen.com/us/en/insights/news/2014/sports-fans-amplify-the-action-across-screens.html

O'Malley, L., & Tynan, C. (2003). Relationship marketing. In J. Barker (Ed.), *The marketing book* (5th ed., pp. 32-52). Burlington, MA: Butterworth-Heinemann.

Perrin, A. (2015). *Social media usage: 2005-2015*. Retrieved from www.pewinternet.org/2015/10/08/social-networking-usage-2005-2015

Pitts, B.G., Fielding, L.W., & Miller, L.K. (1994). Industry segmentation theory and the sport industry: Developing a sport industry segmentation model. *Sport Marketing Quarterly, 3*(1), 15-24.

Pitts, B.G., & Stotlar, D.K. (2007). *Fundamentals of sport marketing* (3rd ed.). Morgantown, WV: Fitness Information Technology.

Pons, F., Larouche, M., Nyeck, S., & Perreault, S. (2001). Role of sport events as ethnocultural emblems: Impact of acculturation and ethnic identity on consumers' orientations toward sporting events. *Sport Marketing Quarterly, 10*, 231-240.

Schawbel, D. (2015). 10 New findings about the millennial consumer. *Forbes*. Retrieved from www.forbes.com/sites/danschawbel/2015/01/20/10-new-findings-about-the-millennial-consumer/2/#546e-b7aa42b8

Shank, M.D. (2015). *Sports marketing: A strategic perspective* (5th ed.). New York, NY: Routledge.

Sports Market Analytics. (2017). *The millennials*. Retrieved from www.sportsmarketanalytics.com/Blog/July-2015/The-Millennials.aspx

Stuart, H., & Muzellec, L. (2004). Corporate makeovers: Can a hyena be rebranded? *Journal of Brand Management, 11*, 472-482.

Tracy, M. (2016, May 24). U.C.L.A. and Under Armour in record sponsorship deal. *The New York Times*. Retrieved from www.nytimes.com/2016/05/25/sports/ucla-under-armour-sponsorship.html

Walsh, P., & Ross, S.D. (2010). Examining brand extensions and their potential to dilute team brand associations. *Sport Marketing Quarterly, 19*, 196-206.

Chapter 13

Brown, N.A., Devlin, M.B., & Billings, A.C. (2013). Fan identification gone extreme: Sports communication variables between fans and sport in the Ultimate Fighting Championship. *International Journal of Sport Communication, 6*, 19-32.

Burmann, C., & Arnhold, U. (2009). *User generated branding: State of the art research*. Wiesbaden, Germany: Gabler Verlag.

Cialdini, R.B., Borden, R.J., Thorne, A., Walker, M.R., Freeman, S., & Sloan, L.R. (1976). Basking in reflected glory: Three (football) field studies. *Journal of Personality and Social Psychology, 34*, 366-375.

de Mooij, M.K. (2004). *Consumer behavior and culture: Consequences for global marketing and advertising*. Thousand Oaks, CA: Sage.

Geurin, A.N., & Burch, L.M. (2017). User-generated branding via social media: An examination of six running brands. *Sport Management Review, 20*(3), 273-284.

Green, B.C. (1996). A social learning approach to youth sport motivation: Initial scale development and validation. *Dissertation Abstracts International, 60*, 203.

Holt, D., & Cameron, D. (2010). *Cultural strategy: Using innovative ideologies to build breakthrough brands*. London, England: Oxford University Press.

Hums, M.A., & MacLean, J.C. (2013). *Governance and policy in sport organizations*. Scottsdale, AZ: Holcomb Hathaway.

Kim, M.K., Zhang, J.J., Jackson, E.N., Connaughton, D.P., & Kim, M. (2013). Modification and revision of the scale of market demand for taekwondo. *Measurement in Physical Education and Exercise Science, 17*, 187-207.

Lam, E.T.C., Zhang, J.J., & Jensen, B.E. (2005). Dimensions of membership satisfaction toward service quality of health-fitness clubs. *Measurement in Physical Education and Exercise Science, 9*(2), 79-111.

Lim, C.H., Chung, J., & Pedersen, P.M. (2012). The influence of online consumer postings on purchase intentions: Investigating electronic word-of-mouth (eWOM) messages and sporting goods. *Sport Management International Journal, 8*(1), 55-75.

Running USA. (2017). *2016 Running USA annual half marathon report*. Retrieved from www.runningusa. org/half-marathon-report-2017

Shank, M.D. (2015). *Sports marketing: A strategic perspective* (5th ed.). New York, NY: Routledge.

Smith, D., & Bar-Eli, M. (Eds.). (2007). *Essential readings in sport and exercise psychology*. Champaign, IL: Human Kinetics.

Thomas, I., & McClung, B. (2016). *MLS sets third consecutive attendance record during '16 season, led again by Sounders*. Retrieved from www.sportsbusinessdaily. com/Daily/Issues/2016/10/24/Leagues-and-Governing-Bodies/MLS.aspx

Trail, G.T., Kim, Y.K., Kwon, H.H., Harrolle, M.G., Braunstein-Minkove, J.R., & Dick, R. (2012). The effects of vicarious achievement on BIRGing and CORFing: Testing, moderating, and mediating effects of team identification. *Sport Management Review, 15*, 345-354.

U.S. Department of Health and Human Services. (2016). *Let's Move!* Retrieved from https://letsmove. obamawhitehouse.archives.gov/resources

Wakefield, K. (2014). *Team sports marketing*. Retrieved from http://teamsportsmarketing.com/the-text

Zhang, J.J. (2015). What to study? That is a question: A conscious thought analysis. *Journal of Sport Management, 29*, 1-10.

Zhang, J.J., Jin, L., Kim, M., & Li, H. (2013). Environmental corporate social responsibility practices within the Asian sport event industry: A case study of the Beijing Olympics. In K. Babiak, J.L.P. Salcines, & G. Walters (Eds.), *Handbook of sport and corporate social responsibility* (pp. 119-134). New York, NY: Routledge.

Chapter 14

Abeza, G., O'Reilly, N., & Nadeau, J. (2014). Sport communication: A multidimensional assessment of the field's development. *International Journal of Sport Communication, 7*, 289-316.

Abeza, G., O'Reilly, N., Seguin, B., & Nzindukiyimana, O. (2015). Social media scholarship in sport management research: A critical review. *Journal of Sport Management, 29*, 601-618.

Battenfield, F. (2013). The culture of communication in athletics. In P.M. Pedersen (Ed.), *Routledge handbook of sport communication* (pp. 441-450). New York, NY: Routledge.

Battenfield, F., & Kent, A. (2007). The culture of communication among intercollegiate sport information professionals. *International Journal of Sport Management and Marketing, 2*, 236-251.

Beaujon, A. (2013). *Report: Sports fans like print newspapers*. Retrieved from www.poynter.org/2013/report-sports-fans-like-print-newspapers/206693

Beck, K. (2012). *Das mediensystem Deutschlands: Strukturen, märkte, regulierung*. Wiesbaden, Germany: Springer.

Billings, A.C., Butterworth, M.L., & Turman, P.D. (2018). *Communication and sport: Surveying the field* (3rd ed.). Thousand Oaks, CA: Sage.

DeVito, J.A. (2017). *Interpersonal messages* (4th ed.). Upper Saddle River, NJ: Pearson Education.

DiMoro, A. (2015). The growing impact of social media on today's sports culture. *Forbes*. Retrieved from www.forbes.com/sites/anthonydimoro/2015/07/02/the-growing-impact-of-social-media-on-todays-sports-culture/#3f5471767d77

Federal Communications Commission. (2016, October 19). *Broadcast station totals as of September 30, 2016*. Retrieved from http://transition.fcc.gov/Daily_Releases/Daily_Business/2016/db1019/DOC-341807A1.pdf

Grunig, J.E., & Hunt, T. (1984). *Managing public relations*. New York, NY: Holt, Rinehart and Winston.

Heinze, K.L., Soderstrom, S., & Zdroik, J. (2014). Toward strategic and authentic corporate social responsibility in professional sport: A case study of the Detroit Lions. *Journal of Sport Management, 28*, 672-686.

Hopwood, M.K. (2005). Public relations practice in English county cricket. *Corporate Communications: An International Journal, 10*, 201-212.

Horky, T. (2009). Was macht den sport zum mediensport? Ein modell zur definition und analyse von mediensportarten. *Sportwissenschaft, 39*(4), 298-308.

Horky, T. (2016). Sports and media in Germany: Historic milestones and key facts about football and sports media in Germany. *Journal of Chengdu Sport University, 42*(2), 1-7. doi:10.15942/j.jcsu.2016.02.001

Internet World Stats. (2017). *Internet users in the world*. Retrieved from www.internetworldstats.com/stats.htm

Lasswell, H.D. (1948). The structure and function of communication in society. In L. Bryson (Ed.), *The communication of ideas* (pp. 37-51). New York, NY: Harper.

Lavigne, P. (2013). *Athlete charities often lack standards*. Retrieved from http://espn.go.com/espn/otl/story/_/id/9109024/top-athletes-charities-often-measure-charity-experts-say-efficient-effective-use-money

Littlejohn, S.W., & Foss, K.A. (2011). *Theories of human communication* (10th ed.). Long Grove, IL: Waveland.

McCombs, M.E., & Shaw, D.L. (1972). The agenda-setting function of mass media. *Public Opinion Quarterly, 32*(6), 176-187.

The Nielsen Company. (2016a). *The total audience report: Q1 2016*. Retrieved from www.nielsen.com/

us/en/insights/reports/2016/the-total-audience-report-q1-2016.html

The Nielsen Company. (2016b). *TV season 2015-2016 in review: The biggest social TV moments.* Retrieved from www.nielsen.com/us/en/insights/news/2016/tv-season-2015-2016-in-review-the-biggest-social-tv-moments.html

Ourand, J. (2016, October 13). Monumental Sports Network officially launches OTT service for DC-area sports. *Street & Smith's SportsBusiness Daily.* Retrieved from www.sportsbusinessdaily.com/Daily/Issues/2016/10/13/Media/Monumental-OTT.aspx

Pedersen, P.M. (2013). Reflections on communication and sport: On strategic communication and management. *Communication and Sport, 1*(1/2), 55-67.

Pedersen, P.M. (2014). The changing role of sports media producers. In A.C. Billings & M. Hardin (Eds.), *Routledge handbook of sport and new media* (pp. 101-109). London, England: Routledge.

Pedersen, P.M. (Ed.). (2015). *Routledge handbook of sport communication.* London, England: Routledge.

Pedersen, P.M., Laucella, P.C., Kian, E.T.M., & Geurin, A.N. (2017). *Strategic sport communication* (2nd ed.). Champaign, IL: Human Kinetics.

Pedersen, P.M., Miloch, K.S., Laucella, P.C., & Fielding, L. (2007). The juxtaposition of sport and communication: Defining the field of sport communication. *International Journal of Sport Management and Marketing, 2*, 193-207.

Pew Research Center. (2016). *State of the news media 2016.* Retrieved from http://assets.pewresearch.org/wp-content/uploads/sites/13/2016/06/State-of-the-News-Media-Report-2016-FINAL.pdf

Schramm, W. (1954). How communication works. In W. Schramm (Ed.), *The process and effects of mass communication* (pp. 3-26). Urbana, IL: University of Illinois Press.

Shannon, C.E., & Weaver, W. (1949). *The mathematical theory of communication.* Urbana, IL: University of Illinois Press.

Stoldt, G.C., Dittmore, S.W., & Branvold, S.E. (2012). *Sport public relations: Managing stakeholder communication* (2nd ed.). Champaign, IL: Human Kinetics.

Time. (2014). *Addicted: Americans spend 11 hours a day on TV, phone, radio and gaming.* Retrieved from http://time.com/16458/nielsen-electronic-media-study-11-hours-a-day/

World Association of Newspapers and News Publishers. (n.d.). *World press trends: Facts and figures.* Retrieved from www.wptdatabase.org/world-press-trends-2015-facts-and-figures

Chapter 15

Associated Press. (2016, September 15). Joining Colin Kaepernick in his cause comes with costs. *USA Today.* Retrieved from www.usatoday.com/story/sports/nfl/2016/09/15/joining-colin-kaepernick-in-his-cause-comes-with-costs/90432330

Associated Press. (2017, April 2). APNewsBreak: Yanks drop to 3rd in payroll; Dodgers lead. *USA Today.* Retrieved from www.usatoday.com/story/sports/mlb/2017/04/02/apnewsbreak-yanks-drop-to-3rd-in-payroll-dodgers-lead/99964672

A.T. Kearney. (2014). *Winning in the business of sports.* Retrieved from www.atkearney.com/documents/10192/5258876/Winning+in+the+Business+of+Sports.pdf/ed85b644-7633-469d-8f7a-99e4a50aadc8

Badenhausen, K. (2015). Average MLB salary nearly double NFL's, but still trails NBA's. *Forbes.* Retrieved from www.forbes.com/sites/kurtbadenhausen/2015/01/23/average-mlb-salary-nearly-double-nfls-but-trails-nba-players/#42fc30c0269e

Barca, J. (2016). Twitter's NFL live streaming debut—commence cable cutting, sports fans. *Forbes.* Retrieved from www.forbes.com/sites/jerrybarca/2016/09/16/twitters-nfl-live-streaming-debut-commence-cable-cutting-sports-fans/#6396e5531c0d

Bennett, B. (2014). *NCAA board votes to allow autonomy.* Retrieved from www.espn.com/college-sports/story/_/id/11321551/ncaa-board-votes-allow-autonomy-five-power-conferences

Burnsed, B. (2015). *Athletics departments that make more than they spend still a minority.* Retrieved from www.ncaa.org/about/resources/media-center/news/athletics-departments-make-more-they-spend-still-minority

Cave, A. (2015, May 13). Discover the potential of sport: A £20 billion industry. *The Telegraph.* Retrieved from www.telegraph.co.uk/sponsored/business/business-sport-series/11604008/potential-of-sport-20billion-industry.html

CBS Sports. (n.d.). *MLB salaries.* Retrieved from www.cbssports.com/mlb/salaries/avgsalaries

Corbett, P. (2015, June 23). Report: Super Bowl lifted Valley economy by $720 million. *The Republic.* Retrieved from www.azcentral.com/story/news/local/glendale/2015/06/23/super-bowl-valley-economic-impact/29193319/

Fisher, E. (2009). Flight of fancy? *Street & Smith's SportsBusiness Journal.* Retrieved from www.sportsbusinessjournal.com/article/62656

Fulks, D.L. (2015). *2004–2014 Revenues and expenses: Divisions I intercollegiate athletic programs report.*

Indianapolis, IN: National Collegiate Athletic Association.

Gaines, C., & Nudelman, M. (2017, September 15). ESPN has lost nearly 13 million subscribers in 6 years, but it is not as bad as it sounds. *Business Insider*. Retrieved from www.businessinsider.com/espn-losing-subscribers-not-ratings-viewers-2017-9

Howard, D.R., & Crompton, J.L. (2004). *Financing sport* (2nd ed.). Morgantown, WV: Fitness Information Technology.

Keat, P.G., Young, P.K., & Erfle, S. (2014). *Managerial economics: Economic tools for today's decision makers* (7th ed.). Upper Saddle River, NJ: Prentice Hall.

McInerney, B. (2016). *Super Bowl benefits host city, but by how much?* Retrieved from www.cnbc.com/2016/01/29/super-bowl-benefits-host-city-but-by-how-much.html

Mills, C. (2016). The new golden age of black athlete activism. *The Daily Beast*. Retrieved from www.thedailybeast.com/articles/2016/10/03/black-athletes-embrace-social-activism.html

NCAA. (2016). *Turner, CBS, and the NCAA reach long-term multimedia rights extension for NCAA Division I men's basketball championship*. Retrieved from www.ncaa.com/news/basketball-men/article/2016-04-12/turner-cbs-and-ncaa-reach-long-term-multimedia-rights

Novy-Williams, E. (2016). *NFL revenue reaches $7.1 billion based on Green Bay report*. Retrieved from www.bloomberg.com/news/articles/2016-06-24/nfl-revenue-reaches-7-1-billion-based-on-green-bay-report

The Organizing Committee of the XXII Olympic Winter Games and XI Paralympic Winter Games of 2014 in Sochi. (2014). *Sochi 2014 official report*. Retrieved from https://library.olympic.org/Default/doc/SYRACUSE/76792/sochi-2014-official-report-sotchi-2014-rapport-officiel-the-organizing -committee-of-the-xxii-olympic

Ozanian, M. (2016a). The NFL's most valuable teams 2016. *Forbes*. Retrieved from www.forbes.com/sites/mikeozanian/2016/09/14/the-nfls-most-valuable-teams-2016/#4fc2efed373b

Ozanian, M. (2016b). The NHL's most valuable teams. *Forbes*. Retrieved from www.forbes.com/sites/mikeozanian/2016/11/30/the-nhls-most-valuable-teams-3/#42a130c31569

Plunkett Research. (n.d.). *Sports and recreation business statistics analysis, business, and industry statistics*. Retrieved from www.plunkettresearch.com/statistics/sports-industry/

Porter, P. (2001, January 15). Super Bowl impact figures a super stretch. *Street & Smith's SportsBusiness Journal*. Retrieved from www.sportsbusinessdaily.com/Journal/Issues/2001/01/20010115/Opinion/Super-Bowl-Impact-Figures-A-Super-Stretch.aspx

Ringler, L. (2016). Tulsa will eliminate men's golf program after season. *Golfweek*. Retrieved from http://golfweek.com/2016/03/25/college-golf-men-tulsa-program-eliminated/

Savitz, H.J. (2014, September 26). Each Ohio State football gameday brings in about $7.15M. *The Lantern*. Retrieved from http://thelantern.com/2014/09/each-ohio-state-football-gameday-brings-in-about-7-15m/

Sports and Fitness Industry Association (SFIA). (2015). *Sports and fitness industry surpasses $84 billion in wholesale sales*. Retrieved from www.sfia.org/press/706_Sports-and-Fitness-Industry-Surpasses-$84-Billion-in-Wholesale-Sales

Study: Economy lessens Super Bowl economic impact. (2009). *Tampa Bay Business Journal*. Retrieved from www.bizjournals.com/tampabay/stories/2009/01/19/daily32.html

The business of baseball. (2016). *Forbes*. Retrieved from www.forbes.com/mlb-valuations/list/

Travis, C. (2016). *ESPN loses 621,000 subscribers; worst month in company history*. Retrieved from www.outkickthecoverage.com/espn-loses-621-000-subscribers-worst-month-in-company-history-102916

Turco, D.M., & Kelsey, C.W. (1992). *Conducting economic impact studies of recreational and parks special events*. Arlington, VA: National Recreation and Park Association.

Tures, J.A. (2016, October 14). Is Colin Kaepernick really the reason for the NFL's ratings decline? *Observer*. Retrieved from http://observer.com/2016/10/is-colin-kaepernick-really-the-reason-for-the-nfls-ratings-decline/

U.S. Census Bureau. (2016, July 14). *Statistical abstract of the United States: 2016*. Retrieved from https://www.census.gov/library/publications/time-series/statistical_abstracts.html

Wade Rupard Forum News Service. (2016, October 3). Future of 8 UND sports up in the air as committee considers cuts. *The Bismarck Tribune*. Retrieved from http://bismarcktribune.com/news/state-and-regional/future-of-und-sports-up-in-the-air-as-committee/article_a081501e-51db-5938-86ce-7bcc7275ede9.html

Walsh, P. (2016, March 3). In all-sport meeting, St. Cloud State athletes told 6 programs being eliminated. *StarTribune*. Retrieved from www.startribune.com/st-cloud-state-dropping-6-sports-programs/370796061/

Zimmerman, D. (1997). Subsidizing stadiums: Who benefits, who pays? In R.G. Noll & A. Zimbalist (Eds.),

Sports, jobs, and taxes (pp. 119-145). Washington, DC: Brookings Institution Press.

Chapter 16

Ammon, R., Jr., Southall, R., & Nagel, M.S. (2016). *Sport facility management: Organizing events and mitigating risks* (3rd ed.). Morgantown, WV: Fitness Information Technology.

Ammon, R., Jr., & Unruh, N. (2013). Crowd management. In D.J. Cotton & J. Wolohan (Eds.), *Law for recreation and sport managers* (6th ed., pp. 328-339). Dubuque, IA: Kendall/Hunt.

BBC News. (2016). *Qatar abolishes controversial "kafala" labour system.* Retrieved from www.bbc.com/news/world-middle-east-38298393

Brandt, A. (2016). *After the failed stadium vote, what now for the Chargers?* Retrieved from http://mmqb.si.com/mmqb/2016/11/09/nfl-san-diego-failed-stadium-vote-chargers-options

Department of Homeland Security. (n.d.). *SportEvac: Choreographing a stadium stampede.* Retrieved from www.dhs.gov/sportevac-choreographing-stadium-stampede

Filce, R., Hall, S.A., & Phillips, D. (2016). Stadium alcohol management: A best practices approach. *International Journal of Sport Management, Recreation and Tourism, 21,* 48-65.

Flyvbjerg, B., Stewart, A., & Budzier, A. (2016). *The Oxford Olympics study: Cost and cost overrun at the Games* (RP 2016-20). Oxford, England: Said Business School.

Hall, S. (2013). Training needs of sport and event organizations. *The International Centre for Sports Security Journal, 1*(3), 61-67.

Hall, S., Cooper, W.E., Marciani, L., & McGee, J.A. (2012). *Security management for sports and special events: An interagency approach.* Champaign, IL: Human Kinetics.

Human Rights Watch. (2017, September 27). *Qatar: Take urgent action to protect constructions workers.* Retrieved from https://www.hrw.org/news/2017/09/27/qatar-take-urgent-action-protect-construction-workers

Mercedes-Benz Stadium. (2016). *How Mercedes-Benz Stadium will be funded.* Retrieved from http://mercedesbenzstadium.com/stadium-info/funding

Merrick, R. (2016, January 15). Standing sections at English football stadiums could return if trial in Scotland is successful. *The Daily Mirror.* Retrieved from www.mirror.co.uk/sport/football/news/standing-sections-english-football-stadiums-7184142

Myers, S.L. (2014, January 27). Russians debate sticker price of Sochi Games. *The New York Times.* Retrieved from www.nytimes.com/2014/01/27/world/europe/russians-debate-sticker-price-of-sochi-games.html?r=0

Payne, M. (2016, November 9). Alcohol banned from stadiums, streets at 2022 World Cup in Qatar. *The Washington Post.* Retrieved from www.washingtonpost.com/news/early-lead/wp/2016/11/09/alcohol-banned-from-stadiums-streets-at-2022-world-cup-in-qatar/

Sawyer, T.H. (Ed.). (2013). *Facility planning and design for health, physical activity, recreation, and sport* (13th ed.). Urbana, IL: Sagamore.

Schrotenboer, B. (2016, October 27). Where do Chargers go if voters reject stadium bid? *USA Today.* Retrieved from www.usatoday.com/story/sports/nfl/chargers/2016/10/25/stadium-ballot-measure-vote-downtown-los-angeles-dean-spanos/92727440

Schwarz, E.C., Hall, S., & Shibli, S. (2015). *Sport facility operations management: A global perspective* (2nd ed.). London, England: Routledge, Taylor & Francis Group.

Seattle Seahawks. (2017). *Fan code of conduct.* Retrieved from www.seahawks.com/gameday/gameday-policies-and-information#code

Steinbach, P. (2004). Special operations. *Athletic Business, 28*(8), 24-28.

Sutton, B. (2012). Sport organizations must deal with feedback more effectively. *Street & Smith's Sports-Business Journal.* Retrieved from http://m.sportsbusinessdaily.com/Journal/Issues/2012/02/13/Opinion/Sutton-Impact.aspx

Volner, D. (2016). No. 3 Michigan at No. 2 Ohio State: ABC's presentation of the game culminates ESPN's weeklong, all platform coverage of marquee matchup. Retrieved from http://espnmediazone.com/us/press-releases/2016/11/no-3-michigan-no-2-ohio-state-abcs-presentation-game-culminates-espns-weeklong-platform-coverage-marquee-matchup/

Yoshida, M. (2017). Consumer experience quality: A review and extension of the sport management literature. *Sport Management Review, 20,* 427-442.

Chapter 17

Alexander v. Yale, 631 F.2d 178 (2nd Cir. 1980).

Anderson, N., & Clement, S. (2015, June 12). College sexual assault: 1 in 5 college women say they were violated. *The Washington Post.* Retrieved from www.washingtonpost.com/sf/local/2015/06/12/1-in-5-women-say-they-were-violated

Association of American Universities. (2015). *Report on the AAU Campus Climate Survey on Sexual Assault and Sexual Misconduct.* Retrieved from www.aau.edu/uploadedFiles/AAU_Publications/AAU_Reports/Sexual_Assault_Campus_Survey/Report%20 on%20the%20AAU%20Campus%20Climate%20 Survey%20on%20Sexual%20Assault%20and%20 Sexual%20Misconduct.pdf

Benjamin, C. (2016). The 65 most valuable college sports apparel deals. *Forbes.* Retrieved from www.forbes. com/sites/carlybenjamin/2016/07/12/the-65-most-valuable-college-sports-apparel-deals/#700bf3ef6087

Boston Celtics Ltd. P'ship v. Shaw, 908 F.2d 1041 (1st Cir. 1990).

Caputo, E., Pettegrew, H., Bennett, M., & Keehan, A. (2015). *Confronting campus sexual assault: An examination of higher education claims.* Retrieved from www.ue.orgsexual_assault_claim_study.pdf

Chaffee, Z. (1930). The internal affairs of associations not for profit. *Harvard Law Review, 43,* 993-1029.

Chemerinsky, E. (2006). *Constitutional law: Principles and policies.* New York, NY: Aspen.

Connors, J.W. (2009). Treating like subdecisions alike: The scope of stare decisis as applied to the judicial method. *Columbia Law Review, 108*(3), 681-715.

Federal Trade Commission (FTC). (2009). *FTC publishes final guides governing endorsements and testimonials.* Retrieved from www.ftc.gov/opa/2009/10/ endortest.shtm

Federal Trade Commission (FTC). (2015a). *The FTC's endorsement guides: What people are asking.* Retrieved from www.ftc.gov/system/files/documents/plain-language/pdf-0205-endorsement-guides-faqs_0.pdf

Federal Trade Commission (FTC). (2015b). *Native advertising: A guide for businesses.* Retrieved from www.ftc.gov/tips-advice/business-center/guidance/ native-advertising-guide-businesses

Hambrick, M.E., & Mahoney, T.Q. (2012). "It's incredible—trust me": Exploring the role of celebrity athletes as marketers in online social networks. *International Journal of Sport Management and Marketing, 10,* 161-179.

Heitner, D. (2015). Congress wisely puts legal status of fantasy sports under review. *Forbes.* Retrieved from www.forbes.com/sites/darrenheitner/2015/09/15/ congress-wisely-puts-legal-status-of-fantasy-sports-under-review/#4d6f3a7c5eab

Hoch, D. (2016). *Dealing with social media in a high school athletics program.* Retrieved from www.nfhs. org/articles/dealing-with-social-media-in-a-high-school-athletics-program

Hull, M.R. (2010). Sports leagues new social media policies: Enforcement under copyright law and state law. *Columbia Journal of Law and the Arts, 34,* 457-490.

International Olympic Committee. (n.d.). *Social media, blogging, and Internet guidelines.* Retrieved from www.olympic.org/social-media-and-internet-guidelines

Koller, P. (2006). The concept of law and its conceptions. *Ratio Juris, 19*(2), 180-196.

Krebs, C.P., Lindquist, C.H., Warner, T.D., Fisher, B.S., & Martin, S.L. (2007). *The campus sexual assault study.* Retrieved from www.ncjrs.gov/pdffiles1/nij/ grants/22153.pdf

Lavigne, P., & Noren, N. (2014). *Athletes, assaults, and inaction.* Retrieved from http://espn.go.com/espn/otl/ story/_/id/11381416/missouri-tulsa-southern-idaho-face-allegations-did-not-investigate-title-ix-cases

Law. (n.d.). *Nolo's plain English law dictionary.* Retrieved from www.nolo.com/dictionary/law-term. html

Lombardi, K. (2014). *Flurry of new legislation targets sexual assault on campus.* Retrieved from www.publicintegrity.org/2014/07/30/15185/flurry-new-legislation-targets-sexual-assault-campus

McKelvey, S., & Masteralexis, J. (2011). This tweet sponsored by . . . : The application of the new FTC guides to the social media world of professional athletes. *Virginia Sports and Entertainment Law Journal, 11,* 222-246.

Mervosh, S. (2017, February 6). Baylor sex assault scandal: Everything you need to know to understand what happened. *The Dallas Morning News.* Retrieved from www.dallasnews.com/news/baylor/2016/12/22/ baylor-sexassault-scandal-everything-need-know-understand-happened

Moorman, A.M. (2016). *A legal analysis of emerging provisions in college athletic apparel agreements: Cash, royalties, product, and innovation.* Oral presentation and abstract at the Sport Marketing Association annual conference, Indianapolis, Indiana.

Moorman, A.M., & Osborne, B. (2016). Are institutions of higher education failing to protect students? An analysis of Title IX's sexual violence protections and college athletics. *Marquette Sports Law Review, 26,* 545-582.

National Collegiate Athletic Association (NCAA). (n.d.). *Gender equity/Title IX important facts.* Retrieved from www.ncaa.org/about/resources/inclusion/gender-equity/title-ix-important-facts

National Conference of State Legislatures. (2015). *Traumatic brain injury legislation.* Retrieved from www.ncsl.org/research/health/traumatic-brain-injury-legislation.aspx#1

Oliver v. National Collegiate Athletic Association, 155 Ohio Misc.2d 17 (2009).

Precedent. (n.d.). *Nolo's plain English law dictionary.* Retrieved from www.nolo.com/dictionary/precedent-term.html

Ross, S.F., Karcher, R.T., & Kensinger, S.B. (2014). Judicial review of NCAA eligibility decisions: Evaluation of the restitution rule and a call for arbitration. *Journal of College and University Law, 40*(1), 79-113.

Sanderson, J. (2011). To tweet or not to tweet: Exploring Division 1 athletic departments' social-media policies. *International Journal of Sport Communication, 4,* 492-513.

Sellers, S.M. (2016). *Where is sports concussion litigation headed?* Retrieved from www.bna.com/sports-concussion-litigation-n57982067520

Sharp, L., Moorman, A., & Claussen, C. (2014). *Sport law: A managerial approach* (3rd ed.). London, England: Routledge.

Spengler, J.O., Anderson, P.M., Connaughton, D.P., & Baker, T.A., III. (2009). *Introduction to sport law.* Champaign, IL: Human Kinetics.

Title IX of the Education Amendments of 1972, 20 USC § 1681–1688 (2017).

Unlawful Internet Gambling Enforcement Act (UIGEA), 31 USC § 5361–5367 (2006).

U.S. Department of Education. (2011). *Dear colleague letter: Sexual violence.* Retrieved from www2.ed.gov/about/offices/list/ocr/letters/colleague_201104.pdf

U.S. Department of Education. (2016). *U.S. Department of Education levies historic fine against Penn State over handling of sexual misconduct incidents.* Retrieved from www.ed.gov/news/press-releases/us-department-education-levies-historic-fine-against-penn-state-over-handling-sexual-misconduct-incidents

Chapter 18

Acosta, R.V., & Carpenter, L.J. (2014). *Women in intercollegiate sport—a longitudinal, national study: Thirty-seven year update 1977-2014.* Retrieved from www.acostacarpenter.org

Armour, M., & Levitt, D.R. (2013). *Baseball demographics, 1947-2012.* Retrieved from http://sabr.org/bioproj/topic/baseball-demographics-1947-2012

Australian Broadcasting Company. (2016). *#Coverthe-athlete hashtag takes aim at sexist coverage of female athletes.* Retrieved from www.abc.net.au/news/2016-08-17/rio-2016-social-media-goes-after-sexist-coverage/7760352

Coakley, J. (2015). *Sports in society: Issues and controversies* (11th ed.). New York, NY: McGraw-Hill Higher Education.

Cooky, C., Messner, M.A., & Hextrum, R.H. (2013). Women play sport, but not on TV: A longitudinal study of televised news media. *Communication & Sport, 1,* 203-230.

Cyphers, L., & Fagan, K. (2011). *Unhealthy climate: Some coaches' homophobia is polluting the recruiting trail.* Retrieved from http://sports.espn.go.com/ncw/news/story?page=Mag15unhealthyclimate

Davis-Delano, L.R. (2007). Eliminating Native American mascots: Ingredients for success. *Journal of Sport and Social Issues, 31,* 340-373.

Federation of International Football Association (FIFA). (2015). *Record-breaking FIFA Women's World Cup tops 750 million TV viewers.* Retrieved from www.fifa.com/womensworldcup/news/y=2015/m=12/news=record-breaking-fifa-women-s-world-cup-tops-750-million-tv-viewers-2745963.html

Fink, J., Kane, M.J., & LaVoi, N.M. (2014). The freedom to choose: Elite female athletes' preferred representations within endorsement opportunities. *Journal of Sport Management, 28,* 207-219.

Fink, J.S. (2008). Sex and gender diversity in sport: Concluding comments. *Sex Roles, 58,* 146-147.

Gates, G.J. (2017, January 11). In U.S., more adults identify as LGBT. Retrieved from http://news.gallup.com/poll/201731/lgbt-identification-rises.aspx

Griffin, P. (1992). Changing the game: Homophobia, sexism and lesbians in sport. *Quest, 44,* 251-265.

Groden, C. (2016). This is how much a 2016 Super Bowl ad costs. *Fortune.* Retrieved from http://fortune.com/2015/08/06/super-bowl-ad-cost/

Hardin, M., Zhong, B., & Corrigan, T.F. (2012). The funhouse mirror: The blogosphere's reflection. In T. Dumova & R. Fiordo (Eds.), *Blogging in the global society: Cultural, political and geographical aspects* (pp. 55-71). Hershey, PA: IGI Global.

Iannotta, J., & Kane, M.J. (2002). Sexual stories as resistance narratives in women's sports: Reconceptualizing identity performance. *Sociology of Sport Journal, 19,* 347-369.

Jacobs, C. (2015). *Sports and fitness industry surpasses $84 billion in wholesale sales.* Retrieved from www.sfia.org/press/706_Sports-and-Fitness-Industry-Surpasses-$84-Billion-in-Wholesale-Sales

Kane, M.J. (2011). Sex sells sex, not women's sports. *The Nation Magazine, 293*(7), 28-29.

Kauer, K., & Krane, V. (2006). "Scary dykes" and "feminine queens": Stereotypes and female collegiate athletes. *Women in Sport & Physical Activity Journal, 15,* 42-55.

Lapchick, R. (2015). *The 2014 Associated Press sports editors racial and gender report card.* Retrieved from http://nebula.wsimg.com/038bb0ccc9436494ebee1430174c13a0?AccessKeyId=DAC3A56D-8FB782449D2A&disposition=0&alloworigin=1

Lapchick, R., & Baker, D. (2016). *The 2015 racial and gender report card: College sport.* Retrieved from http://nebula.wsimg.com/5050ddee56f2fc-c884660e4a03297317?AccessKeyId=DAC3A56D-8FB782449D2A&disposition=0&alloworigin=1

Lapchick, R., Malveaux, C., Davison, E., & Grant, C. (2016). *The 2016 racial and gender report card: National Football League.* Retrieved from http://nebula.wsimg.com/1abf21ec51fd8daf-becfc2e0319a6091?AccessKeyId=DAC3A56D-8FB782449D2A&disposition=0&alloworigin=1

LaVoi, N.M. (2016). *Women in sports coaching.* London, England: Routledge.

LaVoi, N.M., & Calhoun, A.S. (2014). Digital media and female athletes. In A.C. Billings & M. Hardin (Eds.), *Routledge handbook of sport and new media* (pp. 320-330). New York, NY: Routledge.

McCarthy, J. (2015, May 19). Record high 60% of Americans support same-sex marriage. Retrieved from http://news.gallup.com/poll/183272/record-high-americans-support-sex-marriage.aspx

Mumcu, C., & Lough, N. (2017). Are fans proud of the WNBA Pride campaign? *Sport Marketing Quarterly, 24,* 42-54.

National Collegiate Athletic Association (NCAA). (2014). *1981-82–2013-14 NCAA sports sponsorship and participation rates report.* Retrieved from www.ncaapublications.com/productdownloads/PR1314.pdf

National Collegiate Athletic Association (NCAA). (2016). *2016 NCAA women's basketball attendance report.* Retrieved from http://fs.ncaa.org/Docs/stats/w_basketball_RB/reports/Attend/2016.pdf

National Federation of State High School Athletic Associations (NFHS). (2017). *2016-17 high school athletics participation survey.* Retrieved from http://www.nfhs.org/ParticipationStatistics/PDF/2016-17_Participation_Survey_Results.pdf

Pharr, J., & Lough, N. (2016). Examining the relationship between sport and health among USA women: An analysis of the Behavioral Risk Factor Surveillance System. *Journal of Sport and Health Science, 5*(4), 403-409.

Sage, G.H., & Eitzen, D.S. (2016). *Sociology of North American sport* (10th ed.). New York, NY: Oxford University Press.

Sandomir, R. (2016, February 6). Viewership of Super Bowl falls short of record. *The New York Times.* Retrieved from www.nytimes.com/2016/02/09/sports/football/viewership-of-super-bowl-falls-short-of-record.html?_r=0

Sport and Fitness Industry Association (SFIA). (n.d.). *Cost of inactivity counter.* Retrieved from http://www.phitamerica.org/Cost_of_Inactivity_Counter.htm

Staurowsky, E.J. (2004). Privilege at play: On the legal and social fictions that sustain American Indian sport imagery. *Journal of Sport and Social Issues, 28,* 11-29.

Thul, C.M., LaVoi, N.M., Hazelwood, T.F., & Hussein, F. (2016). "We have a right to the gym": Physical activity experiences of East African immigrant girls. In M. Messner & M. Musto (Eds.), *Child's play: Sport in kids' worlds* (pp. 165-178). New Brunswick, NJ: Rutgers University Press.

Witeck, B. (2016, July 20). *America's LGBT 2015 buying power estimated at $917 billion.* Retrieved from www.nlgja.org/outnewswire/2016/07/20/americas-lgbt-2015-buying-power-estimated-at-917-billion/

Witz, B. (2016, September 1). This time, Colin Kaepernick takes a stand by kneeling. *The New York Times.* Retrieved from www.nytimes.com/2016/09/02/sports/football/colin-kaepernick-kneels-national-anthem-protest.html

Chapter 19

Bates, L. (2016, August 22). The hotly contested Olympic medal table of sexism. *The Guardian.* Retrieved from www.theguardian.com/lifeandstyle/womens-blog/2016/aug/22/the-hotly-contested-olympic-medal-table-of-sexism

Bevir, M. (2009). *Key concepts in governance.* Thousand Oaks, CA: Sage.

Bland, B. (2016). *China's $2bn football buying spree has fans fearful of results.* Retrieved from www.ft.com/content/e246a8f2-6a9d-11e6-a0b1-d87a9fea034f

Cohen, D. (2016). *Rio 2016: 1.5 billion Facebook interactions; 916 million on Instagram.* Retrieved from http://www.adweek.com/digital/rio-2016-wrapup-facebook-instagram

Dowling, E. (2012). *Final social TV data for the 2012 London Olympics.* Retrieved from https://bluefinlabs.com/blog/2012/08/13/final-social-tv-data-for-the-2012-london-olympics

Fédération Internationale de Football Association (FIFA). (2014a). *Developing football for all.* Retrieved from www.fifa.com/development/videos/y=2014/m=11/video=developing-football-for-all-2477115.html

Fédération Internationale de Football Association (FIFA). (2014b). *Harrison: Football turf is integral to Canada 2015.* Retrieved from www.fifa.com/womensworldcup/news/y=2014/m=10/news=harrison-football-turf-is-integral-to-canada-2015-2461003.html

Fédération Internationale de Football Association (FIFA). (n.d.). *Women's football.* Retrieved from www.fifa.com/womens-football/mission.html

Galanis, S. (2015). *US Women's team earns $2m for World Cup win; German men earned $35m.* Retrieved from http://nesn.com/2015/07/u-s-womens-team-earns-2m-for-world-cup-win-german-men-earned-35m

Houlihan, B. (2004). Civil rights, doping control and the World Anti-Doping Code. *Sport in Society, 7*(3), 420-437.

Institute on Governance. (2017). *Defining governance.* Retrieved from https://iog.ca/what-is-governance/

International Association of Athletics Federations (IAAF). (2011). *IAAF to introduce eligibility rules for females with hyperandrogenism.* Retrieved from www.iaaf.org/news/iaaf-news/iaaf-to-introduce-eligibility-rules-for-femal-1

International Olympic Committee (IOC). (2015). *Use of a participant's image for advertising purposes during the Rio 2016 Olympic Games.* Retrieved from https://stillmed.olympic.org/media/Document%20Library/OlympicOrg/IOC/What-We-Do/Protecting-Clean-Athletes/Athletes-Space/Rule-40-Rio-2016-QA-for-Athletes.pdf#_ga=2.65748270.123909219.1510073459-690158230.1510073459

International Olympic Committee (IOC). (n.d.-a). IOC executive members. Retrieved from www.olympic.org/executive-board

International Olympic Committee (IOC). (n.d.-b). Members. Retrieved from www.olympic.org/ioc-members-list

Lough, N., & Mumcu, C. (2015). Marketing women's sports: A European versus North American perspective. In S. Chadwick, N. Chanavat, & M. Desbordes (Eds.), *Routledge handbook of sport management* (pp. 355-368). London, England: Routledge.

Major League Baseball (MLB). (2017, April 3). *Opening day rosters feature record 259 players born outside the U.S.* Retrieved from http://m.mlb.com/news/article/222084690/opening-day-rosters-feature-record-259-players-born-outside-the-us/

Merriam-Webster. (n.d.). *Democracy.* Retrieved from https://www.merriam-webster.com/dictionary/democracy

National Basketball Association (NBA). (2017a). *NBA rosters feature 108 international players from record 42 countries and territories.* Retrieved from www.nba.com/article/2017/10/17/nba-international-players-2017-18-season-record-countries#/

National Basketball Association (NBA). (2017b). *NBA All-Star 2017 by the numbers.* Retrieved from http://pr.nba.com/nba-star-2017-numbers/

NBC Sports. (2016). *NBC's Rio Olympics is the most successful media event in history.* Retrieved from http://nbcsportsgrouppressbox.com/2016/08/22/nbcs-rio-olympics-is-the-most-successful-media-event-in-history

Padawer, R. (2016). The humiliating practice of sex-testing female athletes. *The New York Times Magazine.* Retrieved from www.nytimes.com/2016/07/03/magazine/the-humiliating-practice-of-sex-testing-female-athletes.html?_r=0

Powell, J. (2016). *Social media, second screen and video streaming to transform Rio 2016 for viewers around the world.* Retrieved from www.live-production.tv/news/sports/rio-2016-social-media-second-screens-and-video-streaming.html

QuantHockey. (2017). *NHL totals by nationality 2017-18 stats.* Retrieved from www.quanthockey.com/nhl/nationality-totals/nhl-players-2017-18-stats.html

Russell, C. (2016). *Could gender equality be the real legacy of Rio?* Retrieved from www.espn.com/espnw/culture/article/17432409/could-gender-equality-real-legacy-2016-rio-olympics

Thornton, T. (2012). *London 2012: The thrills (and agony) of the social Olympics.* Retrieved from www.pbs.org/mediashift/2012/07/london-2012-the-thrills-and-agony-of-the-social-olympics-208

Whiteside, K. (2012, August 23). After London, athletes still pushing for Rule 40 change. *USA Today.* Retrieved from http://usatoday30.usatoday.com/sports/olympics/london/story/2012-08-23/olympics-rule-40-michael-phelpos-lashinda-demus/57225924/1

Women's National Basketball Association (WNBA). (2017). *WNBA players playing overseas.* Retrieved from www.wnba.com/wnba-players-playing-overseas/

World Commission on Environment and Development. (1987). *Our common future.* Oxford, England: Oxford University Press.

Yuan, M. (2017, January 29). Lakers top team in NBA merchandise sales in China. *ESPN Streak.* Retrieved from www.espn.com/nba/story/_/id/18571714/kobe-bryant-stephen-curry-top-nba-jersey-sales-china

Chapter 20

American Statistical Association (ASA). (2016). *Ethical guidelines for statistical practice.* Retrieved from www.amstat.org/asa/files/pdfs/EthicalGuidelines.pdf

Berri, D.J., Brook, S.L., & Fenn, A.J. (2011). From college to the pros: Predicting the NBA amateur player draft. *Journal of Productivity Analysis, 35*(1), 25-35.

Berri, D.J., & Schmidt, M.B. (2010). *Stumbling on wins: Two economists explore the pitfalls on the road to victory in professional sports.* Princeton, NJ: Financial Times Press.

Berri, D.J., & Simmons, R. (2009). Race and the evaluation of signal callers in the National Football League. *Journal of Sports Economics, 10*(1), 23-43.

Bradbury, J.C. (2008). Statistics performance analysis in sport. In B.R. Humphreys & D.R. Howard (Eds.), *The business of sport: Bridging research and practice* (Vol. 3, pp. 41-56). Westport, CT: Praeger.

Brustein, J. (2010, June 27). Star pitchers in a duel? Tickets will cost more. *The New York Times*. Retrieved from www.nytimes.com/2010/06/28/technology/28tickets.html

Caro, C.A., & Machtmes, R. (2013). Testing the utility of the Pythagorean expectation formula on Division One college football: An examination and comparison to the Morey model. *Journal of Business & Economics Research, 11*(12), 537-542.

Charski, M. (2013). *Orlando Magic applies analytics to retain season ticket holders*. Retrieved from http://data-informed.com/orlando-magic-applies-analytics-to-retain-season-ticketholders/

Cochran, J., & Blackstock, R. (2009). Pythagoras and the National Hockey League. *Journal of Quantitative Analysis in Sports, 5*(2), 1-13.

Davenport, C., & Woolner, K. (1999). *Revisiting the Pythagorean theorem—putting Bill James' Pythagorean theorem to the test*. Retrieved from www.baseballprospectus.com/article.php?articleid=342

Davenport, T.H., & Harris, J.G. (2007). *Competing on analytics: The new science of winning*. Cambridge, MA: Harvard Business Press.

Greenberg, N. (2016, March 22). What are Pomeroy college basketball ratings? *The Washington Post*. Retrieved from www.washingtonpost.com/pb/what-are-pomeroy-college-basketball-ratings/fc7bff57-b177-4c12-8912-69d0fcaf2e63_note.html

Hamilton, H.H. (2011). *An extension of the Pythagorean expectation for association football*. Atlanta, GA: Soccermetrics Research. Retrieved from www.soccermetrics.net/wp-content/uploads/2013/08/football-pythagorean-article.pdf

Harris, J., & Berri, D.J. (2015). Predicting the WNBA draft: What matters most from college performance? *International Journal of Sport Finance, 10*(4), 299-310.

Harriss, D.J., & Atkinson, G. (2009). Ethical standards in sport and exercise science research. *International Journal of Sports Medicine, 30*(10), 701-702.

Harriss, D.J., & Atkinson, G. (2011). Ethical standards in sport and exercise science research: Update. *International Journal of Sports Medicine, 32*(11), 819-821.

Harriss, D.J., & Atkinson, G. (2013). Ethical standards in sport and exercise science research: 2014 update. *International Journal of Sports Medicine, 34*(12), 1025-1028.

Heumann, J. (2016). An improvement to the baseball statistic "Pythagorean wins." *Journal of Sports Analytics, 2*(1), 49-59.

Kaplan, D. (2015). Dynamic ticket pricing makes successful debut. *Street & Smith's SportsBusiness Journal*. Retrieved from www.sportsbusinessdaily.com/Journal/Issues/2015/10/26/Leagues-and-Governing-Bodies/NFL-dynamic.aspx

Kubatko, J. (2013). *Pythagoras of the hardwood*. Retrieved from http://statitudes.com/blog/2013/09/09/pythagoras-of-the-hardwood

Lewis, M. (2003). *Moneyball: The art of winning an unfair game*. New York, NY: W.W. Norton & Company.

Massey, C., & Thaler, R.H. (2013). The loser's curse: Decision making and market efficiency in the National Football League draft. *Management Science, 59*(7), 1479-1495.

Schatz, A. (2003). *Pythagoras on the gridiron*. Retrieved from www.footballoutsiders.com/stat-analysis/2003/pythagoras-gridiron

Scully, G.W. (1974). Pay and performance in Major League Baseball. *The American Economic Review, 64*(6), 915-930.

Spanberg, E. (2016). Placing values on social media engagement. *Street & Smith's SportsBusiness Journal*. Retrieved from www.sportsbusinessdaily.com/Journal/Issues/2016/02/22/In-Depth/Social-media.aspx

Turnkey Intelligence. (2015). *Sports data systems study*. Haddonfield, NJ: Author. Retrieved from http://intel.turnkeyse.com/2015/03/13/2014-sports-data-systems

Chapter 21

Alavy, K., Gaskell, A., Leach, S., & Szymanski, S. (2010). On the edge of your seat: Demand for football on television and the uncertainty of outcome hypothesis. *International Journal of Sport Finance, 5*(2), 75-95.

Andrew, D.P.S., Pedersen, P.M., & McEvoy, C.D. (2011). *Research methods and design in sport management*. Champaign, IL: Human Kinetics.

Blum, R. (2016). *AP newsbreak: MLB average salary $4.4 million after 4.4 pct rise*. Retrieved from http://bigstory.ap.org/article/43161e78d26b4865a187fb-cf9a2d08ff/ap-newsbreak-mlb-average-salary-44m-after-44-pct-rise

Cialdini, R.B., Borden, R.J., Thorne, A., Walker, M.R., Freeman, S., & Sloan, L.R. (1976). Basking in reflected glory: Three (football) studies. *Journal of Personality and Social Psychology, 34*, 366-375.

Creswell, J.W. (2014). *Research design: Qualitative, quantitative, and mixed methods approaches* (4th ed.). Thousand Oaks, CA: Sage.

Culhane, J. (2015). The DraftKings crash: Insider trading scandals could bring down daily fantasy sports. *Slate*. Retrieved from www.slate.com/articles/sports/sports_nut/2015/10/the_insider_trading_scandals_could_bring_down_draftkings_and_fanduel.html

Davenport, T.H., & Patil, D.J. (2012). Data scientist: The sexiest job of the 21st century. *Harvard Business Review, 90*(10), 70-76.

DeSchriver, T.D., Rascher, D.A., & Shapiro, S.L. (2016). If we build it, will they come? Examining the effect of expansion teams and soccer-specific stadiums on Major League Soccer attendance. *Sport, Business and Management: An International Journal, 6*(2), 205-227.

Frisby, W., Reid, C., Millar, S., & Hoeber, L. (2005). Putting "participatory" into participatory forms of action research. *Journal of Sport Management, 19*, 367-386.

Hoeber, L., & Kerwin, S. (2013). Exploring the experiences of female sport fans: A collaborative self-ethnography. *Sport Management Review, 16*(3), 326-336.

Holloway, D. (2016). How Rio ratings surprised NBC and will impact future Olympics. *Variety.* Retrieved from http://variety.com/2016/tv/news/2016-olympics-ratings-rio-nbc-1201843200

Hoover, A. (2016, November 22). Many teens can't tell real news from fake, study finds. *The Christian Science Monitor.* Retrieved from www.csmonitor.com/Technology/2016/1122/Many-teens-can-t-tell-real-news-from-fake-study-finds

Huff, D. (1954). *How to lie with statistics.* New York, NY: Norton.

Hutchinson, A. (2016). *How the 2016 Rio Olympics dominated social media.* Retrieved from www.socialmediatoday.com/social-networks/how-2016-rio-olympics-dominated-social-media-infographic

IBM. (n.d.). *What is big data?* Retrieved from www-01.ibm.com/software/data/bigdata/what-is-big-data.html

Jones, I. (2015). *Research methods for sports studies.* New York, NY: Routledge.

Kelley, K., Harrolle, M.G., & Casper, J.M. (2014). Estimating consumer spending on tickets, merchandise, and food and beverage: A case study of a NHL team. *Journal of Sport Management, 28*, 253-265.

McDonald, M., & Rascher, D.A. (2000). Does bat day make cents? The effect of promotions on the demand for baseball. *Journal of Sport Management, 14*, 8-27.

Meier, H.E., Konjer, M., & Leinwather, M. (2016). The demand for women's league soccer in Germany. *European Sport Management Quarterly, 16*(1), 1-19.

Milne, G.R., & McDonald, M.A. (1999). *Sport marketing: Managing the exchange process.* Sudbury, MA: Jones and Bartlett.

Muret, D. (2015a). Concessionaires go deep with analytics. *Street & Smith's SportsBusiness Journal.* Retrieved from www.sportsbusinessdaily.com/Journal/Issues/2015/02/23/In-Depth/Analytics.aspx

Muret, D. (2015b). Levi's Stadium numbers don't lie. *Street & Smith's SportsBusiness Journal.* Retrieved from www.sportsbusinessdaily.com/Journal/Issues/2015/02/23/In-Depth/Levis-Stadium.aspx

Reason, P., & Bradbury, H. (2007). *Handbook of action research.* Thousand Oaks, CA: Sage.

Reinboth, M., & Duda, J.L. (2006). Perceived motivational climate, need satisfaction and indices of well-being in team sports: A longitudinal perspective. *Psychology of Sport and Exercise, 7*(3), 269-286.

Research. (n.d.). *Merriam-Webster.* Retrieved from www.merriam-webster.com/dictionary/research

Schmidt, M.B., & Berri, D.J. (2004). The impact of labor strikes on consumer demand: An application to professional sports. *The American Economic Review, 94*(1), 344-357.

Smith, M. (2014). SEC schools retool stadiums based on results of broad survey. *Street & Smith's SportsBusiness Journal.* Retrieved from www.sportsbusinessdaily.com/Journal/Issues/2014/09/29/Colleges/SEC-fans.aspx

Smith, M. (2016). Kraft-Learfield union has name, client. *Street & Smith's SportsBusiness Journal.* Retrieved from www.sportsbusinessdaily.com/Journal/Issues/2016/09/26/Colleges/KlearIntel.aspx?

Stanford History Education Group. (2016). *Evaluating information: The cornerstone of civic online reasoning.* Retrieved from https://sheg.stanford.edu/upload/V3LessonPlans/Executive%20Summary%2011.21.16.pdf

Trail, G.T., & James, J.D. (2001). The motivation scale for sport consumption: Assessment of the scale's psychometric properties. *Journal of Sport Behavior, 24*, 108-127.

Trail, G.T., & Kim, Y.K. (2011). Factors influencing spectator sports consumption: NCAA women's college basketball. *International Journal of Sports Marketing and Sponsorship, 13*(1), 55-77.

Tyler, B.D., & Cobbs, J.B. (2015). Rival conceptions of rivalry: Why some competitions mean more than others. *European Sport Management Quarterly, 15*(2), 227-248.

Wann, D.L. (1995). Preliminary validation of the sport fan motivation scale. *Journal of Sport and Social Issues, 19*, 377-396.

Index

About the Editors

Courtesy of Indiana University.

Paul M. Pedersen, PhD, is a professor of sport management and the director of the sport management program in the School of Public Health at Indiana University – Bloomington (IU). He has worked as a sports writer, sport management consultant, and sport business columnist. Pedersen's primary areas of scholarly interest and research are the symbiotic relationship between sport and communication, and the activities and practices of various sport organization personnel.

A research fellow of the North American Society for Sport Management (NASSM), Pedersen has published eight books (including *The Routledge Handbook of Sport Communication, Research Methods and Design in Sport Management*, and *Strategic Sport Communication*) and over 95 articles in peer-reviewed outlets such as the *Journal of Sport Management, European Sport Management Quarterly, Sport Marketing Quarterly, International Journal of Sports Marketing and Sponsorship, Sociology of Sport Journal, International Review for the Sociology of Sport*, and *Journal of Sports Economics*. He has also been a part of more than 100 refereed presentations at professional conferences and more than 50 invited presentations, including invited addresses in China, Denmark, Hungary, Norway, and South Korea. He has been interviewed and quoted in publications as diverse as *The New York Times* and *China Daily*.

Founder and editor in chief of the *International Journal of Sport Communication*, he serves on the editorial board of 10 journals. A 2011 inductee into the Golden Eagle Hall of Fame (East High School in Pueblo, Colorado), Pedersen lives in Bloomington, Indiana, with his wife, Jennifer, and their two youngest children, Brock and Carlie. Their oldest son, Zack, is a student at IU, and their oldest daughter, Hallie, has recently accepted a position in Chicago.

Courtesy of Colleen Patterson, Brock University.

Lucie Thibault, PhD, is a professor in the department of sport management at Brock University in Ontario, Canada. She has taught at Brock since 2002. Thibault has also taught at the University of British Columbia and the University of Ottawa. In her quarter century of teaching, Thibault has taught courses in organizational theory, organizational behavior, ethics in sport, globalization of sport, and policy and social issues in sport.

Thibault serves on the editorial board of the *International Journal of Sport Policy and Politics* as well as the *European Sport Management Quarterly*. She has held the roles of associate editor and editor of the *Journal of Sport Management*. She is a member of the North American Society for Sport Management (NASSM) and was named a research fellow of NASSM in 2001. In 2008, Thibault was awarded the Earle F. Zeigler Lecture Award from NASSM for her scholarly and leadership contributions to the field.

Thibault's research interests lie in the formation, management, and evaluation of cross-sectoral partnerships in sport organizations. She also investigates the role of the Canadian government in sport excellence and sport participation and government involvement in developing sport policy. She has been an invited speaker at many conferences around the world. Her research has appeared in numerous scholarly journals, including the *Journal of Sport Management, International Review for the Sociology of Sport, Journal of Sport and Social Issues, Human Relations, Leisure Studies, European Sport Management Quarterly, International Journal for Sport Policy and Politics*, and *Nonprofit and Voluntary Sector Quarterly*.

Thibault resides in the Niagara region of Ontario.

About the Contributors

Robertha Abney, PhD, is an associate professor at Slippery Rock University (SRU) in the department of sport management. She received her doctoral degree in athletic administration from the University of Iowa. Her areas of research include role models and mentoring women in sport (womentoring) and the status of minorities and women in leadership roles in sport. At SRU she teaches courses in leadership in athletic administration and sport management, sport management and ethics, sport communication and technology, global sport management, and introduction to sport management. Dr. Abney has written several chapters in sport management textbooks. She was the associate athletic director and senior woman administrator at SRU for 17 years. She served on the following committees within the NCAA: Division II Management Council, Management Council Subcommittee, Committee on Infractions, Administrative Review Subcommittee, Championship Task Force Committee, and Project Team to Review Issues Related to Diversity. She also served on the American Alliance for Health, Physical Education, Recreation and Dance Awards Committee. Dr. Abney is a past president of the National Association for Girls and Women in Sport and is a member of the North American Society for Sport Management. In addition to serving on the Commission on Sport Management Accreditation's Board of Commissioners, she was elected to serve as the organization's chair in 2013. Her photo appears courtesy of Herman A. Boler.

Nola Agha, PhD, is an associate professor in the Sport Management Program at the University of San Francisco (USF). She holds a BS from Indiana University – Bloomington (IU), an MA in sport management from USF, and a doctorate in management

from the Mark H. McCormack Department of Sport Management at the University of Massachusetts Amherst. She has taught a master's-level course in research methods since 2010. Dr. Agha's primary research focuses on the economic impacts of teams and stadiums, the efficiency and equity outcomes of stadium subsidies, and a variety of issues related to minor league baseball. She brings a multidisciplinary approach to her research that combines her training in economics and management. She has published sport-related articles in the *Journal of Sports Economics*, *Sport Management Review*, *Managerial and Decision Economics*, *Contemporary Economic Policy*, *European Sport Management Quarterly*, and more. Dr. Agha worked in international business operations for several years and has consulted to the sport industry by conducting economic impact studies, competitive analyses, and feasibility studies for clients in MLB, the NBA, and minor league sports. Her photo appears courtesy of University of San Francisco.

Ketra L. Armstrong, PhD, is the associate dean for graduate affairs, professor of sport management in the School of Kinesiology, and affiliate faculty in women's studies and Afroamerican and African studies at the University of Michigan (UM). She is also the UM faculty athletics

representative. Dr. Armstrong's scholarship converges on the topics of race, gender, and the social psychology of managing, marketing, and participating in sport. Her research has been featured in numerous journals (e.g., *Journal of Sport Management*, *Sport Marketing Quarterly*, *Journal of Sport and Social Issues*, *Journal of Sport Behavior*, *Innovative Marketing*, *Journal of Black Psychology*, *Journal of Black Studies*, *Western Journal of Black Studies*). She coauthored an article that received the 2004 outstanding research award by the Sport Marketing Association, and she conducted national research for *Essence Magazine* on Black women's fitness. In 2008, she was inducted as a research fellow by the North

American Society for Sport Management. In 2011, an article she coauthored, "Market Analyses of Race and Sport Consumption," was selected among the top 20 articles published in the past 20 years by *Sport Marketing Quarterly*. She was inducted as a 2015 Fellow in the National Academy of Kinesiology. Over the years, she has performed integral roles in advising and consulting, research, management, marketing, and media relations for numerous youth, community, collegiate, professional, and international sport events. She is the former president of the National Association for Girls and Women in Sport. Her photo appears courtesy of Ketra L. Armstrong, University of Michigan.

Kathy Babiak, PhD, is an associate professor of sport management at the University of Michigan (UM). She completed her doctoral degree at the University of British Columbia, where she explored the implementation, management, and evaluation of cross-sector partnerships  in the Canadian sport system. From this doctoral work, a natural extension of her research became focusing on socially responsible issues in cross-sector partnerships. Her most recent research has explored underlying motives that drive sport organizations to engage in socially responsible practices and strategic aspects related to social involvement (such as community investment, philanthropy, and environmental sustainability) in commercial and nonprofit sport organizations. Her work appears in journals such as the *Journal of Sport Management*, *Corporate Social Responsibility and Environmental Management*, *Journal of Business Ethics*, and *Sport Management Review*. Dr. Babiak's coedited book, *The Handbook of Corporate Responsibility in Sport: Principles and Practice*, was published in 2013. This book offers a comprehensive survey of theories and concepts of corporate social responsibility as applied to sport and considers the social, strategic, ethical, and environmental aspects of social responsibility in the field of sport. She has taught undergraduate and graduate classes related to organizations and business, including strategic management, human resource management, and organizational behavior. Babiak is a North American Society for Sport Management research fellow and is also currently launching the Center for Sport and Social Innovation at UM. Her photo appears courtesy of KGT Photography.

Natasha T. Brison, JD, PhD, is an assistant professor of sport management in the department of health and kinesiology at Texas A&M University. Dr. Brison received her MS in sport administration from Georgia State University and a JD and a PhD in kinesiology with an emphasis in sport management and policy from the University of Georgia. As a PhD student, she received the Bernard Maloy Student Research Award from the Sport and Recreation Law Association (SRLA) for her research paper "Tweets and Crumpets: Examining UK and US Regulation of Athlete Endorsements and Social Media Marketing." Her primary research expertise is in sport marketing and the law with a focus on how advertising and marketing regulations affect sport brands. Her secondary research interest involves sport entity branding creation and management. Dr. Brison's work has been published in the *International Journal of Sports Marketing and Sponsorship*, *Sport Marketing Quarterly*, *Journal of Legal Aspects of Sport*, and *Marquette Sports Law Review*. She has presented at conferences and invited lectures in the United States, Canada, Amsterdam, Ireland, France, and China. In 2017, Dr. Brison received the SRLA's Lori K. Miller Young Professional award, which recognizes a young professional who exhibits a dedication to the study and instruction of the legal aspects of sport and recreation and service to the field and SRLA. Dr. Brison serves as the associate editor for the *Journal of Legal Aspects of Sport* and is a member of the review board for the *Journal of Global Sport Management*. Her photo appears courtesy of Texas A&M Sport Management.

Laura J. Burton, PhD, is an associate professor of sport management in the department of educational leadership in the Neag School of Education at the University of Connecticut. She teaches courses in management, leadership, finance, and HR management within the sport  management program. Dr. Burton's research interests include understanding leadership in organizations, particularly sport organizations, and exploring development, access, and success in leadership. In her work, she focuses on issues of gender in leadership contexts and, specifically, how stereotypes and discrimination affect women in sport leadership. Dr. Burton currently serves as the editor of the *Journal of Intercollegiate Sport* and has published in the *Journal of Sport Management*, *Sport Management Review*, *Harvard Education Review*, and *Sex Roles*. She coedited *Sport Leadership in the 21st Century* (2014) with Greg Kane and John Borland and *Women in Sport Leadership* (2017) with Sarah Leberman. Her photo appears courtesy of the Neag School of Education, University of Connecticut.

Corinne M. Daprano, PhD, is an associate professor in sport management and chair of the department of health and sport science at the University of Dayton in Ohio. Dr. Daprano graduated from The Ohio State University, and she has more than 25 years of experience work-  ing in the sport and recreation industry. Her research interests include Paralympic sport, sport for development, and organizational behavior in sport and health organizations. At the University of Dayton, she teaches undergraduate courses in principles of management, organizational behavior, sport law, international sport business, and sport sociology. Dr. Daprano has published articles in *Sport Management Review*, *Recreational Sports Journal*, *Quest*, and *Future Focus*. She coauthored a book chapter on the topic of service learning, and she has made numerous presentations at local, regional, national, and international conferences on volunteer management, Paralympic sport, and civic engagement. Dr. Daprano serves on the editorial review board of *Teaching, Research, and Media in Kinesiology*. She is a member of the North American Society for Sport Management and the Sport and Recreation Law Association. Her photo appears courtesy of the University of Dayton.

Windy Dees, PhD, is an associate professor of sport administration in the department of kinesiology and sport sciences at the University of Miami in Coral Gables, Florida. She earned her doctorate at Texas A&M University with an emphasis in marketing and specializations in sport sponsorship and event management. Prior  to obtaining her PhD, she was an account executive for Synergy Sports Marketing where she serviced corporate sponsorships and conducted hospitality and event management services for several professional golfing events. This experience has led to a research specialization in the areas of sponsorship effectiveness and event marketing. Dr. Dees has published numerous book chapters and more than 25 peer-reviewed research manuscripts in a variety of sport and tourism journals, including such outlets as the *Journal of Sponsorship and Event Management*. She is also coauthor of *LAW for Recreation and Sport Managers*. She is a member of the executive board (president in 2018-19) for the Sport Marketing Association, an editorial board member for the *Sport Marketing Quarterly*, and the executive editor of the *Global Sport Business Journal*. Her photo appears courtesy of Jenny Abreu Photography.

Timothy D. DeSchriver, EdD, is an associate professor of sport management in the Alfred Lerner College of Business and Economics at the University of Delaware. He earned his doctoral degree in physical education with an emphasis in sport administration from the  University of Northern Colorado (UNC). He has worked as a field economist for the U.S. Department of Labor and has served as interim associate athletic director at UNC. He also spent three years as an assistant professor at Western Carolina University. He currently teaches classes on sport finance and sport marketing at the undergraduate and graduate levels. Dr. DeSchriver's research interests are sport consumer demand, professional sport ownership incentives, and sport facility financing. He has published articles in the *Journal of Sport Management*, *Eastern Economic Journal*, *Sport Marketing Quarterly*, *International Sports Journal*, and *Street & Smith's SportsBusiness Journal*. He has been involved in research projects for the NCAA, the New York Red Bulls, the Major Indoor Soccer League, and the National Steeplechase Association. He was also coauthor of the textbook *Sport Finance*. Dr. DeSchriver is a member of the North American Society for Sport Management (NASSM) and the Sport Marketing Association, and he has served as the NASSM treasurer. He has made numerous presentations at national and international conferences. Before taking his position at the University of Delaware, Dr. DeSchriver was an assistant professor at the University of Massachusetts at Amherst. His photo appears courtesy of the University of Delaware.

Stephen W. Dittmore, PhD, is an associate professor and assistant department head in the department of health, human performance, and recreation at the University of Arkansas, where he teaches graduate courses in the recreation and sport management program. He earned his doctorate from  the University of Louisville. Dr. Dittmore's research has appeared in the *Journal of Sport Management, International Journal of Sport Communication, Sport Marketing Quarterly,* and *Sport Management Review.* He coauthored *Sport Public Relations: Managing Stakeholder Communication,* which is now in its second edition. Dr. Dittmore has 10 years of practitioner experience in various sport public relations roles, and he served as a director of the Salt Lake City Organizing Committee for the 2002 Olympic Winter Games. His photo appears courtesy of the University of Arkansas.

Jess C. Dixon, PhD, is an associate professor of sport management and the graduate program coordinator in the department of kinesiology at the University of Windsor in Ontario. His primary research and scholarly interests are in strategic management in sport. His secondary inter-  ests include executive leadership and human resource management in sport, sport finance and economics, and sport management pedagogy. He currently teaches classes in sport management, strategic management in sport, human resource management, and sport finance. He has experience working within the golf and retail sporting goods industries and with a boutique sport agency. He belongs to the North American Society for Sport Management and is the editor of *Case Studies in Sport Management.* His photo appears courtesy of the University of Windsor.

Marlene A. Dixon, PhD, is a professor at Texas A&M University. Her research expertise is in sport and life quality. In this area, she examines the ways that sport can be better designed and implemented to enhance the life quality of sport providers and par-  ticipants. Her most recent works include investigations of the characteristics of effective sport for development programs for youth (particularly girls), examinations of the work and family lives of intercollegiate coaches, and the role of sport in community building. Dr. Dixon completed her doctorate at The Ohio State University and served for eight years in the sport management department at The University of Texas at Austin. She has more than 50 publications in a variety of journals, including the *Journal of Sport Management, Sport Management Review, Research Quarterly for Exercise and Sport, Sex Roles,* and *Quest.* She has been named a research fellow in the North American Society for Sport Management. Her primary teaching areas are social and cultural aspects of sport, sport finance, and human resource management. She also enjoys mentoring graduate students and directing projects. Before beginning her formal academic career, Dr. Dixon coached basketball and volleyball at the college level. She also competed as a varsity athlete in basketball and volleyball at Trinity University. She enjoys running, playing basketball, hiking, and fishing with her husband and three children. Her photo appears courtesy of Marlene A. Dixon.

Brendan Dwyer, PhD, is an associate professor at the Center for Sport Leadership at Virginia Commonwealth University. He received his doctorate in sport administration from the University of Northern Colorado. Dr. Dwyer's research interests center

around sport consumer behavior with a distinct focus on the media consumption habits of fantasy sport participants and behavioral patterns of ticket purchasers. Currently, he has more than 40 articles published in journals such as the *Journal of Sport Management*, *Sport Marketing Quarterly*, *Sport Management Review*, *European Sport Marketing Quarterly*, and the *Journal of Gambling Studies*. Dr. Dwyer won the 2009 North American Society for Sport Management (NASSM) Student Research Competition for his dissertation titled "Divided Loyalty? An Analysis of Fantasy Football Involvement and Attitudinal Loyalty to Individual NFL Teams." He has also won the Sport Marketing Association's Best Professional Paper four times (2010, 2013, 2014, 2016), and in 2016, he became a NASSM Research Fellow. He currently serves on four editorial boards and is an associate editor for *Sport Marketing Quarterly*. In addition to teaching and research, Dr. Dwyer has worked with a number of sport organizations, including the Fantasy Sports Trade Association, the U.S. Olympic Committee, the Washington Redskins, Richmond International Raceway, Richmond Sports Backers, Special Olympics Virginia, Running USA, the Denver Nuggets, Colorado Avalanche, Colorado State University Athletics, University of Northern Colorado Athletics, Shanghai Football Association, Richmond Strikers, and VCU Athletics. His photo appears courtesy of Brendan Dwyer.

Justin Evanovich, PhD, is an assistant clinical professor in the department of educational leadership within the Neag School of Education at the University of Connecticut. Dr. Evanovich received his doctorate in sport management and sociology from the University of  Connecticut. He also serves as the managing director of Husky Sport (www.huskysport.uconn.edu; @UConnHuskySport). Husky Sport provides UConn staff and students a unique and intentional structure for collaboration with community and campus partners to plan, deliver, and evaluate youth development programs aimed at enhancing exposure, knowledge, and access to sport and physical activity, healthy nutrition, and academic achievement, as part of positive lifestyles and opportunities. His areas of engaged

scholarship include sport-based youth development, campus–community partnerships, K-12 teacher preparation, critical social theory and practice, diversity and equity in teaching and learning, and service learning. His research collaborations have been published in *Sage Research Methods Case Studies*, *Journal of Intercollegiate Sport*, *Sport Management Education Journal*, *Sport Management Review*, and *Journal of Childhood Obesity*. Dr. Evanovich has been fortunate to have a lifelong involvement in sport and physical activity within socially diverse schools, communities, and teams. His photo appears courtesy of John Schumacher.

Sheranne Fairley, PhD, works in the Business School at the University of Queensland, Australia. Her primary research interests are in sport and event tourism and volunteering. Dr. Fairley's secondary research streams focus on event leveraging and the globalization of  sport. She has conducted research and consultancy projects in the United States, China, Japan, and Australia. Dr. Fairley is an associate editor of *Sport Management Review* and *Leisure Sciences*. She is on the editorial board of the *Journal of Sport Management*, *Journal of Sport & Tourism*, *Sport & Entertainment Review*, and *Global Journal of Sport Management*. Dr. Fairley has published in the *Journal of Sport Management*, *Sport Management Review*, *Current Issues in Tourism*, *Journal of Sport & Tourism*, *Marketing Intelligence and Planning*, and *Event Management*. She teaches classes in event marketing and international event management. Her photo appears courtesy of the University of Queensland.

Eric W. Forsyth, PhD, is a professor at Bemidji State University in Minnesota. He received his doctorate in sport administration from the University of New Mexico with a minor in marketing management. Dr. Forsyth's two primary duties are teaching courses in sport management and

supervising field experiences. He is a founding member of the interscholastic athletic administration graduate curriculum standards endorsed by the National Association for Sport and Physical Education and the National Interscholastic Athletic Administrators Association (NIAAA). Given his passion for interscholastic athletics, he has published numerous articles in juried and trade journals, presented at various national and international conferences, and written several text chapters on issues related to high school athletics. Dr. Forsyth is the coeditor of the textbook *NIAAA's Guide to Interscholastic Athletic Administration*. He received the distinction as a certified master athletic administrator through the NIAAA certification program. His most memorable role was serving as president of the Minnesota AAHPERD Association. When Dr. Forsyth is not in the classroom, you can bet he is in the woods during hunting season; he has written stories about his bear hunting adventures that have appeared in outdoor magazines and two hunting and fishing company profiles that were published in a sport brand textbook. Despite all his successes in his field, Dr. Forsyth considers himself truly accomplished when his wife considers him a good husband and his children consider him a good father. His photo appears courtesy of Eric Forsyth.

Andrea N. Geurin, PhD, is a clinical associate professor in the Tisch Institute for Sports Management, Media, and Business at New York University. She earned her doctoral degree in sport management from Indiana University – Bloomington (IU) in 2008. She has published

extensively on the topics of sport communication and marketing specifically focusing on athletes' and sport organizations' use of social media and media portrayals of athletes of differing races, genders, and nationalities. Her work has appeared in more than 50 peer-reviewed academic journal articles (e.g., *Journal of Sport Management*, *Sport Management Review*, *Sport Marketing Quarterly*, and *International Journal of Sport Communication*) and book chapters. In 2017, she coauthored her first book with Drs. Paul M. Pedersen, Pamela Laucella, and Ted Kian titled *Strategic Sport Communication* (second edition). She has presented her research at conferences and invited lectures in the United States, Canada, Mexico, Ger-

many, Ireland, Norway, Spain, Australia, and New Zealand. In 2015, she was named a North American Society for Sport Management (NASSM) Research Fellow, which recognized her outstanding research contributions in the field of sport management. In addition to her research, Dr. Geurin has held several leadership positions with professional sport management associations such as NASSM and the Sport Marketing Association. She also serves on the editorial boards of six academic sport management journals. Her photo appears courtesy of NYU.

Heather Gibson, PhD, is a professor in the department of tourism, recreation, and sport management at the University of Florida. She has an international reputation as a scholar in sport tourism and has written many foundational papers for work in this area. Her edu-

cational background is in sport and tourism studies. She earned her doctoral degree in sport, leisure, and exercise science from the University of Connecticut. She has published conceptual and empirical work on sport tourism, and she is the author of one of the most widely cited articles in sport tourism, "Sport Tourism: A Critical Analysis of Research," which was published in the *Sport Management Review* in 1998. Dr. Gibson, together with Dr. Laurence Chalip of the University of Illinois at Urbana–Champaign, was instrumental in initially bringing sport tourism to the attention of sport management professionals in the North American Society for Sport Management. She is a fellow of the Academy of Leisure Sciences and managing editor of the journal *Leisure Studies*. She is a member of the European Association for Sport Management, World Leisure, and the Leisure Studies Association. Her photo appears courtesy of Ray Carson, University of Florida.

Elizabeth A. Gregg, PhD, is an associate professor of sport management and chair of the department of leadership, school counseling, and sport management at the University of North Florida. Dr. Gregg attended the University of Evansville where she

completed an undergraduate degree in sport studies and was a member of the women's golf team. She attended graduate school at Indiana University – Bloomington (IU) where she completed two master of science degrees in sport administration and higher education administration and student affairs and a doctorate with a concentration in sport management. Dr. Gregg regularly teaches classes in issues in sport, introduction to sport management, foundations of sport management, and leadership. Her research interests include issues in intercollegiate athletics, sport history, women in sport, and branding. Dr. Gregg's research has been published in the *Journal of Legal Aspects in Sport*, *International Journal of Sport Communication*, *Sport Management Education Journal*, *Journal of Contemporary Athletics*, and others. In addition to serving as a reviewer for the *International Journal of Sport Communication*, *Sport Management Review*, and *Journal of Hospitality, Leisure, Sport & Tourism*, she is a member of the Sport Marketing Association and the North American Society for Sport Management. Her photo appears courtesy of Elizabeth A. Gregg.

Stacey A. Hall, PhD, is an associate professor and associate dean of the college of business at the University of Southern Mississippi. Dr. Hall's expertise is in sport safety and security management. She has published articles in leading international sport management, homeland security, and emergency management journals and has coauthored two textbooks: *Global Sport Facility Operations Management* and *Security Management for Sports and Special Events*. In addition, she has been invited to publish in national magazines such as *Athletic Management*, *Athletic Administration*, and *Security Magazine*. Dr. Hall has been referred to as one of the nation's leading experts in sport security and has been interviewed in *USA Today* and *ESPN the Magazine* and on CBS New York, and she appeared on a live national broadcast of ESPN's *Outside the Lines*. Dr. Hall has been the principal investigator on grant awards of more than US$4 million. Funded projects include awards from the U.S. Department of Homeland Security

to develop risk management curriculum for sport security personnel at NCAA institutions, conduct risk assessments at college sport stadia, and develop training programs for professional sport venue staff. Dr. Hall teaches undergraduate and graduate sport management courses in economics, finance, and security. She developed an emphasis area in sport security management for the master's program at Southern Miss and a Graduate Certificate Program in Sport Security Management. Her photo appears courtesy of the University of Southern Mississippi.

Marion E. Hambrick, PhD, is an associate professor of sport administration at the University of Louisville in Kentucky. Dr. Hambrick has a BA in finance from Transylvania University, an MBA in finance from the University of Kentucky, and a doctorate in educational leadership and organizational development with an emphasis in sport administration from the University of Louisville. He has worked for General Electric in its finance and corporate audit departments. He currently teaches classes on sport finance at the undergraduate and graduate levels. Dr. Hambrick's research interests are social media usage in sports and innovations in the sporting goods industry. He has published articles in the *International Journal of Sport Communication*, *Journal of Sports Media*, *Sport Marketing Quarterly*, *International Journal of Sport Management and Marketing*, and *Case Studies in Sport Management*. Dr. Hambrick is a member of the North American Society for Sport Management and the International Association for Communication and Sport. His photo appears courtesy of Tom Fougerousse/University of Louisville.

David P. Hedlund, PhD, is an assistant professor of sport management and the codirector of the St. John's University Sports Analytics Seminar at St. John's University in New York. Dr. Hedlund received his doctorate from Florida State University with emphasis in sport marketing, consumer behavior, and a certificate in measurement and statistics. Dr. Hedlund has more than 20 years of domestic and international experience in sport, coaching, business, education, and analytics. Prior to earning his PhD, Dr. Hedlund played soccer at the international level and was a professional soccer coach. In recent years, Dr. Hedlund has publicly and privately presented and published more than 50 research studies, presentations, and articles while undertaking multiple analytics projects in college and professional sport. Dr. Hedlund has supervised, advised, or acted as an external examiner for more than 10 undergraduate, master's, and doctoral students' theses or dissertations. In addition to providing media interviews, advising, and consulting, Dr. Hedlund also acts as a reviewer for sport, business, and coaching journals and conferences, and he has worked as an advisory board member for non- and for-profit sport ventures. Detailed information can be found on DavidHedlund.com. His photo appears courtesy of David P. Hedlund.

Kathryn Heinze, PhD, is an assistant professor of sport management at the University of Michigan (UM). Dr. Heinze earned her MA and PhD in management and organizations from the Kellogg School of Management at Northwestern University and her BA in organizational  studies from UM. Her research examines organization and institutional change in sport and health and wellness. In particular, she uses institutional and social movement theory to examine how and why individuals and organizations enact, lead, and respond to institutional change. Dr. Heinze's research is increasingly focused on how sport organizations and the sport industry are affected by, manage, or promote institutional change around social issues such as community development, environmental sustainability, and player health and wellness. Her work has been published in a variety of journals, including *Administrative Science Quarterly* (*ASQ*), *Organization Science, Organization Studies,* and *Journal of Sport Management.* Dr. Heinze was honored with the American Sociological Association Geertz Prize for Best Article (2009) and the *ASQ* Award for Scholarly Contribution (2014). Her photo appears courtesy of Kellogg School of Management.

Mary Jo Kane, PhD, is professor and director of the Tucker Center for Research on Girls & Women in Sport in the School of Kinesiology at the University of Minnesota. She received her doctorate from the University of Illinois at Urbana–Champaign with  an emphasis in sport sociology. Dr. Kane is an internationally recognized scholar who has published extensively on issues related to sport and gender and particularly media representations of women's sports. Dr. Kane is the recipient of the first endowed chair related to women in sport: The Dorothy McNeill Tucker Chair for Women in Sport & Exercise Science. In 2001, she was elected by her peers to become a fellow in the National Academy of Kinesiology, which is the highest academic honor in her field. Dr. Kane is a past recipient of the Scholar of the Year Award from the Women's Sports Foundation. In 2012, she received a Distinguished Service Award from the Minnesota Coalition of Women in Athletic Leadership; this award is given to individuals who exemplify the highest levels of commitment to breaking barriers for girls and women in sports. In 2015, Dr. Kane received the Distinguished Service Award from the North American Society for the Sociology of Sport, and in 2017, she was named one of the 100 most influential sports educators by the Institute for International Sport. Dr. Kane serves on the editorial review boards of *Communication & Sport* and the *Journal of Sport and Social Issues.* Her photo appears courtesy of the University of Minnesota.

Millicent Kennelly, PhD, is a senior lecturer in sport and event management in the department of tourism, sport, and hotel management at Griffith University, Australia. Dr. Kennelly has a BA (Hons) in human movement studies from the University of Technology Sydney and received  her doctorate from Griffith University. Her research interests include sport tourism, participation in sport, and sport event stakeholders and management. Dr. Kennelly is currently on the editorial review board for the *Journal of Sport & Tourism* and serves on the board of the Sport Management Association of Australia and New Zealand. She has published in a range of journals, including the *Journal of Sport Management*, *Sport Management Review*, *Leisure Sciences*, *Journal of Leisure Research*, and the *International Journal of Contemporary Hospitality Management*. Her photo appears courtesy of Griffith University.

Shannon Kerwin, PhD,  received her doctorate from Western University in Canada. She spent two years as an assistant professor at the University of Florida, where she taught graduate-level management and leadership in sport. During this time, she also sat on numerous graduate student committees. Dr. Kerwin is now an assistant professor at Brock University, where her research interest rests in management and leadership within sport organizations. Specifically, Dr. Kerwin has looked at the influence of value congruence on organizational outcomes, the role of conflict in the effectiveness of volunteer boards, and leadership within the context of sport teams and organizational culture. She has delivered presentations at national and international conferences and has published in *Small Group Research*, *Journal of Sport Management*, and *Journal of Leisure Research*. Dr. Kerwin is an editorial board member of *Sport Management Review* and the *Journal of Sport Management* and an active member of the North American Society for Sport Management (NASSM), and she was named an NASSM research fellow in 2015. Her photo appears courtesy of Colleen Patterson, Brock University.

Amy Chan Hyung Kim, PhD, is an assistant professor in the department of sport management at Florida State University. She received her doctorate from The Ohio State University. Her primary research interest lies in health promotion through community-based sport  programs from a social epidemiological perspective. In addition, Dr. Kim investigates knowledge development in the field of sport management using bibliometric analysis. She has taught a number of undergraduate and graduate courses, including

introduction to sport management, human resource management in sport, facility and event management, strategic management in sport organizations, and research methods in sport management. In her free time, Dr. Kim enjoys playing various sports and attending sporting events. Her photo appears courtesy of Florida State University.

Catherine "Kt" Lahey, MBA, MSBM, currently serves as senior director, brands, for Wasserman; she joined the company in 2012. In her current role, she spearheads strategic consulting efforts across the global strategy and team sports pillars for client American Express.  Before joining the American Express team, she oversaw multipillar strategic efforts as well as the motorsports platform of long-time Wasserman client Nationwide. Prior to joining Wasserman, Lahey spent five years in corporate partnerships at International Speedway Corporation where she developed and implemented business solutions for a group of key corporate partners, including Ford and Sprint. She is a graduate of the DeVos Sport Business Management Program at the University of Central Florida and Stetson University, where she earned the J. Ollie Edmunds Distinguished Scholarship. She currently resides in Westerville, Ohio, with her fiancé Brett and his daughters, Megan and Hope. Her photo appears courtesy of Wasserman.

Nicole M. LaVoi, PhD, is the codirector of the Tucker Center for Research on Girls & Women in Sport and senior lecturer in social and behavioral science in the School of Kinesiology at the University of Minnesota. Prior to returning to Minnesota  in 2005, Dr. LaVoi was a research associate in the Mendelson Center for Sport, Character & Culture at the University of Notre Dame and an assistant professor and head women's tennis coach at Wellesley College. Through her multidisciplinary research, she answers critical questions that can make a difference in the lives of sport stakeholders and particularly girls and women. A leading scholar on female coaches, Dr. LaVoi has published numerous book chapters, research reports, and peer reviewed articles across multiple disciplines. Her seminal research includes the fifth annual *Women in College Coaching Report Card*, which is aimed at retaining and increasing the percentage of women in the coaching profession, and a groundbreaking book, *Women in Sports Coaching* (2016). She also collaborates with colleagues on media representations of women in sport, and she coproduced an Emmy-winning best sport documentary titled *Media Coverage and Female Athletes: Women Play Sports, Just Not in the Media* (2013). As a public scholar, she speaks frequently to sport stakeholders, hosts the annual Women Coaches Symposium, and serves on national advisory boards for the Women's Sport Foundation, espnW, and the Alliance of Women Coaches. She maintains a digital media presence through Twitter (@DrSportPsych) and her personal blog, *One Sport Voice* (www.nicolemlavoi.com). Her photo appears courtesy of LÖLE Twin Cities.

Ming Li, EdD, is dean of the College of Education and Human Development and a professor in sport management at Western Michigan University. He received his bachelor's degree from Guangzhou Sport University, his master's degree from Hangzhou University, and his doctorate in sport administration from the University of Kansas. His research interests are in financial and economic aspects of sport and in management of sport business in a global context. Dean Li served on the editorial board of the *Journal of Sport Management* and *Sport Marketing Quarterly*. He has published 29 articles in refereed journals, 11 book chapters, and 3 books (*Economics of Sport*, *Research Methods in Sport Management*, and *International Sport Management*). Dr. Li has made numerous refereed presentations at state, national, and international conferences. He has served as president of the Alliance for Sport Business (ASB), chair of the Board of Commissioners of the Commission on Sport Management Accreditation, and president of the North American Society for Sport Management (NASSM). Dr. Li worked for the Atlanta Committee for the Olympic Games as an Olympic Envoy in 1996. In November 2011, he served as a consultant for the sports department of the Organizing Committee for the Asian Games held in Guangzhou, China. He was the recipient of the Garth Paton Distinguished Service

Award bestowed by NASSM, the Founding President Award presented by ASB, and the 2017 Giving Back Diversity Leadership Award recognized by *Insight into Diversity*. His photo appears courtesy of Western Michigan University.

Nancy Lough, EdD, is professor and coordinator of the higher education program at the University of Nevada, Las Vegas (UNLV). Dr. Lough has a BA in health and physical education from Adams State University, an MEd in kinesiology from Stephen F. Austin State University, and a doctorate in sport management from the University of Northern Colorado. Her sport experience includes competing as a scholarship athlete and working as a college coach in Texas and California, being an associate athletic director in Colorado, and being the director of an NCAA National Championship. Prior to coming to UNLV, Dr. Lough served as faculty at the University of New Mexico, Iowa State University, and Kent State University. She is the coauthor of the *Handbook of Sport Marketing Research* with Dr. Bill Sutton and is an expert on sport marketing, sponsorship, leadership development, and gender parity within sport organizations. Dr. Lough was the first female president (2013-2015) of the Sport Marketing Association (SMA) after serving as the editor (2010-2012) for *Sport Marketing Quarterly* (*SMQ*). Two of her publications were in the top 20 articles in the first 20 years of *SMQ*, and she is an SMA research fellow (2015). Her photo appears courtesy of University of Nevada, Las Vegas.

Jezali Lubenetski, MBA, MSBM, joined Wasserman in 2008 and currently serves as vice president, brands. In her role, she heads up Wasserman's longest tenured retainer account, American Express, and leads the strategic oversight and growth of the account across sports and entertainment. During her time at Wasserman, Lubenetski has worked with numerous clients, including PepsiCo, Nationwide Insurance, T-Mobile, Lenovo, and others. In 2012, Lubenetski was honored for her accomplishments by *Forbes* in its annual "30 Under 30," which is a list of the young disruptors, innovators, and entrepreneurs in the sport industry. She resides in Raleigh with her husband, JD, and their daughter, Maisie. Her photo appears courtesy of Wasserman.

Daniel F. Mahony, PhD, is a professor of sport management and the president of Winthrop University in Rock Hill, South Carolina. Dr. Mahony has a BS in accounting from Virginia Tech, an MS in sport management from West Virginia University, and a doctorate in sport  management from The Ohio State University. He has worked for the accounting firm Peat Marwick Main & Co., the North Hunterdon High School athletic department, the West Virginia University athletic department, and the University of Cincinnati athletic department. Before becoming president of Winthrop University, he was also dean of the college of education, health and human services at Kent State University for seven years and a faculty member and administrator at the University of Louisville for 13 years. Dr. Mahony is an active researcher and has published more than 60 articles in various journals, including the *Journal of Sport Management*, *Sport Management Review*, *Sport Marketing Quarterly*, *International Journal of Sport Marketing and Sponsorship*, *International Journal of Sport Management*, and *Journal of Sport and Social Issues*. He was also coauthor of *Economics of Sport*. Dr. Mahony served as president of the North American Society for Sport Management (NASSM) from 2003 to 2004. He received the 2007 Earle F. Zeigler award from NASSM and has been an NASSM research fellow since 2003. His photo appears courtesy of Winthrop University.

Tywan G. Martin, PhD, is an assistant professor of sport management in the department of kinesiology and sport sciences in the School of Education and Human Development at the University of Miami in Florida. He earned his doctorate from Indiana  University – Bloomington (IU). While at IU, Dr. Martin received the prestigious Groups Student Support Services Fellowship and a School of Health, Physical Education and Recreation minority scholarship award. His primary research focus is on the influence, persuasion, and impact of media messages on consumer behavior across a variety of platforms (e.g., magazines, television, social media, mobile devices). In addition, his research examines brand perception and how associated thoughts and ideas about sport brands are used to influence fan behavior. Dr. Martin has taught many undergraduate and graduate courses that are directly in line with his research interests. He has a wealth of experience as a former student affairs administrator who mentored numerous student-athletes and general admission students. Dr. Martin has worked extensively in the sport industry, most notably as a basketball camp coordinator at the high school, collegiate, and professional levels. In his free time, he enjoys reading, writing, watching movies, working out, and attending live entertainment events. His photo appears courtesy of Jenny Abreu Photography.

Brian P. McCullough, PhD, is an assistant professor in the sport administration and leadership program at Seattle University. He is also the coordinator of the online sport sustainability leadership certificate program, which addresses the global concern for increased environmental  and ecological sustainability in the sport industry. The online program draws students from around the globe. His research focuses on environmental sustainability within the sport industry. Specifically, his research interests concentrate on the managerial decision-making processes involving environmental sustainability initiatives among upper management and using the context of sport to influence environmental behaviors of sport spectators on game day and in everyday life. His research has been published in the *Journal of Sport Management*, *Sport & Communication*, *International Journal of Sport Management and Marketing*, and *Quest*. Most recently, he published his first book, *Introduction to Environmental Sport Management*. Dr. McCullough is also the founder of Forwarding Sport Sustainability, LLC (2014), which was created to offer consulting services to sport organizations that are theoretically based, data driven, and practically applied to allow them to advance their sustainability efforts. McCullough earned his PhD and master's degree in sport management from Texas A&M University and his bachelor's in sport management from Ithaca College. His photo appears courtesy of Seattle University.

Jacqueline McDowell, PhD, is an assistant professor of sport management at George Mason University in the School of Recreation, Health, and Tourism. She received her doctorate in kinesiology from Texas A&M University. Prior to pursuing her doctorate and becoming  a college professor, she taught high school biology, was a head track-and-field and cross-country coach, and was an assistant volleyball and basketball coach. Dr. McDowell currently serves on the editorial board for the *Sport Management Education Journal* and has published numerous book chapters and articles in academic journals that include *Sex Roles, International Journal of Sport Management, Journal of Intercollegiate Sport, Journal of Leisure Research,* and *Quest.* Dr. McDowell's research focuses on issues of diversity and inclusion in sport and recreation organizations with an emphasis on investigating and developing strategies and programs that can be implemented to remove barriers to employment and sport participation. Within this research line, she has focused on the organizational experiences of women of color who serve in athletic administration and coaching positions. Dr. McDowell's emerging research stream investigates the utility of lifetime sports and sport programs in reducing health risks. Her photo appears courtesy of George Mason University.

Jennifer E. (Bruening) McGarry, PhD, earned her PhD from The Ohio State University (2000) and has been a part of the sport management program at the University of Connecticut since 2002. She currently serves as the head of the department of  educational leadership. She is a research fellow with Northeastern University's Center for the Study of Sport in Society and a North American Society for Sport Management research fellow. Dr. McGarry's scholarship has focused primarily on the barriers and supports for women and racially underrepresented groups in sport. Dr. McGarry is also the program founder and director for Husky Sport, which has received operational funding from the U.S. Department of Education SNAP-Ed program since 2004. Husky Sport has program and research components. The program connects mentors (UConn students) who collaboratively plan sessions with teachers and staff at K-8 schools and community organizations in Hartford, Connecticut. These sessions emphasize access to sport and physical activity and advocate good nutrition and healthy lifestyles. Research has focused on the effect of involvement in such programs on the K-8 students and the college student mentors. For more information, see www.huskysport.uconn.edu. Her photo appears courtesy of University of Connecticut.

Kevin Mongeon, PhD, is an assistant professor of sport management at Brock University where he teaches courses in sport analytics, sport economics, and statistics. Dr. Mongeon received his PhD in economics from Washington State University. His primary areas of schol-  arship are in the fields of sport economics, sport analytics, and behavioral economics. Dr. Mongeon develops economic models and uses econometrics to test hypotheses and understand behaviors on real-world markets with a focus on sporting markets. He has published on league design, fan preferences, and salary and ethnicity discrimination in the NHL, and he has provided expert testimony related to Canadian Hockey League players. He received a grant to apply computer programming, big data, and Bayesian econometric techniques to test whether sport bettors exhibit behavioral biases. He is an invited speaker on the topic of sport analytics and provides consulting services to professional sporting organizations. His photo appears courtesy of Colleen Patterson, Brock University.

Anita M. Moorman, JD, is a professor in sport administration at the University of Louisville where she teaches sport law and legal aspects of sport. She joined the faculty in 1996. Professor Moorman holds a law degree from Southern Methodist University.  Before beginning her academic pursuits, she practiced law in Oklahoma City in the areas of commercial and corporate litigation for 10 years. Professor Moorman also holds an MS in sport management from the University of Oklahoma and a BS in political science from Oklahoma State University. She is the coeditor of a feature column in *Sport Marketing Quarterly* titled "Sport Marketing and the Law" and is coauthor of the text *Sport Law: A Managerial Approach*, which entered its third edition in 2014. Professor Moorman's research interests include discrimination in sport and legal and ethical issues related to sport marketing practices, brand protection, and intellectual property issues in sport. She has published more than 30 articles in academic journals, including the *Journal of Sport Management, Sport Management Review, Sport Marketing Quarterly, Journal of Legal Aspects of Sport, Journal of Physical Education, Recreation & Dance, Leisure Science, International Sport Journal, Journal of Sport and Social Issues, Journal of the Academy of Marketing Science,* and *ACSM's Health and Fitness Journal.* She has given more than 70 presentations at national and international conferences. Her photo appears courtesy of the University of Louisville.

Ceyda Mumcu, PhD, is an assistant professor of sport management in the College of Business at the University of New Haven in Connecticut. She received her doctoral degree in sport administration from the University of New Mexico. Dr. Mumcu's research is focused  on marketing and consumer behavior in sport, the special nature of women's sports and its marketing applications, marketing research and analytics in sport, and comparison of sports in international contexts, structural differences, cultures, and tradi-

tions. Her work has appeared in a variety of journals, including *Sport Marketing Quarterly, Journal of Applied Sport Management, International Journal of Sport Management, Journal of Sport Behavior,* and *Street & Smith's SportsBusiness Journal.* Dr. Mumcu's edited book, *Sport Analytics: A Data-Driven Approach to Sport Business and Management,* was published in 2016. She has been involved in research projects for the WNBA, the New England Black Wolves, the CT Open, and the City of New Haven. At the University of New Haven, she teaches sport marketing, marketing research in sport, international sport management, and strategic sport management to undergraduate and graduate students. Before coming to the United States, she played professional basketball for eight years in the Turkish Women's Basketball League. Her photo appears courtesy of the University of New Haven.

Brianna L. Newland, DSM, is an assistant professor of sport management in the Alfred Lerner College of Business & Economics at the University of Delaware (UD). Before joining the team at UD, Dr. Newland spent two years as an assistant professor in event management in  the College of Business at Victoria University (VU) in Melbourne, Australia. Her research explores the patterns of sport participation and delivery and the development of sport. This includes research on what fosters or hinders adult participation in sport and how sport events can be leveraged to develop sport and tourism. Dr. Newland has been published in the *Journal of Sport Management, Sport Management Review, Sport Marketing Quarterly, Journal of Sport & Tourism, Sport & Entertainment Review,* and *Managing Leisure.* She is also coeditor of a textbook titled *Sport Facility and Event Management.* She serves as the associate editor for *Sport & Entertainment Review* and on the editorial board for the *Journal of Applied Sport Management.* Dr. Newland has presented at the North American Society for Sport Management, the Sport Management Association of Australia and New Zealand, the North American Society for the Sociology of Sport, and the Sport Marketing Association annual conferences. Dr. Newland completed a postdoctoral fellowship at the University of Texas at Austin and then served as a lecturer in sport management in the department of kinesiology and health. She holds a doctorate in sport management and a master's degree in exercise physiology and nutritional sciences. Her photo appears courtesy of the University of Delaware.

Amanda L. Paule-Koba, PhD, is an associate professor of sport management at Bowling Green State University in Ohio. She earned her doctoral degree from Michigan State University in the sociology of sport and obtained her master's and bachelor's degrees from  Miami University. Prior to earning her PhD, Dr. Paule-Koba worked for ProCamps, a company that runs professional athletes' youth sport camps and events. She was responsible for communicating with national and international corporate sponsors, marketing the camps nationally and internationally, and executing premier youth sport camps across the United States and in Canada. Dr. Paule-Koba also worked for the Anthony Muñoz Foundation and was responsible for assisting with the execution of the inaugural leadership seminar, the celebrity golf outing and dinner, and a youth football camp. She was also the consultant for the DisAbility Sports Festival and was vital in identifying potential sponsors and developing sponsorship packages. Currently, Dr. Paule-Koba is on the executive board for the nonprofit NWO Apraxia Support. She is responsible for the organization's finances and obtaining sponsorship for its events. Dr. Paule-Koba is an active scholar who examines issues in intercollegiate sport (such as the recruitment process and academic clustering), gender equity policies, and Title IX. She has been published in leading academic journals such as the *Journal of Sport Management*, *Research Quarterly for Exercise and Sport*, *International Journal of Sport Management*, and *Journal of Intercollegiate Sport*. Her photo appears courtesy of Bowling Green State University.

Brenda G. Pitts, EdD, professor at Georgia State University, is well-known nationally and globally in sport marketing and sport business management. She was among the first research fellows of the North American Society for Sport Management  and the Sport Marketing Association and was the honored recipient of the 2016 Diversity Award, the prestigious Dr. Earle F. Zeigler Scholar Award, the Distinguished Sport Management Educator award, and the Dr. Garth Paton Distinguished Service Award. She has delivered over 250 presentations at conferences around the world and is published widely in 17 books (some in different languages) and over 200 papers in such scholarly journals as *Sport Management Education Journal*, *Journal of Sport Management*, *Sport Marketing Quarterly*, *Journal of Vacation Marketing*, *International Journal of Sports Marketing and Sponsorship*, *Women in Sport and Physical Activity*, *International Journal of Sport Management*, *Journal of Legal Aspects of Sport*, *Sport Management International Journal*, and *Journal of Hospitality, Leisure, Sport & Tourism Education*. She loves and plays all kinds of sports. Earlier she played in the first Women's Professional Basketball Association, was one of the first scholarship basketball players at the University of Alabama, and is an Inductee in the Huntsville Sports Hall of Fame, the Women's Basketball Hall of Fame, and a nominee for the Alabama Sports Hall of Fame. She enjoys spending time with her wife, Melita, and playing with their furry kids, Jazz the Corgi, Tucker the Terrier, and Blu the cat. Her photo appears courtesy of Brenda Pitts.

R. Christopher Reynolds, PhD, JD, is the director of athletics at Bradley University in Illinois and has held this role since 2015. Before arriving at Bradley, Reynolds held the position of deputy director of athletics for operations and administration at Northwestern University and  served on the athletic director's executive staff. He has more than 20 years of experience working in athletic administration at Division I institutions in the following areas: university relations, department leadership, strategic planning, professional unit management, financial affairs, budget design and management, compliance and risk management, academic life, student-athlete well-being, sport program administration, hiring of coaches, external operations, marketing plans, branding, corporate sponsors, planning and construction of facilities, business operations, human resources, community relations, and all facets of athletic development. Reynolds has taught graduate-level courses in sport marketing, sport law, NCAA compliance, and issues in sport and higher education. He has served as chair of the NCAA Committee on Sportsmanship and Ethical Conduct, taught as an adjunct faculty member at Indiana University – Bloomington (IU) and Western Michigan University, conducted leadership development workshops for Nike, Inc. and the NCAA, and serves on the NCAA Division I Men's Basketball Competition Committee. Reynolds completed his PhD in sport management (2012), his law degree (1996), and his undergraduate degree (1993) from IU. His photo appears courtesy of Bradley University.

Sally R. Ross, PhD, is an associate professor of sport management at Grand Valley State University in Allendale, Michigan. Prior to earning her doctoral degree from the University of Illinois at Urbana–Champaign, Dr. Ross gained extensive practical experience in

college athletic administration as an assistant athletic director responsible for overseeing student-athlete support services at her alma mater. Before taking on that role, Dr. Ross was an academic counselor and life skills coordinator for student-athletes and was an academic advisor for the department of recreation, sport, and tourism at the University of Illinois at Urbana–Champaign. Her research interests include girls' and women's experiences and opportunities in sport, media representations of athletes, and the social responsibility of sport entities. Her work has been published in *Qualitative Research in Sport, Exercise and Health*, *Quest*, *Sex Roles*, *Sport Marketing Quarterly*, *International Journal of Sport Marketing and Sponsorship*, and *Sport Management Education Journal*. Dr. Ross has taught undergraduate and graduate courses in a variety of areas, including foundations of sport and leisure management, athletic administration, event and facility management, sport ethics, and sociocultural issues in sport. A former Big Ten All-Conference and Academic All-Conference student-athlete, Dr. Ross was the recipient of the Distinguished Alumnus Award from the University of Illinois volleyball program. She is a member of the North American Society for Sport Management and the North American Society for the Sociology of Sport and is a faculty affiliate with the Collegiate Sport Research Institute. Her photo appears courtesy of Grand Valley State University.

Amanda Siegrist, JD, has a legal and sport management background. She earned her Juris Doctor from NKU Salmon P. Chase College of Law and has been admitted to the State Bar of Ohio. Siegrist graduated summa cum laude with a BS in sport sciences from Wingate University. While maintaining responsibilities at KMG Sports Agency as a contract attorney, Siegrist is an assistant professor of recreation and sport management at Coastal Carolina University and teaches courses in sport law at the graduate and undergraduate levels. Her industry experience includes being cocounsel on multimillion-dollar contracts for prominent coaches and players in the industry such as Chase Blackburn, Bob Huggins, Andy Kennedy, and Frank Martin. She has also acted as event manager for camps and charity events for KMG clients ranging from NBA and NFL camps to charity golf outings and more. Her photo appears courtesy of Coastal Carolina University Photography.

Susan E.C. Simmons, PhD, is the director of career services and student engagement at the Indiana University School of Public Health in Bloomington. Dr. Simmons manages career services across five departments and facilitates the career planning process for undergraduates,

graduate students, and alumni. She has served on a university-wide Career Services Council for over a decade and is a founding member of the Indiana University – Bloomington Campus Metrics Committee to track career outcome data at the campus level. Dr. Simmons is an active member of the National Association of Colleges and Employers (NACE) and presented on the topic of career metrics at the NACE national conference in Anaheim, California, in 2015. Dr. Simmons has extensive experience in internship coordination and career coaching as well as certification in MBTI assessment and interpretation. While serving as the coordinator of career services in the department of kinesiology for seven years, Dr. Simmons managed all aspects of the internship program, including all internships in the sport marketing and management and sport communication programs. Prior to working in university career services, Dr. Simmons held faculty positions where she taught in the fields of anatomy, physiology, and exercise physiology. She holds a doctoral degree in human performance from Indiana University – Bloomington (IU) in the area of exercise physiology with a minor in bioanthropology. Her photo appears courtesy of Indiana University – Bloomington.

Danielle Smith, MBA, MSBM, is in her second tenure with Wasserman; she started as a graduate intern in 2007 and joined again in 2014. As senior director, brands, Smith works on a variety of Fortune 100 brands, including American Express and AT&T. Her primary
expertise is in brand strategy, property negotiation, talent identification and negotiation, and property management across sports, music, and cause. Before returning to Wasserman, Smith led the events and corporate marketing efforts for The V Foundation for Cancer Research. Smith received her graduate degrees from the DeVos Program at the University of Central Florida and wears her Terrapin pride proudly as an undergraduate from the University of Maryland. She resides in Raleigh, North Carolina, with her husband, Chris, and two boys, Tyler and Cooper. Smith's photo appears courtesy of Wasserman.

Ryan Spalding, PhD, is an assistant professor of sport management in the Girard School of Business at Merrimack College. Dr. Spalding has a BS in aeronautical and astronautical engineering from Purdue University, an MS in aeronautics and astronautics from Stanford University,
and an MBA, MS in sport management, and PhD in management from the University of Massachusetts Amherst. Combining his quantitative background from his former aerospace engineering career with

his training in business and sport management, Dr. Spalding's research and teaching interests are in sport analytics, sport economics, sport finance, and research methods. While at UMass as a lecturer, Dr. Spalding created and taught the first sport analytics course in the prestigious Mark H. McCormack Department of Sport Management in the Isenberg School of Management. He belongs to the North American Society for Sport Management and regularly presents at its annual conference. His photo appears courtesy of Yi Yang.

Ellen J. Staurowsky, EdD, is professor of sport management at Drexel University in Pennsylvania and interim associate director for the Center for Hospitality and Sport Management. She received her doctoral degree in sport management from Temple University. On more than
200 occasions, Dr. Staurowsky has presented to learned societies, professional associations, and conferences on gender equity and Title IX, pay equity and equal employment opportunity, the exploitation of college athletes and their rights, and the misappropriation of American Indian imagery in sport. She has published numerous articles in scholarly and professional journals. She is coauthor of *College Athletes for Hire: The Evolution and Legacy of the NCAA Amateur Myth*. In 2016, she published the edited text *Women in Sport: A Journey from Liberation to Celebration*. Dr. Staurowsky serves on editorial boards for the *Applied Research in Coaching and Athletics Journal*, *Journal of Intercollegiate Sport*, *Journal of Issues in Intercollegiate Athletics*, *Journal of Sport Management*, and *Women in Sport and Physical Activity Journal*. She is past president of the North American Society for the Sociology of Sport and the Research Consortium and is a former board member for the North American Society for Sport Management. She is also on the executive board of the College Sport Research Institute. She is a former college field hockey and lacrosse coach at Oberlin College and was the director of athletics at Daniel Webster College and William Smith College for nine years. Her photo appears courtesy of Drexel University.

G. Clayton (Clay) Stoldt, EdD, is associate dean in the College of Education and a professor of sport management at Wichita State University in Kansas. He teaches classes in sport public relations and sport marketing. Dr. Stoldt is the coauthor of *Sport Public Relations: Managing Stakeholder Communication* (2nd edition). His research activities have focused on sport public relations issues such as the roles of sport public relations professionals, the influence of social media, and the application of advanced public relations practices in the field. He serves on the editorial boards for the *International Journal of Sport Communication* and the *Journal of Applied Sport Management*. He received his doctorate from the University of Oklahoma. His master's degree was in sport management and his bachelor's degree was in journalism and mass communication. Before coming to Wichita State University, Dr. Stoldt worked in the athletic department at Oklahoma City University, where he served as sports information director, radio play-by-play broadcaster, and development officer. He also served as an adjunct instructor at Oklahoma City University and the University of Oklahoma. His photo appears courtesy of Wichita State University.

Ashleigh-Jane Thompson, PhD, is a lecturer at La Trobe University (Australia) where she teaches in the sport management program. Her research examines the use of new media by sport organizations and athletes as well as the impact of social media on sport fandom. She has been published in journals such as *Communication & Sport*, *International Journal of Sport Communication*, *International Journal of Sport Management*, and *Journal of Applied Sport Management*. In addition, her research has been presented at international conferences in countries such as Australia, Ireland, New Zealand, the United States, and the United

Kingdom. Dr. Thompson is a member of the International Association for Communication and Sport and the Sport Management Association of Australia and New Zealand (SMAANZ). She currently serves on the SMAANZ board and on the editorial board of the *International Journal of Sport Communication*. In addition to her scholarly pursuits, Dr. Thompson maintains active connections with the sport industry by partnering with sport organizations for research projects and volunteering as a media operations assistant at national and international sporting events. Her photo appears courtesy of Ashleigh-Jane Thompson.

Sylvia Trendafilova, PhD, is an associate professor of sport management in the department of kinesiology, recreation, and sport studies at the University of Tennessee. She earned her PhD in sport management at the University of Texas at Austin. She also holds a BS in physics (minor in mathematics) from Sofia University and an MS in environmental studies and another in sport management, both from Baylor University. Dr. Trendafilova's main area of research focuses on the sustainable management of sport and explores corporate social responsibility and the benefits these activities have on different sport organizations. She is also interested in the theory of collective action and its applications in the realm of sport. Her work is informed by theories from political economy, sociology, and behavioral analysis. She has presented nationally and internationally and is serving on the advisory board of the International Center for Sustainable Management of Tourism, Sport and Events. Her work has been published in peer-reviewed journals, and she contributed to M. Parent and T. Slack's book *International Perspectives on the Management of Sport* and to J.L. Paramio, K. Babiak, and G. Walters' book *The Routledge Handbook of Sport and Corporate Social Responsibility*. Dr. Trendafilova teaches graduate classes in several areas, including human recourses management, sport marketing, research methods, and environmental sustainability in sport. Her photo appears courtesy of University of Tennessee, Knoxville.

Patrick Walsh, PhD, is an associate professor of sport management in the David B. Falk College of Sport and Human Dynamics at Syracuse University in New York. His research focuses on the brand management practices of sport organizations. In particular, Dr. Walsh has

examined topics such as the effectiveness of brand extensions in sport, the brand associations consumers hold for sport organizations, and the use of sport video games and social media as marketing and branding tools. Dr. Walsh is a research fellow of the Sport Marketing Association, and his work has been published in journals such as the *Journal of Sport Management*, *Sport Marketing Quarterly* (SMQ), and *Sport Management Review*. He also serves on the editorial boards of *SMQ*, *International Journal of Sport Management*, and *Journal of Global Sport Management*. Prior to entering academia, Dr. Walsh worked with the Buffalo Bills of the NFL and was an associate with Velocity Sports and Entertainment (now MKTG) where he developed and executed strategic marketing plans for sponsors of major professional and collegiate sport properties. His photo appears courtesy of Steve Satori, Syracuse University.

Nicholas M. Watanabe, PhD, is an assistant professor of big data and analytics in the department of sport and entertainment management at the University of South Carolina. He obtained his doctorate from the University of Illinois at Urbana–Champaign, and his research

focuses on the intersection of economics, management, and communication in sport. He has been published in forums such as the *Journal of Sport Management*, *Sport Marketing Quarterly*, *International Journal of Sport Finance*, and *Oxford Handbook of Sports Economics Research*. Dr. Watanabe is on the editorial board for the *Journal of Sport Management*, *Journal of Issues in Intercollegiate Athletics*, and *Managing Sport and Leisure*. His research and expertise have been featured in the *Boston Globe*, *Yahoo! News*, *The New York Times*, and the *Los Angeles Times*, and he has also spoken internationally on the business of sport at Beijing Sport University in China and the University of Western Cape in South Africa. Previously, Dr. Watanabe worked for the Chicago Fire of Major League Soccer. His photo appears courtesy of the University of Mississippi.

Warren A. Whisenant, PhD, is a professor of sport management and is the chair in the department of kinesiology and sport sciences at the University of Miami in Florida. Dr. Whisenant, a North American Society for Sport Management research fellow, obtained his doc-

torate at Florida State University. He also holds an MA in kinesiology and an MBA in management from Sam Houston State University. He is a cofounding member of the Global Sport Business Association and founding editor of the *Global Sport Business Journal*. His research, most of which has focused on gender issues in sport and organizational justice issues in interscholastic athletics, has been published in journals such as the *Journal of Sport Management*, *International Journal of Sport Management*, *Sex Roles*, and *Global Sport Business Journal*. Dr. Whisenant's professional background includes more than 20 years of experience with three global organizations: Hewitt Associates, KFC-USA, and Frito Lay, Inc. His roles within those businesses were as an advanced project and process consultant, a director of restaurant operations (1 of 16 in North America), and a regional sales manager, respectively. In each of these positions, he was actively involved with numerous sponsorship and promotional activities with professional and collegiate sport organizations. His photo appears courtesy of the University of Miami.

Cara Wright, PhD, is the director of business operations for the Los Angeles Clippers' G League team, the Agua Caliente Clippers of Ontario. The Clippers are the 26th NBA G League expansion team and 2017-18 marks the team's inaugural season.

Dr. Wright manages all marketing, financial, broadcast, media, community relations, and day-to-day operations for the team's front office. Previously, she was an associate athletic director and senior woman administration (SWA) at Alabama A&M University (AAMU). Dr. Wright was instrumental in restructuring the internal operations of the athletic department and managed all correspondence and reporting with the Southwest Athletic Conference as well as with the NCAA. She was an active member in the Women Leaders in College Sports, the National Association of Collegiate Directors of Athletics, and Junior League in Huntsville, Alabama, and she founded her own group for Women of Color in Sport. Wright was also an assistant professor at AAMU in the university's undergraduate sport management program and sought to create opportunities for students to connect with the sport industry. She also has worked for the not-for-profit College Mentors for Kids as a regional director of development and community engagement and with Pacers Sports & Entertainment, primarily with the Indiana Fever in the WNBA champion team's front office. Dr. Wright has taught as an adjunct in sport management for several years and obtained her doctorate from Indiana University – Bloomington (IU). Her photo appears courtesy of Alabama A&M University Athletic Department.

James J. Zhang, PED, is a professor of sport management at the University of Georgia. His primary research interests are applied measurement and applied studies examining sport consumer and organizational behaviors. Dr. Zhang has published extensively and is a fre-

quent presenter at international and national conferences. He has served the profession in various leadership roles such as the president of North American Society for Sport Management (NASSM), sport management section editor of *Measurement in Physical Education and Exercise Science*, and chair of the Measurement and Evaluation Council of the American Alliance for Health, Physical Education, Recreation and Dance (AAHPERD). He has received prestigious recognitions such as fellow of National Academy of Kinesiology, fellow of NASSM, the Dr. Earle F. Zeigler Lecture Award, fellow of the Sport Marketing Association, the J.B. Nash Scholar from the AAHPERD, the University of Florida Research Foundation Professorship, the Measurement and Evaluation Council Honor Award of the AAHPERD, and Southern District Scholar of the AAHPERD. He is a distinguished Oriental scholar named by the City of Shanghai and has recently been named the honorary dean of the College of Sport Economics and Management by Shanghai University of Sport. His photo appears courtesy of Julia L. Wei.